THE GREAT MOVIES III

T H E
{GREAT MOVIES}
III

ROGER EBERT

The University of Chicago Press

Chicago and London

Roger Ebert is the Pulitzer Prize–winning film critic of the *Chicago Sun-Times*. Starting in 1975, he cohosted a long-running weekly movie-review program on television, first with Gene Siskel and then with Richard Roeper. He is the author of numerous books on film, including *The Great Movies*, *The Great Movies II*, *Awake in the Dark: The Best of Roger Ebert*, and *Scorsese by Ebert*, the last two titles published by the University of Chicago Press.

The University of Chicago Press, Chicago 60637
The University of Chicago Press, Ltd., London
© 2010 by The Ebert Company, Ltd.
Foreword © 2010 by The University of Chicago
All rights reserved. Published 2010
Printed in the United States of America

19 18 17 16 15 14 13 12 11 10   1 2 3 4 5

ISBN-13: 978-0-226-18208-7 (cloth)
ISBN-10: 0-226-18208-8 (cloth)

Previous versions of these essays have appeared in the *Chicago Sun-Times,* 2004–2009.

Library of Congress Cataloging-in-Publication Data

Ebert, Roger.
  The great movies III/Roger Ebert.
    p. cm.
  ISBN-13: 978-0-226-18208-7 (cloth : alk. paper)
  ISBN-10: 0-226-18208-8 (cloth : alk. paper) 1. Motion pictures.   I. Title. II. Title: Great movies three. III. Title: Great movies 3.
  PN1994 .E2323 2010
  791.43′75—dc22

                                                    2010009016

♾ The paper used in this publication meets the minimum requirements of the American National Standard for Information Sciences—Permanence of Paper for Printed Library Materials, ANSI Z39.48-1992.

CONTENTS

CONTENTS

CONTENTS

FOREWORD

Roger Ebert has won a readership paralleled by no other film critic in history. His devoted audience numbers in the tens, perhaps hundreds, of thousands. A visit to the Commentary section of his blog shows that he has attracted articulate, thoughtful readers of all ages. They find his writing—not only his film writing but also his essays on humor, science, and spirituality—little short of inspiring.

His endurance alone offers lessons in courage. Despite health problems that would lead most people to retirement, he has simply revved up. Apart from his usual reviewing, his attendance at film festivals and symposia, his coordination of an annual film festival, and globetrotting that would exhaust a youngster, he has managed to turn out another suite of essays on film classics—*The Great Movies III*.

Quantity isn't all. You can argue that since his illness, Ebert's writing has become even more relaxed, conversational, and brilliant. We are, I think it's clear, watching a writer at the peak of his powers. But what accounts for his indelible appeal? I'd argue that he has become something unique: a "man of letters" whose voice comes from the world of cinema.

I apologize for the gender solecism, but "person of letters" sounds forced, and "*littérateur*" is too stiff. Traditionally, the man of letters was neither academic nor journalist. He was a deeply informed essayist, one who stepped back from the passions of the moment to understand, through his humane knowledge, the deeper impulses coursing through culture. Prototypically, this sort of intellectual came from the literary arts, as Hazlitt and De Quincy did, but Pater, Ruskin, and other critics furnish parallels in the visual arts, and of course we have Shaw on music and drama. In modern times, I'd add Dwight Macdonald and Lionel Trilling. The calling isn't only masculine: we need think only of Susan Sontag and Angela Carter.

Ebert is the first "man of letters" I can think of whose insight is distilled not from book culture but from the most important art medium of the twentieth century. His ideas are steeped in cinema. Just as the traditional man of letters saw the world through the prism of book culture, Roger reflects on religion, history, and human relationships by means of what cinema has shown him of human life.

Not that Ebert disdains literary tradition; he is a voracious reader of fiction, history, and science (especially Darwinism), and he can deploy allusions with ease. But his frame of reference, I believe—so typical of the Movie Generation that emerged in the 1960s—is that of films and filmmakers. From this perspective, movies are more than entertainment, more even than exalting or disturbing works of art. Taken in all their variety, films can shape our most fundamental feelings and guide us toward a deeper understanding of the world and our place in it. Movies constitute a shared culture, a kaleidoscopic filter through which life takes on fresh meanings. This is the sensibility that, in my opinion, forms the framework of the *Great Movies* collections.

Ebert would probably reply that he is centrally a journalist: tied to the moment, paced for deadlines, writing for people who want informed opinion about what's playing this weekend. But he'd have to admit that he has also written extended essays that were more than ephemeral "think pieces." The *Great Movies* anthologies go further, into the classic realm of the occasional essay, where the man of letters really gets to show his stuff.

The essays in all three volumes are belletristic in the best sense. A particular film is at once an artwork to be interpreted and an experience to be evoked on the page. Historical and personal background is smoothly integrated into a survey of key instants onscreen, and these are delineated with a crispness that can make your scalp prickle. This is appreciative, celebratory criticism at its best. Read one of these essays, and you want to see the film immediately, even if you've seen it many times before.

At the level of analytical commentary, Ebert can summon up a scene in a sentence. He has sharp eyes and ears. He notices details in the background of shots; he can specify a director's compositional strategies. (The rest of us have to use frame stills.) He cuts to the heart of a movie by quoting a line. In *Rebel Without a Cause*, everybody remembers the moment when James Dean cries out to his bickering parents: "You're tearing me apart!" But we remember it because it's a cliché. Ebert reminds us of what follows, a more eccentric line that mirrors Jim's adolescent confusion: "You say one thing, he says another, and everybody changes back again." And this detail moves Ebert into considered reflection on how this scene and others like it open onto a malaise that goes deeper than 1950s suburban discontent, a glimpse of an existential doubt that life itself means anything.

This yawning uncertainty yields a movie that is compelling in its (probably unintentional) disjunctions. "Like its hero, *Rebel Without a Cause* desperately wants to say something and doesn't know what it is. If it did, it would lose its fascination." Ebert is alert to such tensions, finding them in *The Big Red One*, *The Red Shoes*, *The Scarlet Empress*, and other classics. Along with celebrating formal perfection, Ebert acknowledges that ambitious films often unleash impulses that they can't contain. The discordances demand that we think through the implications of what we're seeing.

Again and again, then, powerful ideas arise from Ebert's exploration of the world offered onscreen. He assumes that a great film will, directly or tacitly, raise permanent concerns about love, trust, moral commitment, and death. Most obviously, there are the Bergman films, which always put ultimate issues at their center. These tease Ebert into some of his most eloquent writing. "The events in *Fanny and Alexander* may be seen through the prism of the children's memories, so that half-understood and half-forgotten events have been reconstructed into a new fable that explains their lives."

Likewise, Welles has never shirked a chance to explore issues of deep concern to human life. For Ebert, *Chimes at Midnight* is not only a supreme work of Welles's late years; it's also an autobiographical testament and a meditation on power and loyalty. For Ebert, Welles treats Shakespeare's play as setting Falstaff's unsparing vitality against the compromises of political responsibility.

But less solemn work stirs Ebert to thought as well. *Groundhog Day*, which seems to be admired by every person I sit beside on a plane, provokes Ebert to some unique observations. Bill Murray, he points out, not only makes the film wonderful: "He does a more difficult thing, which is to make it bearable." Ebert goes on to describe the actor's "detached melancholy": "He is deeply suspicious of joy, he sees sincerity as a weapon that can be used against him . . . Hamlet in a sitcom world." From this Ebert moves smoothly to contemplate the film as "a parable for our materialistic age," an anti–New Age vision of a spirituality that doesn't come easily. Instead of a happy ending, the film offers a hero who remains flawed: "He becomes a better Phil, not a different Phil."

In the nineteenth century, literature offered itself as the central art for making sense of history, society, and personal relationships. Art, said Zola, was nature seen through a temperament. We learned to call a personal problem Jamesian in its intricacy, or to label a friend as straight out of Dickens or Jane Austen. Accordingly, the man of letters delicately traced the interface between modern life and the arts dedicated to interpreting it. But movies—and here's another gospel of the Film Generation—furnish our culture's touchstones. Now we recognize another person as Rupert Pupkin or Alvy Singer; a faculty meeting reminds us of the Marx Brothers or *The Godfather*. Once, at a committee meeting, I said of a project: "I have a bad feeling about this." Immediately a colleague said: "That's the first time I heard you quote *Star Wars*." I had no idea I was doing it.

Ebert understands that movies have become our lingua franca, our window and rangefinder and microscope. By thinking hard about them, he shows us how the pleasures and challenges of cinema open us up to wisdom. The great movies both teach and please, and each anchors us so firmly in its coordinates that we see our ornery world, for the moment, transformed into something bright, sharp, and comprehensible.

Pervaded by the love of film and the love of ideas, Ebert's *Great Movies* essays do what one variety of belletristic writing has always done. They trigger unexpected thought with a minimum of apparent effort. Chiseled *aperçus* lead to deeper enjoyment and greater reflection on how the world would look if the artwork's premises were perfectly universal. This may be a lot to hang on a batch of film essays, but I think that their blend of incisiveness, lack of pretension, and openhearted celebration fully warrant it. Roger Ebert demonstrates that film viewing, undertaken with zest, opens a path to understanding life.

DAVID BORDWELL

INTRODUCTION

You might be surprised by how many people have told me they're working their way through my books of Great Movies one film at a time. That's not to suggest these books are in any way definitive. I loathe "best of" lists, which are not the best of anything except what someone was able to come up with that day. I look at a list of the "100 greatest horror films," or musicals, or whatever, and I want to ask the list maker, "But how do you *know?*" There are great films in my books, and films that are not great, but there is no film here to which I didn't respond strongly. That's the reassurance I can offer.

I believe good movies are a civilizing force. They allow us to empathize with those whose lives are different than our own. I like to say they open windows in our box of space and time. Here's a third book filled with windows.

I was just now looking over the hundred titles in this third volume, and I wanted to watch most of them again. That's not a figure of speech. Although the sainted Pauline Kael was adamant about never watching a movie twice, I think of a good film similarly to a favorite music album that I might listen to time and again. In a sense, a movie is a *place* for me. I go there. Just as I return time and again to London, I return to *Fitzcarraldo*, *Dark City*, *Late Spring*, and Bergman's trilogy *Through a Glass Darkly*, *The Silence*, and *Winter Light*.

In fact, there is a fourth Bergman in this book, *Fanny and Alexander*—his films have been very important to me recently. I have no desire to belabor my adventures with health during the period since *The Great Movies II*, but I went through a period of seeing and writing about no movies at all. The first film I saw in a theater after a period of abstinence was *Indiana Jones and the Kingdom of the Crystal Skull*. On reflection, that was an excellent choice. It was gloriously what it was. You won't find it in this book—or the next one, if there is one—but it's still an excellent choice.

After returning home from the hospital, I resumed my usual schedule. Above all that included a Great Movie essay every other week. Most of them I watched on DVD; several, like *The Godfather: Part II*, on big screens. Some I was able to see in theaters. I saw Melville's *Touchez Pas au Grisbi* (reviewed in *GM II*) in a revival house in Seattle while I was there getting dosed with radiation. Like the others, it conferred the gift of taking me to another place. It also confirmed my affection for Melville and Jean Gabin.

Soon after I returned home I turned to Bergman, who is a filmmaker for thoughtful moods. The new Criterion discs of his trilogy have been restored to an astonishing black-and-white beauty, and I fell into them. It's conventional to write of "his great cinematographer, Sven Nykvist," but my God, he *is* great, and I found myself trying to describe the perfection of his lighting. I responded strongly to Bergman's passion about fundamental questions of life and death, guilt, mortality, and what he regards as the silence of God. I'd seen all these films on first release, but at an older age, having walked through the valley, I saw them quite differently. Norman Cousins famously found during an illness that comedy helped heal him. For me, it was Bergman. In those months I wasn't finding many things funny.

Indeed, looking over the list, I'm surprised to see only four pure comedy entries, the Chuck Jones cartoons, *My Man Godfrey*, Chaplin's *The Great Dictator*, and Harold Lloyd's *Safety Last*. A good case can be made for *The Scarlet Empress* and *Playtime*. There are lots of smiles in *The Bandwagon*, *My Fair Lady*, *Top Hat*, and *Thief of Bagdad*, but you can't call them comedies. *Groundhog Day* is sort of a comedy, and sort of a profound exploration of why time makes it possible for us to connect with others.

For that matter, some of the funniest film scenes don't play as comedy at all. In my review of *Touchez Pas au Grisbi*, I describe a scene where the Gabin character returns to his secret gangster's hideout, a room with a comfy charm, a phonograph, fresh clothes, and even guest pajamas. He has a voiceover, a monologue about his old pal who has stupidly made it necessary for him to go into hiding. He's angry but affectionate. Gabin mirrors his inner monologue with subtle body language. The scene has truth in it but is also funny, although no one in the audience laughs. There's that kind of comedy, too.

People often ask me, "Do you ever change your mind about a movie?" Hardly ever, although I may refine my opinion. Among the films here, I've changed on *The Godfather: Part II* and *Blade Runner*. My original review of *Part II* puts me in mind of the "brain cloud" that besets Tom Hanks in *Joe versus the Volcano*. I was simply wrong. In the case of *Blade Runner*, I think the director's cut by Ridley Scott simply plays much better.

I also turned around on *Groundhog Day*, which made it into this book when I belatedly caught on that it wasn't about the weatherman's predicament but about the nature of time and will. Perhaps when I first saw it I allowed myself to be distracted by Bill Murray's mainstream comedy reputation. But someone in film school somewhere is probably even now writing a thesis about how Murray's famous cameos represent an injection of his philosophy into those pictures. The cameos may be the subversive flowering of what he was trying to express more conventionally in *The Razor's Edge*, and what also underlies *Groundhog Dog*, a spiritual view of existence that helps give weight to the basically comic presentation.

I see another group of pictures here I'm fond of: the strange films. So many movies repeat the same tired formulas that I find myself grateful for one that does something unexpected and new, and does it well. Consider *Leolo, Withnail and I, Exotica*, and Jodorowsky's fevered *Santa Sangre*. The strangest of all is Bela Tarr's *Werckmeister Harmonies*, although some readers may not be persuaded by my claim, "If you have not walked out after 20 or 30 minutes, you will thereafter not be able to move from your seat."

A few other titles require mention. *A Woman's Tale* is a masterwork by the wrongly overlooked Australian director Paul Cox. *Moolade* is the last film by the Senegalese director Ousmane Sembene, who I met at eighty-one in the lobby of my small Cannes hotel, puffing contentedly on a Sherlock Holmes pipe. In this group I include the problematical *Triumph of the Will*. This is a movie I had been struggling with because it forced me to confront the ultimate question, "What is a great film, anyway?"

Then there is *A Prairie Home Companion*, which I believe, wrongly or not, Robert Altman may have made as a farewell of sorts. He died while I was in a coma, and my wife didn't tell me for two months. Rightly so. From the day I saw the premiere of *MASH*, Altman graced my personal cinema as an example of an exemplary filmmaker, a man whose life and films were in complete sympathy.

I ruffled some feathers after *Transformers: Revenge of the Fallen* was released in 2009. It was so stupid it was almost criminal. Noting that some of its fans considered it one of the greatest films ever made, I suggested perhaps they were not "sufficiently evolved." Oh, did that make people angry. What snobbery! Who did I think I was?

I was indeed a snob, if you agree with this definition: "A person who believes that their tastes in a particular area are superior to those of other people." I do. That is not ego. It is a faith that after writing and teaching about films for more than forty years, my tastes are more evolved than those of a fanboy. We are so terrified these days of showing disrespect for low taste. You can admire Miley Cyrus (God love her), but if I prefer Billie Holiday, why, I'm a snob. It is quite possible to devise a defense of *T2RF*, as its fans affectionately call it. One persuasive critic likened it to pop art. Well, okay. He had an argument, he had his reasons, he considered it in a particular context. But to argue I am a snob for not *loving T2RF* as much as "everybody does" values less thought and experience over more.

What am I getting at here? The way to know more about anything is to deepen your experience of it. I have no way of proving it, but I would bet you a shiny new dime that it is impossible to start out loving *T2RF*, experience the films in this book, and end by loving it.

{ THE GREAT MOVIES III }

{ 3 Women }

And so I descend once more into the mysterious depths of *3 Women*, a film that was imagined in a dream. Robert Altman's 1977 masterpiece tells the story of three women whose identities blur, shift, and merge until finally, in an enigmatic last scene, they have formed a family, or perhaps have become one person. I have seen it many times, been through it twice in shot-by-shot analysis, and yet it always seems to be happening as I watch it. Recurring dreams are like that: we have had them before, but have not finished with them, and we return because they contain unsolved enigmas.

Shelley Duvall, Sissy Spacek, and Janice Rule play the three women, who live in an apartment complex in the California desert. Duvall plays Millie Lammoreaux, who works as a therapist in a senior care center; Spacek plays Pinky Rose, who gets a job there and becomes Millie's roommate. Rule is Willie Hart, the pregnant wife of the building owner, who moves within a sad silence, holding herself apart from the others, and paints on the bottom of the pool godlike creatures, bizarre and fantastical men and women who menace one another.

There are men all around, but only one drifts drunkenly into focus. This is Edgar (Robert Fortier), Willie's husband, who speaks gruffly in a low, sardonic voice, and defines himself with guns, motorcycles, and beer. He has an awkward jocular style based on his pose as a chivalrous gunslinger, but is a drunk and a lech and seems hardly able to see his wife. The other men, at work and around the pool in the evening, are objects of Millie's fascination, and she seems always in a state of preparing for dates and dinners that never happen.

In the opening scenes, the three women represent three roles that women often play. Willie is the mother, pregnant with sad knowledge, an earth goddess who drifts across the desert landscape in a world of her own. Millie is a chirpy consumerette who studies the women's magazines, "co-ordinates" her wardrobe by wearing yellows and whites, plans her meals by the time it takes to prepare them, and obsessively shares recipes. Pinky arrives in the movie unformed and childlike; she blows bubbles into her Coke through the straw, she impishly walks in step behind the twins who work at the senior center, she makes faces, she tells Millie "You're the most perfect person I've ever met."

The early passages of the film focus on Millie's relentlessly cheerful attempts to ingratiate herself with her neighbors and co-workers, who ignore her and then ridicule her among themselves. She dreams of dates with Tom, who presides over the grill at poolside dinners, and with the doctors in the hospital across the street from the senior center, but we cringe when she joins the doctors in their commissary for lunch and sits between two of them, who talk right through her. In a movie filled with mirrors, reflections, and multiple images, Millie always seems to be primping, making minute adjustments to her clothes and hair, perfecting her makeup, admiring herself in reflection while no one else seems to quite see her.

Millie is ordered to show Pinky the ropes at work. Their dialogue in the scene is precise and exactly heard, the American idiom. Preparing to take her into the heated exercise pool, Millie asks Pinky, "What's wrong with you?" Pinky doesn't think anything is. "Well there has to be something wrong with you, or otherwise why would you be here?" Pinky finally figures out that Millie is addressing her as a hypothetical patient, for purposes of demonstration. "Oooh, my head!" she says like a child. "Oooh, my legs hurt!" Later, she suddenly plunges underwater and Millie has to drag her up, looking around uneasily to see if anyone noticed.

There is water all through the movie. Altman says the opening shot represents the amniotic fluid surrounding a fetus. The second shot shows old people descending slowly into the exercise pool—returning to the water from where their lives began. A wavy line that drifts across the screen from time to time might be an umbilical cord. Willie's sinister images live at the bottom of the swimming pool, and at a crucial turning point Pinky jumps into the pool from the balcony, is knocked out, rescued, and taken to the hospital.

Altman says Ingmar Bergman's *Persona* was one of his influences, and we can see that in the way Pinky does secret things to hurt Millie, spies on her secrets, and eventually tries to absorb and steal her identity. *Persona* has a central moment of violence in which the film seems to break and the story must begin again, and Pinky's dive into the pool works in the same way, as a definitive tear in the structure of the film. It reassembles itself with Pinky in control. She wears Millie's clothes, uses her social security number, reads her diary. In an early scene, Millie assigned them each a twin bed, and now Pinky moves over and takes Millie's bed. Millie calls her "Pinky" and she explodes: "How many times do I have to tell you? My name's not Pinky! It's Mildred!"

Shelley Duvall's reaction shots during these developments are a study in unease. Millie knows something sinister is happening, but is confused and baffled by Pinky's behavior. Consider the strange scene in the hospital, when two visitors (John Cromwell and Ruth Nelson) appear and identify themselves as Pinky's parents. Pinky says she doesn't know them and has never seen them before. Certainly they look too old to be her parents (Cromwell was in his nineties when the film was made). Who, then, are they? Imposters? Grandparents or adoptive parents? We never really know. Pinky arrives in the desert without a past and essentially without an identity, and simply takes Millie's. And all the while, at a deeper, instinctive level, the Willie character exists beneath their consciousness and will eventually absorb them both.

I saw the film first at Cannes, where it won the best actress award for Duvall (she also later won the Los Angeles Film Critics award, and

Spacek won with the New York Film Critics Circle award). Altman told me the story came to him in a dream: "All complete. The story, the casting, everything." He wrote it down and tried to film it as he dreamed it. Like many dreams, it ends without concluding, and seems to shift toward deeper and more disturbing implications just before fading out. In his DVD commentary, Altman speculates about the film's meaning just as a viewer might, acknowledges that some aspects remain a mystery to him, and provides a startling possibility about the film's last shot. The camera pulls away from the house where the three women now live, and pans over to a pile of discarded tires. "If you were to ask me where I think Edgar is at the end of the film," Altman says, "I think he's buried under those tires."

But of course nothing concrete in the film supports that. No matter. The movie is whole and complete without being lucid and logical. It circles back on itself, Altman says. There are scenes of acute social observation, including the degrees of cruelty that Millie must endure, and details of specific behavior, as when Pinky squirts a cheese spread on crackers, and then spills a bottled shrimp cocktail on her dress. The senior center is run by a couple who seem to have traded genders; the doctor seems effeminate, and his female administrator seems masculine. Much is made of specifics: how to use the time clock, how to get off early on Fridays, how "we don't like the twins." Sometimes the details repeat as in a dream—the way Millie's yellow dresses always get caught in her car door, for example. Gerald Busby's ominous atonal score is a counterpoint to such daily events.

And against these realistic details Altman marshals the force of dreams. In dreams we test new identities, cast our friends in shifting roles, and find ourselves inexplicably at new jobs or in new places where the rules are explained but we never quite understand them. Here the dream is perhaps shared by all three women, each one imagining the other two, each one lacking what the others possess. As men rumble without consequence in the background, they feel their way through mystery toward each other, Willie with sad resignation, Pinky with avid emotional hunger, and Millie, poor Millie, because she knows not what else to do.

{ ACE IN THE HOLE }

There's not a soft or sentimental passage in Billy Wilder's *Ace in the Hole* (1951), a portrait of rotten journalism and the public's insatiable appetite for it. It's easy to blame the press for its portraits of self-destructing celebrities, philandering preachers, corrupt politicians, or bragging serial killers, but who loves those stories? The public does. Wilder, true to this vision and ahead of his time, made a movie in which the only good men are the victim and his doctor. Instead of blaming the journalist who masterminds a media circus, he is equally hard on sightseers who pay twenty-five cents admission. Nobody gets off the hook here. The movie stars Kirk Douglas, an actor who could freeze the blood when he wanted to, in his most savage role. Yes, he made comedies and played heroes, but he could be merciless, his face curling into scorn and bitterness. He plays Charles Tatum, a skilled reporter with a drinking problem, who has been fired in eleven markets (slander, adultery, boozing) when his car breaks down in Albuquerque and he cons his way into a job at the local paper.

The break he's waiting for comes a year later. Dispatched to a remote town to cover a rattlesnake competition, he stops in a desert hamlet and discovers that the owner of the trading post has been trapped in an abandoned silver mine by a cave-in. Tatum forgets the rattlesnakes and talks his way into the tunnel to talk to Leo Minosa (Richard Benedict), whose legs are pinned under timbers. When Tatum comes out again, he sees the future: he will nail down possession of the story, spin it out as long as he can, and milk it for money, fame, and his old job back East.

Confronted by a corrupt local sheriff and mining experts, Tatum takes charge by force of will, issuing orders and slapping around deputies with so much confidence he gets away with it. Learning that Minosa could be rescued in a day or two if workers simply shored up the mine tunnel and brought him out, Tatum cooks up a cockamamie scheme to lengthen the process: rescuers will drill straight down to the trapped man, through solid rock.

The newspaperman moves into Minosa's trading post and starts issuing orders. He finds that the man's wife, a one-time Baltimore bar girl named Lorraine (Jan Sterling), has raided the cash register and plans to take the next bus out of town. He slaps her hard, and orders her to stay and portray a grieving spouse. He needs her for his story. Even though the film has been little seen and appeared for the first time on home video only last month, it produced one of those famous hard-boiled movie lines everybody seems to have heard; ordered to attend a prayer service for her husband, Lorraine sneers, "I don't go to church. Kneeling bags my nylons."

Wilder (1906–2002) came to *Ace in the Hole* right after *Sunset Boulevard* (1950), which had eleven Oscar nominations and won three. Known for his biting cynicism and hard edges in such masterpieces as *Double Indemnity* (1944) and *The Lost Weekend* (1945), he outdid himself with *Ace in the Hole*. The film's harsh portrait of an American media circus appalled the critics and repelled the public; it failed on first release, and after it won European festivals and was retitled *The Big Carnival*, it failed again.

There's not a wasted shot in Wilder's film, which is single-mindedly economical. Students of Arthur Schmidt's editing could learn from the way every shot does its duty. There's not even a gratuitous reaction shot. The black-and-white cinematography by Charles Lang is the inevitable choice; this story would curdle color. And notice how no time is wasted with needless exposition. A wire-service ticker turns up near the mine, without comment. A press tent goes up and speaks for itself.

Although the film is fifty-six years old, I found while watching it again that it still has all its power. It hasn't aged because Wilder and his co-writers, Walter Newman and Lesser Samuels, were so lean and mean. The dialogue delivers perfectly timed punches: "I can handle big news and little news. And if there's no news, I'll go out and bite a dog."

That's what Tatum does with the Minosa story. Not content with the drama of a man trapped underground, Tatum discovers the mountain is an Indian burial ground and adds speculations about a mummy's curse. Soon gawkers are arriving from all over the country, and there are those who have arrived to exploit them: hot dog stands, cotton candy vendors, a carnival with a merry-go-round.

Meanwhile, Minosa grows weaker and depends on Tatum for his contact with the surface. The pounding drill, growing closer, tortures him. Rival newsmen complain about Tatum's role: he controls access to the rescue, the story, and the wife. With every day that passes, the story grows bigger. And Tatum manufactures news on a slow day. He plunges into the cave with a priest and a doctor, and finds out from Leo about his anniversary present for the wife who despises him. It's a fur scarf. Tatum hands it to her and tells her to wear it. She hates it. He almost chokes her with it. She wears it.

Kirk Douglas (born in 1916) was and still is a ferocious competitor. Little wonder one of his first screen roles was as a boxer in *Champion* (1949). When I interviewed him for *Esquire* in 1969, the role of a champion was his central theme: "It doesn't matter if you're a nice guy or you're a bastard. What matters is, you won't bend!" His focus and energy as Chuck Tatum is almost scary. There is nothing dated about Douglas's performance. It's as right-now as a sharpened knife.

Tatum drives relentlessly toward his goal of money and fame, and if there's a moment when we think he might take pity on Minosa, that's just Wilder, yanking our chains. The way Tatum's thinking evolves about the trapped man is a study in subtlety of direction, writing, and acting. In a lesser movie, Tatum would share our sympathy for the pathetic man. Here, he's on a parabola in that direction but wants it to intersect with the moment of his own greatest fame.

Wilder, born in Austria, a refugee from Hitler, certainly became one of America's greatest directors. But he never bought into the American dream. What he saw in Europe warned him off dreams. Although *Ace in the Hole* has always been considered one of his greatest films, its rejection by the marketplace isn't surprising: moviegoers like crime, like suspense, like violence, but they like happy endings, and Wilder is telling them to wake up and smell the coffee.

When the film was released, the press complained about its portrait of news practices and standards, even though the story was inspired by a real media circus when a man named Floyd Collins was trapped in a Kentucky cave. Today, it is hard to imagine some segments of the press not recognizing their hunger for sensation. The same might be said of the public; after the movie was finished, the studio sold admissions to its mountain sets outside Gallup, New Mexico.

{ ADAPTATION }

Charlie Kaufman's screenplay for *Adaptation* (2002) has it three ways. It is wickedly playful in its construction, it gets the story told, and it doubles back and kids itself. There is also the sense that to some degree it's true: that it records the torments of a screenwriter who doesn't know how the hell to write a movie about orchids. And it has the audacity to introduce characters we know are based on real people and has them do shocking things.

Even the DVD maintains the illusion of life colliding with art. The case contains a Columbia interoffice memo, seemingly included by accident, not even referring to this movie. And it is startling to see an ant crawling across the main menu until you get to the dialogue line, "I wish I were an ant."

The movie is the second collaboration between Kaufman and director Spike Jonze, after the equally brilliant *Being John Malkovich* (1999). Jonze spends most of his time making music videos and documentaries, but when he makes a movie, it's a spellbinder, and he has the serene confidence to wade into this Kaufman screenplay and know that he can pull it off.

The movie is inspired by *The Orchid Thief*, by Susan Orlean, a best seller expanded from an article in the *New Yorker*. It involves mankind's fascination for these extraordinary flowers, the blood that has been spilled in collecting them, their boundless illustration of Darwin's ideas about natural selection, and a contemporary orchid hunter in Florida who is a strange, compelling man. Considered simply like that, the book might have inspired a *National Geographic* special.

It could also have been a straight fiction film about the life and times of John Laroche, a Miami eccentric who hit upon the idea of collecting endangered species of orchids from swampland that was Seminole territory. By using real Seminoles to obtain his specimens, he exploited their legal right to use their own ancestral lands. Laroche himself is a student of orchids, and he narrates a poetic passage about the limitless shapes that orchids can take in attracting insects—imitating their shapes and coloring, while all the while neither the flower nor the insect realizes what is happening. There is even one orchid so strangely shaped that Darwin hypothesized a moth with a twelve-inch proboscis that could dip down into its long, hollow tube. Such a moth was actually found.

So you see how the movie could have been a doc. But the title is a pun, referring both to Darwinian principle of adaptation and the ordeal of adapting a book into a screenplay. Although its soul is comic, and it indulges in shameless invention, it is also the most accurate film I have seen about this process—exaggerated, yes, but true. We meet Charlie Kaufman and his (fictitious) twin brother, Donald, both played by Nicolas Cage, who finds subtle ways so that we can always tell them apart. They're like the twins in the old joke, one pessimistic, one optimistic ("There must be a pony in here somewhere").

The movie opens with Charlie's voiceover cataloging his flaws: he's too fat, balding, needs exercise, has no talent, etc. So inspired is Donald by his brother's struggle that he decides to write one of his own, after taking the famous screenwriting seminars of Robert McKee (Brian Cox). Charlie has only scorn for McKee and great doubts about Donald's story idea, which involves a madman and a woman who are the same person with multiple personalities. But how, asks Charlie, do you put them in the same scene together, when one has the other locked in the basement?

Charlie sweats blood over his screenplay. His copy of the book is thick with Post-It notes, the text painted with yellow and red highlighters. He has highlighted about everything. In a sneaky way, a good part of the movie is just Charlie reading the book to us. Then he develops an erotic fixation with the author, Susan (Meryl Streep), masturbating while imagining her bending tenderly to administer to him. He even flies to New York to meet her, but is paralyzed with shyness.

The third major character is John Laroche (Oscar winner Chris Cooper), a swamp rat with no front teeth who lives at home with his dad and describes himself as "probably the most brilliant man I know." At one time, he tells Susan, he had the largest collection of Dutch mirrors in the world. At another, he had a rare collection of tropical fish. He is the only man he knows who can breed the rare Ghost Orchid under glass. When he tires of an obsession, he drops it cold. "Finished with fish," he says, and in context, it's one of the movie's funniest lines.

Having placed these characters onstage (as well as a studio executive played by Tilda Swinton, an agent played by Jay Tavare, and various Indians and park rangers), Kaufman intercuts their scenes with scenes of himself creating them, and scenes from a McKee story conference. He lists all the things he hates in blockbusters: the chase, the shootings, the sex.

And now I must tread carefully, so as not to spoil surprises (everything I've described so far is just the setup). Without going into details, what Kaufman does is create scenes that merge fact with his creative despair, his erotic imagination, and the very kinds of scenes he loathes. Some of these scenes are possibly libelous. The real Orlean and Laroche must have signed waivers abandoning every possible legal recourse; they were very good sports. The scenes are also wildly audacious and hilarious, and you have the instinct that a few of them, such as Laroche driving Orlean in his van and taking her into the swamp, are "based on" truth. That's quite a van, by the way; it not only smells like things are growing in it, but they are.

I will observe that the final chapter on the DVD menu is titled "Deus Ex Machina." Wikipedia splendidly explains the term: "improbable contrivance in a story characterized by a sudden unexpected solution to a seemingly intractable problem." That is exactly what it is, writing Kaufman out of an impossible hole by violating all of his standards.

The performances are wonderful. When Streep's character ingests an obscure Indian drug, wriggles her toes, and does a phone-tone duet with Laroche, you wonder what other actress could have done it so well. Watch Swinton's studio executive closely during her first luncheon with Charlie. As he describes his grandiose and inflamed ideas, she ties to smile twice, in rapid succession, both smiles breaking down into doubts. Body movements very small, very perfect. Cooper pulls off the feat of making a repulsive character into a plausible romantic object for the author, because of Laroche's brilliance and enthusiasm. At first sight, he would rank last on any list of lovers for an elegant *New Yorker* writer.

And Cage. There are often lists of the great living male movie stars: De Niro, Nicholson, and Pacino, usually. How often do you see the name of Nicolas Cage? He should always be up there. He's daring and fearless in his choice of roles, and unafraid to crawl out on a limb, saw it off, and remain suspended in air. No one else can project inner trembling so effectively. Recall the opening scenes in *Leaving Las Vegas*. See him in Scorsese's *Bringing Out the Dead*. Think of the title character in *The Weather Man*. Watch him melting down in *Adaptation*. And then remember that he can also do a parachuting Elvis impersonator (*Honeymoon in Vegas*), a wild rock 'n' roller (*Wild at Heart*), a lovesick one-handed baker (*Moonstruck*), a straight-arrow Secret Service agent (*Guarding Tess*), and on and on.

He always seems so earnest. However improbable his character, he never winks at the audience. He is committed to the character with every atom and plays him as if he were him. His success in making Charlie Kaufman a neurotic mess and Donald Kaufman a carefree success story, in the same movie, comes largely from this gift. There are slight cosmetic differences between the two: Charlie usually needs a shave, Donald has a little more hair. But the real reason we can tell the twins apart, even when they're in the same trick shot, comes from within: Cage can tell them apart. He is always Charlie when he plays Charlie, always Donald when he plays Donald. Look and see.

{ AFTER DARK, MY SWEET }

There is something wrong with Collie, but it's hard to put your finger on it. He tells the bartender he pours a good glass of beer, and the bartender feels like throwing him out of the bar. He looks like a bum, clutching that parcel wrapped in brown paper, but he's young and handsome and will tell you that he's an ex-serviceman with a year and a half of community college. He walks unsteadily out of the blinding sunlight of the desert and into a run-down suburb of Palm Springs, where his destiny is sitting in the same bar, smoking a cigarette.

Her name is Mrs. Fay Anderson. She is pretty clearly an alcoholic. Why else, after Collie beats the bartender senseless, would she follow him down the street in her car and offer him a ride? She does this not because she is drunk, but because widowhood and drinking have put her into the orbit of Uncle Bud, a man whose moneymaking plans require someone like Collie: needy, vulnerable, presentable, persuadable. Individually, these three people are hopeless loners. Together, they are a danger, because they are just smart enough to think up plans they're stupid enough to try.

After Dark, My Sweet (1990) tells their story as an inevitable progress toward failure and doom. What makes the story fascinating is the subterranean way Collie understands everything that is going wrong, understands Mrs. Fay Anderson is a good person and needs to be protected, and protects

15

her in a way so subtle she may still be wondering if he did what she thinks he did.

The movie, based on a novel by Jim Thompson, the poet of circa-1950 pulp noir, has a stubborn, sullen truth to it, focusing on its handful of characters during the course of a particularly incompetent kidnapping. The story is so intimate that everything depends on the performances, and Jason Patric, Rachel Ward, and Bruce Dern, and a character actor named George Dickerson, bring a grim, poetic sadness to the story. Film noir, we are reminded, is not about action and victory, but about incompetence and defeat. If it has a happy ending, something went wrong.

After Fay (Ward) picks up Collie (Patric), she offers him the use of a house trailer at the far end of her dying palm plantation, a kiss on the doorstep, and a lot of drinking companionship. Through her he meets Uncle Bud (Dern), who says he is a former police detective with "connections on the force," and who seems to have no life at all apart from sitting in Fay's living room enlisting them in his scheme to kidnap the son of a rich local man. Fay tells Collie to get away, get out of town: "His scheme's been cooking for months, and if you go away, it will keep right on boiling until it boils away."

Flashbacks inform us that Collie is a former boxer who was in one fight too many—both for his own mental acuity and for the life of the fighter he beat to death. In an all-night diner, he stumbles into Doc Goldman (Dickerson), who takes one look at him and guesses, correctly, he is AWOL from a mental institution. The Doc has a concerned and kindly manner, which masks sexual desire; he invites Collie into his home, offers to let him stay, gives him employment. But Collie cannot take that form of captivity, and returns one morning to Fay's door.

Now Uncle Bud goes into overdrive. He briefs them on his kidnap plan as if it were one of those clever strategies in a heist movie, and not simply a matter of sending Collie to pick up a rich kid in a schoolyard. Collie wonders if maybe there's a way to get the money without the kidnapping: like, maybe, Uncle Bud could foil the kidnapping and collect a reward. The problem, says Uncle Bud, is that the plan doesn't look right unless the hero produces the kidnapper. That would be Collie. At the same time Bud rejects the plan, Collie senses that he sees an angle in it. Get rid of Collie, and the money is only split two ways.

It may seem I've revealed too much of the plot, but *After Dark, My Sweet* is not about the plot but about the personal and moral decisions that Collie and Fay make in light of how the plot unfolds. The closing twenty minutes of this movie contain masterful storytelling, with important decisions arriving silently, by implication. The last sixty seconds are brilliantly complex, as Collie steps a few feet away into the desert to think things through, and does, and improvises a chain of events that is inevitable, heroic, sad, and flawless.

The movie was directed by James Foley, born 1953, a USC film-school graduate, and one of the most underappreciated filmmakers of his generation. His *At Close Range* (1986) contained career-defining performances by Sean Penn and Christopher Walken; his *Glengarry Glen Ross* (1992) was the powerful adaptation of David Mamet's play about real-estate salesmen, with its electric performances by Jack Lemmon, Al Pacino, and Alec Baldwin; his *Confidence* (2003) had that unforgettable Dustin Hoffman performance as a hyperactive strip-club operator.

After Dark, My Sweet is the movie that eluded audiences; it grossed less than $3 million, has been almost forgotten, and remains one of the purest and most uncompromising of modern films noir. It captures above all the lonely, exhausted lives of its characters.

Faye lives in a suburban home that looks half-furnished, as if she is moving in, or out. The water in the pool is thick with leaves. We see a lot of drinking in the house, but no eating. How did Uncle Bud drift into her life? We gather he drifts as a mode of living. How does she feel about his kidnapping scheme? Before Collie came along, it gave them something to vaguely plan. She thinks Bud is a fool, but her life is too unfocused for resistance. When she and Collie finally have sex, the sequence is punctuated by fades into darkness, as if they are seeking oblivion as much as pleasure.

Collie is the central character, the one who retains the ability to decide what he will and should do. Jason Patric's performance is perfectly tuned to give us a man who finds that, with some effort, he can function in the world, but that he has lost the confidence to prevail. He supplies a narration from the Thompson novel that allows us a glimpse inside his mind. That's useful, because although he repeatedly tells people that he hates to be thought of as stupid, the narration proves that he thinks more than he reveals. The subplot involving Doc Goldman is a tragedy within a tragedy, above all for the doctor, a pathetic little man with a yearning for the impossible and a bad sense of timing.

Jason Patric, in movies like this and *Rush* (1991), *Your Friends and Neighbors* (1998), *Narc* (2002), and *The Alamo* (2004), shows a tough complexity that subverts his good looks or turns them to dark dramatic advantage. True, he was also in *Speed 2* (1997), but as the only critic who liked that movie, I cannot complain.

Rachel Ward, remembered for *The Thorn Birds* on TV, creates a wounded and drifting Faye, a woman without hope or purpose, her beautiful face rising bravely to a world of those too exhausted or damaged to be moved by it. The precise evolution of her feelings during the final scene is crucial, but I was also touched by her tenderness in earlier scenes; she plays a kind woman who has been deposited into an ugly situation by the inertia and hopelessness of alcoholism. As for Bruce Dern, there is a calculation in the way the movie denies him a life outside the immediate plot. Yes, we get a glimpse of an associate or two at long range, but here is a man who functions for Collie and Faye only in terms of his need to use them. Uncle Bud, who is nobody's uncle and probably not named Bud, projects the patient intelligence of a man who can convince you of one thing and himself of another.

That ambivalence is the essence of Thompson's novel and Foley's film: it begins with exhaustion and despair, stirs itself into half-hearted evil, and then in a final desperate sequence finds barely enough heroism to bring itself to a stop again. I have seen *After Dark, My Sweet* four times, and it only deepens with the retelling.

{ AFTER HOURS }

After Hours approaches the notion of pure filmmaking; it's a nearly flawless example of—itself. It lacks, as nearly as I can determine, a lesson or message, and is content to show the hero facing a series of interlocking challenges to his safety and sanity. It is *The Perils of Pauline* told boldly and well.

Critics have called it "Kafkaesque" almost as a reflex, but that is a descriptive term, not an explanatory one. Is the film a cautionary tale about life in the city? To what purpose? New York may offer a variety of strange people awake after midnight, but they seldom find themselves intertwined in a bizarre series of coincidences, all focused on the same individual. You're not paranoid if people really are plotting against you, but strangers do not plot against you to make you paranoid. The film has been described as dream logic, but it might as well be called screwball logic; apart from the nightmarish and bizarre nature of his experiences, what happens to Paul Hackett is like what happens to Buster Keaton: just one damned thing after another.

The project was not personally developed by director Martin Scorsese, who was involved at the time in struggles over *The Last Temptation of Christ*. Paramount's abrupt cancellation of that film four weeks before the start of production (the sets had been built, the costumes prepared) sent Scorsese into deep frustration. "My idea then was to pull back, and not to become hysterical and try to kill people," he told his friend Mary Pat Kelly. "So the trick then was to try to do something."

After rejecting piles of scripts, he received one from producers Amy Robinson and Griffin Dunne, who thought it could be made for $4 million. It had been written by Joseph Minion, then a graduate student at Columbia, and Scorsese was later to recall that Minion's teacher, the Yugoslavian director Dusan Makavejev, gave it an *A*. He decided to make it: "I thought it would be interesting to see if I could go back and do something in a very fast way. All style. An exercise completely in style. And to show they hadn't killed my spirit."

It was the first film of what would become his long collaboration with German cinematographer Michael Ballhaus, who had worked with Fassbinder and therefore knew all about low budgets, fast shooting schedules, and passionate directors. It was shot entirely at night, sometimes with on-the-spot improvisation of camera movements, as in the famous shot where Paul Hackett (Dunne), the hero, rings the bell of Kiki Bridges (Linda Fiorentino) and she throws down her keys, and Scorsese uses a POV shot of the keys dropping toward Paul.

In pre-digital days, that really had to happen. They tried fastening the camera to a board and dropping it toward Paul with ropes to stop it at the last moment (Dunne was risking his life), but after that approach produced out-of-focus footage, Ballhaus came up with a terrifyingly fast crane move. Other shots, Scorsese said, were in the spirit of Hitchcock, fetishizing close-ups of objects like light switches, keys, locks, and especially faces. Because we believe a close-up underlines something of importance to a character, Scorsese exploited that knowledge with unmotivated close-ups; Paul thought something critical had happened, but much of the time it had not. In an unconscious way, an audience raised on classic film grammar would share his expectation and disappointment. Pure filmmaking.

Another device was to offhandedly suggest alarming possibilities about characters, as when Kiki describes burns, and Paul finds a graphic medical textbook about burn victims in the bedroom of Marcy (Rosanna Arquette), the girl he has gone to meet at Kiki's apartment. Are the burns accidental or deliberate? The possibility is there, because Kiki is into sadomasochism. Trying to find a shared conversational topic, Paul tells Marcy the story of the time he was a little boy in the hospital and was left for a time in the burn unit, but blindfolded and warned not to remove the blindfold. He did, and what he saw horrified him. Strange, that entering the lives of two women obsessed with burns, he would have his own burn story, but coincidence and synchronicity are the engines of the plot.

After Hours could be called a "hypertext" film, in which disparate elements of the plot are associated in an occult way. In *After Hours*, such elements as a suicide, a method of sculpture, a plaster-of-paris bagel, a $20 bill, and a string of burglaries all reveal connections that only exist because Paul's adventures link them. This generates the film's sinister undertone, as in a scene where he tries to explain all the things that have befallen him, and fails, perhaps because they sound too absurd even to him. One thing many viewers of the film have reported is the high (some say almost unpleasant) level of suspense in *After Hours*, which is technically a comedy but plays like a satanic version of the classic Hitchcock plot formula, the Innocent Man Wrongly Accused.

With different filmmakers and other actors, the film might have played more safely, like *Adventures in Babysitting*. But there is an intensity and drive in Scorsese's direction that gives it desperation; it really seems to matter that this devastated hero struggle on and survive. Scorsese has suggested that Paul's implacable run of bad luck reflected his own frustration during the *Last Temptation of Christ* experience.

Executives kept reassuring Scorsese that all was going well with that film, backers said they had the money, Paramount green-lighted it, agents promised it was a "go," everything was in place, and then time after time an unexpected development would threaten everything. In *After Hours*, each new person Paul meets promises that they will take care of him, make him happy, lend him money, give him a place to stay, let him use the phone, trust him with their keys, drive him home—and every offer of mercy turns into an unanticipated danger. The film could be read as an emotional autobiography of that period in Scorsese's life. The director said he began filming without an ending. IMDb claims, "One idea that made it to the storyboard stage had Paul crawling into June's womb to hide from the angry mob, with

June (Verna Bloom, the lonely woman in the bar) giving 'birth' to him on the West Side Highway." An ending Scorsese actually filmed had Paul still trapped inside the sculpture as the truck driven by the burglars (Cheech and Chong) roared away. Scorsese said he showed that version to his father, who was angry: "You can't let him die!"

That was the same message he had been hearing for weeks from Michael Powell, the great British director who had come on board as a consultant and was soon to marry Scorsese's editor, Thelma Schoonmaker. Powell kept repeating that Paul not only had to live at the end, but to end up back at his office. And so he does, although after Paul returns to the office, close examination of the very final credit shots show that he has disappeared from his desk.

After Hours is not routinely included in lists of Scorsese's master-pieces. Its appearance on DVD was long delayed. On IMDb's ranking of his films by user vote (a notoriously unreliable but sometimes interesting reflection of popular opinion), it ranks sixteenth. But I recall how I felt after the first time I saw it: wrung out. Yes, no matter that it was a satire, a black comedy, an exercise in style, it worked above all as a story that flew in the face of common sense, but it hooked me. I've seen it several times since, I know how it ends, and despite my suspicion of "happy endings," I agree that Paul could not have been left to die. I no longer feel the suspense, of course, because I know what will happen. But I feel the same admiration. "An exercise completely in style," Scorsese said. But he could not quite hold it to that. He had to make a great film because, perhaps, at that time in his life, with the collapse of *The Last Temptation*, he was ready to, he needed to, and he could.

{ THE AGE OF INNOCENCE }

"It was the spirit of it—the spirit of the exquisite romantic pain. The idea that the mere touching of a woman's hand would suffice. The idea that seeing her across the room would keep him alive for another year." So Martin Scorsese told me one autumn afternoon, as we drank tea in the library of his New York town house, a house like the ones inhabited by the characters in his film *The Age of Innocence*.

He was explaining why the director of *Taxi Driver* and *Raging Bull* had made a film about characters defined by the social codes of New York society in the 1870s. We had both read the Edith Wharton novel, and so really no explanation was necessary. We understood that passion and violence can exist in places where absolute decorum rules; that Jake LaMotta, smashing his fists into the walls of his cell in *Raging Bull*, found a release that Newland Archer could not discover anywhere in the sitting rooms and dinners and nights at the opera that defined his life in *The Age of Innocence*.

Archer was a man who loved one woman and married another, because it was the right thing to do. Or, more accurately, because everyone in his world thought it was the right thing to do, and made sure that he did it. The film employs a narration (read by Joanne Woodward) that reflects the way Wharton addresses us directly in the novel, telling us how Archer was trapped. Listen to her: "They all lived in a kind of hieroglyphic world. The real thing was never said or done or even thought, but only represented by a set of arbitrary signs."

Those words could also describe the world of the Mafia in Scorsese's films. Scorsese told me that in reading Wharton's novel, "What has always stuck in my head is the brutality under the manners. People hide what they mean under the surface of language. In the subculture I was around when I grew up in Little Italy, when somebody was killed, there was a finality to it. It was usually done by the hands of a friend. And in a funny way, it was almost like ritualistic slaughter, a sacrifice. But New York society in the 1870s didn't have that. It was so cold-blooded. I don't know which is preferable."

The Age of Innocence is one of Scorsese's greatest films, improperly appreciated because, like *Kundun* (1997), it stands outside the main line of his work. Its story of a man of tradition who spends a lifetime of unrequited love resembles one of Scorsese's favorite films, Michael Powell's *The Life and Death of Colonel Blimp*.

The story: Newland Archer (Daniel Day-Lewis) is planning a proper marriage to the respectable society virgin May Welland (Winona Ryder). Then the Countess Ellen Olenska (Michelle Pfeiffer) returns to New York, and her presence stirs him beyond all measure. Ellen is an American, May's cousin, who unwisely married a Polish count. The count took her fortune and mistreated her, she left him and has fled back to New York—where in the movie's opening scene she joins her relatives, including May and May's mother, in their box at the opera.

This causes a shock in society circles; the Wellands are boldly and publicly standing by the Countess in the face of malicious gossip, and Newland Archer admires it. Observe how Scorsese sets up the dynamic of the film before a word has been spoken between Newland and May or Ellen. It involves a point-of-view sequence, and Scorsese told me: "We look through his opera glasses, seeing what he sees. But not just in regular time. We did stop-frame photography, exposing one frame at a time and printing each frame three times and then dissolving between each three frames. It looks sort of like what you see when you look through an opera glass, but with heightened attention. He scans the audience and then backs up and stops on her. With all the different experimenting we did, that took almost a year to get right."

Archer prematurely announces his engagement to May, perhaps because he senses the danger in his attraction to Ellen. But as he sees more of Ellen, he is excited not only physically but especially by her unconventional mind and tastes. In Europe, she moved among writers and artists; in New York, Newland has a library where he treasures his books and paintings in solitude, because there is no one to share his artistic yearnings. He has a safe job in a boring law office, and only in his library, or during conversation with the Countess, does he feel that his true feelings are engaged.

She is attracted to him for the same reason: in a society of ancient customs and prejudices, enforced by malicious gossip, she believes Archer to be the only man in New York she could love. Ellen tells him, "All this blind obeying of tradition, somebody else's tradition, is thoroughly needless. It seems stupid to have discovered America only to make it a copy of another country." Again, later: "Does no one here want to know the truth, Mr. Archer? The real loneliness is living among all these kind people who ask you only to pretend."

I recently read *The Age of Innocence* again, impressed by how accurately the screenplay (by Jay Cocks and Scorsese) reflects the book. Scorsese has two great strengths in adapting it. The first is visual. Working with the masterful cinematographer Michael Ballhaus, he shows a society encrusted by its possessions. Everything is gilt or silver, crystal or velvet or ivory. The Victorian rooms are jammed with furniture, paintings, candelabra, statuary, plants, feathers, cushions, bric-a-brac, and people costumed to adorn the furnishings.

These people always seem to be posing for their portraits, but Scorsese employs his invariable device of a constantly moving camera to undermine their poses. The camera may be moving so subtly we can hardly tell (unless we watch the sides of the screen), but it is always moving. A still camera implies an observation, a moving camera an observer. The film's narrator observes and comments, and so does the camera, voyeuristically. Occasionally, Scorsese adds old-fashioned touches like iris shots to underline key moments. Or he'll circle an area in brightness and darken the rest, to spotlight the emotion in a sea of ennui.

His second strength is a complete command of tone. Like her friend Henry James, Edith Wharton seldom allowed her characters to state bluntly what they were thinking. They talked around it, inhibited by society and perhaps afraid of their own thoughts. Wharton, however, allows herself a narrator who does state the plain truth. At a key point in the story, May, now Archer's wife, makes comments that reveal how frankly she views the world, and then quickly returns to her tame and naive persona. The narrator tells us what Archer cannot, that he wonders "how such depths of feeling could coexist with such an absence of imagination."

Consider the most crucial passage in the film. Archer has decided to take a decisive step, to break away from his flawless but banal wife, be with the Countess, and accept the consequences. Then the prospects of the Countess change dramatically, and his wife tells him something he did not expect to hear. He is an intelligent man and realizes at once what has been done, how it cannot be undone, and what as a gentleman he must do. His fate is sealed. As he regards the future, the narrator tells us what cannot, in this world, possibly be said in dialogue: he guessed himself to have been, for months, the center of countless silently observing eyes and patiently listening ears. He understood that, somehow, the separation between himself and the partner of his guilt had been achieved. And he knew that now the whole tribe had rallied around his wife. He was a prisoner in the center of an armed camp.

The film ends with a sense of loss, sadness, and resignation, reminding me of the elegiac feeling in Orson Welles's *The Magnificent Ambersons*. The final scene, on a park bench in Paris, sums up not only the movie but Scorsese's reason for making it; it contains a revelation showing that love is more complex and secret than we imagine. Archer's son Ted says his mother told him his father could be trusted because "when she asked you to, you gave up the thing you wanted most." Archer replies, "She never asked me." We reflect, first, that she never did, and, second, that she never needed to.

{ ARMY OF SHADOWS }

Jean-Pierre Melville's *Army of Shadows* is about members of the French Resistance who persist in the face of despair. Rarely has a film shown so truly that place in the heart where hope lives with fatalism. It is not a film about daring raids and exploding trains, but about cold, hungry, desperate men and women who move invisibly through the Nazi occupation of France. Their army is indeed made of shadows: they use false names, they have no addresses, they can be betrayed in an instant by a traitor or an accident. They know they will probably die.

This is not a war film. It is about a state of mind. Under the Vichy government of the World War I hero Petain, France officially permitted the Nazi occupation. Most Frenchmen accepted it as the price of immunity from German armies. DeGaulle runs the Free French movement from London but is a voice on the radio and commands no troops—none except for those in the Resistance, who pose as ordinary citizens, lead two lives, spy on the Germans, provide information to the Allies, and sometimes carry out guerrilla raids against the enemy.

Many films have shown such actions. Melville, who was himself a member of the Resistance, is not interested in making an action film. Action releases tension and makes it external. His film is about the war within the minds of Resistance members, who must live with constant fear, persist in the face of futility, accept the deaths of their comrades, and expect no reward, except the knowledge that they are doing the right thing. Because many die under false names, their sacrifices are never known; in the film, two brothers never discover that they are both in the Resistance, and one dies anonymously.

As one of his films after another is rediscovered, Melville is moving into the ranks of the greatest directors. He was not much honored in his lifetime. We now know from his gangster film *Bob le Flambeur* (1955) that he was an early father of the New Wave—before Godard, Truffaut, Malle. He used actual locations, dolly shots with a camera mounted on a bicycle, unknown actors and unrehearsed street scenes, everyday incidents instead of heightened melodrama. In *Le Samourai* (1967), at a time when movie hit men were larger than life, he reduced the existence of a professional assassin (Alain Delon) to ritual, solitude, simplicity, and understatement. And in *Le Cercle Rouge* (1970), he showed police and gangsters who know how a man must win the respect of those few others who understand the code. His films, with their precision of image and movement, are startlingly beautiful.

Now we have the American premiere of perhaps his greatest film (I have not seen them all, but I will). When *Army of Shadows* was released in 1969, it was denounced by the left-wing Parisian critics as "Gaullist," because it has a brief scene involving DeGaulle and because it involves a Resistance supporting his cause; by the late 1960s, DeGaulle was considered a reactionary relic. The movie was hardly seen at the time. This restored 35mm print, now in art theaters around the country, may be thirty-seven years old, but it is the best foreign film of the year.

It follows the activities of a small cell of Resistance fighters based in Lyons and Paris. Most of them have never met their leader, a philosopher named Luc Jardie (Paul Meurisse). Their immediate commander is Philippe Gerbier, played by Lino Ventura with a hawk nose and physical bulk, introspection, and implacable determination. To overact for Ventura would be an embarrassment. Working with him is a woman named Mathilde (Simone Signoret), and those known as Francois (Jean-Pierre Cassel), Le Masque (Claude Mann), and Felix (Paul Crauchet).

"Does your husband know of your activities?" Mathilde is asked one day. "Certainly not. And neither does my child." Signoret plays her as a mistress of disguise, able to be a dowdy fishwife, a bold whore, even a German nurse who with two comrades drives an ambulance into a Nazi prison and says she has orders to transport Felix to Paris. The greatness of her deception comes not as she impersonates the German-speaking nurse, but when she is told Felix is too ill to be moved. She instantly accepts that, nods curtly, says "I'll report that," and leaves. To offer the slightest quarrel would betray them.

The members of this group move between safe houses, often in the countryside. When they determine they have a traitor among them, they take him to a rented house, only to learn that new neighbors have moved in. They would hear a gunshot. A knife? There is no knife. "There is a towel in the kitchen," Gerbier says. We see the man strangled, and rarely has an onscreen death seemed more straightforward, and final.

To protect the security of the Resistance, it is necessary to kill not only traitors but those who have been compromised. There is a death late in the film that comes as a wound to the viewer; we accept that it is necessary, but we do not believe it will happen. For this death of one of the bravest of the group, the leader Luc Jardie insists on coming out of hiding because the victim "must see me in the car." That much is owed: respect, acknowledgment, and then oblivion.

There are moments of respite. Airplanes fly from England to a landing field on the grounds of a baron (Jean-Marie Robain) to exchange personnel and bring in supplies and instructions. Gerbier and Jardie are taken to London for a brief ceremony with DeGaulle and see *Gone with the Wind*. Then they are back in France.

Yes, there are moments of excitement, but they hinge on decisions, not actions. Gerbier at one point is taken prisoner and sent to be executed. The Nazis march their prisoners to a long indoor parade ground. Machine guns are set up at one end. The prisoners are told to start running. Anyone who reaches the far wall without being hit will be spared—to die another day. Gerbier argues with himself about whether he should choose to run. That is existentialism in extremis.

Because he worked in the Resistance (and because he was working from a well-informed 1943 Joseph Kessel novel), Melville knew that life for a fighter was not a series of romantic scenes played in trench coats, but ambiguous everyday encounters that could result in death. After Gerbier escapes from Gestapo headquarters, he walks into a barber shop to have his mustache removed. The barber has a poster of Petain on his wall. Not a word is said between the two men. A sweating man at night who wants his mustache removed is a suspect. As Gerbier pays and readies to leave, the barber simply hands him an overcoat of another color.

Such a moment feels realistic, and is perhaps based on a real event. But "I had no intention of making a film about the Resistance," Melville told the interviewer Rui Nogueira. "So with one exception—the German occupation—I excluded all realism." The exploits of his heroes are not meant so much to reflect real events as to evoke real states of mind. The only big German scene is the opening shot, of German troops marching on the Champs-Elysees. It is one of the shots he is proudest of, Melville said, and to make it he had to win an exemption from a law that prohibited German uniforms on the boulevard.

How did the Resistance fighters feel, risking their lives for a country that had officially surrendered? What were their rewards? In 1940, Melville says, the Resistance in all numbered only six hundred. Many of them died under torture, including Jean Moulin, the original of Luc Jardie. Kessel: "Since he was no longer able to speak, one of the Gestapo chiefs, Klaus Barbie, handed him a piece of paper on which he had written, 'Are you Jean Moulins?' Jean Moulin's only reply was to take the pencil from Colonel Barbie and cross out the 's.'"

{ ATLANTIC CITY }

I might have thought *Atlantic City* was more of a fantasy had I not lived for several weeks circa 1970 in a hotel near Sunset Strip named the Sunset Marquis. It is now a luxury hotel of the same name, but at that time a room was $19 a night, and the residents included Tiny Tim, Van Heflin, and Elaine May. You dialed room service, you got Greenblatt's Deli. A scrap-iron dealer named Jack Sachs presided as the "mayor" from his poolside efficiency. He ran the cocktail hour as his personal salon, supplying whiskey to the circulating population of show-biz folks—Jackie Gayle, Roy Scheider, Harold Ramis—on their way up, down, or sideways.

A similar establishment provides the location for Louis Malle's *Atlantic City* (1980), which takes place in an apartment house near the Boardwalk. It's slated for demolition, and all around are vacant lots filled with rubble and the sky-cranes of new construction. Every exterior shot seems to have a background of debris being shoved out of upper windows, or bulldozers clearing vacant lots.

In this doomed building live three people: an oyster-bar waitress named Sally (Susan Sarandon), an aging numbers runner named Lou (Burt Lancaster), and a widow named Grace (Kate Reid), who came to the city forty years ago for a Betty Grable look-alike contest and depends on Lou to run her errands, some of a sexual nature. She lives in an apartment so filled

31

with photographs, stuffed animals, feather boas, geegaws, silk festoons, and glitz that you might think it is a fantasy, but not me, because I saw Tiny Tim's apartment one morning when the maid left the door standing open.

Lou claims to have been big-time in Vegas in the old days, "a cell-mate of Bugsy Siegel," no less. Now he walks a daily route through Atlantic City's urban decay, taking twenty-five-cent bets on the numbers. It's implied that a stipend from Grace keeps him afloat. At night he stands behind the blinds of his darkened apartment and watches as Sally engages in an after-work ritual. She cuts fresh lemons and caresses her skin to take away the shellfish smell.

Later, after they know each other, Lou confesses that he used to watch her. She says she knew there was somebody, but didn't know who. "What did you see when you looked at me?" she asks. He describes her ritual in great detail, and when the camera cuts back to her, she has opened her blouse, as if his words were stage directions.

Into this closed world come two loose cannons, Dave and Chrissie. Dave was once married to Sally, then ran away with Chrissie, Sally's younger sister. They're a better match, equally spaced out; Sally on the other hand wants to succeed. "Teach me stuff," she asks Lou at one point.

She's taking lessons in blackjack from a casino boss (Michel Piccoli). Dave has stolen some drugs in Philadelphia, wants to sell them in Atlantic City, and has a contact named Alfie (Al Waxman) who runs a permanent poker game in a hotel room. Gangsters from Philadelphia inevitably come looking for their drugs and for Dave, who becomes dead. Chrissie becomes the confidant of Grace, Lou inherits the drugs and makes the deals, and then he buys himself a new white suit and sets himself up as a knight in shining armor to protect Sally from the guys who killed her ex-husband.

There is nothing particularly new in this screenplay, written by the playwright John Guare, and assembled from drugs, colorful characters, a decaying city, memories of the past. What makes *Atlantic City* sweet— and that's the word for it—is the gentleness with which Lou handles his last chance at amounting to something, and the wisdom with which Sally handles Lou. Lou wants to take the drug money as a gift from the gods and recreate his glory days. The question is, were there really glory days? A gangster as important as Lou claims to have been should be, by now, either rich or dead.

Lou is not a letch. He has dignity, the same kind of instinctive aristocratic self-regard that made Lancaster's performance in Visconti's *The Leopard* (1963) so authentic. When you embody dignity, you don't need to play it. There is a moment in the hotel room with the poker players when he casually uses the side of his arm to brush away someone who invades his space. And a moment when he says quietly to another man, "Don't touch the suit." That he can seriously see himself as the lover of the much younger Sally is more plausible when he uses the word "protector."

When he actually does protect her, his dreams seem within reach. The giveaway is that he's so elated when he defends her from an attack by two hoods. A real gangster, a real buddy of Bugsy's, a real former hit-man, would not be as excited as a kid. Yet Lou's childlike delight at his own startling behavior is part of the man he really is: like the narrator of Scorsese's *GoodFellas*, he admires and envies gangsters and likes to be a big shot.

Louis Malle (1932–95) was a French New Wave pioneer who alternated between documentaries and fiction, between France and America. His first feature, *Elevator to the Gallows* (1958), grew directly from the 1950s French noir period that gave us Jacques Becker, Jean-Pierre Melville, and the late flowering of the actor Jean Gabin. Their French noirs were more elegies than adventures, more concerned with failure than triumph, less interested in action than the close observation of the daily behavior of their heroes. The best scene in Becker's *Touchez Pas au Grisbi* shows Gabin preparing a late-night dinner of pate for the old pal he has loyally supported through one fiasco after another. After dinner, he gives him a toothbrush and pajamas.

For Lancaster's character, the association with Grace begins with the fact that she needs Lou to survive. To conceal her desperation, she insults and criticizes him like a diva, and he sees right through her. Grace the aging beauty (and perhaps retired whore) finds a natural rapport with Chrissie the hippie, who believes in reincarnation and foot reflexology. They're far apart in age, style, and beliefs, but they both construct fantasies to wall off the grim reality surrounding them.

As for Lou and Sally, there is something tender and subtle going on. Neither was born yesterday. Both have dreams. Both have lived with disappointment. Even though they could be lovers, they have no future together, and maybe no future separately. They don't need to say this to each other. When he helps her, it is because she needs help, and equally because he needs to help. His payoff is not living happily ever after, but in having an eyewitness who knows that at least once during his descent into obscurity he stepped up to the plate and acted as he thinks a man should act—a man like the men he admires, who may have been criminals but were powerful and respected. The movie does not deny reality; it ends with what must happen, in the way it must happen, given what has gone before.

The British critic Philip French, who knew Malle since his first film, thinks *Atlantic City* is the best of his American projects, although I would choose *My Dinner with Andre* (1981), and Stanley Kauffmann thinks *Vanya on 42nd Street* (1994), Malle's last film, is the only successful film of a Chekhov play. When I told a French film official last autumn that I had just seen and admired *Elevator to the Gallows*, I received not a smile but a scornful "pffft!" Perhaps Malle alienated his countrymen by moving to America, by marrying Candice Bergen, by taking on so many American stories (*Pretty Baby, Alamo Bay*). Malle did not follow his New Wave origins into ideological extremities, like Godard, but like his German contemporary Fassbinder frankly desired large audiences.

What's interesting, even with a seemingly commercial project like *Atlantic City*, is how resolutely he stayed with the human dimension of his story and let the drug plot supply an almost casual background. Here is a movie where reincarnation is treated at least as seriously as cocaine, and the white suit even more so.

{ Au Revoir les Enfants }

There is such exhilaration in the heedless energy of the schoolboys. They tumble up and down stairs, stand on stilts for playground wars, eagerly study naughty postcards, read novels at night by flashlight, and are even merry as they pour into the cellars during an air raid. One of the foundations of Louis Malle's *Au Revoir les Enfants* (1987) is how naturally he evokes the daily life of a French boarding school in 1944. His central story shows young life hurtling forward; he knows, because he was there, that some of these lives will be exterminated.

The film centers on the friendship of two boys of twelve, Julien Quentin and Jean Bonnet. They are played by Gaspard Manesse and Raphael Fejto. They had never acted before and barely acted again. Julien's father is always absent at his factory; his glamorous mother wants him safely away from Paris, and sends him by train to a Catholic school for rich children. Here he will find priests and teachers he respects, and classrooms where the students actually seem happy. One day after Christmas, a new student arrives: Jean.

Of course the others pick on the newcomer, and Julien joins in. Sometimes at that age fights are a form of expressing friendship, and often enough they end in laughter. They both love to read. Gradually, through a series of signs so subtle the other boys never pick up on them, Julien learns that Jean is concealing a secret. Is it the way he avoids questions about his family? The fact that he doesn't recite the prayers with everyone else, and skips choir practice? Julien notices that when Jean kneels at the altar rail, the priest quietly passes without giving him a communion wafer. In Jean's locker, Julien finds a book from which the name has not entirely been removed. The name is Kippelstein.

Julien knows almost nothing about Jews. "Why do we hate them?" he asks his older brother, Francois. "They're smarter than we are, and they killed Jesus." Julien doesn't understand: "But it was the Romans who killed Jesus." He does, however, feel some envy after he fails a piano lesson with the pretty Mlle. Davenne (Irene Jacob), and then Jean sits down and begins to play with ease and beauty. From time to time, the single awkward notes of Julien's tortured piano lesson will be heard on the soundtrack, as when Jean gets a better essay score than Julien. When Julien sits for a long time in a bathtub, in close-up, we hear the notes again as the camera focuses on his face. We imagine he is piecing together everything he knows, and deciding to keep Jean's secret.

It is near the end of the war. Marshal Petain's collaborationist French government has lost popularity and an American invasion seems imminent. "Nobody likes Petain anymore," someone says during parents' weekend. Nazis patrol the district but are not always monsters. Julien asks his mother to invite Jean to join them and Francois at lunch, and when an old Jewish man at another table is confronted by French fascists, German officers at another table order them out of the room and tell the old man to continue with his meal.

In the film's most important sequence, Julien is involved in a treasure hunt in a forest of deep shadows, large rock outcroppings, and an ominous early twilight. He gets lost, and it feels a little like *Picnic at Hanging Rock*. He finds the treasure in a dark, hidden cave, and then he finds Jean. "Are there wolves in this forest?" Jean asks. They encounter a boar, who snuffles at them and waddles away. Walking home after curfew, they are seen by two Germans in a car. Jean begins to run, but the Germans catch both boys, give them a blanket to stay warm and return to them to the school. "You see, we Bavarians are Catholics also," they say.

Yes, but the long day in the forest is the story of Julien's year, the story of lost wandering, surrounded by unnamed dangers. He competes with the other students, is isolated, discovers a secret, and can share it with only one other student, Jean Bonnet. The two boys never talk about Julien keeping Jean's secret; it doesn't need saying. "Are you ever afraid?" Julien asks. "All the time," says Jean.

Au Revoir les Enfants is based on a wartime memory of Louis Malle (1932–95), who attended this very school, le Petit-College d'Avon, which was attached to a Carmelite monastery near Fountainebleau. The school, like many Catholic schools and other organizations, took in Jewish children under assumed names to shelter them from the Nazis; partly as a result, some 75 percent of French Jews survived the war, according to an essay by Francis J. Murphy.

Malle never forgot the day when Nazis raided the Petit-College and arrested three Jewish students and the headmaster (Father Jacques in life, Father Jean in the film). The students and their teachers lined up in the courtyard as the little group was marched off the grounds; the priest looked back at them and said, "Au revoir, les enfants." Goodbye, children. The three boys died at Auschwitz. The priest, whose birth name was Lucien Bunuel, nursed others and shared his rations at the Mauthausen camp, where he died four weeks after the war ended.

I remember the day *Au Revoir les Enfants* was shown for the first time, at the 1987 Telluride Film Festival. I had come to know Louis Malle a little since a dinner we had in 1972; he was the most approachable of great directors. I was almost the first person he saw after the screening. I remember him weeping as he clasped my hands and said, "This film is my story. Now it is told at last."

Louis Malle was a pioneer of the French New Wave. His *Elevator to the Gallows* (1958) followed Jeanne Moreau through Paris using available light and a camera on a bicycle, which were then revolutionary techniques. His *The Lovers* (1958) and *Zazie in the Metro* (1960) were simultaneous with the other early New Wave films. Later in his career, he made powerful but more conventional narrative films like *Au Revoir les Enfants, Murmur of the Heart* (1971), *Pretty Baby* (1978), and *Atlantic City* (1980). His *Lacombe,*

Lucien (1974), about a working-class youth who falls in with the Nazis, may have been inspired in part by the character of Joseph, the kitchen helper in *Au Revoir*. As he gained worldwide success, Malle fell out of favor with some French critics because his films were popular and accessible, and also because he married Candice Bergen, although their love was true and she was his rock as he died in 1995 of lymphoma. Until the end, he was willing to experiment, as in *My Dinner with Andre* (1981), and the remarkable *Vanya on 42nd Street* (1994), a film about a rehearsal that Stanley Kauffmann thinks is the best adaptation of Chekhov ever filmed.

It is difficult to say exactly what Malle thought Julien's role (or his own) was in the capture of the Jewish students. In the film, a Nazi enters the classroom and demands to know if there are any Jews present. Julien unintentionally betrays Jean. I wrote in my original review: "Which of us cannot remember a moment when we did or said precisely the wrong thing, irretrievably, irreparably? The instant the action was completed or the words were spoken we burned with shame and regret, but what we had done never could be repaired." Yes, but it is not clear that Julien is entirely responsible for Jean's capture. "They would have caught me, anyway," he tells Julien, giving him his treasured books.

The film ends in a long close-up of Julien, reminding us of the last shot of Truffaut's *The 400 Blows*, and we hear Malle's voice on the soundtrack: "More than forty years have passed, but I'll remember every second of that January morning until the day I die." After the speech ends, the camera stays on Julien's face for twenty-five more seconds, and on the soundtrack the piano is heard once again, this time quiet, sad, and correct.

{ BABEL }

England and America are two countries separated by a common language.

GEORGE BERNARD SHAW

Even more separated are cultures that do not share languages, values, frames of reference, or physical realities. *Babel* weaves stories from Morocco, America, Mexico, and Japan, all connected by the thoughtless act of a child, and demonstrates how each culture works against itself to compound the repercussions. It is the third and most powerful of Alejandro Gonzalez Inarritu's trilogy of films in which the action is connected or influenced in invisible ways. Sometimes these are called "hyperlink films." After *Amores Perros* (2000) and *21 Grams* (2003), it shows his mastery of the form, and it surprises us by offering human insight rather than obligatory tragedy.

Without revealing too much, let me chronologically piece together the stories. A Japanese businessman goes on a hunting trip in Morocco, and tips his guide with a rifle. The guide sells the rifle to a friend, who needs it to kill the jackals attacking his sheep. The friend's son shoots toward a tourist bus at a great distance. An American tourist is wounded. The tourist's Mexican nanny, in San Diego, is told to stay with their two children, but doesn't want to miss her son's wedding, and takes the children along with her to Mexico. Police enquiries about the Japanese businessman's rifle lead to consequences for his disturbed daughter.

Yes, but there is so much more to *Babel* than the through-line of the plot. The movie is not, as we might expect, about how each culture wreaks hatred and violence on another, but about how each culture tries to behave well, and is handicapped by misperceptions. *Babel* could have been a routine recital of man's inhumanity to man, but Inarritu, the writer-director, has something deeper and kinder to say: when we are strangers in a strange land, we can bring trouble upon ourselves and our hosts. Before our latest Mars probe blasted off, it was scrubbed to avoid carrying Earth microbes to the other planet. All of the characters in this film are carriers of cultural microbes.

Consider the plight of Yussef (Boubker Ait El Caid), the Moroccan boy. He lives happily with his family, tends sheep, plays with his brother Ahmed. Two alien microbes come into his world: a high-powered rifle and a tourist bus. Over a great distance, he childishly shoots at one with the other, and seriously wounds Susan (Cate Blanchett), an American tourist. Her husband, Richard (Brad Pitt), demands doctors, ambulances, helicopters, but has to settle for a friendly local man who takes Susan into his home and summons what the village has in the way of medical care.

American authorities immediately brand the shooting as a terrorist act. The Moroccan government refuses to send a helicopter because it insists it harbors no terrorists. This becomes a worldwide news story, told in cable cliches. The other tourists on the bus, led by an outraged Brit, insists on leaving the couple behind, in part because the bus driver insists on saving gas by not turning on the air conditioning—this in a land where the locals have no choice but to live with the heat. As ripples from the original event spread wider, the original reality gets lost.

The American couple lives forty-five minutes north of the Mexican border. Susan has arranged for her sister to watch their children while the nanny (Adriana Barraza) attends her son's wedding. But the sister cannot come, the nanny cannot find a substitute, and in desperation she gets her nephew (Gael Garcia Bernal) to drive them all to the wedding. Returning to America, they are properly questioned by U.S. border authorities, but the nephew (who has been drinking, and knows his aunt is an unregistered worker) runs the border, is pursued, and leaves the nanny and children in the desert intending to return. How could the nanny take the children to Mexico? How could she miss her son's wedding? Yes, but how could the nephew leave them in the desert? He drank at the wedding.

Contrary to our expectations, the U.S. border guards are not the villains. Nor, really, is the nanny. Nor did the American couple do anything wrong. Susan was essentially wounded by culture clash. Her husband could not empathize with the nanny's desire to attend her son's wedding because he was too disturbed about his wife ("I'll pay for a bigger wedding," he says). The nanny thought the children, whom she loved, would be safe with her and her family. The nephew should not have been drinking, but it was his cousin's wedding and such things have been known to happen. The border guards were correct in questioning two Mexicans, one inebriated, traveling after midnight with young children not their own.

I could go through each of the stories in this way, showing how carefully Inarritu portrays the motivations of his characters. Richard, the Pitt character, behaves like an ugly American in one sense, and in another like a man terrified of losing his wife. He is insulting, sometimes without realizing it, to his generous hosts. Nor should he assume no one in Morocco speaks English. When Moroccan authorities go looking for the shooter, they behave as we expect, and the sheepherder's family behaves as we would also expect, and children will be children.

In Inarritu's *21 Grams*, I thought the interlocking stories spun a little out of his control. Everything finally fit together, in a very good film, but there was sometimes the sense that we were more disoriented than the film really wanted us to be. *Amores Perros*, with its three stories, was easy to follow, and now *Babel* finds Inarritu in full command of his technique: the writing and editing moves between the stories with full logical and emotional clarity, and the film builds to a stunning impact because it does not hammer us with heroes and villains but asks us to empathize with all of its characters. They all have their reasons, they all work with only limited information, they all win our sympathy.

There were a few complaints when the film was released that the Japanese plot was hauled into the movie against its will. Not at all. The point of *Babel* is that none need necessarily have met, that the odds against all of these events are high, but that they happened, and there you are. There is even the theme of adolescent sexual insecurity to link Japan with Morocco. And the behavior of police officers in both countries, who are doing their jobs blamelessly, based on the information they have. And with various adults, including the passengers on the bus, there is the reality of men accustomed to having their way, finding themselves in a place where no one knows or cares who they are.

Technically, *Babel* may seem to be an example of the Idiot Plot, in which at many points one word or sentence could clear everything up. But these characters are not idiots, and desperately want to utter that word or sentence, but are prevented because of (a) the language barrier, (b) their cultural assumptions, (c) the inability of others to comprehend what they are actually saying, and (d) how in that case everyone falls into an established script made of prejudice and misunderstanding. Inarritu films more in sorrow than anger, and spares most of his characters tragic retribution because he loves and understands them too much to simply grind them in a plot. This is a film about people who do what we might do—if we were them. We are not, but then it is useful to reflect that they are not us, either.

Inarritu (born 1963) is one of three friends I have taken to calling the New Mexican Cinema, although other names should and will be included. Guillermo del Toro made *Pan's Labyrinth*, and Alfonso Cuaron *Children of Men*, and with *Babel* those three titles are among the adornments of recent cinema. For unknown reasons a country (France, Sweden, Brazil, South Korea, Iran, Germany) will suddenly produce a brilliant generation, and that is happening right now in Mexico. That these Mexicans are also completely at home in English is our gain, but not their loss, because outside the United States most audiences are long accustomed to dubbing, even into their own languages.

{ THE BAND WAGON }

The opening credits of Vincente Minnelli's *The Band Wagon* play over a top hat and cane, which would remind us of Fred Astaire even if he weren't the star of the movie. Then we join an auction of movie memorabilia. The top hat and cane don't sell, even when the auctioneer pleads, "Fifty cents, anyone?" They belonged to a has-been hoofer named Tony Hunter, and now we see him, played by Astaire, on a train to New York City. Maybe he can make a comeback on Broadway. From the way he sings "By Myself," he doesn't seem hopeful.

The Band Wagon (1953) came only a year after the same writers, Betty Comden and Adolph Green, wrote *Singin' in the Rain*. Both are great backstage musicals, one about Hollywood, the other about Broadway, one starring Gene Kelly, the other Fred Astaire. *Singin' in the Rain* is a comedy, but *The Band Wagon* has a note of melancholy along with its smiles, a sadness always present among Broadway veterans, who have seen more failure than success, who know the show always closes and that the backstage family breaks up and returns to the limbo of auditions and out-of-town tryouts.

The movie takes a would-be musical through all the stages of writing, casting, production, choreography, rehearsals, failure on the road, and eventual triumph on Broadway. It's so happily aware of its genre that we actually do hear mention of renting a barn and putting on a show. But it draws on experience with the actual working conditions of Broadway professionals, just as *Singin' in the Rain* knew a lot about how movies are made. *Singin' in the Rain* was the work of a fresh newcomer (Stanley Donen was twenty-eight when he directed it). *The Band Wagon* is informed by a Minnelli who, at fifty, had logged a long tour of duty in show biz, not least as the husband of the complicated Judy Garland.

When Astaire made *The Band Wagon*, he was fifty-four years old but hardly washed up. In recent years, he had made *Easter Parade* and *Royal Wedding*, and his future held *Funny Face* and *Silk Stockings*. But in the movie as in life, he is insecure about his gifts; "Fred rehearsed until he drove you crazy," remembers co-star Nanette Fabray, and he was uneasy about co-starring with Cyd Charisse. "She's rather tall, isn't she?" he worries in the movie, and Fabray assures him, "It's a stage illusion."

It wasn't. Charisse was fully as tall as Astaire, taller with heels, and she had classical dance training; Astaire's Tony Hunter complains about "this little ballerina's snide insinuation that I'm only a hoofer." Real insecurities and rivalries were right beneath the surface of the fictional ones created by Comden and Green, and real personalities are not far offscreen; they even based the writers Lily and Lester Marton on themselves (Minnelli cast them as Oscar Levant, who looked like Green, and Fabray, who had Comden's spirit).

The Astaire and Charisse characters are brought together by Jeffrey Cordova (Jack Buchanan), a director-producer-star with artistic pretensions, who thinks the lively little musical by the Martons should be reworked as a version of *Faust*. The Cordova character is said to be inspired by Jose Ferrer, who at the time was starring in one Broadway show and producing three others, but in the ego and the big plans there's also an echo of Orson Welles.

Buchanan, an actor from Scotland who kids his own patrician stage presence, has fun with a character who lacks any practical knowledge about what a production can afford and what an audience will endure. (One of the movie's charms is the moment when he concedes he is wrong and Astaire is right, and they do a soft-shoe to "I Guess I'll Have to Change My Plan.")

Astaire and Charisse get into a furious fight the first time they meet, and then, in the scene where the movie's magic first begins to work, they make up wordlessly in the "Dancing in the Dark" sequence under a full moon in Central Park. (The critic Douglas Pratt recommends watching this scene with the audio turned off: "It is haunting.") Here and throughout the movie, Charisse is a sexy and capable partner for Astaire, who said somewhat enigmatically, "When you dance with her, you stay danced with."

The overblown Faustian musical is a flop in New Haven; a stagehand observes, "You've got more scenery in this show than there is in Yellowstone National Park." As the depressed actors and dancers gather in a hotel suite, they cheer themselves with the "I Love Louisa" musical number, "but only for the time it takes them to sing and dance," writes the critic Joe McElhaney. "The moment the song is finished everyone goes into a depressed slump."

Levant in fact looks like he's depressed most of the time. A real-life hypochondriac whose character recites a list of complaints early in the movie, Levant was a friend and good-luck mascot for Arthur Freed, the key producer during MGM's golden age. That's how he got so many good supporting roles (as in *An American in Paris*), despite often looking grumpy and exhausted. "Oscar needed someone to yell at," Fabray remembers in an interview on the DVD. When he blew a line, he'd blame it on somebody—usually picking on Fabray, who was appearing in her first movie. After she told him to go to hell, she says, he backed off.

All of the interviews with the surviving cast members suggest the film was an unhappy shoot, although they don't quite say why. Minnelli's offstage marriage problems with Garland may have been one reason, Astaire's ambivalence about Charisse might have been another, Levant's daily appearance represented what he liked to call "a pharmaceutical miracle," and Buchanan was undergoing painful dental surgery. Still, a great musical emerged from the shambles, just as it does in the story.

Despite the elegance of "Dancing in the Dark" and the long "Girl Hunt" ballet sequence toward the end (with Astaire as a private eye and Charisse a slinky dame in red), my favorite musical number is an early one, "Shine on Your Shoes." Liza Minnelli, then seven, followed her father around during the filming, and remembers him scouting Penn Station for ideas about the soundstage sets.

Minnelli saw Leroy Daniels, a real shoeshine man who sang and danced as he worked, and that not only inspired the number, but got Daniels a trip to Hollywood and a scene where he co-stars with Astaire. He's a gifted performer, his timing as precise as Astaire's, and perhaps because he's the real thing, we sense a freshness and joy. Note, too, Astaire's casual strength when he lifts himself on the arms of the chair so he can kick in mid-air.

Most of the scene's charm is because of Astaire and Daniels, but some, too, was contributed by Minnelli. McElhaney recommends watching the "Shine on Your Shoes" number, but not focusing on Astaire and Daniels: "Instead, only take note of the direction of the extras; watch it again, and only note the function of the decor and the camera movements; then watch it one final time putting all of these elements together." What that exercise would illustrate is that for Minnelli, the whole screen was always in play, not just the foreground and the stars.

Many of the movie's songs, by Arthur Schwartz and Howard Deitz, already existed; MGM in those days didn't simply recycle Broadway hits but created new musicals from scratch, often using songs it already owned. That works here because, after dumping the Faustian musical, the performers decide to put on a revue. One song written new for the movie would become a touchstone: Deitz and Schwartz's "That's Entertainment," which celebrates show business in a way as joyous but not as zany as Donald O'Connor's "Make 'em Laugh" in *Singin' in the Rain*. One of their older songs that makes an unconvincing reappearance is "Louisiana Hayride," originally written in 1932; although in a revue anything, so to speak, goes, the hayride seems like a stretch.

Another musical sequence, the bizarre "Triplets," shows Astaire, Fabray, and Buchanan all apparently midgets dressed as babies, sliding down from their high chairs and dancing. Since we see their feet hit the floor and special effects seem impossible, how did they do it? By balancing on artificial legs strapped to their knees, Fabray reports; they fell dozens of times before getting it right, and relied on pain killers.

All of these backstage details seem like a distraction from the magic of *The Band Wagon*, but part of the film's appeal comes from our sense that what we see is not far removed from the actual process of making the movie. It's entertainment, all right, but it's also hard work, and Astaire chain smokes all the way through it. "I don't think a dancer should smoke," Charisse tells him early in the film, but by the end, she's bumming a cigarette.

{ BARAKA }

If man sends another *Voyager* to the distant stars and it can carry only one film on board, that film might be *Baraka*. It uses no language, so needs no translation. It speaks in magnificent images, natural sounds, and music both composed and discovered. It regards our planet and the life upon it. It stands outside of historical time. To another race, it would communicate: this is what you would see if you came here. Of course this will all long since have disappeared when the spacecraft is discovered.

The film was photographed over fourteen months by director Ron Fricke, who invented a time-lapse camera system to use for it. In 1992, it was the first film since 1970 to be photographed in Todd-AO, a 65mm system, and now, it seems to have been the last. The restored 2008 Blu-ray is the finest video disc I have ever viewed or ever imagined. It was made from the Todd-AO print, which was digitally restored to a perfection arguably superior to the original film. It is the first 8K resolution video ever made of a 65mm film, on the world's only scanner capable of it. It is comparable to what is perceptible to the human eye, the restorers say. *Baraka* by itself is sufficient reason to acquire a Blu-ray player.

The film consists of awesome sights, joyful, sad, always in their own way beautiful. By that I do not mean picturesque. A friend came into the room while I was watching the film, saw a close-up of the head of a Gila monster and said, "That's beautiful." I asked if she liked lizards. "I hate lizards," she said, shuddering. She wasn't thinking about lizards. She was observing the iridescent scales of the creature's head. Beauty is in the eye of the beholder. We are the beholder.

A large gathering of men, shaped in a rough circle, join in synchronous dancing, bowing, standing, kneeling, sitting, standing, their arms in the air, their fingers fluttering like the wings of birds, their voices a rhythmic chatter. Asia, somewhere. They face a statue of the Buddha. Their movements are more complex and intricately timed than the drummers at the opening ceremonies of the Beijing Olympics. More inspiring, also, because they have chosen to do this as worship and have not been drilled. They have perfected their ritual, and in their faces we do not see strain or determination, despite the physical ordeal, but contentment and joy. Their movements have the energy of deep enjoyment.

There's the indescribable beauty of aborigines, their bodies bearing necklaces, bracelets, and body ornaments made from countless tiny beads, their arms and faces painted in intricate patterns of innumerable dots. They dip a cheap plastic comb in paint and rotate it across their skin to leave the dots. Their hypnotic dancing somehow reverberates with the Asian dancers. We see the bright scarlet paint on the brow of a young Amazonian girl, peering solemnly from bright green leaves. A young woman of the Maasai tribe in Kenya is clothed in a beauty to render "designer fashions" threadbare.

More images: the sorrowful fall in slow motion of an ancient and lofty tree in the rain forest. The sad poetic beauty in slow motion of a chain of explosions for a strip mine. The despoiling of the land by the deep mine pits. The undeniable beauty of the access roads circling down to the pit bottoms, one line atop another. A virgin forest seen from high above, looking down on wave after wave of birds, hundreds of thousands of them from horizon to horizon.

Scavengers, in an enormous garbage dump in India, claw at the refuse to make a living, competing with birds and dogs. Women, boys, and girls. Barefoot. Bold boys climb atop a dump truck to slide down with fresh garbage and grab at treasure. There's not a T-shirt to be seen. They are all garbed in the cheapest fabrics of India, a land where a woman can crawl from a cardboard box on the sidewalk and stand up looking elegantly dressed.

Eggs, thousands of them, float by on a conveyor belt. Recently hatched chicks, dressed in yellow down, tumble from a conveyor belt down a chute onto another belt. Their eyes are wide, they look about amazed, their tiny wings flutter. This is the most freedom they will ever know. They are sorted, tossed into funnels, spin down in a spiral, emerge one at a time to be marked with dye, and have the tips of their beaks burned off. This process, one second per chick, is repeated time after time by workers. Endless rows of chickens stacked atop each other in boxes too small to allow them to move. Girls and young women, thousands of them, as far as the eye can see, make cigarettes by hand in a South American sweatshop. Too close to stretch. Workers assemble computer parts in a Japanese factory, thousands of them, each one repeating a small action all day along, one who is working with a bandaged hand, three of its fingers too short.

In the factories, the high-angle camera shows rows of these workers reaching to the vanishing point. These are not computer graphics. The images result from painstaking care and perfectionist detail in the filming and restoration, and thoughtful camera placement. Consider a shot from above looking down on the great hall of Grand Central Station. Two movements at once: commuters dashing across the floor in speeded-up time, while the camera pans across them in slow motion. It is easy enough to achieve fast motion, but how difficult with a camera that is panning with exquisite slowness. There's an overhead shot of an intersection in Tokyo, with alternating swarms of thousands of cars and thousands of pedestrians. Escalators on the subway system, a speeded-up shot, pour out travelers as the conveyor belt poured chicks.

An orangutan stands shoulder-deep in a warm pool, steam rising around it. We regard it. The eyes look old and thoughtful. The sky is filled with stars. The same thoughtful eyes again. What is it thinking? W. G. Sebold: "Men and animals regard each other across a gulf of mutual incomprehension." What are the people thinking? The man waits for a light to change in Tokyo, inhaling his cigarette. Prostitutes gather outside their brothel. Steelworkers are covered with grime. Monks, girls at a subway stop, kabuki dancers. Why does no one make eye contact with the camera during crowded street scenes? Where was the big Todd-AO camera? How was it concealed? Why did it not frighten a herd of springboks, standing at rest in perfect focus?

Will the aliens viewing this film comprehend some of the scenes? Tiny bright plumes in a desert are revealed as the burning oil fields of Kuwait. Mothballed B-52 bombers reach to the horizon. Manhattan. Corpses are burned on the banks of the Ganges. Will they know the donkeys are pulling a cart much too heavy for them? They will probably understand mountains, waterfalls, volcanoes. Do we? *Baraka* is paced so we can contemplate the places we will never go, the places we are destroying, the places where we might find renewal. It is like a prayer.

"Baraka" is a Sufi word meaning "a blessing, or the breath, or the essence of life, from which the evolutionary process unfolds." In Islam generally, it is "a quality or force emanating originally from Allah but capable of transmission to objects or to human beings." In Judaism, it is a ceremonial blessing. In Swahili, it means "blessing." In French slang, it means "good luck." In Serbian and Bulgarian, it means "shack." In Turkish, it means "barracks." All over the world, it is the name of a character in the Mortal Kombat video game.

THE BATTLE OF ALGIERS

The most common form of warfare since 1945 has involved irregular resistance fighters attacking conventional forces and then disappearing back into the population. Bombs planted by civilians, often women and children, have served as deadly weapons in this war. The United States, France, Russia, Israel, Northern Ireland, South Africa, and several South American states have all had their experiences with urban guerrillas.

George W. Bush complained in his first televised debate with Senator John Kerry that he thought Saddam's army would stand and fight, but it melted away into the city streets. He blamed some of the problems in Iraq on the fact that the initial U.S. victory came too easily and quickly; if the lessons of other conflicts are a guide, it may be too soon to declare that victory. The army disappeared, but it didn't leave.

Gillo Pontecorvo's *The Battle of Algiers*, filmed in 1965, released in late 1967, is the crucial film about this new kind of warfare. It involves the proving-ground of the emerging tactics in Algeria from 1954 to 1962, as France tried and failed to contain a nationalist uprising. Methods that were successful in Algeria would be adapted by Castro and Guevara in Cuba, by the Vietcong, the Palestinians, the IRA, and South African militants, and are currently being employed in Iraq. One conventional response has been the capture, interrogation, and sometimes torture of the fighters, who are pressured to betray the names and plans of their co-conspirators.

This theory is described by a French military commander in *The Battle of Algiers*: terrorist groups are like tapeworms—they keep reviving unless you destroy the head. That's not easy, because the groups are broken up into cells so that no member knows the names of more than a few others. As a consequence, neither side can really know how many (or how few) insurgents are involved.

The Battle of Algiers is "a training film for urban guerrillas," Jimmy Breslin declared on TV in 1968. Certainly it was shown by the Black Panthers and the IRA to their members, and in September 2003 the *New York Times* reported that the movie was being shown in the Pentagon to military and civilian experts. *Times* reporter Michael Kaufman wrote that Pentagon audiences were "urged to consider and discuss the implicit issues at the core of the film—the problematic but alluring efficacy of brutal and repressive means in fighting clandestine terrorists in places like Algeria and Iraq." In short, the possibilities of torture.

Pontecorvo's film was released at the peak of antiwar sentiment in the United States, and had a surprising box-office success; it played for fourteen weeks in Chicago. It was described at the time as "impartial," alternating between the stories of the Algerian National Liberation Front (FLN) and the French police and paratroopers assigned to destroy it. "Pontecorvo has taken his stance," I wrote in my 1968 review, "somewhere between the FLN and the French, although his sympathies are on the side of the Nationalists. He is aware that innocent civilians die and are tortured on both sides, that bombs cannot choose their victims, that both armies have heroes, and that everyone fighting a war can supply rational arguments to prove he is on the side of morality."

True up to a point. But watching the movie again on the new Criterion DVD, I believe Pontecorvo's sympathies were clearly with the FLN. The resistance opens with FLN members walking up to French policemen in the street and shooting them dead, often in the back. Bombs are used against police strongholds. These actions are seen in silence, but when the French respond by blowing up the home of a terrorist, the score by Ennio

Morricone becomes mournful as survivors pick through the debris. His score withholds sympathy for the dead police.

Pontecorvo does, however, show the French leadership in a relatively objective light. In a film that was cast almost entirely with local non-actors, he uses the Paris stage veteran Jean Martin to play Colonel Mathieu, commander of paratroopers sent in to back up the police. Mathieu, himself a member of the French resistance to the Nazis, later a veteran of the French defeat in Indochina, knows a thing or two about urban warfare. He is calm, analytical, strategic in his thinking, and considers the FLN to be the enemy, not a malevolent force. As French public opinion turns against the war, he is besieged by reporters, one of whom quotes the philosopher Jean-Paul Sartre.

"Why are the Sartres always born on the other side?" Colonel Mathieu complains.

"You like Sartre?" asks a journalist.

"No, but I like him even less as an enemy."

Pontecorvo's film remains even today a triumph of realistic production values. Filming on location in Algiers, using the real locations in the European quarter and the Casbah (which sheltered the FLN), he achieved such a convincing actuality that he found it necessary to issue a disclaimer: there is "not one foot" of documentary or newsreel footage in his two hours of film. Everything was shot live, even riot scenes in which police battle civilian demonstrators.

He cuts back and forth between Colonel Mathieu and other military and civilian leaders and a raggedy band of FLN fighters, of which the key figure may be Ali la Pointe (Braham Haggiag), a reform-school boy and professional criminal who converts to the FLN after witnessing a beheading in prison. Back on the streets, Ali receives instructions (carried by a small boy) to shoot a policeman who meets daily with an Algerian informer. A woman standing outside a cafe will hand him a gun.

Ali finds the cafe, the policeman, the woman, and the gun, but when he pulls the trigger, the gun is not loaded. He feels betrayed by the FLN, but the woman takes him to her contact, who explains the reasoning: they did not know if they could trust him. Ali might have been recruited by the French in prison. The reason they told him to shoot the cop instead of the informer is that, if he were a police stooge, the police wouldn't object to the murder of a civilian, but they wouldn't let an informer shoot a French policeman. By pulling the trigger, Ali has symbolically committed a murder, earning his entry into the FLN.

This reasoning is chilling, and carries a terrible weight of logic. The strength of *The Battle of Algiers*, the reason it is being viewed in the Pentagon thirty-five years after its making, is that it is lucid and dispassionate in its examination of the tactics of both sides. It shows the French setting up roadblocks and checkpoints between the Casbah and the European quarter. Then it follows three women, one with a child, who walk right past the checkpoints with bombs in their purses. One woman plants her bomb in a cafe and then, in a disturbing scene, watches the customers eating, drinking, smoking, and talking—customers who will soon be dead. The parallel with bombings in Israel, the U.K., and Iraq is prophetic and chilling.

Colonel Mathieu does his job well. His chart of FLN cells has squares that are gradually filled in until, with the final defeat of Ali and three others, trapped in their hiding place, he declares victory. The FLN has been eliminated. Two years later, the film notes, "for no particular reason that anyone could explain," the uprising began again as mobs poured out of the Casbah and overwhelmed the police. In 1962, the French granted Algeria its freedom.

What lessons a modern viewer can gain from the film depends on who is watching and what they want to see. Those who study the French tactics should note that they failed. Although the American use of torture at Abu Ghraib has been credited, at least, with producing the names and locations of many enemy fighters, the scale of urban warfare in Iraq is escalating. A few days before I wrote this review, some thirty-five children were killed by a bomb while being given candy by Americans. The moral paradox is that many Iraqis will blame the deaths on us, because if we were not there, the bombing would not have taken place. Certainly the bombers were the murderers. But *The Battle of Algiers* shows now, as it did when it was made, that for nationalist resistance movements, the end justifies the means. President Bush said something in the debate that this film abundantly illustrates: fighting terrorism is hard work.

{ BERGMAN'S TRILOGY 1 }
Through a Glass Darkly

The great subject of the cinema, Ingmar Bergman believed, is the human face. He'd been watching Antonioni on television, he told me during an interview, and realized it wasn't what Antonioni said that absorbed him, but the man's face. Bergman was not thinking about anything as simple as a close-up, I believe. He was thinking about the study of the face, the intense gaze, the face as window to the soul. Faces are central to all of his films, but they are absolutely essential to the power of what has come to be called his Silence of God trilogy: *Through a Glass Darkly* (1961), *Winter Light* (1962), and *The Silence* (1963).

In the conventional language of cinema, a close-up is part of the grammar, used to make a point, show a reaction, emphasize an emotion. Close-ups fit into the rhythm of the cutting of a scene. But in these three films, and many others, Bergman was not using his close shots that way. His characters are often alone, or in twos. They are not looking at anything in particular—or, perhaps, they're looking inside themselves. He requires great concentration on the part of his actors, as in *Through a Glass Darkly*, where Harriet Andersson's face is held in the foreground and another character in the background for a long span of time in which she focuses on a point in space somewhere to screen right, and never blinks, nor does an eyeball so much as move. The shot communicates the power of her obsession, with her belief that voices are calling to her.

Frequently Bergman uses what I think of as "the basic Bergman two-shot," which is a reductive term for a strategy of great power. He places two faces on the screen, in very close physical juxtaposition, but the characters are not looking at each other. Each is focused on some unspecified point offscreen, each is looking in a different direction. They are so close, and yet so separated. It is the visual equivalent of the fundamental belief of his cinema: that we try to reach out to one another, but more often than not are held back by compulsions within ourselves.

In framing these shots, Bergman works hand-in-hand with his cinematographer, Sven Nykvist, one of the greatest artists of his craft. Nykvist makes us realize that most movies simply illuminate faces, while he lights them. Especially since the advent of television, movies have used a lighting style that flattens the image and makes it all seem on one plane. One reason we like film noir is that it uses angles, shadows, and strategic lighting more boldly. In a Bergman film, if you freeze a frame on one of his two-shots, you'll see that Nykvist has lighted each face separately, and often not from the same source; he uses the lights to create a band of shadow that is like a dark line drawn between the faces, separating them.

You can see this happening all during *Through a Glass Darkly*, which tells the story of a father, his daughter and son, and the daughter's husband, isolated on a remote Swedish island for a summer vacation. They're living in a run-down cottage. The opening scenes are deliberately banal, as they emerge from a dip in the sea and debate about who will fix dinner and who will put out the nets. But deeper currents emerge. We hear about the "sickness" of the daughter, Karin (Harriet Andersson). It is never named, but is clearly schizophrenia. She has been treated and is going through a period of recovery. Her husband, Martin (Max von Sydow), loves her but feels powerless to help her. Her brother, nicknamed Minus (Lars Passgard), is balanced at the entry to adolescent sexuality, and is very aware of the physical reality of his sister. The father, David (Gunnar Bjornstrand), is an author, highly regarded, who has just returned from a stay in Switzerland. He is cool and distant.

During the course of the first evening, the children will put on a play for their father, which has as its subject the impotence of art. It can be seen as a veiled attack on his novels. Later, Minus asks Karin if she noticed how offended their father was. Not particularly. The characters separate, the married couple together, the other two in their rooms. It is a long Swedish summer night; when darkness falls, the sun is already rising again.

This perpetual daylight has an eerie effect. Everything that happens is like a waking dream. Karin rises up from her bed and climbs the stairs to a shabby upper floor, and enters a room. She seems almost in a trance. She clings to the wall and traces out figures in the wallpaper. When she is found, she at first seems disturbed, but then cheers up and acts normally. Later she will tell her brother that voices called to her, that the wallpaper opened a door, that those on the other side were waiting for something, and that she thinks it might have been God. Still later, famously, she says she saw God, and he was a spider.

Left alone in her father's room, she reads his journal, where he confesses his obsession with his daughter's illness, notes that it is "incurable," and confesses he is interested in how he could use it in his work. This deeply upsets her. Earlier she had teased her brother after catching him looking at a pinup magazine. He had accused her of wearing seductive clothes. Now her brother goes seeking her on the beach and finds her huddled inside the wreck of a burned-out boat. There is an extraordinary scene, making great use of meticulously lighted two-shots, emphasizing their closeness and their separation. At the end of the scene, there is an implication that an act of incest occurs, although Bergman is deliberately obscure.

There have been other fraught scenes—between Karin and Martin, for example, who she has drawn apart from physically. And between Martin and David. Finally all comes down to Karin having a relapse. An ambulance is called; it is a helicopter, which apparently she experiences as a spider descending from the sky.

You can freeze almost any frame of this film and be looking at a striking still photograph. Nothing is done casually. Verticals are employed to partition characters into a limited part of the screen. Diagonals indicate discord. The characters move into and out of view around the cottage as if in a play. The visual orchestration underlines the disturbance of Karin's mental illness, and the no smaller turmoil within the minds of the others.

I was impressed time and again by how painstakingly the film had been made. Nykvist's lighting is essentially another character. How he sees, how he shades, how he conceals, all sum up into how we are to feel about the characters. The same film photographed by another cinematographer might seem shallow, even silly. Certainly Bergman attracted his share of parody. But this film, shot this way, surprises us by how much power it builds.

Peter Cowie, an expert on Bergman, appears in a short subject on the Criterion DVD and says the trilogy was Bergman's way of unloading the "baggage" of his religious upbringing; his father was a strict Lutheran minister. Bergman still has a great deal of that upbringing left over for his other films, which often deal with mortality, guilt, sin, God, and demons. But in these three, there is a focus almost painfully intense.

Through a Glass Darkly would be followed by *Winter Light*, about a minister who despairs of God's silence, and by *The Silence*, about two sisters and the child of one, stranded in a strange town and haunted by old hatreds and wounds. Long stretches of that film are silent, or at least lacking in dialogue, as the boy prowls a hotel's corridors, making fantasies of his own to displace the disturbance being trapped between the two sisters. In all of these films, we're struck by Bergman's deep concern that humans see the world as through a glass, darkly, and are unable to perceive its meaning.

BERGMAN'S TRILOGY 2
Winter Light

On the day Ingmar Bergman died, the first film of his that came into my mind was *Winter Light*. Odd, because I had not seen it since teaching a film class in the 1970s. In the weeks that passed, I found it lingering there, asking to be seen again. What did I remember about it? That it was part of Bergman's Silence of God trilogy. That it was about a pastor who was unable to comfort a man in dread of nuclear holocaust. That the pastor rejected a woman who sought to comfort him. That Bergman and his cinematographer, Sven Nykvist, sat in a rural church for a winter day to note how the sunlight moved through the space. In short, I hardly remembered the film at all, because those sparse memories were not enough to ignite a need to see it again. Yet I felt one. Finally I took *Winter Light* (1962) down from the shelf, watched it again, and was awestruck by its bleak, courageous power.

It is, first of all, much more complex than the broad outlines I held in memory. It is about more than God, silent or not. It is about the silence of a man, Pastor Tomas Ericsson (Gunnar Bjornstrand), who speaks enough in the film but is unable to say anything of use to himself or anyone else. About another man, the fisherman Jonas (Max von Sydow), obsessed by evil in the world, who calls God's bluff, so to speak, by killing himself. About Marta, a schoolteacher (Ingrid Thulin) who cares for the pastor,

60

loves him, worries about him, and is thanked by coldness and hostility. And it is about two monologues in which the pastor and the teacher describe their real feelings, and deeply wound each other.

But it is also about faith. The pastor is assisted in his duties by two men. One, the organist, is a clock-watcher, eager to see a service over with, already packing away his music while playing the final notes. The other, Algot (Allan Edwall), a man whose body has been crippled by a railroad accident, is the sexton who rings the bells, lights the candles, helps with the vestments. He has a monologue, too, about the passion of Christ, and he is the only character in the film who seems to have allowed the Christ story into his meaningful daily thoughts.

The film's visual style is one of rigorous simplicity. Nykvist does not use a single camera movement for effect. He only wants to regard, to show. His compositions, while sometimes dramatic, are mostly static. He uses slow push-ins and pull-outs to underline dialogue of intensity. His gaze is so unblinking that sequences with the potential to be boring, like the opening scenes of the consecration and distribution of hosts and wine, become fascinating: more is going on here than ritual, and there are buried currents between the communicants. Nykvist focuses above all on faces, in close-up and medium shot, and they are even the real subject of longer shots, recalling Bergman's belief that the human face is the most fascinating study for the cinema.

Pastor Tomas never smiles. He is sick, for one thing (and Peter Cowie reveals in an introduction that the actor Bjornstrand really had the flu during the filming). But more than that, he is cold, detached, unable to care. Marta, in contrast, trembles in close-ups with suppressed tenderness and grief. The younger actress Gunnel Lindblom, as the pregnant Karin, the fisherman's wife, looks vulnerable and confused. The fisherman Jonas looks as if he has already seen his end.

The sexton, the little twisted man, alone has a face that is alive with wonder at the mystery of faith. He has been reading the Gospels, he says, and thinks the emphasis on Christ's suffering on the cross is all wrong. Christ only suffered a few hours, he says, while he, Algot, has suffered more and longer, and it is not so bad. No, the real suffering of Christ came when his disciples betrayed him at Gethsemane, and when he cried out to a father who seemed to have forsaken him. He suffered because he feared no one had heard or understood his message. Christ suffered because he, too, was dismayed by the silence of God.

Pastor Tomas is stiff and harsh as he recites the words of the service, before a congregation of perhaps eight people, including two who are paid to be there and Marta, who does not believe in God. After the service, he is dismissive and curt. But when Karin asks him to speak with her husband, who has been troubled by his fears, the pastor agrees; Jonas will drive Karin home to their three children, and return. "I really hope he returns," Tomas says more than once. He reads a letter Marta has left for him, and Bergman shows Thulin reciting the entire letter in a six-minute close-up that is true, sad, and hard upon herself, but by implication merciless about Tomas.

Later, when Jonas returns and describes his fears that the world will end in nuclear destruction, all Tomas can say is, "We must trust in the Lord." Then, when Tomas stands up, Nykvist's camera tilts down to his fingers on the desk, hesitating, trembling, and then Tomas confesses to Jonas: he feels he is a bad pastor, he is anguished by the silence of God, he has lost his faith. Jonas leaves, and soon word comes that he drove to a nearby river and shot himself with his rifle.

Tomas resolves to visit Karin and the family. Marta drives him. They stop at her home for cold medicine, and she embraces him and urges him to accept her love. Tomas rejects her, citing his one true love, his wife who died four years earlier. And then, in a passage of lacerating cruelty, he enumerates everything he finds disgusting about Marta—her fussing, her weeping, her rashes on hands and head (recalling the wounds of Christ). He is pitiless, then storms out, hesitates, and unexpectedly asks her to join him in going to the fisherman's widow.

There is more silence here than the silence of God. Tomas's late wife is wrapped in the silence of the grave. Tomas is silent to the need of the fisherman. He cannot respond to Marta's love except by stern silence and rejection. Fredrik, the church organist, is silent in the way he pays no attention to the service and wishes for it to be over. Those who are not silent, such as the fisherman and his wife, ask for help and receive none.

But then there is Algot, the crooked sexton. He alone of all these people seems to have given more thought to the suffering of Christ than to his own suffering. His insights into Christ's passion are convincing and empathetic, but the pastor cannot hear him, he is wrapped in his own cold indifference.

Cowie speaks of a moment when Marta and Tomas are stopped on the road for a train to pass. "My parents dreamed of me becoming a pastor," he tells her. Cowie thinks that the pastor stands for Bergman at that moment—Bergman, the son of a strict Lutheran who listened to his father's sanctimonious sermons in church and then came home to cruel punishments.

I wonder if there are other ways in which Bergman speaks through the character of the pastor. We know that he was much married, and thought of himself before his women. In his screenplay for *Faithless* (2000), directed by Liv Ullmann, he plays an old director who hires an actress to help him visualize a story about how he mistreated women, and wants to be forgiven. Is *Winter Light* also not a portrait of a man who is cruel to a woman who only wants to love and help him? Is it not the cry of an artist who fears his message has not been heard? Is his art the father who has forsaken him? Has he been powerless to help those who came to him in real need, while focusing on his career and his reputation?

To the degree that *Winter Light* is autobiographical, and that we will never know, it is the portrait of a man who thought he was God, and failed himself.

BERGMAN'S TRILOGY 3
The Silence

Two women and a boy share a compartment on a train. It is an unhappy journey, and we sense tension and dislike between the women. The boy wanders out into the corridor, stares at other passengers, watches as another train passes by, its cars carrying armored tanks. The train stops in an unnamed city, and the three check into a hotel. So begins Ingmar Bergman's *The Silence* (1963), the third part of his Silence of God trilogy. If *Winter Light* (1962) directly referred to God's silence, and *Through a Glass Darkly* (1961) did so by implication, there is no theology in *The Silence*—only a world bereft of it.

We learn about the characters indirectly, through their dialogue; a reference to their father reveals that they are sisters. One is Ester (Ingrid Thulin), a translator, a woman who looks severe, pained, disappointed. She is dying. The other is Anna (Gunnel Lindblom), younger, more voluptuous, impatient with this journey. Although they are apparently going "home," there is no indication of where they were or why they went there, and no clear idea of where they are. Even Ester, the translator, doesn't recognize the language, and in a European grand hotel, it is odd that the hall porter speaks no German or English.

The boy, not yet an adolescent, is Johan (Jorgen Lindstrom). He has an angelic face and a sweet nature. He is Anna's son, but apparently has long lived in the middle between the two spiteful sisters. The reason for their spite is never specified, but goes back to childhood and obscurely involves their father. Now that Ester is dying, Anna has little pity for her and flaunts the fact that she is going out into the city—for sex, we somehow understand, or at least as a show of disloyalty.

The film is oblique. Most of the rest of the story involves reading between the lines. I could turn analytical and point out that Anna, who picks up a man and has sex with him in the hotel, represents Body, and that Ester, who works and reads in bed and at the table in her room, represents Mind. The doorway between their rooms is the portal through which they stage their rivalry, and only Johan passes back and forth thoughtlessly.

I think the boy is the key to the film—in what way, I'm not sure. Perhaps the instinctive sympathy he feels for both women is intended to show us a whole person, not parceled into flesh and thought. His scenes in the film, and they are numerous and lengthy, permit a subtle humor and charm to creep in. He doesn't smile much, isn't a clown, observes gravely the adult world around him. At one point, he stops in a corridor and pees, and as he walks away he glances back at the puddle with a certain satisfaction. It is perhaps an expression of resentment and frustration, and nothing else he does accounts for it.

He spends a lot of time exploring the long, stately corridors of the strangely deserted hotel. He encounters few people. There is an electrician, who scowls at him when he threatens the man with his cap pistol. A troupe of dwarf vaudevillians, who invite him into their room, garb him in a dress, and bounce on the bed to entertain him. And, most intriguingly, there's the ancient, bent, ingratiating hall porter (Hakan Jahnberg). This old man occupies a small cubbyhole on the floor, where he takes his meals, sneaks drinks from a flask, and responds to Ester, who rings fiercely for service. There is a beautiful shot when the porter sneaks up on Johan from behind and pounces on him, tickling him, so that Johan squeals and runs away. The porter stiffly tries to pursue him, but Johan disappears around a corner. Still in one unbroken shot, the porter turns and passes the camera, as Johan surprisingly appears in a doorway behind him.

The film was photographed by Sven Nykvist, Bergman's great

longtime collaborator, and I wonder if I can be excused for noticing in Johan's scenes in the hotel corridors a faint echo of Jacques Tati. The porter bears some slight resemblance to Monsieur Hulot, the boy represents the anarchic winds that were always blowing him off course, and the corridors, filmed with such exact precision, are the geometric spaces that Tati loved to violate with human activity.

The porter is a great help to Ester. Although they have not a word in common, he understands that she wants a bottle of liquor, and then food. Chain smoking, guzzling the drink, she cries out that she does not want to die alone, away from home. She is terrified of suffocating. The porter cleans up the mess after she spills the bottle in the bed. He brings her a glass of water, supporting her while she drinks it. He even keeps her company, reading his newspaper, and in his face, there is worry and concern. As he enters the frame, he is like a spectral visitor stooping down to inquire, but his heart is good. It is an extraordinary performance, containing not a word we can understand.

When Anna leaves the hotel, she carries herself on the streets and into a bar like a woman asking to be picked up. She enters a theater balcony and sees a couple having sexual intercourse right in front of her. She is disgusted and leaves. Later she picks up a man and brings him to the hotel. Johan sees them together, but she hardly cares. He tells Ester what he has seen. In a way he is asking for an explanation. He is placed in the sad position of being a child too young to process the information in his life, which he somehow senses is urgent.

The juxtaposition of the child with the scenes of adult behavior is disquieting, although we note that Bergman used the usual strategy for separating the boy into separate shots so he would not see and hear what we do. The film itself was scandalous at the time, with nudity and unusual sexual frankness. Bergman is somehow always thought of as cerebral and detached, but shocking carnality is often a part of his work; one thing he more rarely offers, however, is a sincere and tender romantic scene.

Throughout the film, Bergman's emphasis, as so often, is on the face. He usually has Johan, the outsider, the onlooker, in a one-shot, often full face. He usually sees the women from the side, or at an angle, oblique to one another. Nykvist's lighting is precise. He will hold half a face in shadow, or light from behind at an angle, or light the faces in a two-shot separately. There's one shot where Ester stands at a window, and the shadow of the window frame throws a cross upon her face. Not unusual, until we note from the position of the frame and the shadow that the light source is from below, and since she is looking out in the full of day, it should be from above. Nykvist is always at work, finding his effects, concealing his techniques.

Over the film hangs a tone of foreboding. The tanks on the train are matched, later, by a single massive tank that rumbles down the street in front of the hotel, pauses, and then passes on. There are no explosions, no battles, but war always seems at hand. When Ester's illness reaches a crisis, there is an odd loud moaning on the soundtrack. An air-raid warning? The music of hell? We do not know. But at the end, when Anna coldly tells her sister that she and Johan are leaving on the next train, Johan returns to promise Ester, "We'll be back." The child carries hope in the film. The problem is for hope to survive into adulthood. If you did not believe that God was silent, it would.

THE BEST YEARS OF
OUR LIVES

Homer thinks maybe they should stop at his Uncle Butch's saloon for a drink before they get home. "You're home now, kid," the older man Al tells him. Three military veterans have just returned to their hometown of Boone City, somewhere in the Midwest, and each in his own way is dreading his approaching reunion. Al's dialogue brings down the curtain on the apprehensive first act of William Wyler's *The Best Years of Our Lives* (1946), the first film to win eight Academy Awards (one honorary) and at the time second only to *Gone with the Wind* at the U.S. box office. Seen more than six decades later, it feels surprisingly modern: lean, direct, honest about issues that Hollywood then studiously avoided. After the war years of patriotism and heroism in the movies, this was a sobering look at the problems veterans faced when they returned home.

The movie centers on the stories of the three men. Al Stephenson (Fredric March), in his forties, was an infantryman and is now returning to his family and the bank where he worked. Fred Derry (Dana Andrews) was a crew member on a bomber. Homer Parrish (Harold Russell) was a Navy man who lost both hands and now uses steel hooks. "You gotta hand it to the Navy," Fred tells Al, as they watch Homer walk slowly from their taxi to his front door, "they sure trained that kid how to use those hooks." Al says: "They couldn't train him to put his arms around his girl, or to stroke her hair."

That's why Homer wanted to stop for the drink. When he left for the war, he had an understanding with Wilma (Cathy O'Donnell), the girl next door, but now he fears how she will react to his artificial hands. The other men have fears, too. Fred, raised in a shack by the tracks and working as a drugstore soda jerk when he enlisted, quickly married the sexy Marie (Virginia Mayo), who has stopped writing him. Al has been married for twenty years to Milly (Myrna Loy), and has a son, Rob (Michael Hall), and a daughter, Peggy (Teresa Wright). They welcome him home with love and hugs, but he doesn't feel right; his children have changed, his life has changed, and after Rob goes to bed he suddenly remembers Butch's bar and suggests his wife and daughter join him for a celebration.

The other two men also turn up at Butch's. Homer couldn't take the exaggerated kindness and suppressed grief he thought he sensed from his parents and Wilma. Fred didn't find anyone at home at Marie's apartment. The three men get plastered together, with Al's wife looking on with su-perhuman understanding. That's the night Fred and Peggy have their first conversation, and begin to fall in love.

The movie's screenplay, by Robert Sherwood, moves confidently among the problems faced by the three men; unhurried and relatively low-key, this isn't a fevered docudrama. It becomes clear to Fred that Marie is a party girl who isn't interested in life on his drugstore paycheck of $32.50. Homer coldly tries to force away Wilma because he doesn't want her pity. Al gets a promotion at the bank, and is in charge of giving loans under the G.I. Bill, but rebels when he's asked to trust an applicant's collateral more than his character. Al turns to drink, and has a half-sloshed, half-heroic moment when he speaks his mind at a company dinner.

The film makes no effort to paint these men as extraordinary. Their lives, their characters, their prospects are all more or less average, and Wyler doesn't pump in superfluous drama. That's why the movie is so effective, and maybe why it doesn't seem as dated as some 1946 dramas. But Wyler employed remarkable visuals to make some of his points. He was working with the great cinematographer Gregg Toland, known for his deep-focus photography on such films as *Citizen Kane*, and often Wyler uses deep-focus instead of cutting, so that the meaning of a scene can reveal itself to us, instead of being pounded down with close-ups. Consider a scene in Butch's where Homer proudly shows how Butch (Hoagy Carmichael) has taught him to play piano with his hooks. Al and Fred look on, and then Fred walks to a phone booth in the far background to make a crucial call. The camera doesn't move, but our eyes follow Fred's movement to the booth, and we focus on a decision he is making.

One of the movie's most famous sequences involves Fred deciding to leave town in search of work, and going to the airport. While waiting for his military transport flight, he wanders into a vast graveyard of mothballed warplanes. This scene is heartbreaking. Once Fred flew these planes, and now they, and their pilots, are no longer needed. The payoff of the scene is deeply ironic.

And consider the film's extended closing scene, when Homer and Wilma get married. Fred and Peggy are among the guests. Earlier they have told each other that they are in love, and Peggy vowed to her parents she would break up Fred's mistaken and miserable marriage. But Al warned Fred away from his daughter—one reason he was leaving town, even though the tawdry Marie is filing for divorce.

Wyler shows the entire marriage ceremony, all the way through, starting with Carmichael playing the wedding march and the lovers exchanging vows. There are two parallel lines of suspense. One involves the marriage itself, and whether Homer's hooks can slip a ring on Wilma's finger. The other involves Fred and Peggy on opposite sides of the same room, their eyes locked as they hear the wedding vows being pronounced. Deep focus allows Wyler to show both of these events at once, and his framing draws our eyes to the back of the shot, where Teresa Wright, never prettier or more vulnerable, doesn't move a muscle.

The Best Years of Our Lives doesn't use verbal or technical pyrotechnics. It trusts entirely in the strength of its story. One of the sources of its power is the performance by Harold Russell, the handless veteran. Producer Samuel Goldwyn was actually criticized at the time for his "tasteless" use of

Russell, but look at the heartbreaking scene where Homer invites Wilma up to his bedroom—not to make a pass, but to show her what is involved in getting ready for bed. He thinks maybe then she'll understand why he doesn't think he can marry her.

Russell was an untrained actor, but utterly sincere. He says: "This is when I know I'm helpless. My hands are down there on the bed. I can't put them on again without calling to somebody for help. I can't smoke a cigarette or read a book. If that door should blow shut, I can't open it and get out of this room. I'm as dependent as a baby that doesn't know how to get anything except to cry for it." We know Russell is speaking for himself, and the emotional power is overwhelming. O'Donnell's response is pitch-perfect.

Russell won an honorary Oscar, "for bringing hope and courage to his fellow veterans through his appearance." Although he was actually nominated for best supporting actor, the Academy board voted the special award because they thought he didn't have a chance of winning. They were wrong. He won the Oscar, the only time an actor has been given two Oscars for the same role. The film also won for best picture, actor (March), director, screenplay, editing, and score.

As long as we have wars and returning veterans, some of them wounded, *The Best Years of Our Lives* will not be dated. The movie is available on DVD, but there are no bells and whistles, and it calls out for a special edition or the Criterion treatment. I agree with Noel Megahey at DVDTalk.com: "Some other studios might regard a film that won eight Oscars as a major back-catalogue release but not MGM. The DVD presentation of the film is barely even adequate as a barebones release, with ... not a single feature to support the film's historical and cinematic importance."

Note: the film is said to have inspired one of Samuel Goldwyn's famous Goldwynisms: "I don't care if the film doesn't make a nickel. I just want every man, woman, and child in America to see it."

{ THE BIG RED ONE }

Eventually the veterans in the rifle squad stop bothering to learn the names of the new kids who arrive to bring them up to strength. They get killed so quickly, it's not worth the trouble. But the sergeant and four of his men make it all the way through the war, or almost, anyway—from North Africa to Sicily to Omaha Beach on D-Day to Belgium and finally to Germany and the liberation of a death camp.

Is it unlikely these five would be survivors? Not to Sam Fuller, who wrote and directed *The Big Red One* (1980), based on his own combat memories. "I wanted to do the story of a survivor," he told me when the movie premiered at Cannes, "because all war stories are told by survivors."

Fuller was a cigar-chomping, tough-talking, wiry little guy who started out as a teenage New York crime reporter, lying about his age to get the job. He wrote pulp novels, he talked tough, he fought all the way through the war, and he carried around memories of the First Infantry Division, the *Big Red One*. He made a lot of other movies first, hard-boiled war movies like *Steel Helmet* and *Fixed Bayonets* (both 1951), noir classics like *Pickup on South Street* (1953), and cult B pictures like *Shock Corridor* (1963) and *The Naked Kiss* (1964).

Finally he got his chance at his dream project. He had a limited budget, $4 million, but he shot and shot and shot, because like all newspapermen he couldn't bear to waste a good story. Yes, the movie is episodic. War is episodic. He said he couldn't stand war pictures that had a story arc where everything led up to a big scene. In the real war, you lived in the present. There was no connection between what happened to you last week and what was happening today, because you had no direction over your life and neither did anyone else.

Fuller's original cut of the film came to 270 minutes. It was cut to 113 minutes, which broke his heart, but what was left worked well enough that he was proud of it. He talked about restoring his original version, but he died in 1997 without getting that done. Now the film critic Richard Schickel has overseen a reconstruction that brings the film up to 158 minutes, and it reveals a richness and pacing missing in the earlier version; one suspects that the 270-minute version was a rough cut even Fuller would have trimmed. The restored *Big Red One* is able to suggest the scope and duration of the war, the way it's one damned thing after another, the distances traveled, the pile-up of experiences that are numbing most of the time but occasionally produce an episode as perfect as a short story.

Fuller centers everything on the sergeant, played by Lee Marvin with the rock-solid authority of a man who had seen action as a Marine in the Pacific, and called his other big war movie, *The Dirty Dozen*, a "dummy moneymaker." Fuller always wanted Marvin for the role. A studio insisted on John Wayne, but Fuller said he'd rather not make the picture than use Wayne. He was correct. This is Marvin's picture, and he dominates it not with heroics and speechmaking but with competence, patience, realism, and a certain tender sadness. There's a scene where a soldier is shot in the groin, and the sergeant finds something in the mud and tosses it away: "That was just one of your balls, Smitty. That's why they give you two."

The long-lasting squad members are Zab (Robert Carradine), a cigar-chewing pulp writer who is obviously playing Fuller; Griff (Mark Hamill), who doesn't like killing but has a change of heart; Vinci (Bobby DiCicco); and Johnson (Kelly Ward). There's a scene where one of the anonymous new replacements is reading a paperback titled *The Dark Deadline*, and Zab tries to tell him he wrote the book. The kid doesn't grasp the concept. He's dead before he finishes the book.

The film starts with the horror of World War I, as a shell-shocked Army horse runs maddened across a battlefield. That's where we meet Marvin's character for the first time. He apparently becomes a lifer in the Army, is promoted to sergeant, leads these kids through the next war. We learn nothing about him—not if he's married, not if he has a family, not even his name. In another sense, we learn everything about him. Fuller and Marvin never give the sergeant those obligatory campfire speeches describing his history and beliefs, and instead develop the character by showing how he behaves at important moments. He captures a German sniper, for example, and finds out the gunman is only a kid from Hitler's desperate last-ditch "children's army." The sergeant would have routinely shot another sniper. This one, he spanks.

There are details Fuller must have remembered from the time, such as the landing in Africa at a position defended by soldiers from the Nazi-sympathizing Vichy government of France. "If you're Vichy, fight us," the Americans shout over loud-speakers. "If you're Frenchmen, join us." The scene draws a class distinction between officers and men in the French lines. There is no distinction between the American sergeant and his men.

Some episodes sound like something Fuller would tell you over a beer. Like the time the squad hides in a cave and one German after another appears in the opening—some to pee, others to have a look. The Americans pick them off one by one. They're in desperate danger themselves, but the cave becomes their shooting gallery. And there's a scene where they deliver a baby in a German tank they've just captured; in his heartfelt review of the film, Charles Taylor of Salon.com notices "one genuinely surreal detail: hanging belts of ammunition used as stirrups, the bullets pointed at the pregnant woman's belly."

There is a moment during the landing at Omaha Beach that no one forgets after seeing the film. A soldier's arm has been torn off, and sticks in the sand, a wristwatch still in place. From time to time, Fuller cuts back to the watch; we can see how much time has passed. Steven Spielberg, who undoubtedly screened *The Big Red One* while preparing *Saving Private Ryan*, is not a director who often needs to feel envy, but he must have coveted that shot.

What we understand, finally, is that the entire war comes down to these five men, because it is their entire war. Nobody wades ashore with ten thousand men. They wade ashore all by themselves. By limiting the scope of the action, Fuller was able to make the movie look completely convincing on his limited budget, using Ireland for the scenes set in Belgium and Israel for all the other scenes. We see tanks and planes and Germans and landing craft when we need to, but the focus is on the faces of the squad members.

Talking with Fuller, I quoted Truffaut's dictum that all war movies are pro-war, because no matter what their "message" is, they make the action look exciting. Fuller snorted. "Pro or anti, what the hell difference does it make to the guy who gets his ass shot off? The movie is very simple. It's a series of combat experiences, and the times of waiting in between. Lee Marvin plays a carpenter of death. The sergeants of this world have been dealing death to young men for ten thousand years. He's a symbol of all those years and all those sergeants, no matter what their names were or what they called their rank in other languages. That's why he has no name in the movie.

"The movie deals with death in a way that might be unfamiliar to people who know nothing of war except what they learned in war movies. I believe that fear doesn't delay death, and so it is fruitless. A guy is hit. So, he's hit. That's that. I don't cry because that guy over there got hit. I cry because I'm gonna get hit next. All that phony heroism is a bunch of baloney when they're shooting at you. But you have to be honest with a corpse, and that is the emotion that the movie shows rubbing off on four young men."

Yes, it does. And that's why Griff, the squad member who doesn't like killing, pumps twenty rounds into a Nazi in one of the final scenes. He is a killer, shooting at a murderer.

Blade Runner: The Final Cut

In an earlier review of *Blade Runner*, I wrote: "It looks fabulous, it uses special effects to create a new world of its own, but it is thin in its human story." This seems a strange complaint, given that so much of the movie concerns who is, and is not, human, and what it means to be human anyway. Even one character we can safely assume is human, the reptilian Tyrell, czar of the corporation that manufactures replicants, strikes me as a possible replicant. And of the hero, Deckard (Harrison Ford), all we can say for sure is that director Ridley Scott has left clues in various versions of his film that can be used to prove that Deckard is a human—or a replicant.

Now study that paragraph again and notice I have committed a journalistic misdemeanor. I have referred to replicants without ever establishing what a replicant is. It is a tribute to the influence and reach of *Blade Runner* that twenty-five years after its release virtually everyone reading this knows about replicants. Reviews of *The Wizard of Oz* never define Munchkins, do they? This is a seminal film, building on older classics like *Metropolis* or *Things to Come*, but establishing a pervasive view of the future that has influenced science fiction films ever since. Its key legacies are: giant global corporations, environmental decay, overcrowding, technological progress at the top, poverty or slavery at the bottom—and, curiously, almost always a film noir vision. Look at *Dark City, Total Recall, Brazil, 12 Monkeys,* or *Gattaca* and you will see its progeny.

I have never quite embraced *Blade Runner,* admiring it at arm's length, but now it is time to cave in and admit it to the canon. Ridley Scott has released a "definitive version" subtitled *Blade Runner: The Final Cut,* which will go first to theaters and then be released December 18 in three DVD editions, including a "Five-Disc Ultimate Collector's Edition" that includes, according to a press release, "All 4 Previous Cuts, Including the Ultra-Rare 'Workprint' Version!" plus the usual deleted scenes, documentaries, bells and whistles.

The biggest change Scott made in earlier versions was to drop the voiceover narration from the 1982 original. Spoken by Ford, channeling Philip Marlowe, it explained things on behalf of a studio nervous that we wouldn't understand the film. Since much of the interest in the film has been generated by what we weren't sure we understood, that turned out to be no problem. The ending has been tweaked from bleak to romantic to existential to an assortment of the above, and shots have come and gone, but for me the most important change in the 2007 version is in the print itself.

Scott has resisted the temptation to go back and replace analog special effects with new CGI work (which disturbed many fans of George Lucas's *Star Wars*) and has kept Douglas Turnbull's virtuoso original special effects, while enhancing, restoring, cleaning, and scrubbing both visuals and sound so the film reflects a higher technical standard than ever before. It looks so great, you're tempted to say the hell with the story, let's just watch it.

But the story benefits, too, by seeming more to inhabit its world than be laid on top of it. The action follows Deckard, a "blade runner" who is assigned to track down and kill six rebel replicants who have returned illegally from off-worlds to Earth, and are thought to be in Los Angeles. (The movie never actually deals with more than five replicants, however, unless, as the critic Tim Dirks speculates, Deckard might be the sixth.) Replicants, as you know, are androids who are "more human than human," manufactured to perform skilled slave labor on Earth colonies. They are born fully formed, supplied with artificial memories of their "pasts," and set to break down after four years, because after that point they are so smart they have a tendency to develop human emotions and feelings and have the audacity to think of themselves as human. Next thing you know, they'll want the vote, and civil rights. Much of this comes from the original Philip K. Dick story, *Do Androids Dream of Electric Sheep?*

Since replicants in general do not know they are replicants, there can be real poignancy in their lives. We feel sympathy for one in particular, Rachael (Sean Young), who finds herself involved in romance with Deckard. He loves her even though he has reason to believe she is a replicant, but a very good one, almost impossible to detect.

What I have always wondered is why the Tyrell Corporation made their androids so lifelike. Why not give them four arms and settle the matter, and get more work out of them? Is there a buried possibility that Tyrell's long-range plan is to replace humans altogether? Is the whole blade-running caper simply a cover for his scheme? But never mind. What matters to the viewer is that the ground rules seem to be in place, and apply in one of the most extraordinary worlds ever created in a film.

The skies are always dark with airborne filth in this Los Angeles of the future. It usually rains. The infrastructure looks a lot like now, except older and more crowded, and with the addition of vast floating zeppelins, individual flying cars, and towering buildings of unimaginable size. When I first saw the film I was impressed by the giant billboards with moving, speaking faces on them, touting Coca-Cola and other products. Now I walk over to Millennium Park and see giant faces looming above me, smiling, winking, and periodically spitting (but not Coke). As for the flying cars, these have been a staple of sci-fi magazine covers for decades, but remain wildly impractical and dangerous, unless locked into a control grid.

The "human story," as I think of it, involves practical tests to determine if an individual is a replicant or not, and impractical tests (such as love) to determine how much that matters to (a) people, if they are in love with a replicant, and (b) replicants, if they know they are replicants. This has always been a contrived problem, easily avoidable in practical ways, unless (as I suspect) the Tyrell Corporation has more up its sleeves than arms. But to stumble on plot logic seems absurd in a film that is more about vision. And I continue to find it fascinating how film noir, a genre born in the 1940s, has such a hammerlock on the future (look at *Dark City* again). I suspect film noir is so fruitful and suggestive that if you bring it on board, half your set and costume decisions have been made for you, and you know what your tone will be.

Ridley Scott is a considerable director who makes no small plans. His credits include *Alien*, *Legend*, the inexplicable *1492*, *Gladiator*, *Black Hawk Down*, the brilliant *Matchstick Men*, and *American Gangster*. He has the gift of making action on a vast scale seem comprehensible. I have been assured that my problems in the past with *Blade Runner* represent a failure of my own taste and imagination, but if the film was perfect, why has Sir Ridley continued to tinker with it, and now released his fifth version? I guess he's only . . . human.

$\left\{\text{ C A B I R I A }\right\}$

On my last night at Cannes 2006, I climbed to the fifth floor of the Palais du Cinema to see a 180-minute silent epic made in 1914. Giovanni Pastrone's *Cabiria* was famous in its day, a global box-office success, but has fallen into neglect. I have a laserdisc of a battered version with dubbed sound, a version released in 1931 and cut to 123 minutes, but now here was the original film, compiled from prints found in Moscow, Paris, London, New York, and Pastrone's estate, and restored to within three minutes of its original running time. Its visual quality was so good that when a low-quality shot occasionally had to be used, it only helped me appreciate how good the restoration was.

The Cannes screening was prefaced by videotaped remarks from Martin Scorsese, the most passionate film historian among active directors. What he said, essentially, was that Pastrone invented the epic and deserves credit for many of the innovations often credited to D. W. Griffith and Cecil B. DeMille. Among those were the moving camera; Pastrone helped free movies from a static gaze.

What we are now beginning to realize, as more silent films are rediscovered and restored, is that no one film was a breakthrough but excitement and innovation were everywhere in the air; since films from all nations could play anywhere just by changing the languages of the title cards, what directors learned from Sweden tonight was in the films they were making tomorrow in Italy or America.

Although Pastrone pointed the way, certainly Griffith was a greater filmmaker than the Italian, and his *Birth of a Nation* (1915) moves the camera with greater freedom and has a headlong narrative and an exciting use of cross-cutting that Pastrone does not approach. *Cabiria* moves at a stately pace, depends on title cards of perplexing complexity, and introduces so many characters, cities, and plotlines that we are grateful for a princess who becomes a slave and a giant who becomes a hero, because we can follow their stories all the way through.

Yet in its particular way, *Cabiria* is beautiful and enthralling. In his novel *The Book of Illusions*, Paul Auster has a remarkable passage about the appeal of silent films: "They were like poems, like the renderings of dreams, like some intricate choreography of the spirit, and because they were dead, they probably spoke more deeply to us now than they had to the audiences of their time. We watched them across a great chasm of forgetfulness, and the very things that separated them from us were in fact what made them so arresting: their muteness, their absence of color, their fitful, speeded-up rhythms."

I felt that way watching *Cabiria*. The film was made with limitless scope and ambition, with towering sets and thousands of extras, with stunts that (because they were actually performed by stuntmen) have an impact lost in these days of visual effects. Hannibal's elephants actually cross the Alps in this movie. But there is room for the tiny detail; in an early scene, the foreground action takes place before an imposing palace wall, and in the upper right corner of the screen, far in the background, we see a little bridge leading somewhere, and on it the figure of a woman, gesturing. I watched her to see what she was doing and realized: she was acting in a movie. She was playing a woman in the back of the shot, gesturing, and because she was completely unnecessary to the action, she was there only because Pastrone put her there, high above the ground, and told her to gesture so that his shot would give the impression of life going on everywhere in the city.

The princess in the foreground is an eight-year-old Sicilian named Cabiria (Carolina Catena), who survives an eruption of Aetna but is kidnapped, and after various adventures becomes a slave in Carthage. She was originally rescued from the volcano and earthquake by a traveler from Rome named Fulvio (Umberto Mozzato) and his slave, Maciste (Bartolomeo Pagano), and they discover her again as a grown woman (Lidia Quaranta). Together they plot to free her.

Maciste, who was chained for years to a grindstone, breaks his chains, is imprisoned, forces apart the prison bars, hurls his enemies to their deaths, and in the process becomes one of the first Italian movie stars. Pagano, discovered by Pastrone, was a Herculean giant who changed his name to Maciste and went on to star in twenty-four more films, always playing the same North African slave, always in blackface, which alas was conventional at the time. His charisma and screen presence are undeniable, and in a film where one character in a toga and helmet looks much like another, he suggests the movies invented the star system because they needed it.

There are no true close-ups in *Cabiria*, although there are medium and medium-long shots. The typical shot stands back far enough to incorporate a great deal of architecture along with tableaux of characters. The sets for Griffith's *Intolerance* possibly grew so large after he saw *Cabiria*, and DeMille was also fond of enormous sets. When a modern film like *Troy* creates a vast Greek city out of digital information, we aren't fooled. We may be impressed by the visual effect, but we aren't impressed by the achievement. Watching these silent films, we feel a kind of awe, because we see that the sets are really there, and really that size.

The same reality is true of some of the stunts in *Cabiria*. There is a scene where a city's walls are besieged by warriors on ladders, and others in a wicker basket are raised high up at the end of a crane. The city defenders push the ladders off the walls and use lances to overturn the basket. Yes, there are probably piles of straw down below to cushion the warriors as they land, but look how far they fall while they are still onscreen. The risks they are taking are chilling.

Consider another scene where warriors with shields approach a city wall. Eight of them (as I recall) bend double and put their shields on their backs. Six climb onto those shields, bend double, and put their own shields on their backs. Four more stand on them, and two more on them, and at last the hero is able to climb this human pyramid and reach the top of the wall. This is a stunt taking place in one shot before our eyes, and if the legs of one of the warriors had buckled, it would not have been a pretty sight. Because all of this is so palpably real, there is an undeniable sense of wonder in seeing it achieved, as there is when Douglas Fairbanks Sr. or Buster Keaton do their own stunts in shots deliberately photographed so we can see they were not faked.

The glory of this restoration of *Cabiria* is that almost all of it is sharp and clear. My laserdisc version is so murky you can't see and appreciate the beauty of the sets and costumes. Because the film's story moves in a stately fashion, because intertitles introduce more characters and plotlines than are probably necessary, because the acting is broad and the gestures large, we don't get involved emotionally. But there are benefits as well as drawbacks to Pastrone's epic style.

The movie feels old, and by that I mean older than 1914. It feels like a view of ancient times, or at least of those times as imagined a century ago. We are looking into two levels of a time machine. Silent films in general create a reverie state for me; sound films are more realistic, more immediately gripping, but in a silent film I find myself dreamier, more drawn into meditations about the nature of life and time. These people are all dead, but here they are as they were on that day in 1914, boldly telling a story in a new medium, trusting it would reach audiences all over the world, and little suspecting that ninety-two years later moviegoers would still be climbing to the top of another palace, the one at Cannes, to see them.

{ CAT PEOPLE }

C*at People* is constructed almost entirely out of fear. There wasn't a budget for much of anything else. It exists on eight or nine sets, the running time is only seventy-three minutes, it has few special effects, there are no major stars, the violence is implied or dreaded but not much seen. Yet the film, made as a B picture for only $135,000, became RKO's top grosser for 1942, bringing in $4 million, compared to the studio's *Citizen Kane* at $500,000 in 1941. It renewed the careers of its producer Val Lewton, its director Jacques Tourneur, and its star, the French actress Simone Simon; it inspired ten more macabre titles from Lewton's production unit and was copied all over Hollywood—because it was scary, and because it was cheap. What was hard to copy was its artistry.

Cat People wasn't frightening like a slasher movie, using shocks and gore, but frightening in an eerie, mysterious way that was hard to define; the screen harbored unseen threats, and there was an undertone of sexual danger that was more ominous because it was never acted upon. Its heroine is a beautiful woman who never sleeps with her new husband (indeed she never even kisses him) because she fears that passion could turn her into a panther. The film magnifies her dread by exploiting the fear some people have of cats: they're sneaky and devious and creep up on you, and are associated with Satan.

These dark undertones are framed by a story of everyday life. Irena (Simon) is sketching a panther at the zoo when she meets the clean-cut and well-behaved architect Oliver Reed (Kent Smith). He walks her home, she asks him in for tea, and they fall in love. She talks of her village in Serbia, of the belief that it sheltered satanic cultists who could take the form of cats. Good King John tried to kill these cat people, but some fled into the mountains, where they are said to live to this day. Irena secretly fears she is one of those people.

The dialogue, a first screenplay by DeWitt Bodeen, contains lines that hint at the bizarre and the erotic. Oliver tells Irena her perfume is "warm and living." Irena says the roars of the big cats in the nearby zoo are "natural and soothing." As the afternoon lengthens, she finally turns on a light, after saying she finds the dark "friendly." Tourneur and his cinematographer, Nicholas Musuraca, who also worked together on the great film noir *Out of the Past*, are masters of light and shadow. They often place Irena in darkness, cast the silhouettes of other characters on the wall behind her, enclose her with shadows that work like a cage.

Irena and Oliver announce their engagement at a party in a restaurant, where an inexplicable and disturbing thing happens: she is approached by a strange woman (Elizabeth Russell), who affects a catlike appearance and addresses her in Serbian, calling her "sister." We never see this woman again, but her spectre haunts the movie. Are there lesbian notes in her approach to Irena? Perhaps in the sense that she is a powerful animal who challenges Oliver's right to claim a mate?

In their marriage, Irena is fearful, and we understand that she is fearful of herself, of her latent evil. When the extraordinarily patient Oliver observes, "I've never kissed you," Irena tells him: "I've lived in dread of this moment. I've never wanted to love you. I've stayed away from people.... I've fled from the past. Some things you could never know, or understand—evil things." Some of their conversations take place while he stands on one side of her bedroom door and she slumps against the other side.

He begins to work late at the office, where his co-worker Alice (Jane Randolph) is sympathetic. Irena follows him, sees them together, grows jealous, and one of the movie's great sequences shows Alice walking home on a dark and deserted street, followed by footsteps. Nothing precisely happens to her, and we see little but some shadows and some disturbed leaves, but Alice is terrified when she jumps on a bus; she knows she saw something, which she will later describe to Oliver as Irena's "cat form." Her night walk seems to pass the same short span of stone wall again and again; Tourneur edits to make it seem longer. We are aware of the visual trick, yet it evokes a dreamlike quality.

Curiously, Alice, Irena, and Oliver continue as friends, although there is a giveaway moment when they visit a museum together. As he suggests that Irena look at an upstairs exhibit, Oliver uses the word "we" to refer to himself and Alice, not Irena. This slip betrays him. Later that night, Alice goes for a plunge in the swimming pool at her residential club, and in a genuinely terrifying sequence she treads water in the deserted pool while . . . something . . . growls and paces, and then she screams. Notice how light reflected from the surface of the pool causes unsettling patterns to creep along the walls.

Irena has been seeing a psychiatrist. Dr. Judd (Tom Conway), a graduate of the Vincent Price school of therapy, talks to her while her face is detached in a circle of light surrounded by darkness. These sessions are not helpful, and she finds more relief by returning again and again to the leopard cage at the zoo. The genius of the film is in its indirection. It doesn't specifically show us horrible things happening. It toys with us, introducing the elements from which horror could emerge. For example, Oliver gives Irena a kitten, which is terrified of her. Having established dark possibilities, *Cat People* gives us daylight scenes and chirpy supporting characters who don't realize they're skirting danger. At a pet shop run by a woman so cheerful she seems demented, they trade the cat for a canary. The destiny of this canary supplies, in a way, all we need to know about Irena's fundamental nature. Yet she really does love Oliver—love him, and need him, as "the only friend I've ever had." The film evokes the loneliness of the person set aside from humanity, given skills or powers that are a curse; it has the same kind of uneasy sympathy for Irena that Anne Rice has for her vampires. It's not much fun, being a cat woman.

As a group, the films that Val Lewton produced in the 1940s are a landmark in American movie history. Born in the Ukraine, raised in Berlin, a newspaperman and pulp writer, he was a story editor for David O. Selznick before starting his own unit at RKO. Lewton (1904–51) worked with directors who became important (Tourneur, Mark Robson, Robert Wise), but the films were and still are identified as his; I remember the French director Bertrand Tavernier and the American critic Manny Farber at the 1990 Telluride festival, talking about how unusual it was for a producer, not a director, to be the ruling auteur of a group of films.

Lewton may have found his overall approach by happenstance in *Cat People*, which began as a title without a story and developed its minimalist style as a result of the low budget. But he and Tourneur had found a note that worked, and in various ways Lewton found it again in such films as *I Walked with a Zombie* (1943), *The Leopard Man* (1943), *The Curse of the Cat People* (1944), and *The Body Snatcher* (1945). He made "movies that are often more like symbolist poems or obscure fetishistic rituals," wrote Geoffrey O'Brien in the *New York Review of Books*. "They are not so much frightening as unnervingly strange and shot through with a palpable melancholy."

Do the movies still work today, or are they too quiet? Depends on your tastes. Paul Schrader made a much more specific version of *Cat People* in 1982, which I admired for its own qualities, including the use of atmospheric New Orleans locations. But the 1942 movie gets under your skin. There is something subtly alarming about the oddly mannered good-girl behavior of Simone Simon, and the unearthly detachment of Kent Smith as her husband, and the rooms and streets that look not like places but like ideas of places. And something touching about Irena, who has never had a friend, and fears she will kill the only person she loves, and is told she is insane. At the end, Oliver pays her a simple tribute: "She never lied to us."

{ CHIMES AT MIDNIGHT }

T*here live not three good men unhanged in England. And one of them is fat and grows old.*

How can it be that there is an Orson Welles masterpiece that remains all but unseen? I refer not to incomplete or abandoned projects that have gathered legends, but to *Chimes at Midnight* (1965), his film about Falstaff, which has survived in acceptable prints and is ripe for restoration. I saw the film in early 1968, put it on my list of that year's best films, saw it again on 16mm in a Welles class I taught, and then could not see it for thirty-five years.

It dropped so completely out of sight that there is no video version in America, Britain, or France. Preparing to attend the epic production of both parts of Shakespeare's *Henry IV* at the Chicago Shakespeare Theater, I wanted to see it again and found it available on DVD from Spain and Brazil. Both versions carry the original English-language soundtrack; the Brazilian disc is clear enough and a thing of beauty. What luck that Welles shot in black-and-white, so there was no color to fade.

This is a magnificent film, clearly among Welles's greatest work, joining *Citizen Kane, The Magnificent Ambersons, Touch of Evil,* and (I would argue) *The Trial*. It is also magnificent Shakespeare, focusing on Falstaff through the two *Henry IV* plays to his offstage death in *Henry V*. Although the plays are much abridged, it is said there is not a word in the film not written by Shakespeare.

Falstaff, "this huge hill of flesh," is one of Shakespeare's greatest characters—the equal, argues Harold Bloom, of Hamlet. He so dominates the *Henry IV* plays that although Shakespeare promised he would return in *Henry V*, he reconsidered; the fat knight would have sounded the wrong note in that heroic tale, and so we learn from Mistress Quickly of his death, as he "babbl'd of green fields."

Welles was born to play Falstaff, not only because of the physical similarity but because of the rich voice, sonorous and amused, and the shared life experience. Both men lived long and too well, were at odds with the powers at court, and were constantly in debt. Both knew disappointment, and one of the most sublime moments in Welles's career is simply the expression on his face at the coronation of *Henry V*, when he cries out "God save thee, my sweet boy," and the new king replies, "I know thee not, old man."

Prince Hal, later Henry V, is played in the film by Keith Baxter, who looks dissolute enough in the roistering at the Boars Head Tavern, but as early as act 1, scene 2 is an unpleasant hypocrite in the monologue where he admits his present misdeeds but promises to reform at the right time. In Shakespeare, this is a soliloquy; in Welles, Falstaff listens in the back of the shot and is forewarned. Later, in an echo of that composition, the prince looks impatiently toward the field of battle as Falstaff, behind him, questions the concept of honor. That each man hears the other's intended soliloquy adds a dimension to both.

Welles as director uses some of his familiar visual strategies; the vast interiors of Henry IV's castles contrast with the low ceilings and cluttered rooms of bawdy houses, just as the vast space of Kane's great hall contrasts with the low ceilings and dancing girls of the *New York Inquirer*. Royalty in *Chimes at Midnight* is framed by vast cathedral vaults, with high windows casting diagonals of light. Welles uses dramatic camera angles, craning to look up at the trumpeters atop the battlements as Henry IV rides off to battle.

At Mistress Quickly's, on the other hand, Falstaff and his roisterers have great freedom of movement involving doorways and posts, barrels and vertiginous staircases, barking dogs and laughing wenches. He and other actors circle verticals and one another as they speak, just as Welles and Joseph Cotten circled in *Citizen Kane* and *The Third Man*. And watch the use of deep focus when he begins a shot with Hal seated in the background and, as news of his father's death is conveyed, Hal stands and moves forward, finally looming over the camera in foreground. All one shot.

The scene of the battle of Shrewsbury is justly famous. It lasts fully ten minutes, chaotic action at a brutal pitch, horses and men confused in smoke and fog, steel crashing against steel, cries of pain, desperate struggles, confused limbs caked in mud and blood, men falling exhausted or dead. Barbara Leaming, one of Welles's biographers, says the scene was created by careful framing; Welles at no time had more than about a hundred extras, yet seems to have a multitude, and the violence of the struggle was studied by Mel Gibson before he directed *Braveheart*.

The battle is intercut with shots of a fat man in armor, hurrying and scurrying out of the way and finally playing dead. When Hal finds Falstaff flat on his back, he cries out, "What, old acquaintance! Could not all this flesh keep in a little life?" We know Falstaff is not dead, and Welles finds a way to let Hal know, too: the frost on the old man's breath puffs out from beneath his visor. Yes, it was cold. Welles shot on location in Spain, in winter; his first shot shows Falstaff as a tiny figure in a vast field of snow, his last shows Falstaff's coffin being pushed across snow toward his grave, and in several of John Gielgud's speeches as Henry IV, we can see the frost on his breath.

That Gielgud played the king and others such as Margaret Rutherford (Mistress Quickly), Jeanne Moreau (Doll Tearsheet), and Fernando Rey (Worcester) also appeared in the film is a tribute to Welles's reputation, for on a budget of less than $1 million he was, like Falstaff, not prompt to pay. Gielgud plays Henry IV as a dying man almost from his earliest scenes, plagued with guilt because of how he won his throne. His son is no consolation; the king envies Northumberland his son Henry Percy, known as Hotspur (Norman Rodway), and wishes "would I have his Harry, and he mine." He excoriates the thief and whoremonger Hal and his low companions, none lower in deportment or loftier in essential humanity than Falstaff.

How good is Falstaff? Consider the way warm affection illuminates the face of Jeanne Moreau as Doll Tearsheet caresses and tickles her beloved old rogue. Note the boundless affection Falstaff has for all around him, so real that even Quickly forgives his debts and allows him to contract new ones.

Such scenes illuminate the life Welles poured into *Chimes at Midnight*. He came early to Shakespeare; he edited and published editions of some of the plays while still at prep school. On stage and screen, he was also Othello and Macbeth, his voice fell naturally into iambic rumbles, he was large enough for heroes and so small he could disappear before Henry V's scorn. He once asked an audience, reduced by a snowstorm: "Why are there so many of me and so few of you?"

There was not something Falstaffian about Welles, there was everything. As a young man he conquered all that came before him (at Shrewsbury a knight meekly surrenders to the old man, awed by his leftover reputation). Welles grew fat and in debt, took jobs unworthy of him, was trailed by sycophants and leeches, yet was loved by good women and honored by those who could see him clearly. And he battled on, Quixotic as well as Falstaffian, commencing grand schemes and sometimes actually finishing them (indeed, his *Don Quixote* can now be seen in intriguing but incomplete form).

The crucial point about *Chimes at Midnight* is that although it was rejected by audiences and many critics on its release, although some of the dialogue is out of sync and needs to be adjusted, although many of the actors become doubles whenever they turn their backs, although he dubbed many of the voices himself, although the film was assembled painstakingly from scenes shot when he found the cash—although all of these things are true, it is a finished film, it realizes his vision, it is the Falstaff he was born to direct and play, and it is a masterpiece. Now to restore it and give it back to the world.

{ CHOP SHOP }

Chop Shop has such an immediate sense of time and space that it comes as a slight shock to understand that the time is now and the place is in the shadow of the late Shea Stadium—or, more accurately, next to the right-field parking lot. This area is known as the Iron Triangle, a crowded, ramshackle bazaar of auto-parts shops. We see it through the eyes of Alejandro, universally known as Ale, a twelve-year-old who lives and works there. If you squint a little to turn the automobiles into carriages, this would be a story by Dickens.

Ale is enterprising and optimistic. In exchange for his work, he lives in a knocked-together plywood room under the roof of a shop owned by a man named Rob. He gets $5 for every passing car he flags onto the premises. This income he supplements by selling candy on the subway, peddling bootlegged DVDs, stealing hubcaps, and snatching purses. He is not a criminal. He is a survivor. He goes at things as he has taught himself, and will make the record in his own way: first to knock, first admitted, sometimes an innocent knock, sometimes not so innocent.

That is how Saul Bellow wrote of Augie March. *Chop Shop* (2007) also evokes F. Scott Fitzgerald, who wrote about this very area in *The Great Gatsby*. He named it the valley of ashes. In the 1920s, it was the wasteland on the way from East and West Egg to Manhattan: *occasionally, a line of gray cars crawls along an invisible track, gives out a ghastly creak, and comes to rest, and immediately the ash-gray men swarm up with leaden spades and stir up an impenetrable cloud, which screens their obscure operations from your sight.*

Ale is in the tradition of American symbols of upward striving. A Latino, he is in the line of those poor Jews, Irish, and Italians who landed in New York and hustled for a living. He is an immensely strong boy, and a vulnerable kid. He seems to be an orphan, but he has a sister, Isamar, four years older, and he visibly glows when she comes to live with him. He has been preparing this home for them. When she complains it is small, he is cheerful: it has a little refrigerator. It has a microwave. She will be happy.

Bahrani immersed himself in the Iron Triangle while writing his screenplay. Only one of his actors had ever worked in a movie before; Ahmad Razvi, who plays a shady operator, had been in one, Bahrani's own *Man Push Cart* (2005). Ale's boss, Rob Sowulski, owns and operates the shop where Ale lives. Everyone you see works in the Iron Triangle, except for Ale (Alejandro Polanco) and Isamar (Isamar Gonzales), who are schoolkids. What is remarkable is the way, after careful preparation and multiple takes, Bahrani finds performances in them that are so natural and convincing, they put professional actors to shame.

He depends on preparation and his visual sense, collaborating always with the same meticulous cinematographer, Michael Simmonds. In April 2009, I joined Bahrani in a shot-by-shot analysis of the film at the University of Colorado at Boulder. It was an illuminating experience. I knew that it was a great film, a universal film, and how well it worked. Bahrani knew why it worked, and was brave enough to discuss his methods, which directors are often reluctant to do.

The screenplay was revised over and again, removing all unnecessary digressions and obvious "look at me" moments. The three-act structure was so deeply embedded in the events, they seemed to flow inevitably. Specific turning points were used in important scenes; sometimes they were no more than a subtle change in tone, but they were emotionally decisive. Much was made of Antonioni painting some grass for *Blow Up*, because it was not green enough. Bahrani and Simmonds composed every shot with acute attention to detail. Often foreground elements forced characters toward the left, more problematic, side of the screen. No auto junk in the background was there by chance. In the lighting of faces, they took Bergman's Sven Nykvist as their ideal. There is a pickup truck that has a small sticker of a soccer ball on its back gate. Bahrani and Simmonds discussed whether it should be there: "Was it contributing, or distracting?"

Although there was rehearsal, he said, he avoided drilling his actors. He told them what to say, and they tended to slip into their own word choices. Ale and Isamar discuss a pair of brand-name sneakers. The screenplay used the word "real." Isamar used the word "official," the correct street word. Some shots were captured unobserved; the movie used no clapboard to begin and end shots, and Bahrani and Simmonds could communicate with a nod or a gesture. The high-def camera was always around, and Simmonds was always peering through it to set up shots; sometimes the actors were unaware they were being filmed. Bahrani also likes long shots with the camera far enough back so it is not evident. As Ale grabs a purse (from a cast member) on a walkway leading to the parking lot, nobody else in the shot knows they are in a movie.

Chop Shop is about a hard coming of age. Ale's dream is that he and his sister will buy a taco truck and go into business on their own. He saves every dollar. She won't have to work in Ahmad's truck anymore. In a heart-breaking scene, Ale glimpses how she has started to augment her income. He never directly confronts her. He works harder to make money, to buy her things, to make money less necessary to her. He is a brother, but also, in a sense, a husband. He wants to take responsibility. He learns some inescapable realities about the limitations of his power and undergoes a shift into tacitly understanding why she earns as she does. He will be thirteen soon, and then twenty-three, and one day we are sure he will own a taco truck, but not now, and certainly not the shabby truck he has set his dreams on. Reality is taking him on the first steps toward the American Dream, and they are lower steps than we like to imagine.

Ramin Bahrani was born in 1975 in Winston-Salem, North Carolina, and is not, as has been misreported by many, including me, an immigrant from Iran. His parents came from Iran. His father is a psychiatrist in Winston-Salem, practicing much among poor blacks and whites. Bahrani says neither he nor his family has experienced racism there, although at school, there were "whites, blacks, and my brother and me." His parents have instilled a love of Persian poetry. Once during a conversation, he mentioned the poems of Hafez of Shiraz (1315–90), which are used as an oracle like the I Ching by many Persians. I asked if I could present a question to Hafez. He told me not to speak it aloud. He telephoned his father in North Carolina, who opened his volume at random and took fifteen minutes to translate what he found there. It was relevant.

It may be this dual heritage that inspires Bahrani to look more closely at the many new Americans among us. *Man Push Cart* was about the Pakistani operator of a Manhattan sidewalk bagel cart. Such carts are part of the daily routines of many New Yorkers, who may rarely look at those behind the counter. His 2008 film, *Goodbye Solo*, is about a Senegalese-American taxi driver in Winston-Salem, and an old man who hires him for a trip that worries him. The taxi driver is played by Souleymane Sy Savane, from the Ivory Coast. The old man is played by Red West, who met Elvis Presley in high school and was his longtime bodyguard. Only in America.

CHUCK JONES: THREE CARTOONS

A film director, like an orchestra conductor, is the lord of his domain, and no director has more power than a director of animated films. He is set free from the rules of the physical universe and the limitations of human actors, and can tell any story his mind can conceive. That's no doubt why Chuck Jones, after creating the characters of the Road Runner and Wile E. Coyote, immediately wrote down the rules of what could and could not happen in their universe. If anything could happen (and it could), the comedy would be lost in anarchy.

Jones and other masters of the cartoon short subject created a world apart from the real world and also apart from feature-length animation, which tended to be more story-driven. In their films, which were usually about seven minutes long, comic scenarios were driven by eternal conflicts between a character and his desires: Elmer Fudd wanted to shoot a wabbit, and over and over he tried, and over and over he was outwitted (except once, as we will see).

There was a time when the feature was invariably preceded by a cartoon, and audiences smiled when they heard the theme music for Looney Tunes and Merrie Melodies from Warner Bros. Cartoons have long since been replaced by fifteen minutes of trailers in many theaters, an emblem of the greed of exhibitors and their contempt for their audiences. In those golden days, the cartoon (and even a newsreel and a short subject) was a gift from the management.

There are several main lines in cartoon shorts: Disney (Mickey, Donald, and Goofy), Warner Bros. (Bugs, Daffy, Elmer, Tweety and Sylvester, the Road Runner), MGM (Tom and Jerry), and UPA (Mr. Magoo). Many of these little films are available on DVD, lovingly restored (Roy E. Disney personally supervised a series of Disney classics, which come packaged in aluminum canisters). To choose one director or a few titles from the cartoon universe is daunting, but I'll choose Chuck Jones, because I knew him and because three of his cartoons have been included in the National Film Registry of the Library of Congress: "Duck Amuck" (1953), "One Froggy Evening" (1955), and "What's Opera, Doc?" (1957).

With commentary tracks, interviews, and documentaries, the Warner Bros. Looney Tunes Golden Collections on DVD surround the films with the legend and lore of Termite Terrace, where the animators and their writers and assistants labored in the 1930s and 1940s under the unloved producer Leon Schlesinger. He was an independent contractor supplying cartoons to Warners, and he required every animator (including Jones, Tex Avery, Friz Freleng, and Bob Clampett) to produce ten cartoons a year, one every five weeks, with two weeks for vacation. Schlesinger sold out to Warners in the mid-40s, but lived on in the legends of the Termites.

I met Jones (1912–2002) and his wife, Marian, many times at the Telluride Film Festival, and spent a week with them on the QEII during Telluride's twenty-fifth-anniversary cruise. I heard again and again about Schlesinger, his cluelessness, his rigidity, his time clocks, and especially his weird Trumpian comb-over. "Leon never did figure out that he was the inspiration for Daffy Duck," Jones chuckled. At last, in a 1940 Friz Freleng short named "You Ought to Be in Pictures" in one of the Warner's collections, I've seen Schlesinger for the first time, and, oddly enough, he looks a little like Elmer Fudd and, yes, he has the most unconvincing hair I have ever seen.

The animators sometimes bent Schlesinger's rules to make more ambitious cartoons. Working with Michael Maltese, the writer of all three of the National Registry cartoons, Jones knocked off a Road Runner short in three weeks flat to steal time for "One Froggy Evening," which required extra attention for its singing and dancing frog. More time was needed, too, for "What's Opera, Doc?" in which Elmer Fudd plays a Wagnerian warrior and Bugs Bunny, in drag with blond pigtails, is Brunnhilde.

Of the three titles, the strangest is "Duck Amuck," which plays with the reality of the genre. In it Daffy Duck is aware he's a character in a cartoon and shouts angry tirades against his animator, who strikes back with pencil, eraser, and paint brush. Daffy begins as a dueling musketeer but suddenly runs out of background and is marooned on an empty white screen. He demands a backdrop, and a brush enters the frame to paint a farm. Daffy, a trouper, starts singing "Daffy Duck, He Had a Farm." But the backgrounds change with sadistic glee: snow, a beach in Hawaii. Then he is erased. He reappears with a guitar but cannot make his music heard, and holds up a sign saying "Sound, Please!" He gets a machine gun and a klaxon.

"I've never been so humiliated in my life," Daffy complains. There's more. He's on a desert island that's a speck in the distance. "Give me a close-up!" he demands. The island is framed in a small box surrounding the speck with black. "This is a close-up?" The camera zooms to his bloodshot eyes. Soon "The End" appears on the screen, and Daffy angrily pushes the letters offscreen and gets into a fight with curtains of black ink that threaten to obscure him. It's a fight to the finish between a cartoon character and his medium, with a twist at the end when we find out who the animator is.

The subtext of "Duck Amuck" is Daffy's desire to be the star of the studio, and his career-long rivalry with Bugs Bunny, who came along just as Daffy was becoming Warner's star. In both "Duck Amuck" and "What's Opera, Doc?" Jones gives himself freedom to rewrite cartoon conventions.

In the opera spoof, bits of half a dozen Wagner operas create a pastiche of romantic turmoil as Elmer woos Bugs. There are sensational shots (the opening lightning storm) and quieter moments that surprise us, as when Elmer Fudd seems sad and takes the plot seriously. For the first time, we feel sorry for this creature who exists to be the foil of Bugs. There is a scene where Bugs appears to be dead, tears drop from a flower on a broken stem, and Elmer mourns, "Poor little wabbit." Jones seems perilously close to breaking through the ritual of the Elmer-Bugs feud into the reality of their endless Sisyphean rivalry. At the end, amazingly, Elmer is not defeated, but strides off in his helmet and with his spear, the wabbit under his arm. Doesn't that break all the rules?

Bugs then asks us, "Well, what did you expect in an opera? A happy ending?"

"One Froggy Evening" is a parable starting with the old joke about a guy with a talking frog. A construction worker opens a time capsule from a demolished building and finds a frog who puts on a top hat and dances while singing "Hello, My Ragtime Gal." Later, he will perform an Irish ballad and the aria "Largo al factotum" from *The Barber of Seville.*

Dollar signs dance around the construction worker's head as he imagines the frog as a box-office bonanza. But the frog will sing only for the worker; it clams up and goes limp when anyone else is listening. In despair, the worker seals the frog inside another time capsule, and we see it being discovered by another worker, a century in the future, who is also delighted by its act.

There are tragedies in conflict here: (a) a frog who is a song-and-dance star, who has been locked in the dark for decades but cannot perform in public; and (b) a worker who dreams of wealth and is considered a fool and a liar. The story of "One Froggy Evening" involves an endless loop of frustration. Jones bent the rules to sneak it around Schlesinger, and it was hailed as a masterpiece—so popular that although the frog appeared in only one cartoon, he was later given a name (Michigan J. Frog, the middle initial in honor of *Time* magazine film critic Jay Cocks) and became a logo for the WB Network.

Cartoons were limited not only in length but in detail; they were made at a time when every frame had to be drawn by hand, and implacable producers like Schlesinger kept an eye on the time clock. Backgrounds tended to be static unless motion was essential; the animators focused on the characters, and it is remarkable what precision of behavior and personality they achieved. In body language, as much as in the voices supplied by such gifted artists as Mel Blanc, the characters expressed themselves, and to look at the elegant nonchalance of Bugs or the frenzied determination of Daffy is to see a universe of emotion conveyed in animation where economy met style.

These cartoons, and all the cartoons from the same tradition, seemed doomed to play for a week and then disappear (although sometimes there would be a collection of "Five Color Cartoons" before a kiddie matinee, and London's Piccadilly Circus had a theater that played only cartoons). Then, just as the studios pulled the plug on cartoon shorts, color TV came along to give them a new life, and now on cable and DVD they seem immortal. There are two ways to regard them: as silly little entertainments, or as an art form that in its own small way, its limitations permitting an infinity of imagination, approaches perfection.

Thanks to reader Mark Kitchen, who suggested cartoons as Great Movies, and credit to the commentary tracks and supplementary material on the Warner Bros. Looney Tunes Golden Collection volumes 1 and 2.

{ COOL HAND LUKE }

All these years after the release of *Cool Hand Luke* in 1967, all you have to do is say, "What we have here is—failure to communicate." Everyone knows the line, and everyone can identify the film, even those who may not have seen it. And here's the curious part. As they make the connection, they'll invariably smile, as if recalling a pleasant experience, a good time at the movies. Have you seen *Cool Hand Luke* lately? I have. Rarely has an important movie star suffered more, in a film wall-to-wall with physical punishment, psychological cruelty, hopelessness, and equal parts of sadism and masochism.

It is a great film. On that most of us can agree. But such a film could not possibly be made in more recent decades, not one starring Brad Pitt or Tom Cruise or other actors comparable to Paul Newman's stature. It is simply too painful. I can imagine a voice at a studio pitch meeting: "Nobody wants to see that." Much was made by many critics, myself included, of Newman's "anti-hero" stature in *Luke* and other films he made around the same time: *The Hustler*, *Hud*, even *Butch Cassidy and the Sundance Kid*. I'm no longer sure he's an anti-hero in *Cool Hand Luke*. I think he's more of a willing martyr, a man so obsessed with the wrongness of the world that he invites death to prove himself correct. Louis Armstrong once said, "There are some folks that, if they don't know, you can't tell 'em." The brutal guards who rule the work camp where Luke is a prisoner demonstrate time and again that if he escapes, he will be captured and punished to within an inch of his life. Since he knows that, is he seeking punishment?

The film is an effective physical production, set in the South but filmed around Stockton, California, in a bleak rural landscape. Fifty prisoners, counted daily, are assigned to a work gang under the fierce eyes of the Captain (Strother Martin) and the never-seen eyes of Boss Godfrey (Morgan Woodward), whose reflecting sunglasses get him described as "the man with no eyes." (That he does not speak adds to his stature as a fearsome icon.) The gang is ruled by its top dog, a prisoner named Dragline (George Kennedy). The newcomer Luke loses little time in challenging Dragline's authority, and they have a boxing match during which Dragline beats him almost to death. It is a point of pride to Luke that he hauls himself to his feet and refuses to admit defeat, and this, we discover, will be his method throughout the movie: he can't win, but he can continue to absorb punishment indefinitely.

The director, Stuart Rosenberg, working with the great cinematographer Conrad Hall, evokes the punishing heat of the location, where shirts stick to skin and dust sticks to everything. The prisoners cut weeds, dig ditches, and tar roads—in the road job, urged on by Luke to shove gravel on fresh oil so quickly the boss can hardly keep up. Another example of taking the moral high ground by physical travail. In the bunkhouse, Dragline, respecting Luke's stubbornness in their fight, becomes Luke's biggest admirer, and the kind of dynamic is set up that we might recognize from other prison movies; character actors (Robert Drivas, Luke Askew, Warren Finnerty, Dennis Hopper) play assigned roles in the groups that witness and admire Luke.

The movie is "crowd-pleasing," says the critic Tim Dirks, and James Berardinelli speaks of such "comic" scenes as the one where Luke eats fifty hardboiled eggs. I saw the movie at the time and can testify that it is crowd-pleasing, and in my review from 1967, I wrote that Luke was "always smiling, always ready for a little fun. He eats fifty hard-boiled eggs on a bet and collects all the money in the camp. That Luke, he's a cool hand." What was I thinking? Today, the egg-eating scene strikes me as all but unwatchable.

The physical suffering and danger are sickening, no less so than Luke's punishment of being made to dig and fill in the same grave-shaped hole time and again. "Why did you have to say fifty eggs?" Dragline asks him. "Why not . . . thirty-nine?" Well, there are fifty prisoners, of course.

When Luke collapses on a table after eating the eggs, he takes the posture of Christ on the cross. Yes, he is a Christ figure, and on the last night of the story, in a little rural church, he addresses his Father on the subject of whether he has been forsaken. Will he die for the sins of his fellow prisoners? That's making it too simple, I think, although at the end there is the curious eyewitness report by Dragline, who is already trying to recast the Gospel according to Luke to reflect a symbolic victory. Luke is shot dead by No Eyes, and looks stunned as it happens, but here is Dragline's revisionism: "He was smiling. That's right. You know, that Luke smile of his. He had it on his face right to the very end."

This and other dialogue suggests that Dragline is more than half in love with Luke, who acted out all their dreams and desires, and even turned up, improbably, with a couple of chorus girls in a magazine photo. As Dragline tells him, "Oh Luke, you wild, beautiful thing. You crazy handful of nothin'." He's right about the handful, but the first part of the description seems a strange thing for one prisoner to say about another.

Could another actor than Paul Newman have played the role and gotten away with it? Of the stars at the time, I would not be able to supply one. Warren Beatty? Steve McQueen? Lee Marvin? They would have the presence and stamina, but would have lacked the smile. The physical presence of Paul Newman is the reason this movie works: the smile, the innocent blue eyes, the lack of strutting. Look at his gentle behavior in the touching scene with his mother (Jo Van Fleet), a scene that evokes the scene with Bonnie's mother in *Bonnie and Clyde*. Both parents and both children know they will never see each other again, and in a way are apologizing. Newman as a star had a powerful unforced charisma: we liked him. Could Kennedy have described Lee Marvin as "you wild, beautiful thing"?

Much was also made in 1967 of the movie as an "anti-establishment" statement. The year 1967 was at the center of the Vietnam era, and Luke was against the establishment, but I cannot rebuild the period in my memory to make *Cool Hand Luke* work as a statement about Vietnam. Strother Martin as LBJ? But my mind returns to the symbolism of Boss Godfrey, the man with the mirroring sunglasses who never speaks. He reminds me of another famous pair of glasses in fiction. In F. Scott Fitzgerald's *The Great Gatsby*, the road into town passes through an industrial wasteland overseen by a gigantic billboard of never-blinking yellow eyeglasses, through which stare the eyes of Dr. T. J. Eckleburg. Some see Eckleburg's eyes as the eyes of God. I don't know. I know that Luke calls out to God at the end: "It's beginnin' to look like you got things fixed so I can't never win out. Inside, outside, all them rules and regulations and bosses. You made me like I am. Just where am I supposed to fit in? Ol' Man, I gotta tell ya. I started out pretty strong and fast. But it's beginnin' to get to me. When does it end?"

He gets his answer quickly enough, but what other answer could he have expected? The problem between Luke and God is nothing more than a failure to communicate. Having seen this powerful, punishing movie again freshly, I reflect that in 1967 I didn't approach it with the proper pessimism. Today, it seems to be God does a fairly good job of getting his message across. There's an old vaudeville joke. "Doc, it hurts when I do this." "Then don't do that no more."

{CRIMES AND MISDEMEANORS}

I *remember my father telling me, "The eyes of God are on us always."*

The man who remembers is Judah Rosenthal, a respected ophthalmologist and community leader. As Woody Allen's *Crimes and Misdemeanors* opens, he is being honored at a banquet. He lives on three acres in Connecticut, drives a Jaguar, built a new wing on the hospital. During the course of the movie he will be responsible for the murder of a woman who loves him.

She dies not because of his passion but for his convenience. In this darkest and most cynical Allen comedy—yes, comedy—he not only gets away with murder but even finds it possible, after a few months, to view the experience in a positive light. If the eyes of God are on him always, what does that say about God?

Woody Allen has made more than forty movies; the best are *Annie Hall* (1976), *Hannah and Her Sisters* (1987), *Crimes and Misdemeanors* (1989), and *Match Point*, which premiered at Cannes 2005. The new film resembles *Crimes and Misdemeanors* in the way it involves a man who commits murder to cover up an affair, but *Match Point* is more firmly a film noir, and *Crimes* is frankly a complaint against God for turning a blind eye on evil.

Judah, played by Martin Landau as a man of probity and vast self-importance, is, or thinks he is, a moral man. That has not prevented him from having an affair for two years with Dolores (Anjelica Huston), a flight attendant with whom he has walked on the beach and discussed marriage. But Judah will never divorce his wife, Miriam (Claire Bloom), to marry Dolores. Nor is he capable of confessing his sin to Miriam: "Miriam won't forgive me," he tells a rabbi. "She'll be broken. She idealizes me." That the conversation with the rabbi is imaginary takes away nothing from its ruthlessness. What Judah is arguing is that Dolores must die because if Miriam found out about the affair it would—what? Destroy Miriam? Dolores? No, it would destroy his image and stature in the eyes of his wife and his community, and he thinks that is worth killing for.

To be sure, Judah backs into murder. Dolores has been acting dangerously. She sent a letter to Miriam that Judah only barely intercepted. She called from a gas station ten minutes down the road, threatening to come to his house and tell Miriam "what she needs to know." Judah discusses his problem with his brother Jack (Jerry Orbach), who has connections with the Mafia. "They'll handle it," Jack tells him. Handle? "I can't believe I'm talking about a human being," Judah says. "She's not just an insect to be stepped on. . . ."

Yet he steps on her. Dolores knows about certain "financial improprieties" that Judah has committed; funds from one place were useful in another. Threatened with exposure on both fronts, Judah makes a call to Jack, and Jack calls back: "It's taken care of." Now listen to Judah: "I can't speak. I'm in shock. God have mercy on us, Jack." How about a little mercy for Dolores? Judah has mastered the art of ameliorating his crime by being shocked at it. Yes, he had Dolores killed—but if he feels terrible about it, doesn't that prove he's not an entirely bad man?

The movie intercuts this tragic story with a comedy, also about adultery. The technique is Shakespearean: the crimes of kings are mirrored for comic effect in the foibles of the lower orders. Allen plays Cliff Stern, a maker of documentaries of stultifying boredom; in one, an old man in thick glasses discusses metaphysics. Cliff is married to Wendy (Joanna Gleason). She has two brothers: Ben (Sam Waterston), the rabbi, who is going blind and is being treated by Judah, and Lester (Alan Alda), the creator of incredibly successful TV sitcoms.

Cliff detests Lester. Consider the scene where we first see the two men together; Lester is on the left flanked by his sister and another woman, holding court. Cliff is on the right, slightly more in the foreground, and half-turned away from the action and toward us. He seems barely able to prevent himself from turning to the camera and telling us directly what a jerk Lester is. The visual strategy is subtle but wonderful: Allen delivers a monologue using only body language.

Cliff is offered a job directing a documentary about Lester. "You weren't my first choice," the Alda character cheerfully tells him. "I'm doing it as a favor to my sister." While making the film, Cliff meets a production assistant named Halley (Mia Farrow) and falls for her. They have a little non-affair; Cliff is not made for big affairs, but for modest displays of erotic self-deprecation. He proposes marriage to her, despite the fact that he has barely kissed her and is obviously married to Wendy.

So now we have two married men discussing marriage with other women. That Judah will not really marry Dolores destroys her ("I was at a low point when I met you!" she cries in raw emotion. "You turned every-thing around!"). That Cliff might actually marry Halley, or thinks he might, is fielded by her with tact: she announces a trip to London, thinks they ought to "have some time apart," and returns engaged to—yes, Lester. Cliff is morally offended by her choice, despite the inarguable fact that Lester is single and available (and also rich and successful), and Cliff is married, poor, and has been fired from the documentary after a scene comparing Lester to Mussolini.

The Woody Allen scenes provide the kind of stand-up self-analysis and kvetching that his characters are famous for. But what happens in the Martin Landau scenes are as calmly shocking as anything Allen has ever done. In that imaginary conversation with the rabbi, Judah refers to his brother's offer to "take care" of Dolores. "God is a luxury I can't afford," he says. "Jack lives in the real world. You live in the kingdom of heaven." After Judah learns that Dolores has been killed, he visits Dolores's apartment, sees that she is indeed dead, and takes her address book and other papers that might link him with her.

"Four months later," we're told in a subtitle, the principal characters are gathered at a wedding. Cliff wanders off, outraged at seeing Halley with the despised Lester. Why should a worthless parasite like Lester get the girl? Judah wanders in the same direction, and the two men have a curious conversation. It turns on the idea of a perfect murder. Judah describes "a murder plot" to Cliff. It is the murder he has gotten away with.

But how does it feel to be responsible for the death of another person? Can you live with yourself? "Suddenly it's not an empty universe at all," Judah tells Cliff. God occupies it, and has eyes, and sees. "The man is an inch away from confessing to the police." Then suddenly one morning, he wakes up, the sun is shining, his life is good, and he has returned to "his protected world of wealth and privilege." The moral of this story? "We define ourselves by the choices we make," Judah says. By choosing to have Dolores murdered, Judah has defined himself as a man of wealth and privilege, respected by society, "idolized" by his wife, and a murderer. He can live with that.

The implications of *Crimes and Misdemeanors* are bleak and hopeless. The evil are rewarded, the blameless are punished, and the rabbi goes blind. To be sure, justice is done in the low-road plot: Cliff does not succeed in leaving his wife to marry a girl for whom he would be the worst possible partner, and the rich and triumphant Lester gets the girl and will possibly make her happy, or at least rich. But in the main story Dolores lies in her grave, and Judah finds that life goes on—for him, at least. For Martin Landau, the performance is a masterpiece of smooth, practiced diplomacy, as he glides through life and leaves his problems behind. Landau is never more effective than when he is shocked and dismayed at his own behavior. It's as if he's regarding himself from outside, with a kind of fascination. He sees what he does, and does nothing to stop it. In his own world, he is the eyes of God.

{ CRUMB }

Crumb is a meeting between two eccentrics in sympathy with each other. The artist R. Crumb created such bizarre images in his underground comic books that the art critic Robert Hughes named him "the Brueghel of the last half of the 20th century." The director Terry Zwigoff knew him before he had any notion of making this documentary. They shared a love for obscure musicians on 78 rpm records from the 1920s and 1930s, and they once played in the same band. Long before he knew the inhabitants of Crumb's childhood home would be the keys to this film, Zwigoff had slept the night there and met Crumb's brother Charles, who is perhaps the key to the whole Crumb story.

The old 78s led Zwigoff to his first film, *Louie Bluie* (1986), about a musician named Howard Armstrong, whose forgotten recordings from the 1930s fascinated him. Learning that Armstrong was still alive, he made a film about a man who was ageless, gifted in music and art, a clown and mimic, a life force. Zwigoff was now a filmmaker, and knew that his next subject was obviously his fellow music lover, Robert Crumb.

This was not obvious to Crumb, a legendary underground artist from San Francisco whose "Keep on Truckin'" image had become a 1960s icon, and whose cover for Janis Joplin's *Cheap Thrills* album was a classic even apart from the music it enclosed. Crumb had little interest in success, turned down countless offers to license "Keep on Truckin'," turned down an offer to host *Saturday Night Live* with his band, drew compulsively all the time, produced small-press graphic novels of startling, often pornographic, weirdness, and listened to his old records.

Zwigoff told me he "called in every favor he owed me" to persuade Crumb to be in his film: he spent nine years on the documentary "while averaging an income of about $200 a month and living with back pain so intense that I spent three years with a loaded gun on the pillow next to my bed, trying to get up the nerve to kill myself." I am apparently responsible for the urban legend that Zwigoff told Crumb, "Make this film or I will shoot myself." That never happened, but it may be true that Zwigoff's life was saved because he did make the film.

Among documentaries about artists, *Crumb* (1994) is unusual in having access to the key players and biographical artifacts of Crumb's entire life. Crumb himself is entirely forthcoming on camera, uninhibited, honest. We meet both of his wives, who talk cheerfully about the way their images and secrets were incorporated, sometimes directly, into Crumb's work. We see the high school yearbook portraits of classmates immortalized into grotesques and sadists, sometimes under their own names. Most crucially, we enter Crumb's boyhood home in New Jersey, still occupied by his mother and his brother Charles, and in San Francisco we visit his brother Max. His two sisters refuse to participate.

We leave the film convinced there are no secrets still concealed in this family. We know that Robert's central sexual fantasy was to ride bareback on women with overdeveloped rumps; that Charles remained a virgin and recluse, rarely leaving his bedroom, his erotic imagination forever fixed on Bobby Driscoll in the 1960 film *Treasure Island*; that Max lived in monkish isolation, slept on a bed of nails, and regularly passed a thirty-foot cloth ribbon through his body; that their alcoholic father broke Robert's collarbone when he was a boy, and that the parents fought between themselves so fiercely that their faces were often covered with scratches and bruises. Photographs of the family circa 1950 find parents and five children posed in their Sunday best on a suburban lawn, looking as if they are awaiting the arrival of Diane Arbus.

Charles was the first artist in the family. He hand-drew comic books, and encouraged Robert and Max to draw, against their will at first. Hand-made comics from the period survive and are seen in the film; Robert seems to have saved everything, and Charles did, too, although after his death by overdose, his mother threw out most of his work before Robert could rescue it. Max accumulates little, as befits a monk, but his paintings now draw high prices in galleries. Ironic that Robert and Max gained fame as artists while Charles remained in his room, reading stacks of paperback novels and filling notebooks with endless entries, some of them words, some only elaborate typographical patterns. In an extraordinary scene involving Robert, Charles, and their mother, Beatrice, she sprawls almost flat on a sofa, but like her sons is funny, articulate, and very strange.

Art may have saved Crumb from madness, turning private neurosis into public validation. Zwigoff is unsparing in showing Crumb's more transgressive work; the camera follows panel by panel through comic books as Crumb narrates stories of incest, necrophilia, scatology, assault, mayhem, and sexual couplings as unlikely as they are alarming. To call some of his images sexist, racist, and depraved is putting it mildly.

Zwigoff is fair enough to provide an articulate objection to Crumb's work: good, sane Deirdre English, a former editor of *Mother Jones* magazine, is not shocked as much as saddened and repelled by Crumb's work, which treats women as objects, commodities, victims, mindless (sometimes even headless) conveniences. In defense of Crumb, the art critic Hughes finds a vision of suffering and yearning, of barriers ignored, of inhibitions disregarded, of a psyche turning itself out naked upon the page. Certainly it is true that Crumb's men are treated no better than his women: all are disgusting creatures driven by animalistic lust and depraved need.

His graphic novels have undeniable energy and a visual style that depends on meticulous command of the divide between portrait and caricature. We see his pen at work, we see the materials that inspire some of his images, we see him giving a drawing lesson to his teenage son, Jesse. He is one of those artists whose pen stroke is instantly identifiable as his own. His subjects are not superheroes or comic characters (although Crumb reveals that as a child he masturbated to Bugs Bunny). They are lonely, disenfranchised, pimply, unpopular—all the things we sense Crumb was when he was "the most unpopular kid in high school." In some of his most loathsome caricatures, Crumb is still settling scores with bullies from his adolescence and girls who turned him down.

Yet the women who knew him best seem fond of him, especially his first wife, Dana, and current wife, Aline, who see him (as we do in the film) as a smart and entertaining companion who has transformed his demons into his work. Yes, he has sexual hang-ups, but not ones they find unpleasant or painful. Researching Crumb's fetishes for isolated body parts, especially feet, buttocks, and breasts, Zwigoff visits Dian Hanson, the editor of the *Juggs* and *Leg Show* magazines, who attributes her publishing success to the fact that she actually reads the letters from her readers.

She arranges a fantasy session for Crumb and some of her models, but this scene doesn't work; for Crumb, the point is not realizing his fantasies, but displacing them into obsessive visual caricatures. In this process some of his work becomes a critique of the same values Deirdre English deplores. If pornography dehumanizes and objectifies, then perhaps that is the point of the Crumb story (shown in detail) about a woman whose neck ends with a peg on which a mannequin head can be attached? She is otherwise functional in all the ways Crumb's hero desires. The strip has a shocking climax, when the hero discovers his woman is not without a head after all; it has been shoved down inside her neck, and when it emerges, the woman has a great deal to complain about. Such a work is disgusting and depraved at the same time it is satirical and subversive; it is an overdose of sexism, inspiring not desire but disgust. It is also, let us be honest, satirical in a dark and scary way.

Crumb's art and career would define the limits of this film if it had been made by someone else. What deepens Zwigoff's work are the scenes with the family members. There is in Charles such a gentle sadness, such a resigned acceptance of his emotional imprisonment, that we sense how Robert's art has saved him from a similar destiny. In the fondness of his wives and girlfriends, there is a redemption to be sensed. As the film ends, Crumb is moving with his family to the south of France, where in recent years he has not produced so much, perhaps because, let us speculate, he is happier.

{ DARK CITY }

Dark City by Alex Proyas resembles its great silent predecessor *Metropolis* in asking what it is that makes us human, and why it cannot be changed by decree. Both films are about false worlds created to fabricate ideal societies, and in both the machinery of the rulers is destroyed by the hearts of the ruled. Both are parables in which a dangerous weapon attacks the order of things: a free human who can see what really is, and question it. *Dark City* contains a threat more terrible than any of the horrors in *Metropolis*, because the rulers of the city can control the memories of its citizens; if we are the sum of all that has happened to us, then what are we when nothing has happened to us?

In *Dark City* (1998), all of the human memories are newly fabricated when the hands of the clock reach twelve. This is defined as "midnight," but the term is deceptive, because there is no noon. "First came darkness, then came the Strangers," we are told in the opening narration. In the beginning, there was no light. John Murdoch, the hero, asks Bumstead, the police detective: "When was the last time you remember doing something during the day?" Bumstead is surprised by the question. "You know something?" Murdoch asks him. "I don't think the sun even exists in this place. I've been up for hours and hours, and the night never ends here."

The narration explains that the Strangers came from another galaxy and collected a group of humans to study them. Their civilization is dying. They seek to find the secret of the human heart, or soul, or whatever it is that falls outside their compass. They create a vast artificial city, which can be fabricated, or "tuned," whenever they want to run another experiment.

We see the tuning taking place. All humans lose consciousness. All machinery stops. Changes are made in the city. Skyscrapers are extruded from the primordial materials of the underworld, architecture is devised, rooms are prepared for their inhabitants, props are set in place. Aided by a human scientist, the Strangers inject memories into the foreheads of their test subjects. When humans awaken, they have no memory of the day before; everything they remember has been injected from a communal memory bank. If a man commits murder one day and then is given a new identity, is he still capable of committing murder? Are men inherently good or evil, or is it a matter of how they think of themselves? The Strangers need to know.

Murdoch (Rufus Sewell) has developed an immunity to the devices of the Strangers. His latest memory injection was incomplete. It was administered by Dr. Schreber (Kiefer Sutherland), a scientist who works for the Strangers but has no love for them. Murdoch wakes in a hotel room with the corpse of a dead woman; the script for the day has made him a serial killer of prostitutes. Schreber warns him he is the subject of an experiment but has proven resistant to it. The Strangers are coming for him, and he must flee.

That sets the story into motion: Murdoch wanders through the city, trying to discover its underlying nature; Detective Bumstead (William Hurt) tries to capture him, but will gradually be won over by Murdoch's questions (he is programmed as a cop, but not a very good one; he keeps complaining, "No one ever listens to me"). Then there is the torch singer, Emma (Jennifer Connelly), who remembers that she is John's wife and loves him, and that they met at Shell Beach. Everyone says they know how to go to Shell Beach. But no one seems able to say exactly where it is.

The Strangers occupy the bodies of human cadavers. Most of them are tall; one is in a child's body but is no child. The alien beings themselves, living inside the corpses, look like spiders made of frightened noodles. They can levitate, they can change the matter of the city at will, they have a hive insect organization, they gather in a subterranean cavern to collectively re-tune the city. This cavern has visuals reminding us of two Fritz Lang films: the underworld mechanisms in *Metropolis* (1927) and *M* (1931), with the pale faces of criminals rising row above row into the gloom.

One year, I went through *Dark City* a shot at a time for four days at the Hawaii Film festival, with moviegoers who were as curious as I was. We froze frames, we dissected special effects, we debated the meaning of the film, and our numbers even included a psychiatrist who told us of the original Daniel Schreber, a schizophrenic whose book on his condition influenced Freud and Jung.

Sometimes during the shot-by-shot analysis, we simply froze a frame and regarded it. Some of the street scenes echo paintings by Edward Hopper or Jack Vettriano. This is not only a beautiful film but a generous one, which supplies rich depth and imagination and many more details than are really necessary to tell the story. Small wonder that the name Bumstead appears, perhaps in honor of Henry Bumstead, one of the greatest Hollywood art directors. The world created by the Strangers seems borrowed from 1940s film noir; we see fedoras, cigarettes, neon signs, automats, older cars (and some newer ones—the world is not consistent). Proyas wrote the screenplay with David S. Goyer and Lem Dobbs; the screenplays Dobbs wrote for *Kafka* and Goyer wrote for *Batman Begins* contain some of the same notes sounded here.

Proyas likes deep-focus compositions. Many interior spaces are long and narrow. Exteriors look down one street to the vanishing point, and then the camera pans to look down another street, equally long. The lighting is low-key and moody. The color scheme depends on blacks, browns, shadows, and the pallor of the Strangers; warmer colors exist in human faces, in neon signs, and on the billboard for Shell Beach. "I am simply grateful for this shot," I said in Hawaii more than once. "It is as well-done as it can possibly be." Many other great films give you the same feeling—that their makers were carried far beyond the actual requirements of their work into the passion of creating something wonderful.

I believe more than ever that *Dark City* is one of the great modern films. It preceded *The Matrix* by a year (both films used a few of the same sets in Australia), and on a smaller budget, with special effects that owe as much to imagination as to technology, did what *The Matrix* wanted to do, earlier and with more feeling.

The poignancy of *Dark City* emerges in its love stories. At a crucial point, John Murdoch tells Emma, "Everything you remember, and everything I'm supposed to remember, never really happened." Emma doesn't think that can be true. "I so vividly remember meeting you," she says. "I remember falling in love with you." Yes, she remembers. But this is the first time they have met. "I love you, John," she says. "You can't fake something like that." And Murdoch says, "No, you can't." You can inform someone who they love, and that is what the Strangers have done with their memory injection. But what she feels cannot be injected. That is the part the Strangers do not understand. Emma has a small role but it is at the heart of the movie, because she truly knows love; John has still to discover it—to learn about it from her.

The Strangers are not evil. They simply proceed from alien assumptions. They are not even omnipotent, which is why Murdoch, Bumstead, and Schreber have relative freedom to move about the city. At the end, we feel a little sorry for them. They will die surrounded by happy beings whose secrets they could not discover.

Notice an opening shot that approaches the hotel window behind which we meet Murdoch. The window is a circular dome in a rectangular frame. As clearly as possible, it looks like the "face" of Hal 9000 in *2001*. Hal was a computer that understood everything, except what it was to be human and have emotions. *Dark City* considers the same theme in a film that creates a completely artificial world in which humans teach themselves to be themselves.

{ THE DEAD }

John Huston was dying when he directed *The Dead*. Tethered to an oxygen tank, hunched in a wheelchair, weak with emphysema and heart disease, he was a perfectionist attentive to the slightest nuance of the filming. James Joyce's story, for that matter, is all nuance until the final pages. It leads by subtle signs to a great outpouring of grief and love, but until then, as Huston observed, "The biggest piece of action is trying to pass the port." He began shooting in January 1987, finished in April, and at the end of August, he died. He was eighty-one.

All of this I have from *The Hustons*, by Lawrence Grobel, a biography that charts a scattered and troubled family, yet one that gathered Oscars in three generations, for Walter, John, and Anjelica. John's daughter won hers for a supporting role in his previous film, *Prizzi's Honor* (1985), and now she was playing the crucial role in *The Dead*. John's son Tony, then thirty-seven, was nominated for his screenplay for *The Dead*, and served as his father's assistant, aware of the secret being kept from the world, which was how ill John really was.

Joyce's "The Dead" is one of the greatest short stories in the language, but would seem unfilmable. Its action takes place in Dublin in 1904 at a holiday party given by two elderly sisters and their niece, who have spent their lives performing or teaching music. The guests arrive, we observe them as they observe one another and listen to talk that means more than it says. At the end of the long evening, Gabriel Conroy (Donal McCann), nephew of the Misses Morkan, leaves with his wife, Gretta (Anjelica Huston), to go back to the hotel where they will spend the night before going home to a far suburb in the morning.

All was prologue to their cab ride and an hour or so in the hotel. She tells him a story he has never heard, about a boy who was sweet on her when he was seventeen, a boy named Michael Furey, who died. He was a sickly boy, who stood in the rain on the night before she was to leave Galway and go to a convent school. "I implored of him to go home at once and told him he would get his death in the rain," she remembers. "But he said he did not want to live." When she was only a week in the convent school, he died. "What was it he died of so young?" asks Gabriel. "Consumption, was it?" She replies, "I think he died from me." In his final pages, Joyce enters the mind of Gabriel, who thinks about the dead boy, about his wife's first great love, about how he has never felt a love like that, about those who have died, and about how all the rest of us will die as well—die, with our loves and lusts, our hopes and regrets, our plans and secrets, all dead.

Read with me James Joyce's last paragraph:

A few light taps upon the pane made him turn to the window. It had begun to snow again. He watched sleepily the flakes, silver and dark, falling obliquely against the lamplight. The time had come for him to set out on his journey westward. Yes, the newspapers were right: snow was general all over Ireland. It was falling on every part of the dark central plain, on the treeless hills, on the Bog of Allen and, farther westward, softly falling into the dark mutinous Shannon waves. It was falling, too, upon every part of the lonely churchyard on the hill where Michael Furey lay buried. It lay thickly drifted on the crooked crosses and headstones, on the spears of the little gate, on the barren thorns. His soul swooned slowly as he heard the snow falling faintly through the universe and faintly falling, like the descent of their last end, upon all the living and the dead.

There is, as John Huston realized, no way to translate this epiphany into the action of a movie script. It exists resolutely as thoughts expressed in words. He and Tony in their screenplay did what they had to do, and made it an interior monologue, spoken by the actor Donal McCann, as his wife, having wept, now sleeps on their bed. We note that he thinks of "his" journey, although she will accompany him. He thinks of himself as alone. When I first saw *The Dead*, I thought it brave and deeply felt but "an impossible film," and I wrote: "There is no way in the world any filmmaker can reproduce the thoughts inside Gabriel's head." But of course there was. Huston could do the same thing Joyce did, and simply tell us what Gabriel was thinking.

The film follows the story with almost complete fidelity. A few details are transposed; Gabriel's story about his grandfather's horse is moved forward in the story, and given to Freddy Malins (Donal Donnelly), who arrives drunk but, as Gabriel reassures Mrs. Malins, "nearly all right." Line for line and scene for scene, the movie faithfully reflects the book, even to such details as two young men slipping into the next room for a drink during a piano recital and then returning at its close to applaud loudly.

The turning point comes as everyone is leaving. Gabriel has already descended the stairs when the famous tenor Bartell D'Arcy (Frank Patterson) is finally prevailed upon to sing. Gabriel looks up and sees a figure paused listening on the stair, and eventually realizes it is his wife: "There was grace and mystery in her attitude as if she were a symbol of something," and he thinks, "if he were a painter, he would paint her in that attitude." John Huston is a painter, and does. The song is the same one Michael Furey used to sing, and it awakens Gretta's whole sad train of memory.

There is one line in the story that neither Huston nor anyone else could get into a film, because it is not the thought of Gabriel, but of Joyce. He tells us that as Gabriel regards his sleeping wife in the hotel, "a strange, friendly pity for her entered his soul." That is the phrase upon which the whole story wheels. He has been married for years and thinks he knows her, but suddenly he sees Gretta not in terms of wife, lover, or their history together, but as another human being, one who will also be alone on her journey westward.

The Dead ends in sadness, but it is one of the great romantic films, fearless in its regard for regret and tenderness. John Huston, who lived for years in Ireland and raised Anjelica there until she was sixteen, had an instinctive sympathy for the kindness with which the guests at the Misses Morkan's party accepted one another's lives and failings. They have all fallen short of their hopes, and know it. Freddy Malins is a drunk, but as we see him seated beside his mother, we suspect that she has forced him to pursue defeat. Mr. Brown (Dan O'Herlihy) is a drunk in the classic mold, because of uncomplicated alcoholism. Molly Ivors (Maria McDermottroe), who supports the Republican cause, hurries off early to a meeting, still convinced their problems have political solutions. Aunt Julia (Cathleen Delany), who confesses she had a decent voice years ago, is persuaded to sing, and does so, not very well. Freddy lurches forward to blurt out praise that is so effusive, it embarrasses her in front of the party, but everyone understands that Julia's voice has failed, and that Freddy means well.

Gabriel is the witness to it all. An early shot shows the back of his head, regarding everyone in the room. Later he will see his wife, finally, as the person she really is and always has been. And he will see himself, with his ambitions as a journalist, the bright light of his family, the pride of his aunts, as a paltry fellow resting on unworthy accomplishments. Did these thoughts go through John Huston's mind as he chose his last film and directed it? How could they not? And if all those sad things were true, then he could at least communicate them with grace and poetry, in a film as quiet and forgiving as the falling snow.

{ DIVA }

Peering into obscure corners of Paris, Jean-Jacques Beineix emerged with
an assembly of unlikely, even impossible, characters to populate his *Diva*
(1981), a thriller that is more about how it looks than what happens in it.
Here is an exhilarating film made for no better purpose than to surprise
and fascinate. I remember it at Toronto 1981, where it arrived unknown and
unsung and won, as I recall, the festival's first audience award. Now released
in a restored print, it glistens in its original magnificence.

The plot is both preposterous and delightful, put together out of
elements that seem chosen for their audacity. The central character is a
young postman named Jules (Frederic Andrei), who races the streets on his
moped, delivering special-delivery mail and pausing at an opera recital to
secretly record a performance by a tall, black, gorgeous American soprano
named Cynthia Hawkins (Wilhelmenia Wiggins Fernandez). He has a
professional-quality Nagra recorder hidden in his bag. After the performance, he enters her dressing room with a crowd of well-wishers and steals
her elegant white silk gown.

Hawkins is famous for never having entered a recording studio, and
we later learn she has never heard her own voice. Now Jules has the only
existing tape of her singing; it is priceless, but he wants it only for himself. Unfortunately, he was seen making the recording by two Taiwanese

bootleggers, who want to steal it from him. And his problems grow more complex when two gangsters murder a prostitute on a street where he is making a delivery. She has a tape incriminating the chief of police in a sex-slavery ring, and before she dies, she slips the tape into the carrier bag of his moped. Now four deadly crooks are looking for him.

Jules lives in his own way, in his own shadowy industrial space, which is filled with crashed cars and wall paintings of automobiles. Here he listens to the sublime voice. (Fernandez, an established opera diva, did her own singing and created an early-1980s boom for Catalani's opera *La Wally* and its first-act aria.) One day at a record store, Jules spots a Vietnamese nymphet named Alba (Thuy An Luu) shoplifting a 33 rpm record with a cleverly designed art portfolio, which seems to contain only nude photographs of herself.

He follows her, asks her how she did it, they discover they share a love of opera, and he lets her listen to his recording. She supplies it to a mysterious, cigar-smoking, handsome older man named Gorodish (Richard Bohringer), who lives in an industrial loft of vast size, furnished mostly by a chair, a bed, a bathtub, and an aquarium. Is this man her lover? Her guru? Why does he seem to possess unlimited wealth and power?

Now all the pieces are in place, and what remains is only for the film to spin them in a dazzling kaleidoscope of sex, action, and startling images. *Diva* has been referred to as the first French film in the post–New Wave *cinema du look*, defined by Wikipedia as a group of films "that had a slick visual style and a focus on young, alienated characters that were said to represent the marginalized youth of Francois Mitterrand's France." It was the look itself, rather than the content, that defined the films, and sometimes the plots seemed almost designed to create photographic opportunities.

The films were drawn to untamed non-bourgeois spaces such as industrial wastelands and the Paris Metro rather than tidy indoor spaces. *Subway*, a famous 1985 *cinema du look* by Luc Besson, has a crime plot that takes place largely in the Metro, where a rock concert is even staged. And in *Diva*, the most sensational sequence involves Jules being pursued by the cops and actually racing his moped down the Metro stairs, onto a train, off again, and up another flight of stairs. The photography of this shot helps explain why Philippe Rousselot won the Cesar, or French Oscar, for his cinematography (the film won three more Cesars, for best first work, best music, and best sound).

Not the least of the film's attractions is the unexpected casting. You could say many characters were typecast, but they were largely unknown at the time of the film's release. This was Andrei's first significant role, for example, Fernandez's first and only film, and the first feature of Dominique Pinon, called "Le curé" ("the treatment"). A short young man hiding behind mirrored glasses, an earplug always in his ear, his head shaved, he performs his treatments with a heavy awl, which he throws into the backs of his victims, killing them. He likes to pose with the point of the awl tickling his chin. He doesn't smile.

The presence of Fernandez is awesome; the filmmakers discovered her at a performance of *Carmen* in Paris and found her sufficiently awesome to justify the young postman's obsession with her. The moments when he returns her gown, and then the tape, are handled by her with a subtle balance of astonishment and amusement.

The most mysterious characters in the film are, of course, the rich recluse Gorodish and his bold young friend Alba (this was the first of five films made by Thuy An Luu). The characters are found in a series of popular French thrillers by Delacorta, including *Diva*, where we can learn that he is a musician, she is a fourteen-year-old wise beyond her years, their relationship is unconsummated, and she has a knack for bringing trouble home for him to solve, just as a cat will bring home a mouse, and just as she brings Jules to his lair. In a sense, you could say that Delacorta (real name Daniel Odier) was a co-inventor of the *cinema du look*, since his prose emphasizes slick surfaces, neon colors, unorthodox settings, and characters from the shadows. Here is an idea of his prose, from his 1990 novel *Alba*: "He noticed on the white table a piece of paper adorned with Alba's lovely handwriting. Her practice of the Tao mysteries had made it as deliciously fluid as one of her inspired kisses, the one she called a dawn ottoman."

One peculiarity of the plot is that Beineix withholds much from the characters, but almost nothing from the audience. We know what both sides know, and the result is to focus our attention on the how rather than the why. The film is an "exercise in style," yes, but that need not be a criticism. We go to different films for different reasons, and *Diva* gives us such a sensuous flow of images that we enjoy the characters moving through them. Rousselot's camera itself sometimes seems governed by the images, rather than controlling them.

As the critic David Edelstein observes, "when the bicycle-messenger hero listens to Wilhelmenia Fernandez sing the aria from *La Wally* . . . at that first sublime high note, the camera lifts off and begins to sway. Every time the aria is replayed, the camera moves at the same instant. It has to. This is style as a force of nature."

For Beineix (born 1946), *Diva* was a sensational start to what turned out to be a rather anticlimactic career. In 1984, he was back at Cannes with *The Moon in the Gutter*, which was booed, perhaps for its over-insistence on style; some shots were so elaborate or obviously concocted that they upstaged and even obscured their content. In 1986, he made the sensational *Betty Blue*, which became a huge success in France and still plays as a cult film, primarily, I am convinced, because of its generous nudity. Interestingly, in 1997 for the BBC, he made *Locked-in Syndrome*, a documentary about Jean Dominique Bauby (the subject of *The Diving Bell and the Butterfly*).

{ DOG DAY AFTERNOON }

D*og Day Afternoon* runs a little longer than the average feature, and you think maybe they could have cut an opening montage of life in New York. But no. These shots, stolen from reality, establish a bedrock for the film. It's "naturalistic," says the director, Sidney Lumet. I think he means it has the pace and feel of everyday life. When you begin with the story of a man who sticks up a bank to finance his lover's sex change, when you have a situation that has attracted hundreds of cops and millions of TV viewers, you run the risk of making a sideshow. *Dog Day Afternoon* never makes that mistake. The characters are all believable, sympathetic, convincing. We care for them. In a film about cops and robbers, there are no bad guys. Just people trying to get through a summer afternoon that has taken a strange turn.

It's an actor's picture. Lumet and his editor, Dede Allen, take the time to allow the actors to live within the characters; we forget we're watching performances. Although the movie contains tragedy and the potential for greater tragedy, it is also tremendously funny. But Frank Pierson's Oscar-winning screenplay never pauses for a laugh; the laughter grows organically out of people and situations. You can believe that even with hostages taken and firearms being waved around, such elements of human comedy would nevertheless arise.

One of the funny moments comes at the beginning, when three robbers enter a bank but one of them chickens out and says he can't go through with it. "Stevie," says his partner Sonny, "don't take the car." "But how am I gonna get home?" Stevie whines. Is that real? Yes, because you believe that Stevie would in fact have driven himself home and that Sonny (Al Pacino) would think of that.

Pacino has said the most memorable moment in the movie involves the delivery boy (Lionel Pina) who brings pizza to the robbers and their hostages. He's been watching the drama unfold on live TV, and when he's applauded by the crowd, he does a little skip and jump and says, "I'm a star!" Television turns the moment into what, at that time, was a fairly new event for live broadcasting. Sonny expands in the TV lights, strutting back and forth in front of the bank and unwisely exposing himself to rooftops lined with snipers. His remaining partner, Sal (John Cazale), on the other hand, shrinks within himself. He can't believe he's a bank robber. He can't believe Sonny says he will kill people. He's offended that on TV, which has the facts a little confused, he's described as a homosexual. He can't believe he's expected to get on a jet with the others and fly to safety. He's never flown before. Asked to name a foreign country they can fly to, he says "Wyoming." The line was improvised on the spot by Cazale.

The movie takes place almost entirely within a bank branch and the barbershop across the street, which becomes the police and FBI "command center." Back and forth Lumet's camera moves, on a shuttle of negotiations. The side view down the street in either direction shows their escape route, until it's blocked by a crowd that quickly forms and becomes a character in itself. At one point, making threats on the sidewalk, Pacino shouts "Attica," referring to the infamous massacre of prisoners in an upstate prison. "Attica!" the crowd shouts back, without prompting. They never see Sal, who is trembling, pale, sweaty, frightened. They respond to Sonny, first as a hero and then (when they find out he's gay) with jeers.

Sonny is gay, along with many other things. He is also a son whose mother mercilessly criticizes him, a husband and father whose wife (Judith Malina) won't let him get a word in edgewise. Asked why she didn't come to the bank when he asked for her, she explains on the phone, "I couldn't get a babysitter." She and her husband speak the same New York dialect. Denying that her husband could possibly have robbed a bank, she says: "He mighta done it, his body functions mighta done it, but he, himself, he didn't do it."

Sonny is many things and wants to be all things. The writer Pierson, unable to interview the robber in the real-life story, says he found the key for the character after being told Sonny was the kind of man "who would take care of you." He walks into the bank, waving the rifle but also saying, "I'm a Catholic and I don't want to hurt anyone, understand?" He listens when a teller has to use the toilet and is worried about the bank guard with asthma. He often says, "I'm dyin' here," because the problems of the tellers become his problems.

The most colorful of the tellers is their head, Sylvia (Penelope Allen), who cares for her "girls." Outside the bank and free to escape, she goes back inside: she's staying because she enjoys being the center of attention. "He don't have a plan," she says of Sonny. "It's all a whim." She may be right. Sal certainly has no idea what Sonny is capable of. In an interview on the disc of extras, I learned that Sonny met Sal in a Greenwich Village bar and didn't even really know him very well. We sense that when Sal starts trembling when he learns they'll leave the country by air. "You said if it went wrong, we'd kill ourselves!" he protests. He'd rather die than fly.

More than halfway through the picture, the other key character appears. This is Leon (Chris Sarandon), Sonny's lover. He is adamant: he certainly never asked Sonny to rob a bank to pay for his sex change. Brought into the barbershop and put on the phone with Sonny, he indirectly reveals his emotional inner life. He was in a mental institution. He and Sonny are drifting apart. He can't keep up with Sonny's emotional needs. He sits in the barbershop and talks to Sonny on the phone. This conversation was written as two monologues, Pierson says, and intercut into an exchange that essentially won Sarandon his supporting actor Oscar nomination. Throughout the film, neither man exhibits gay stereotypes. Leon is vulnerable and easily wounded, but not a drama queen. Pacino is matter of fact; in a scene when he dictates his last will to the bank manager (Sully Boyar), he says he loves Leon "more than any man ever loved any other man." He states this as a matter of fact; there's not a whisper of gay spin to it, and indeed even his wife and mother tacitly accept his bisexuality as simply the way he is.

The cops and FBI agents are instrumental to the film, but less fully developed than the people in the bank. Charles Durning plays the NYPD officer in charge, and James Broderick is the chief FBI agent. Neither one is given the kinds of plot elements that usually come with cops in hostage movies. They're unburdened by standard subplots (trouble at home, a conflict with a superior) and just do their jobs; afraid that a bloodbath will erupt, Durning actually runs at cops who won't holster their weapons. Both are matter of fact, direct, playing their roles right down the center. Many of Broderick's most essential moments come in reaction shots. They help demonstrate Lumet's naturalistic approach.

Sidney Lumet is a master filmmaker. His book on directing joins David Mamet's as two contrasting approaches to the subject, both written with clarity and conviction. Starting young by directing live TV, Lumet launched his big-screen career with *12 Angry Men*, based on one of his TV productions. His subjects have ranged widely; he clearly cares for the story above all else and doesn't specialize in genres or themes. If he's known for one aspect of his broad creative career, it is films about New York, including *The Pawnbroker*, *Bye Bye Braverman*, *Serpico* (also starring Pacino), *Q&A*, *Network*, and the suburban *Before the Devil Knows You're Dead*. Here he has created a film made brilliant by its deeply seen characters, in a plot that could have obviously been cheapened and exploited but is always human and true.

THE DOUBLE LIFE
OF VERONIQUE

Here is a film about a feeling. Like all feelings, it is one that can hardly be described in words, although it can be evoked in art. It is the feeling that we are not alone, because there is more than one of us. We are connected at a level far, far beneath thought. We have no understanding of this. It is simply a feeling that we have.

There are theories about events affecting other events at a distance. Chimpanzees on one island are taught a skill, and those on another develop it. Twins say they intuit each other's feelings. The first four-minute mile is run, and then it becomes common. Two vibrating strings on a quantum level seem to be in synchronicity—or are they in two places at once? Krzysztof Kieslowski's *The Double Life of Veronique* (1991) does us the favor of not supplying any explanation for itself, and is not even very clear about what actually happens. It evokes.

It does this above all with the face of Irene Jacob, who plays a Polish woman named Veronica and a French woman named Veronique. Bergman said the human face is the great subject of the cinema. Kieslowski's camera spends a great deal of time regarding Jacob's face. Let's not waste any time observing how beautiful she is. What he is searching for is her soul. Sometimes he asks her to smile, or look pensive or thoughtful, but sometimes he simply shows her thinking. She shows herself vulnerable, romantic, joyous, tender. She has a good face. We become invested in her introspection.

The film opens in Poland with a luminous and happy young woman who goes to Krakow to visit her aunt. While there, her pure, flawless voice wins the attention of a choir director, whose husband is a famous conductor, and Veronica is chosen to sing at a concert. Before that takes place, she is in a square and sees—herself—boarding a bus. She stands transfixed. The other woman, taking snapshots, doesn't see her. The Polish Veronica seems to exist on a plane above the mundane; a flasher exposes himself to her, and she hardly seems to notice, or care.

In Paris, we meet Veronique, a schoolteacher. Attending a marionette performance with her students, she sees the puppeteer in a mirror at the side, and he sees her. "Papa, I am in love," she tells her father. A little later, her father asks her if she is sad. She is, but doesn't know why. We think we know: a shiver in the web of time and space has vibrated from Poland. She and the puppeteer Alexandre (Philippe Volter) are somehow connected; he pursues her with mysterious gifts and tape recordings. She finds him, flees him, is pursued, and love is admitted. Later, she tells him that all her life she has felt she is in two places at once.

We know how that feels. We feel it ourselves. Let us agree you have a favorite cafe in Venice, where you like to sit alone with a book and a cup of coffee. You have never been to Venice, but set that aside: you are there now. You lift your eyes from the book and are filled with a faint feeling of being still at home. You, at home, occupy the table in Venice. In either place, you are in communion with the other.

Alexandre makes two marionettes that look like her. He tells their story. When one was very young, she touched a hot stove. A few days later, the other knew not to. Yes, and why did the Paris Veronique suddenly stop taking music lessons? A Hollywood movie would tell you, and you wouldn't want to know. Kieslowski is more delicate. He doesn't want to know why such things happen, or even if they happen. He wants us to acknowledge we all know how they feel.

Have I made *The Double Life of Veronique* sound as if nothing much happens? The movie has a hypnotic effect. We are drawn into the character, not kept at arm's length with a plot. Both women are good and true and do nothing shameful. There is a shot of Jacob, who pauses for a moment and lifts her head to the sun, and we know what she is experiencing: here I am, my life around me, my hopes high, my trust confident, standing stock still, the sun on my face, living in this moment. It is a holy moment.

This is one of the most beautiful films I've seen. The cinematographer, Slawomir Idziak, finds a glow in Irene Jacob's pre-Raphaelite beauty. He uses a rich palette, including insistent reds and greens that don't "stand" for anything but have the effect of underlining the other colors. The other color, blending with both, is golden yellow, and then there are the skin tones. Jacob, who was twenty-four when the film was made, has a flawless complexion that the camera lingers near to. Her face is a template waiting for experience to be added. She is open to the murmurs of the aether.

The film has some older characters: two fathers, an aunt, the conductor and his wife, a music teacher. These people regard her with wisdom and love. There are no bad people, except the flasher, who shrivels from insignificance. There are also some mysterious people. Who is that woman in the floppy black hat who turns and looks intently at Veronique? I thought for a moment it was Veronica's aunt, but no. Has she seen her somewhere before? We will never know. And do the aunt in Poland and the father in France resemble each other a little, or is it only in attitude? And, don't smile, what does the shoestring in France represent? The one so important it must be sought in the Dumpster?

Krzysztof Kieslowski (1941–96) was a great man. With his writing partner, Krzysztof Piesiewicz, he made films that dealt with spiritual challenges and the uncoiling of fate. His *Decalogue*, released as ten films of fifty-five minutes each, deals with people who know what they want to do but not what they should do. Each film centers somehow on a commandment. Then he made the Three Colors trilogy, *Red*, *White*, and *Blue*, of which the first, also starring Irene Jacob, is the first among equals. Then he retired at fifty-three in 1994, and two years later, he was dead.

He is drawn to coincidence and synchronicity. He is little interested in focusing on a character hurtling from point A in the first act to point C in the third. He is fascinated by point B, and the unseen threads linking it to past and present. His films can be mystical experiences. He trusts us to follow him, to sense his purpose, to leave the theater having shared his openness to a moment. The last thing you want to do after a Kieslowski film is "unravel" the plot. It can't be done. If you try it, you will turn clouds into rain. If there seem to be inconsistencies, it is because life and time itself sometimes try again and take an unexpected turn.

Let me give you an example. The Criterion Collection's two-volume DVD edition, a stunning transfer with a wealth of bonus features, includes as an option the "American ending." We learn that Harvey Weinstein, the film's U.S. distributor, felt unsatisfied with the director's close. He changed nothing earlier but edited in four additional shots, now the last ones in the film. They explain nothing and add nothing. All they demonstrate is that Weinstein thought Kieslowski's final image, of Veronique's hand touching the rough old bark of a tree, could be improved by her running across a lawn to hug her father. This whole film is a hug, the kind you share with a very good friend when you are in sympathy about something that is very important.

{ EASY RIDER }

Nobody went to see *Easy Rider* (1969) only once. It became one of the rallying points of the late '60s, a road picture and a buddy picture, celebrating sex, drugs, rock 'n' roll, and the freedom of the open road. It did a lot of repeat business while the sweet smell of pot drifted through theaters. Seeing the movie years later is like opening a time capsule. It provides little shocks of recognition, as when you realize they aren't playing "Don't Bogart That Joint" for laughs.

Peter Fonda and Dennis Hopper play Captain America and Billy, journeying cross-country on their motorcycles, using a drug deal in Los Angeles to finance a trip to Mardi Gras. The drug is cocaine (sold to a dealer played by rock producer Phil Spector), but their drug of choice is marijuana. Billy gets the giggles around the campfire at night. Captain America, who could handle it better, is cool, quiet, remote, a Christ figure who flies the American flag on his gas tank, his helmet, and the back of his leather jacket. (It would be a year later, after the release of *Joe*, that flag decals were co-opted by the right.)

The making of the movie became a Hollywood legend. Fonda and Hopper took their screenplay (co-written with Terry Southern) to the traditional home of motorcycle movies, American-International Pictures. But Sam Arkoff turned them down, and they finally found funding at Columbia.

The budget was so limited, there was no money for an original score, so Hopper, the director, slapped on a scratch track of rock 'n' roll standards for the first studio screening. The executives loved the sound and insisted the songs be left in, and *Easy Rider* begat countless later movies that were scored with oldies.

Motorcycle movies were not fashionable in 1969, although *Hell's Angels on Wheels* made an attempt in 1967 to break free of the booze-and-violence cliches. Directed by Richard Rush (*The Stunt Man*), it was a largely overlooked precursor to *Easy Rider*, sharing the same cinematographer, Laszlo Kovacs, and even the same little-known actor in a colorful supporting role: Jack Nicholson, who played a gas-station attendant named Poet. *Hell's Angels on Wheels* is a great-looking movie, but it took *Easy Rider* to link two symbols of rebellion—motorcycles and the hippie counterculture—and catch the spirit of the time.

Easy Rider was playing in theaters at about the time Woodstock Nation was gathering in upstate New York. It plays today more as a period piece than as living cinema, but it captures so surely the tone and look of that moment in time. There's heavy symbolism as Fonda throws away his wristwatch before setting off on the journey, and the establishing scenes, as Captain America and Billy stash their loot in a gas tank and set off down the backroads of the Southwest, are slowly paced—heavy on scenery, light on dialogue, pregnant with symbolism and foreboding.

One of their bikes needs work, and they borrow tools at a ranch, leading to a labored visual juxtaposition of wheel-changing and horse-shoeing. Then they have dinner with the weathered rancher and his Mexican American brood, and Fonda delivers the first of many quasi-profound lines he will dole out during the movie: "It's not every man who can live off the land, you know. You can be proud." (The rancher, who might understandably have replied, "Who the hell asked you?" nods gratefully.)

A hitchhiker leads them to a hippie commune that may have seemed inspiring in 1969, but today looks banal. A "performance troupe" sings "Does Your Hair Hang Low?" on a makeshift stage, while stoned would-be hippie farmers wander across the parched earth, scattering seed. "Uh, get any rain here?" Billy asks. "Thank you for a place to make a stand,"

Captain America says. The group leader gives the Captain and Billy a tab of acid and the solemn advice, "When you get to the right place, with the right people—quarter this."

If *Easy Rider* had continued in the vein of its opening scenes, it's a good question whether anyone would remember it today. The film comes alive with the electrifying entry of the Jack Nicholson character, a lawyer named George Hanson whom they meet in a jail cell. (They have been jailed for "parading without a permit" after wheeling their bikes into a small-town parade.)

Historic moments in the cinema are not always this easy to identify: Nicholson had been in movies for years, but his jailhouse dialogue in *Easy Rider* instantly made him a star. "You boys don't look like you're from this part of the country," he says. He's an alcoholic lawyer on good terms with the cops; he arranges their release, supplies the name of a topnotch whorehouse in New Orleans, and says that he's started out for Mardi Gras many times without getting past the state line. That sets up the film's most famous shot: George on the back of Billy's motorcycle, wearing a football helmet.

Nicholson's work in *Easy Rider* created a sensation. Audiences loved his sardonic, irreverent personality and were primed for his next film, *Five Easy Pieces* (1970), with its immortal chicken-salad-sandwich dialogue. Then and now, *Easy Rider* comes alive while the Nicholson character is in the movie. That night around the campfire, he samples grass for the first time ("Lord have mercy, is that what that is?") and then explains his theory that extraterrestrials walk among us. He uses a confiding tone, sharing outrageous information as if he's conferring a favor; it would become his trademark.

George is killed shortly afterward, by rednecks who have seen them in a roadside cafe and decide they look "like refugees from a gorilla love-in." The impact of his death seems shortchanged in the movie, which hurries on to New Orleans.

Captain America and Billy find the legendary whorehouse and drop acid in the cemetery with two hookers (including Karen Black in one of her earliest film roles). It's a bad trip, but maybe they chose the wrong place with the wrong people.

The last act of the movie is preordained. There have been ominous omens along the way (and even a brief flash-forward to Captain America's flaming death). Rednecks in a pickup truck use a shotgun to blast both men from their bikes. The camera climbs high into the sky on a crane, pulling back to show us the inevitable fate, I guess, of anyone who dares to be different.

The symbolic deaths of heroes became common in movies after *Bonnie and Clyde* (1967), and Pauline Kael noted in her *Easy Rider* review that "the movie's sentimental paranoia obviously rang true to a large, young audience's vision. In the late '60s, it was cool to feel that you couldn't win, that everything was rigged and hopeless."

One of the reasons that America inspires so many road pictures is that we have so many roads. One of the reasons we have so many buddy pictures is that Hollywood doesn't understand female characters (there are so many hookers in the movies because, as characters, they share the convenience of their real-life counterparts: they're easy to find and easy to get rid of).

The motorcycle picture was a special kind of road/buddy movie that first came into view with Marlon Brando in *The Wild One* (1954), flourished in the late 1960s, and more or less disappeared a few years later. The movie grew out of pictures like *The Wild Angels* (1966, also starring Fonda), but it also expressed a notion that the counterculture believed in at the time: you could leave the city and return to more natural roots. A sweet idea, but one that did not coexist easily with drugs. In scenes like the one where Hopper and Fonda teach Nicholson how to inhale, there's a quietly approving air, as if life is a treatable disease, and pot is the cure.

But Billy is paranoid, probably because of all the grass he smokes, and in later scenes, they're oblivious to the dangers they invite with their strange appearance. (There's a scene where they excite teenage girls in a restaurant with their aura of sexual danger, and local Good Old Boys feel threatened and plot revenge.)

Many deep thoughts were written in 1969 about Fonda's dialogue in a scene the night before his death. Hopper is ecstatic because they've made it to their destination with their drug money intact. "We blew it," Fonda tells him. "We blew it, man." Heavy. But doesn't the movie play differently today from the way its makers intended? Cocaine in 1969 carried different connotations from those of today, and it is possible to see that Captain America and Billy died not only for our sins, but also for their own.

{ EL NORTE }

At the dawn of the U.S. independent film movement, two of its founders made what *Variety* called its first epic. *El Norte* told the story of a Guatemalan brother and sister who fled persecution at home and journeyed north the length of Mexico with a dream of finding a new home in the United States. They were illegal aliens, but then as now, the California economy could not function without their invisible presence as cheap labor. *El Norte* (1983) tells their story with astonishing visual beauty, with unashamed melodrama, with anger leavened by hope. It is a *Grapes of Wrath* for our time.

The movie was directed by Gregory Nava, produced by Anna Thomas, and co-written by both of them. They were later to make *My Family/Mi Familia* (1995), which traces three generations of a Mexican American family in Los Angeles, and Nava became the executive producer and supervising director of the American Family series on PBS, about an extended Latino family in Los Angeles. But I met Nava and Thomas much earlier, in 1976 at the Chicago Film Festival with their first film, *The Confessions of Amans*. It cost $24,000 and won the prize as best first feature.

That was before Sundance, before IFC, before Miramax. They were the co-founders of the Independent Feature Project, which today holds the Independent Spirit Awards in a vast tent on the beach at Santa Monica,

California. When they founded the IFP, everyone at the meeting would fit comfortably into their living room. And when they made *El Norte*, no film like it had been attempted.

Despite its limited budget, the movie is bursting with energy and ambition. At 139 minutes, it is told in three sections, concerning the early life of the brother and sister, their harrowing trek to "el norte," and their life in Los Angeles. It was shot partly in Mexico, and then, after their exposed footage and an accountant were seized and held for ransom, in California. The filmmakers tell harrowing stories of cash payoffs at gunpoint, and how Nava's parents slipped out of the country carrying some of the dailies.

But the film never reflects that backstage ordeal; it chooses, indeed, to paint its story not in the grim grays of neorealism, but with the palette of Mexico, filled with color and fantasy. An early scene involving clouds of butterflies combines local legend with magical realism, and abundant life comes into the film through the shirts, dresses, ponchos, and blankets of the characters, and through the joyous use of color in their homes and villages.

Nava once explained to me one reason for the Mexican love of color: "The rich browns and reds and yellows make brown skin look beautiful; American interiors are painted an eggshell white that doesn't do much for brown skin or any other kind of skin."

The movie stars two unknowns, David Villalpando as Enrique, and Zaide Silvia Gutierrez as his sister, Rosa. They have the spontaneous, unrehearsed quality of some of the actors in neorealist films like *The Bicycle Thief*, and an infectious optimism and naivete that makes us protective of them. In the opening scenes, they live as their ancestors have for many generations, in a village of beauty and dignity, a true community. Meals by candlelight are followed by the evening stroll on the little local ramblas.

But the people spend long hours at backbreaking labor, picking coffee beans under the harsh eyes of intimidating overseers. Their father, Arturo (Ernesto Gomez Cruz), is trying to organize a workers' union; he is betrayed, and everyone at a union meeting is murdered by government troops. Their mother (Alicia del Lago) disappears. And, yes, events like this are the price we are willing to pay for our morning coffee; I confess when I order my first cup, I do not much think of the Arturos and the union-busting international corporations that make their own laws.

Enrique and Rosa have hidden, and feel forced to flee. They have a good idea of America, they think, from the *Good Housekeeping* magazines treasured by their godmother, Josefita (Stella Quan), who gives them her savings for the journey and describes a land where everyone—even the poor—has a refrigerator and an indoor toilet.

Their progress through Mexico is hard enough, but crossing of the border is a nightmare. They hire a "coyote," a man expert at helping immigrants enter America, and have the good luck to find an honest one. He suggests they crawl into America through an empty drainage pipe, and he will meet them at the other end. He gives them flashlights, they start to crawl, and they're attacked by hordes of screaming rats. The scene is horrifying, not least because it's pretty clear these are real rats. Disease-free rats purchased from a laboratory, yes, but real rats all the same, and although Gutierrez was phobic about rats, she insisted on doing her own scenes, and her panic is real.

As they were crawling through the pipe, it occurred to me that we are fortunate to live in a country people want to enter, instead of escape. And fortunate because so many of our immigrants are the best and the brightest. It takes imagination, ambition, and courage to leave your homeland and start over again in a strange land. One reason that immigrants often seem to do well here is that they were self-selected as brave and determined.

In Los Angeles, Enrique and Rosa enter the job market, Enrique as a dishwasher and busboy, Rosa first in a garment factory and then as a maid. They are undocumented, but necessary; a 2004 movie named *A Day without a Mexican* is a fantasy imagining the collapse of the California economies after all the Enriques and Rosas disappear. In Guatemala, Enrique's father told them that the bosses cared nothing for a man, only for his strong arms. Now in America, trucks from day-labor contractors pull into the motels where Hispanics live, and the men hopefully cluster about, showing their muscles.

The great Mexican American character actress Lupe Ontiveros makes one of her first appearances in this movie. (Jennifer Lopez had her first meaningful movie role in *Mi Familia*, and became a star in Nava's 1997 film *Selena*.) Ontiveros plays Nacha, who becomes Rosa's confidant and protector and counsels her on how to deal with the gringos: "Just smile and say 'yes' to whatever they say."

Rosa tries to smile and say "yes" when her employer confronts her with an unbelievably complicated automatic washing machine, but finally surrenders, and in one of the film's welcome laughs, simply spreads the laundry out on the grass, to dry in the sun.

Another of the film's many strong supporting performances is by Trinidad Silva, as the motel manager and labor broker, who defines situations by imposing his will upon them. He might have had a rich career, but was killed in a traffic accident a few years after the film was made.

The closing scenes use the power of melodrama to involve our emotions, and they succeed; the simplicity and depth of Gutierrez's acting is heartbreaking. I've read reviews criticizing the film for its melodrama, but it occurred to me that the lives of many poor people are melodrama from birth to death. It takes a lot of money to insulate yourself in a less eventful, more controllable, life.

Seen after twenty years, *El Norte* retains its direct power to move and anger. The story needs no updating; it repeats every day. The movie really makes no statement about immigration itself, because policy questions are irrelevant to its characters. They want what we all want, better lives for themselves and their children. Their story is the same story enacted by the German, Irish, and Italian immigrants to America—by all of us, even the Native Americans, who came from Mongolia.

In the years since the film was released, the underlying reality of illegal immigration has remained essentially the same: America forbids it, yet requires it as a source of cheap labor. Someone like Cesar Chavez, who fought for the rights of Chicano farm laborers, was attacked because he revealed the nation's underlying hypocrisy on the subject.

The stories of Enrique and Rosa end sadly, but Nava returned to the subject of immigrant families in *Mi Familia*, where they endure and prevail.

A Mexican American couple played by Jose Sanchez and Jennifer Lopez walk to Los Angeles, move in with an uncle they have never met before, and by the end of their lives, count among their children a nun, a lawyer, a writer, and a gang member shot dead by the police. They agree they have had wonderful lives, and that it would be wrong to ask for too much.

{ EL TOPO }

A man in black rides the desert vastness of Mexico with a naked child in front of him on the saddle. Three hee-hawing gunmen appear from out of hiding, laughing that they have been sent to kill him. The man carefully places the child behind him on the saddle.

So opens Alejandro Jodorowsky's *El Topo* (1970), one of the legendary "lost films," out of circulation for years before it was finally released on a DVD in 2007. A lone rider confronted by gunmen is nothing new in the Western. A naked child is, and adds a queasy undertone of danger and transgression. Jodorowsky finds a way to evoke that uneasiness throughout the film, and all of his work. There is always something incongruous, something unexpected that does not belong.

The lone rider is El Topo. The name translates as "the mole." The movie informs us that a mole spends his life digging tunnels to the sky, only to go blind when it sees the sun. This is not quite true, but truth is not allowed to interfere with its use as a convenient symbol. Will El Topo dig free and go blind? And if he does, what will that mean? Pauline Kael observed that Fellini's *La Dolce Vita* is filled with symbols, and they're all obvious. *El Topo* is filled with symbols, and they're not obvious. I am reminded of one of Ebert's Laws: "If you have to ask what something symbolizes, it doesn't." Or it stands for itself.

143

In my review when the movie opened, I wrote: "Jodorowsky lifts his symbols and mythologies from everywhere: Christianity, Zen, discount-store black magic, you name it. He makes not the slightest attempt to use them so they sort out into a single logical significance. Instead, they're employed in a shifting, prismatic way, casting their light on each other instead of on the film's conclusion. The effect resembles Eliot's *The Waste Land*, and especially Eliot's notion of shoring up fragments of mythology against the ruins of the post-Christian era.

I still agree with that and do not think the symbols add up to a conclusion. But now having seen more of Jodorowsky's work, I think Jodorowsky's method is not without a purpose. What is El Topo seeking in the desert? Why, he is seeking symbols, images, bizarre people and events, with which to fill the film.

The ceaseless shocking images on the screen are what made *El Topo* an underground hit in one New York theater for months in 1970. Not the story, not the performances, not the stars (Jodorowsky himself plays El Topo and the child is his own son). The images. John Lennon and Yoko Ono saw it, loved it, and convinced Beatles manager Allen Klein to buy and release it. The film went on to play all over the world and engender countless interpretations. Jodorowsky encourages such speculation by titling sections of the film after books of the Bible ("Psalms"), and making El Topo perhaps a Christ figure.

The film is also populated, as Jodorowsky's films are, by physically challenged characters; amputees, people with Down syndrome, dwarfs, those whose bodies end at their trunks, men who talk with women's voices, women who talk with men's, a man without legs riding on the shoulders of a man without arms, and one of the most persistent images in the director's work, a symbiosis between a person without arms and another who stands close behind and allows his arms to act as the other's.

Many of these have been exiled to a cave inside a mountain. El Topo, threatened with death, bargains to free them from their cave and digs a tunnel into the mountain. Generations of inbreeding have presumably produced the birth defects on view; no word about how the cave people have been able to eat over the years.

No word, because they are not presented as plausible characters anyway, but as symbols; the mole will dig away from the sun to free them, meaning—what? You tell me. And think again about that naked child in the early scene. Why naked? El Topo has serapes and cloaks aplenty to shield the child from cold or sun. But a man riding with a clothed child would simply represent, well, man and child on horse. If the child is naked, it becomes a Child, a symbol of itself.

Reviews of *El Topo* tend to be infuriating because their authors, myself included, fail to make coherent sense of the film and are reduced to laundry lists of its ingredients. "These quests," I wrote in my original review, "supply most of the film's generous supply of killings, tortures, disembowelments, hangings, boilings, genocides, and so on." Evocative but scarcely helpful. The film exists as an unforgettable experience, but not as a comprehensible one.

Jodorowsky (born 1929) is a man of many talents, all at the service of his bizarre imagination. At Cannes 1988 he handed me a typewritten autobiography: "Was born in Bolivia, of Russian parents, lived in Chile, worked in Paris, was the partner of Marcel Marceau, founded the 'Panic' movement with Fernando Arrabal, directed 100 plays in Mexico, drew a comic strip, made *El Topo*, and now lives in the United States—having not been accepted anywhere, because in Bolivia I was a Russian, in Chile I was a Jew, in Paris I was a Chilean, in Mexico I was French, and now, in America, I am a Mexican."

The 2007 DVD collection of his films (*El Topo*, *Fando y Lis*, *The Holy Mountain*, *La Cravate*, but not *Santa Sangre*, which is separately available) brings him back into focus as a great eccentric original.

I talked with Jodorowsky at Cannes in 1988 and 1989. The first year, he said he had to make *Santa Sangre*, a film about women in a religious cult who cut off their arms to atone for the women he, Jodorowsky, had murdered (not literally; you'll have to look up that interview on my Web site).

The second year, after the Cannes premiere of *Santa Sangre*, I asked him why *El Topo* had been out of circulation. He blamed Allen Klein, the man who had put the film in circulation in the first place.

"He's awaiting my death," Jodorowsky said. "He believes he can make more money from the film after I am dead. He says my film is like wine—it grows better with age. He is waiting like a vulture for me to die."

He elaborated: "For fifteen years, I've tried to talk to him by telephone, and he's always busy. He eats the smoking meat. Smoking meat . . . you know? From the delicatessen?"

Smoked meat?

"Yes. When I call him by telephone they say to me he's eating the smoking meat. I cannot speak with him because he is eating the smoking meat. He's eating for fifteen years the smoking meat."

I looked out over the Mediterranean and pondered that image. A man who is eating for fifteen years the smoking meat. One more image, or perhaps a symbol, I could not explain.

{ THE ENIGMA OF KASPAR HAUSER }

Werner Herzog's films do not depend on "acting" in the conventional sense. He is most content when he finds an actor who embodies the essence of a character, and he studies that essence with a fascinated intensity. Consider the case of Bruno S., a street performer and forklift operator whose last name was long concealed. He is the center of two Herzog films, *The Enigma of Kaspar Hauser* (1974) and *Stroszek* (1977). The son of a prostitute, he was locked for twenty-three years in mental institutions, even though Herzog believes he was never insane.

Bruno is, however, very strange, bull-headed, with the simplicity and stubbornness of a child. In *Kaspar Hauser*, he looks anywhere he wants to, sometimes even craftily sideways at the camera, and then it feels not like he's looking *at* the audience but *through* us. He can possibly play no role other than himself, but that is what Herzog needs him for. On the commentary track Herzog says he was vilified in Germany for taking advantage of an unfortunate, but if you study Bruno sympathetically you may see that, by his lights, he is taking advantage of Herzog. On his commentary track, Herzog describes him as "the unknown soldier of the cinema."

Kaspar Hauser was a real historical figure who in 1828 appeared in a town square early one morning clutching the Bible and an anonymous

147

letter. In the movie, as apparently in reality, an unknown captor kept him locked up in a cellar for about the first twenty years of his life. Adopted by the town and a friendly couple, he learns to read and write and even play the piano (in life Bruno also plays accordion and glockenspiel). Kaspar speaks as a man to whom every day is a mystery: "What are women good for?" "My coming to this world was a terribly hard fall." And think of the concept being expressed when he says, "It dreamed to me . . ."

In Herzog the line between fact and fiction is a shifting one. He cares not for accuracy but for effect, for a transcendent ecstasy. *Kaspar Hauser* tells its story not as a narrative about its hero, but as a mosaic of striking behavior and images: a line of penitents struggling up a hillside, a desert caravan led by a blind man, a stork capturing a worm. These images are unrelated to Kaspar except in the way they reflect and illuminate his struggle. The last thing Herzog is interested in is "solving" this lonely man's mystery. It is the mystery that attracts him.

All through the work of this great director, born in 1942, maker of at least fifty-four films, you can find extraordinary individuals who embody the qualities Herzog wants to evoke. In *Heart of Glass* (1976), challenged to depict a village deprived of its livelihood, he hypnotized the entire cast. In *Land of Silence and Darkness* (1971) and *Even Dwarfs Started Small* (1970), he tried to imagine the inner lives of the blind and deaf, and dwarfs. These people are not the captives of their attributes but freed by them to enter realms that are barred for us.

Herzog made two films about a German named Dieter Dengler, the documentary *Little Dieter Needs to Fly* (1977) and the fiction film *Rescue Dawn* (2006). In the first, Dengler, who enlisted in the Navy, plays himself, retracing a torturous escape through the jungle from a Vietcong prison camp. In the second, he is played by Christian Bale. But Herzog has explained that he made up some of the incidents in the documentary, and the feature is in a way a documentary about the ordeal of making itself; Bale looks like a scarecrow; the real Dengler was down to eighty-five pounds. Bale's performance in a way resembles the dedication of Timothy Treadwell, the man who thought he could walk unprotected among bears in Herzog's *Grizzly Man*, a 2005 documentary based on video footage

Treadwell took before finding himself mistaken. And there is Jouko Ahola, a Finnish weightlifter, twice named the world's strongest man, who Herzog uses as the hero of *Invincible* (2001), about a Polish strong man, Jewish, who poses as an Aryan ideal in Hitler's Berlin. Not an actor, but the right person for the role.

Bale is a professional actor, yes, but hired for what he can embody, as much as for what he can do. Consider also the case of Klaus Kinski, the star of Herzog's films *Aguirre, the Wrath of God* (1972), *Fitzcarraldo* (1982), *Nosferatu* (1979), *Cobra Verde* (1987), and *Woyzeck* (1979). An actor in 135 films, yes, but Kinski told me he had seen only two or three of them. A man of towering rages and terrifying rampages, which at one point allegedly had him at gunpoint with Herzog. The subject of *My Best Fiend* (1999), Herzog's savage documentary about the man he loved and reviled. To see Kinski in a Herzog film is to see a man used not as an actor, but as an instrument through which to force the film.

In some ways the most emblematic film of Herzog's career is *The Great Ecstasy of the Woodcarver Steiner* (1974), a documentary about a ski jumper who must start halfway down the slope, because otherwise he is too good and would fly over the landing zone and into the parking lot. His limitation is his gift, and he dreams of flying forever. So many of Herzog's protagonists, real and fictional, have such dreams of escape, and are so intensely themselves that they carry his purpose unthinkingly.

The Enigma of Kaspar Hauser is a lyrical film about the least lyrical of men. Bruno S. has the solidity of the horses and cows he is often among, and as he confronts the world I was reminded of W. G. Sebold's remark that men and animals regard each other across a gulf of mutual incomprehension. The film's landscapes, its details from nature, its music, all embody the dream world Kaspar entered when he escaped the unchanging reality of his cellar. He never dreamed in the cellar, he explains. I think it was because he knew of nothing else than the cellar to dream about.

The film is often linked with Truffaut's *The Wild Child* (1970), set in the same century, about a boy who emerged from the forest possibly having been raised by animals. A psychologist tries to "civilize" him, but cannot change his essential nature. Kaspar is also the subject of study, and there is a professor in the film who tests Kaspar with the riddle about the two villages, one populated by those who could not tell the truth, and the other by those who could not lie. When you meet a man on a path to the two villages, Kaspar is asked, what is the one question you must ask him to determine which village he comes from? "I would ask him if he is a tree frog," Kaspar answers with some pride.

Then there is the foppish English dandy Lord Stanhope, who introduces Kaspar as his "protégé," only to find that his protégé does not like being on exhibit at fancy dress balls. Kaspar seems happy enough to allow the village to pay off its debts as an exhibit in a sideshow, however, along with a Brazilian flautist who believes that if he ever stops playing, the village will die. To prove he is Brazilian, he speaks in his own tongue, forgetting his prophecy.

The film's German title translates as "Every Man for Himself and God against All." That seems to summarize Kaspar's thinking. The mystery of the captive's origins has occupied investigators ever since he first appeared. Was he the secret heir to a throne? A rich man's love child? We have glimpses of the man who held him prisoner and then set him free, standing behind him and kicking his boots to force him to walk. Who is this man? He is never explained. He may be the embodiment of Kaspar's fate. We may all have somebody behind us, kicking our boots. We are poor mortals, but it dreams to us that we can fly.

{ EXOTICA }

Sex for money sometimes conceals great sadness. It can be sought to treat wounds it cannot heal. I believe that may happen less in actual prostitution than in the parody of prostitution offered in "gentleman's clubs." Whatever is going on is less about sex than psychological need, sometimes on both sides. Atom Egoyan's *Exotica* is a deep, painful film about those closed worlds of stage-managed lust.

It is also a tender film about a lonely and desperate man, and a woman who is kind to him. How desperate and how kind are only slowly revealed. In a technical sense, this is a "hyperlink movie," in which characters are revealed to be connected in ways they may not know about. But Egoyan, who also wrote the film, surprises us in how slowly he reveals the links and even more slowly reveals what the characters know about them. When the film ends, you sit regarding the screen, putting together what you have just learned and using it to think again about what went before.

The critic Bryant Frazer wrote that after the film played in the 1994 New York Film Festival, a woman asked Egoyan what had happened at the end. Egoyan was "visibly perturbed" by the question, he said, but finally responded. Frazer writes, "Here is what the last scene in the film meant, he explained, his four- or five-word declamation a stark and numbing negation of the gentle, almost languid spirit of the film, which invites the

151

audience to its own discovery. The 'what happened' is simple enough to explain, but you can't really understand it unless you're fully caught up in the cinema when it unfolds in front of you."

Frazer is right: there is no mystery at the end, except the mysteries of human nature that Egoyan evokes. What you think about those will define the film's importance to you. For me, they make it a cry of sympathy for people suffering from loss and guilt, and also an affirmation about how others are willing to understand them. A film can only get so far by simply stating its message; if the message is that easily defined, why bother with the film? *Exotica* does what many good films do and implies its troubled feelings. Nothing is solved at the end, except that we have learned to understand the characters.

Exotica takes place in a Toronto strip club, but not one of those hellholes of expense-account executives and drunken bachelor parties. This club seems to fill the special needs of the men who go there, although we learn only about one. He is Francis (Bruce Greenwood), who every night buys the company of Christina (Mia Kirshner). She looks young, dresses in a school uniform, opens her shirt before him, and then they talk softly and intensely.

Watching this is the club DJ, Eric (Elias Koteas), who stands on a perch above the action and contributes an insinuating commentary on the lives below. Also watching, from behind one-way mirrors, is the pregnant Zoe (Arsinée Khanjian), who inherited the club from her mother. The decor creates a tropical club heavy with palm fronds, the music slinks between the tables, the lighting is an oddly muted garishness, gloom cut with neon reds, greens, and blues. Egoyan's camera glides around the room, pausing to regard Francis and Christina. Whatever they're talking about hardly seems to be sex and seems to absorb them equally. The DJ notices this.

Other characters are implicated. The opening shots of the film show customs officers scrutinizing an arrival on a flight from the Far East, through a one-way mirror. This is Thomas, who we discover is smuggling rare macaw eggs. At the airport, a man suggests they share a ride to town and pays his share of the ride with two ballet tickets. Thomas gives one of the tickets to a good-looking gay man outside the theater, and they eventually spend the night together. The man was one of the customs officers. He confiscates the eggs, but wants to see Thomas again. Thomas's pet shop is audited under suspicion of illegal imports—by Francis, who later wants him to help eavesdrop on Christina. You see how the subterranean connections link.

I have made *Exotica* seem to be all complexities. Following the connections is straightforward. Deciding what they mean is the challenge. Egoyan has not unfolded the plot as simply as I summarized it, and he uses other suggestive characters. There is Tracey (Sarah Polley, then fifteen), the young girl Francis hires every night to babysit while he is visiting the club. But it's other than babysitting. At the club, he's a client of Christina, who dresses as a schoolgirl; does this suggest he has a sexual interest in Tracey? What does Tracey's father think of the arrangement?

Enough of the plot. Let's draw back to admire Egoyan's method. If we do not at first understand all of the relationships between the characters, they do not all understand them themselves, and in certain ways never figure them out. That provides the film with hidden emotional currents as powerful as those that are visible. When you think through the film later, you realize how much some of the characters never know, and yet how important it has been to the outcome. Egoyan isn't weaving these strands simply to divert us with a labyrinth; he is suggesting the hidden ways in which we affect other lives with our choices and behavior even though unaware.

Beneath everything pulses the atmosphere of the club Exotica, its promise of sexuality masking deeper needs and obsessions. The grave voice of Leonard Cohen and the starkness of his songs, played by Eric the DJ, seem wrong for a strip club, but not for this one, where not desire but desperation is catered to. The advertising, selling a sexy thriller, is all wrong.

Zoe, the club owner, is in some ways the spirit of the film. She is very pregnant, very happy about it, very convinced that her mother created the club in a special way for a special clientele with special needs. She knows more about some of the clients than they realize. She is worried about the tension between Eric and Christina. She meets with Francis after he is thrown out of the club. She wants to restore peace and order, and I won't tell you why that is so difficult for her.

Atom Egoyan, born in 1960 in Egypt of Armenian parents, brought up in Canada, has consistently stepped outside the mainstream in style and subjects. He's fascinated by how people are kept separated by the realities of culture (ethnicity, gender, background) and walls of images, and how they try to get through or around them. One of the most uncompromising of major directors, he hasn't made a single film for solely commercial reasons.

Egoyan is best known for *The Sweet Hereafter*, which won the grand jury prize at Cannes 1997; *Felicia's Journey* (1998); and *Where the Truth Lies*, that remarkable 2005 film with Kevin Bacon and Colin Firth as a team not unlike Dean Martin and Jerry Lewis, implicated in a murder. He often works with his wife, Arsinée Khanjian, who like Ingrid Bergman has the ability to project carnality and sweetness simultaneously. Egoyan brought his first feature, the $20,000 *Next of Kin*, to the Toronto Film Festival in 1984. He was only twenty-four.

There is a quality in all of his work that resists the superficial and facile. Even at the very start, he wasn't interested in simple storytelling. He is drawn to what Fitzgerald called the dark night of the soul. Secrets, shames, the hidden, and the forbidden coil around his characters, but he is not quick to condemn them. He and Khanjian are warm, friendly, and smile easily, and in the films, you sense love for the characters and the belief that to know more is to forgive more.

{ FANNY AND ALEXANDER }

Ingmar Bergman's *Fanny and Alexander* (1982) was intended to be his last film, and in it, he tends to the business of being young, of being middle aged, of being old, of being a man, woman, Christian, Jew, sane, crazy, rich, poor, religious, profane. He creates a world in which the utmost certainty exists side by side with ghosts and magic, and a gallery of characters who are unforgettable in their peculiarities. Small wonder one of his inspirations was Dickens.

It is 1907, in an unnamed Swedish town. The movie plunges into the Christmas Eve celebration of an enormous family, introducing the characters on the fly as they talk, drink, flirt, and plot. They are surrounded by voluptuousness; the Ekdahl family is wealthy and the matriarch, Helena, lives in an enormous home crowded with antique furniture, rich furnishings, paintings, sculptures, tapestries, rugs, flowers, plants, and clocks—always clocks in a Bergman film, their hours striking in a way that is somehow ominous. One room spills into another, as we see when the half-drunk guests join hands for a song while parading through the flat.

Family intrigues are revealed: Gustav Adolf, Helena's third son, is a philanderer whose adventures are forgiven by his merry, buxom wife, Alma, because she likes him as he is. The second son, Carl, is a failed professor, married to a German woman no one likes (although they should), deeply in debt to his mother. The first son, Oscar, runs the family theater, and is moved to tears in his Christmas Eve speech to the staff before joining the party. Oscar is married to Emilie, a grave beauty, and they have two children, Fanny and Alexander. Much of the film is seen through their eyes, especially Alexander's, but other moments take place entirely within the imaginations of the characters.

Gustav's marriage is eccentric, Carl's is sad, and Oscar's is filled with love—for his family, and the theater. We learn quickly that Gustav is having an affair with Maj, Oscar and Emilie's lame, plump young maid. Alma knows it; indeed, it is openly discussed by everyone in the family. We also learn that Helena, a widow, has been the lover and is still the best friend of Isak Jacobi, a Jewish art dealer and money lender. (Bergman has said there is a little of himself in all the male characters.)

A day or two later, during a rehearsal at the theater, Oscar is playing the ghost of Hamlet's father when he loses his place, forgets his lines, doesn't know where he is. Within a day or so, he is dead of a stroke. All of this is witnessed by the solemn Alexander, who is awakened in the middle of the night by his mother's animal cries of grief. And then it is summer, and everything has changed, and his mother is engaged to marry the Lutheran bishop, Edvard Vergerus, who is a tall and handsome man, everyone agrees, but as Helena sees them leaving after the wedding, she says, "I think we will have our Emilie back before long."

The first third of the story, taking place in winter, was filled with color and life, even life in death. Now Fanny and Alexander are taken to a new world, the bishop's house, which he inhabits with his mother, his sister, and his aunt, and which is whitewashed and barren, with only a few necessary pieces of furniture, locks on every door, bars on the windows.

The maid tells the children that the bishop's first wife and two daughters drowned in the river; Alexander says he has been visited by their ghosts, who told him they drowned trying to escape after being locked up for five days without food and water. The faithless maid reports this story to the bishop, who whips Alexander, but not before a struggle in which the boy stubbornly makes clear his hatred for the bishop.

Already in the film we have seen the ghost of Oscar more than once, morose, pensive, worried about his children. There is a touching scene where his mother wakes from a dream on the veranda of her summer cottage and has a loving conversation with him. (If elements of *Hamlet* creep in, with the ghost of Alexander's father and his mother's hasty remarriage, they are not insisted on, and coil casually beneath the surface of the action.)

Now we see another bit of magic. Isak Jacobi, acting for his friend Helena, enters the bishop's house and offers to buy a trunk, and then smuggles her grandchildren out of the house in the trunk—and yet how can it be, when the bishop runs upstairs to look for them, that the children are also apparently in their room?

Perhaps it all has something to do with the magic arts of the Jacobi family. Isak has two nephews, Aron, who helps in the business, and Ismael, who is "not well" and is kept in a locked room and can be heard singing at night. Brought back to Isak's vast house, which is stacked to the ceiling with treasures to sell or barter, Alexander awakens in the middle of the night to urinate, loses his way back to his room, is startled by a conversation with God, and discovers that God is actually a puppet being manipulated as a joke by Aron. Then he is taken to meet Ismael (played, without explanation, by a girl), and it appears that Ismael can "see" what happens in the bishop's house and can control events there so that the bishop dies horribly by fire.

There are fairy-tale elements here, but *Fanny and Alexander* is above all the story of what Alexander understands is really happening. If magic is real, if ghosts can walk, so be it. Bergman has often allowed the supernatural into his films. In another sense, the events in *Fanny and Alexander* may be seen through the prism of the children's memories, so that half-understood and half-forgotten events have been reconstructed into a new fable that explains their lives.

What's certain is that Bergman somehow glides beyond the mere telling of his story into a kind of hypnotic series of events that have the clarity and fascination of dreams. Rarely have I felt so strongly during a movie that my mind had been shifted into a different kind of reality. The scenes at night in the Jacobi house are as intriguing and mysterious as any

I have seen, quiet and dreamy, and then disturbing when the mad Ismael calmly and sweetly shows Alexander how everything will be resolved.

The movie is astonishingly beautiful. The cinematography is by Bergman's longtime collaborator Sven Nykvist, who surrounds the Ekdahls with color and warmth, and bleeds all of the life out of the bishop's household.

The enormous cast centers on Helena, the grandmother, played by Gunn Wallgren (in a role once intended for Ingrid Bergman). Wallgren is full-lipped, warm, and sexy, and her affection for Isak is life-giving; she was the best thing in the film, Bergman believed. Emilie (Ewa Froling) is the most conflicted character in the story; she marries the bishop for love, is tragically mistaken about what kind of man he is, thinks she can protect her children, and cannot. Her visit to Helena is heartbreaking. The marriage of Gustav (Jarl Kulle) and Alma (Mona Malm) is open enough to permit an extraordinary scene in which Gustav discusses his affair with his wife and Emilie, and they all try to decide what would be best for the maid. The bishop (Jan Malmsjo) is a tragic and evil man, strict because he is fearful and insecure, cruel because he cannot stop himself, in agony because, he confesses to Emilie, he thought everyone admired him, and he realizes he is hated.

This is a long film, at 188 minutes plus an intermission. But the version Bergman prefers is longer still, the 312-minute version he made for Swedish television. Both are available on a Criterion DVD, which includes Bergman's feature-length documentary on the making of the film. To see the film in a theater is the way to first come to it, because the colors and shadows are so rich and the sounds so enveloping.

At the end, I was subdued and yet exhilarated; something had happened to me that was outside language, that was spiritual, that incorporated Bergman's mysticism; one of his characters suggests that our lives flow into each other's, that even a pebble is an idea of God, that there is a level just out of view where everything really happens.

Note: When *Sight and Sound*, the British film magazine, asked the world's directors and critics to select the best films of the previous twenty-five years, *Fanny and Alexander* was third, after Francis Ford Coppola's *Apocalypse Now* and Martin Scorsese's *Raging Bull*.

{ FAUST }

The greatest master of horror in the silent era was a cheerful man, much loved by his collaborators, even though they might lose consciousness from time to time while enveloped in clouds of steam or surrounded by tongues of flame. F. W. Murnau (1888–1931) made two of the greatest films of the supernatural, *Nosferatu* (1922) and *Faust* (1926), both voted among the best horror films of all time on the Internet Movie Database: *Faust* surprisingly in fourth place, just ahead of *The Shining*, *Jaws*, and *Alien*.

Murnau had a bold visual imagination, distinctive even during the era of German Expressionism with its skewed perspectives and twisted rooms and stairs. He painted with light and shadow, sometimes complaining to his loyal cameraman, Carl Hoffmann, that he could see too much—that all should be obscured except the focus of a scene.

Faust, with its supernatural vistas of heaven and hell, is particularly distinctive in the way it uses the whole canvas. Consider the startling early shot of Mephisto, his dark wings obscuring the sky as he hovers above a little village that huddles in the lower right corner. Murnau treated the screen as if it offered a larger space than his contemporaries imagined; long before deep focus, he was creating double exposures like shots in *Faust* where a crowd of villagers in the foreground is echoed by faraway crowds in the upper corners.

His screen encompassed great breadth and depth, so that when Mephisto takes Faust on a flight through the sky, we really do seem to see the earth unreeling beneath them: towns and farms, mountains and rivers. Murnau used a model of the landscape, of course; as his art director, Robert Herlth, remembered, "there were pines and larches made of reeds and rushes, glass-wool clouds, cascades, fields of real turf carefully stuck on plaster. When Murnau saw us at work, he bent his great height to help us make our little rocks and trees."

Like all silent-film directors, Murnau was comfortable with special effects that were obviously artificial. The town beneath the wings of the dark angel is clearly a model, and when characters climb a steep street, there is no attempt to make the sharply angled buildings and rooflines behind them seem real. Such effects, paradoxically, can be more effective than more realistic ones; I sometimes feel, in this age of expert CGI, that I am being shown too much—that technique is pushing aside artistry and imagination. The world of *Faust* is never intended to define a physical universe, but is a landscape of nightmares. When the elderly Faust is magically converted by Mephisto into a young man, there is a slight awkwardness in the way one image is replaced by another, and oddly enough that's creepier and more striking than a smooth modern morph.

Murnau and his contemporaries were inventing their techniques while they were using them. Herlth recalled that while Murnau was filming an opening scene of an archangel enveloped by clouds, the director "was so caught up in the pleasure of doing it that he forgot all about time. The steam had to keep on billowing through the beams of light until the archangel—Werner Fuetterer—was so exhausted he could no longer lift his sword. When Murnau realized what had happened, he shook his head and laughed at himself, then gave everyone a break."

Yes, but he was entranced again in the scene where Camilla Horn, playing the beautiful Gretchen, "had to spend hours tied to the stake, with flames leaping round her from 20 lykopodium burners. When she fainted, she was not acting." And the famous Emil Jannings, who played the doorman in Murnau's *Last Laugh* and is Mephisto here, stood for hours above three powerful fans that blew clouds of soot to make his cloak billow twelve feet above his head. All of these facts I take from the book *Murnau*, by the invaluable critic Lotte Eisner, who never met Murnau but talked to his collaborators after his death in 1931, at forty-three, in a traffic accident.

Faust, the story of a man who sells his soul to the devil, was long a European legend before Goethe spent fifty years writing a two-volume version of the myth. Because Goethe was beloved by the Germans, some audiences for Murnau's film were outraged by the liberties he took with the story, not least in shaky central episodes where Faust falls in love with Gretchen, demands to be made young again, and then woos her while Mephisto distracts her Aunt Marthe with his own romantic designs. Somehow it diminishes Mephisto to assign him carnal desires—particularly since, as an angel, he presumably lacked all inclination and equipment for such pursuits.

The film's greatness resides in its majestic opening scenes and its horrifying conclusion. Most viewers dislike the courtship between Gretchen and young Faust, although it is essential to set up her eventual fate—an ending so bleak that there is not much consolation when the archangel informs Mephisto that "Love" is stronger than all the powers of darkness. Tell that to Gretchen, burning at the stake, and Faust, transformed back into an old man and throwing himself into the flames at her feet to beg forgiveness.

Some of the early scenes remind us of *Nosferatu* in their evocation of a terrified population. Faust (played young and old by Gosta Ekman) is seen as a bearded scholar, surrounded by his books, until the plague strikes the land. From his window, he sees hooded figures carrying corpses to a charnel pit; he is called to the bedside of a dying woman, but all of his wisdom and art are helpless to save her, and after praying to God, he is tempted to invoke Mephisto. There is true horror as he burns his books and stands within a ring of fire to call down the devil; when he finds he has the power to cure dying villagers, he thinks he has made a good bargain, but soon his power intoxicates him.

Mephisto offers him the beautiful Duchess of Parma; he prefers the sweet and innocent Gretchen, and demands the gift of youth so that he can woo her. That way tragedy lies. Mephisto is crafty in his techniques; at first he offers Faust a twenty-four-hour trial of satanic powers, no strings attached, but soon Faust is ready to sign anything to win poor Gretchen. So much for the plague victims.

Silent films like this deal more in broad concepts than in the subtleties of personality. Like Greek myth and comic books, they present characters clearly defined by their strengths and weaknesses. There's no small talk. Ekman creates an elderly Faust in anguish over his inability to cure plague victims and too proud to admit defeat. The young Faust is led astray by the stirrings in his loins, and the function of Gretchen, I am afraid, is to be the innocent victim of his lust; she wanders through a blizzard with her innocent infant and burns at the stake, all because of her love for the unworthy Faust.

It's worth mentioning that William Dieterle, who plays Gretchen's brother, Valentin, fled Hitler, came to Hollywood, and had a long career as a director, distinguished by *The Devil and Daniel Webster* (1941), itself a version of the Faust legend.

Murnau died before he was able to express himself fully in the sound era, where there is no telling what he might have accomplished; soon after he moved to America, his *Sunrise* (1927) shared the first Academy Award for best picture. In death, he is surrounded by legend, not least in E. Elias Merhige's strange film *Shadow of the Vampire* (2000), where John Malkovich plays the director as a man whose star, Max Schreck (Willem Dafoe), is in fact a vampire. Murnau promises Schreck that he can eat the leading lady as his payment, but the vampire grows hungry and devours the cinematographer, and in desperation, Murnau muses, "I do not think we need the writer." The movie is not, by the way, a comedy, but feeds on the real horror that Murnau created. He was an original, and no one else ever made films that looked like his. They are strange and haunted; you reflect that if such satanic dealings were possible, they would probably look very much like this.

{ FITZCARRALDO }

Werner Herzog's *Fitzcarraldo* is one of the great visions of the cinema, and one of the great follies. One would not have been possible without the other. This is a movie about an opera-loving madman who is determined to drag a boat overland from one river system to another. In making the film, Herzog was determined to actually do that, which is more than can be said for Brian Sweeney Fitzgerald, the Irishman whose story inspired him.

Fitzcarraldo (1982) is one of those brave and epic films, like *Apocalypse Now* or *2001*, where we are always aware both of the film, and of the making of the film. Herzog could have used special effects for his scenes of the 360-ton boat being hauled up a muddy forty-degree slope in the jungle, but he believed we could tell the difference: "This is not a plastic boat." Watching the film, watching Fitzcarraldo (Klaus Kinski) raving in the jungle in his white suit and floppy panama hat, watching Indians operating a block-and-tackle system to drag the boat out of the muck, we're struck by the fact that this is actually happening, that this huge boat is inching its way onto land—as Fitzcarraldo (who got his name because the locals could not pronounce "Fitzgerald") serenades the jungle with his scratchy old Caruso recordings.

The story of the making of *Fitzcarraldo* is told in *Burden of Dreams* (1982), a documentary by Les Blank and Maureen Gosling, who spent time in the jungle with Herzog, his mutinous crew, and his eccentric star. After you see the Herzog film and *Burden*, it's clear that everyone associated with the film was marked, or scarred, by the experience; there is an impassioned speech in *Burden* where Herzog denounces the jungle as "vile and base," and says, "It's a land which God, if he exists, has created in anger."

Fitzcarraldo opens on the note of madness, which it will sustain. Out of the dark void of the Amazon comes a boat, its motor dead, the shock-haired Kinski furiously rowing at the prow, while his mistress (Claudia Cardinale) watches anxiously behind him. They are late for the opera. He has made some money with an ice-making machine, she is a madam whose bordello services wealthy rubber traders, and as they talk their way into an opera house, Fitzcarraldo knows his mission in life: he will become rich, build an opera house in the jungle, and hire Caruso to sing in it.

Fortunes in this district are built on rubber. He obtains the rights to four hundred square miles that are thought to be useless because a deadly rapids prevents a boat from reaching them. But if he could bring a boat from another river, his dream could come true. The real Fitzgerald only moved a thirty-two-ton boat between rivers, and he disassembled it first. Hearing the story, Herzog was struck by the image of a boat moving up a hillside, and the rest of the screenplay followed.

His production can be described as a series of emergencies. A border war between Peru and Ecuador prevented him from using his first location. He found another location and shot for four months with Jason Robards playing Fitzcarraldo and Mick Jagger playing his loony sidekick. Then Robards contracted amoebic dysentery and flew home, forbidden by his doctors to return, and Jagger dropped out. Herzog turned to Klaus Kinski, the legendary wild man who had starred in his *Aguirre, the Wrath of God* (1972) and *Nosferatu* (1979). Kinski was a better choice for the role than Robards, for the same reason a real boat was better than a model: Robards would have been playing a madman, but to see Kinski is to be convinced of his ruling angers and demons.

Herzog has always been more fascinated by image than story, and here he sears his images into the film. He worked with indigenous Amazonian Indians, whose faces become one of the important elements of the work. An early scene shows Fitzcarraldo awakened from sleep to find his bed surrounded by children. There is a scene where Indians gaze impassively at the river, not even noticing Fitzcarraldo as he ranges up and down their line, peering wildly into their faces. There is another scene where he and his boat crew eat dinner while Indians crowd into the mess room and stare at them. And scenes simply of faces, watchful, judgmental, trying to divine what drives the man in the white suit.

Herzog admitted that he could have filmed his entire production a day or two outside Quito, the capital of Ecuador. Instead, he filmed in the rain forest, five hundred miles from the nearest sizable city. That allows shots like the one where Fitzcarraldo and his boat captain stand in a platform at the top of the tallest tree, surveying the vastness around them. He has spoken of the "voodoo of location," which caused him to shoot part of his *Nosferatu* in the same places where Murnau filmed his 1926 silent version. He felt the jungle location would "bring out special qualities in the actors and even the crew." This was more true than he could have suspected, and in the fourth year of his struggle to make the film, exhausted, he said, "I am running out of fantasy. I don't know what else can happen now. Even if I get that boat over the mountain, nobody on this earth will convince me to be happy about that, not until the end of my days."

Burden of Dreams tells of arrows shot from the forest, of the boat slipping back down the hill, of the Brazilian engineer resigning and walking away after telling Herzog there was a 70 percent chance that the cables would snap and dozens of lives would be lost. On a commentary track, we learn more horrifying details; a crew member, bitten by a deadly snake, saved his own life by instantly cutting off his foot with the chainsaw he was holding. In an outtake from *Burden*, which Herzog used in *My Best Fiend* (1999), his documentary about his stormy relationship with Kinski, we see the actor raging crazily on the set. *Burden* has an image that will do for the entire production: Herzog wading through mud up to his knees, pulling free each leg to take another step.

The movie is imperfect, but transcendent; this story could not have been filmed on this location in this way and been perfect without being less of a film. The conclusion, the scene with the cigar, for example, is an anticlimax; but then everything must be an anticlimax after the boat goes up the hill. What is crucial is that Herzog does not hurry his story along; he seeks not the progress of the plot, but the resonance of the images. Consider a sequence where the boat actually bangs and crashes its way through the deadly Pongo das Mortes, the Rapids of Death. Another director might have made this a routine action scene, with quick cuts and lots of noise; Herzog makes it a slow and frightful procession down real currents in a real ship, with a phonograph playing Caruso until the needle is knocked loose. It looks more horrifying to see the huge ship slowly floating to its destiny.

Among directors of the last four decades, has anyone created a more impassioned and adventurous career than Werner Herzog? Most people have only seen a few of his films, or none; he cannot be fully appreciated without a familiarity with his many documentaries and more obscure features (such as *Heart of Glass* and *Stroszek*). His 2005 documentary *Grizzly Man*, about a man who spent thirteen summers with the grizzly bears of Alaska, is the spiritual brother of *Fitzcarraldo*—both times, men are driven by obsession to challenge the wilderness. Again and again, in films shot in Africa, Australia, Southeast Asia, and South America, he has been drawn to the farthest reaches of the earth and to the people who live there with their images uncorrupted by the thin gruel of mass media.

"I don't want to live in a world without lions, and without people who are lions," he says in *Burden of Dreams*. At the darkest hour in *Fitzcarraldo*, when Robards fell sick and he had to abandon four months of shooting, Herzog returned to get more backing from investors. They had heard he was finding it impossible to get the ship up the mountain, and asked if it would not be wiser to take his losses and quit. His reply: "How can you ask this question? If I abandon this project, I will be a man without dreams, and I don't want to live like that. I live my life or I end my life with this project." With Herzog, that has often been the case.

{ FORBIDDEN GAMES }

We must turn to the past for a film as innocent as *Forbidden Games* (1952), because our own time is too cynical to support it. Here is a film about children using their powers of fantasy and denial to deal with death in wartime. A modern film would back away from the horror and soften and sentimentalize it. It would become a "children's film." But in all times children have survived experiences that no child should have to endure.

Sometimes they're able to shield their innocence by creating games to process the pain. *Forbidden Games* was attacked and praised by adults for the same reason: because it showed children inventing happiness where none should exist. The Japanese animated film *Grave of the Fireflies* (1988) is another rare film with the courage to walk this path.

The film begins during the Nazi invasion of France in 1940. We meet a five-year-old girl named Paulette, with her parents. The road out of Paris is clogged with those escaping the city. It is being strafed by Nazi fighter planes. Paulette's little dog runs onto a bridge. She chases it, and her parents desperately run after her. Bullets kill both parents and fatally wound the dog. Paulette, lying on the ground next to her mother, reaches out a hand to touch the dead cheek, and then touches her own cheek. She does not cry. She does not quite understand. She holds her puppy. Its legs jerk spasmodically for a long time before it dies.

She is given a ride by strangers. The man throws her dog into the river. She jumps off their cart and runs down to save the dog, and is seen by a local boy named Michel, the young son of the Dolle family, peasants on a nearby farm. She is taken in by the Dolles and immediately becomes Michel's favorite. He will give his blanket to her. He will demand that the family keep her. He will have a playmate.

The love between the two children is almost too pure and simple to be believed—unless you can remember being a child. For some reason, we remember best the children we hated, or who hated us. But with a playmate we can construct a world so compelling that all our thoughts are given to its creation and maintenance. With Jackie, the girl next door, I spent days building a toy village on the dining room floor, around an electric train set. It was so elaborate, so invested with our stories of what each house meant, that when it had to be "cleaned up," we felt a hurt no adult could imagine.

Paulette (Brigitte Fossey) determines to bury her dog. Michel (Georges Poujouly) helps her, because she isn't big enough to handle the hoe she has stolen. The grave is hidden in an abandoned mill. They need a crucifix for it, and Michel hammers one from lumber. Paulette has never really dealt with the deaths of her parents. She acknowledges that they are gone, but they are gone in theory, not practice; that they are truly dead forever seems to elude her. Yet she becomes fascinated with death, and Michel joins her in burying a mole that was captured by an owl. Soon they are burying every dead thing they can find, even worms, even broken plates. At one point, while they are lying side by side on the floor doing his homework, he stabs a cockroach with his pen. "Don't kill him! Don't kill him!" she cries, and he says, "I didn't. It was a bomb that killed him."

Close study of this scene reveals a curious detail. She presses to the ground as she cries out, and we cannot see her face. If we happen to look at Michel's face, we will notice that his lips are moving, although we do not hear his voice. Clearly the scene was constructed in the editing room, matching her voice to visuals that did not match. That's possibly an indication of the difficulties the director, Rene Clement, had in directing children so young in a story so fraught. But for the most part the children are astonishingly natural and convincing, and in an interview much later, Fossey remembered with a smile that Clement asked her to cry "a little more" or "a little less" and she fine tuned her tears.

Their cemetery grows larger. They begin to steal crucifixes to put above the graves. Paulette, who does not know her prayers, or about the stations of the cross, or what a crucifix is, must be Jewish. Michel innocently teaches her, and that knowledge could eventually save her life. There is a comic subplot involving a rural feud between the Dolles and their neighbors, the Gouards, who accuse each other of stealing crucifixes; at one point a fight in the cemetery ends with two brothers fighting and falling into a grave. All the while the secret cemetery in the old mill grows more elaborate.

Forbidden Games was the first feature by Rene Clement; his short film on the same story was seen by the director Jacques Tati, who told him it must become a feature. It came (as Tati did) from outside the French film establishment; its producer, Robert Dorfmann, had powerful enemies.

The film was initially turned down by Cannes, then accepted after a scandal. It was turned down by Venice because it had played at Cannes, but accepted after another uproar, and won the Golden Lion as best film, with a best actress award for Fossey (she grew up to make many more good films). It won an honorary Oscar in 1953. Yet one critic said the film itself should be forbidden. Clement was accused simultaneously of trivializing the war and inflicting its horrors too mercilessly on his actors. Leftist critics accused him of an attack on the working class, although his poor peasant farmers are the most warm and generous of characters.

To be sure, it is remarkable that Fossey was able to weather this experience at five. Poujouly, her co-star, was nine or ten. She remembers doing better than older actresses at the audition because she had no idea what stakes were involved; they were nervous, but she just went ahead and did as she was told. Clement "shot around" her character as much as possible, shooting close-ups of her looking at events so she did not really have to witness them, and she remembers attending the premiere at Cannes and seeing the planes attack the bridge for the first time. She was horrified.

The film is so powerful because it does not compromise on two things: the horror of war and the innocence of childhood. Fossey's face becomes a mirror that refuses to reflect what she must see and feel. She transposes it all into the game of burying the dead and placing crosses over them.

The cinematographer, Robert Juillard, always places a little additional light on her face and blond hair, suggesting an angel without insisting on it. Only gradually do we come to understand the total power that their fantasy has over the children, and what measures they will take in its defense. It is funny, also sad, when Paulette fixates on every crucifix she sees, and Michel confesses the theft of some crucifixes and then pauses on his way out of the confessional to try stealing another one from the altar.

Movies like Clement's *Forbidden Games* cannot work unless they are allowed to be completely simple, without guile, transparent. Despite the scenes I have described, it is never a tearjerker. It doesn't try to create emotions, but to observe them. Paulette cannot speak for herself, and the movie doesn't try to speak for her. That's why it is so powerful: her grief is never addressed, and with the help of a boy who loves her, she surrounds it with a game that no adult could possibly understand, or penetrate.

The beautifully restored new Criterion DVD of the film includes an alternate beginning and ending, filmed but never used, in which the scenario is framed as a "story" from a book that Michel reads to Paulette.

THE GODFATHER: PART II

The musical score plays an even greater role in *The Godfather: Part II* than it did in the original film. Nostalgic, mournful, evoking lost eras, it stirs emotions we shouldn't really feel for this story, and wouldn't, if the score were more conventional for a crime movie. Why should we regret the passing of a regime built on murder, extortion, bribery, theft, and the ruthless will of frightened men? Observe how powerfully Nino Rota's music sways our feelings for the brutal events onscreen.

At the end of Francis Ford Coppola's masterwork *The Godfather* (1972), we have seen Michael Corleone (Al Pacino) change from a young man who wanted to stand apart from his family to one who did not hesitate to take up the reigns of control. In *Part II* (1974), we see him lose his remaining shreds of morality and become an empty shell, insecure and merciless. If the score evokes pity, it is Michael's self-pity. In attempting to fill the shoes of his father, Michael has lost sight of those values that made Don Corleone better than he had to be and has become a new godfather every bit as evil as he has to be. If Rota's score had been energetic and pounding, we might see him as more closely paralleling Tony Montana in a better film, Brian DePalma's *Scarface* (1983). But the score is sad, and music can often evoke emotion more surely and subtly than story. Consider how deeply we are moved by certain operatic arias that are utter nonsense.

The devolution of Michael Corleone is counterpointed by flashbacks to the youth and young manhood of his father, Vito (Robert De Niro). These scenes, taking place in Sicily and old New York, follow the conventional pattern of a young man on the rise and show the Mafia code being burned into the Corleone blood. No false romanticism conceals the necessity of using murder to do business. Such events as Vito's murder of the minor-league New York godfather have their barbarism somewhat softened as Coppola adopts Vito's point of view and follows him as he climbs rooftops to ambush the man and successfully escapes. It is a built-in reality that we tend to identify with a film's POV. Here the murder becomes another rung on Vito's ladder to success.

To be sure, the life of young Vito helps to explain the forming of the adult Don Corleone, and to establish in the film the Sicilian code of omerta. As Michael changes, we see why he feels that he must. He must play the game by its rules. But I am not sure the flashbacks strengthen the film. I would have appreciated separate films about young Vito and the evolution of Michael. Never mind. What we have are two compelling narratives, two superb lead performances, and lasting images. There is even a parallel between the deaths of two elderly dons. Revenge must be obtained.

Coppola is at the top of his form in both films, and if I disapprove of the morality of the central characters, well, so do we all. We agree people should not kill one another, but that doesn't explain why these films are seen again and again, entering a small worldwide canon of films just about everyone seems to have seen. They are grippingly written, directed with confidence and artistry, photographed by Gordon Willis ("The Master of Darkness") in rich, warm tones. The acting in both films is definitive. We can name the characters in a lot of films (Harry Lime, Scarlett O'Hara, Travis Bickle, Charles Foster Kane) but from how many films do we remember the names of six or more characters? Brando, Pacino, De Niro, Duvall, Cazale, Caan, Diane Keaton, Lee Strasberg, Talia Shire, Michael V. Gazzo, and others are well cast, well used, gifted, and correct for their roles.

Simply as a story, the Michael scenes in *The Godfather: Part II* engage our emotions. I admire the way Coppola and his co-writer, Mario Puzo, require us to think along with Michael as he handles delicate decisions involving Hyman Roth (Strasberg), the boss of Miami; Fredo (Cazale), his older brother; and the shooting of Sonny (James Caan). Who has done what? Why? Michael floats various narratives past various principals, misleading them all, or nearly. It's like a game of blindfolded chess; he has to envision the moves without seeing them.

But finally it is all about Michael. Even the attack on the night of his son's first-communion party is on his bedroom, not our bedroom. His wife, Kay (Keaton), leaves him, and his focus does not waver: he will keep his son. Tom Hagen (Duvall), the most trusted confidant of father and son, considered a brother, is finally even suspected. In Michael's life, paranoia is a useful defense mechanism.

Coppola shows Michael breaking down under the pressure. We remember that he was once a proud war hero, a successful college student, building a legitimate lifestyle. But on their wedding day, Kay first began to fully realize what an all-controlling cocoon the Corleone clan was. There would always be things she could not be told about, could not be trusted with. Finally Michael has no one to tell or trust except his elderly mother (Morgana King). Michael's desperation in that intense conversation explains everything about the film's final shot.

So *Part II* is finally a sad film, a lament for loss, certainly. It is a contrast with the earlier film, in which Don Corleone is seen defending old values against modern hungers. Young Vito was a murderer, too, as we more fully see in the Sicily and New York scenes of *Part II*. But he had grown wise and diplomatic, and when he dies beside the tomato patch, yes, we feel regret. An age has closed. We feel no regret at Michael's decline. The crucial difference between the two films is that Vito is sympathetic, and Michael becomes a villain. That is not a criticism but an observation.

The "best films" balloting on IMDb.com lacks credibility because popularity is the primary criteria. But hundreds of thousands do indeed vote, and as I write, the top four films, in order, are *The Shawshank Redemption*, *The Godfather*, *The Dark Knight*, and *The Godfather: Part II*. Of all of the reviews I have ever written, my three-star review of *Part II* has stirred the most disagreement. Sometimes it is simply cited as proof of my worthless-ness. I've been told by many that *Part II* is a rare sequel that is better than the original. Have I changed my mind? No. I have read my review of *Part II* and would not change a word.

Then why is it a "great movie"? Because it must be seen as a piece with the unqualified greatness of *The Godfather*. The two can hardly be con-sidered apart (*Part III* is another matter). When the characters in a film take on a virtual reality for us, when a character in another film made thirty years later can say *The Godfather* contains all the lessons in life you need to know, when an audience understands why that statement could be made, a film has become a cultural bedrock. No doubt not all of the gospels are equally "good," but we would not do without any of them.

The Godfather: Part II then becomes a film that everyone who values movies at all should see. And as I write this, it can be seen in astonishingly good prints. The Godfather trilogy has been painstakingly digitally restored by Robert Harris, a master in his field. I have seen the restored *Godfather* in the new 35mm print and *Part II* in the new Blu-ray DVD. Having first seen both at their world premieres, I would argue that they have never looked better. For films of such visual richness, that is a reason to rejoice.

And now I come back to the music. More than ever, I am convinced it is instrumental to the power and emotional effect of the films. I cannot imagine them without their Nino Rota scores. Against all our objective rea-son, they instruct us how to feel about the films. Now listen very carefully to the first notes as the big car drives into Miami. You will hear an evocative echo of Bernard Hermann's score for *Citizen Kane*, another film about a man who got everything he wanted and then lost it.

{THE GREAT DICTATOR}

In 1938, the world's most famous movie star began to prepare a film about the monster of the twentieth century. Charlie Chaplin looked a little like Adolf Hitler, in part because Hitler had chosen the same toothbrush moustache as the Little Tramp. Exploiting that resemblance, Chaplin devised a satire in which the dictator and a Jewish barber from the ghetto would be mistaken for each other. The result, released in 1940, was *The Great Dictator*, Chaplin's first talking picture and the highest-grossing of his career, although it would cause him great difficulties and indirectly lead to his long exile from the United States.

In 1938, Hitler was not yet recognized in all quarters as the embodiment of evil. Powerful isolationist forces in America preached a policy of nonintervention in the troubles of Europe, and rumors of Hitler's policy to exterminate the Jews were welcomed by anti-Semitic groups. Some of Hitler's earliest opponents, including anti-Franco American volunteers in the Spanish Civil War, were later seen as "premature antifascists"; by fighting against fascism when Hitler was still considered an ally, they raised suspicion that they might be communists. *The Great Dictator* ended with a long speech denouncing dictatorships and extolling democracy and individual freedoms. This sounded to the left like bedrock American values, but to some on the right, it sounded pinko.

If Chaplin had not been "premature," however, it is unlikely he would have made the film at all. Once the horrors of the Holocaust began to be known, Hitler was no longer funny, not at all. The Marx Brothers, ahead of the curve, made *Duck Soup* in 1933, with Groucho playing the dictator Rufus T. Firefly in a comedy that had ominous undertones about what was already underway in Europe. And as late as 1942, the German exile Ernst Lubitsch made *To Be or Not to Be*, with Jack Benny as an actor who becomes embroiled in the Nazi occupation of Poland.

Chaplin's film, aimed obviously and scornfully at Hitler himself, could only have been funny, he says in his autobiography, if he had not yet known the full extent of the Nazi evil. As it was, the film's mockery of Hitler got it banned in Spain, Italy, and neutral Ireland. But in America and elsewhere, it played with an impact that, today, may be hard to imagine. There had never been any fictional character as universally beloved as the Little Tramp, and although Chaplin was technically not playing the Tramp in *The Great Dictator*, he looked just like him, this time not in a comic fable but a political satire.

The plot is one of those concoctions that makes the action barely possible. The hero, a barber-soldier in World War I, saves the life of a German pilot named Schultz and flies him to safety, all the time not even knowing he was the enemy. Their crash landing gives the barber amnesia, and for twenty years he doesn't know who he is. Then he recovers and returns to his barber shop in the country of Tomania (say it aloud), only to discover that the dictator Hynkel has come to power, not under the swastika, but under the double cross. His storm troopers are moving through the ghetto, smashing windows and rounding up Jews (the term "concentration camp" is used early, matter-of-factly). But the barber's shop is spared by the intervention of Schultz, now an assistant minister, who recognizes him.

The barber (never named, just like the Tramp) is in love with the maid Hannah (Paulette Goddard, Chaplin's estranged wife at the time). And he is befriended by his former neighbors. But he and the disloyal Schultz are eventually put in a concentration camp, and then Hynkel has a boating mishap, is mistaken for the barber, and locked into the camp just as the barber and Schultz escape—with Hynkel's uniform. Now the barber is assumed by everyone to be the dictator.

In the classic Chaplin tradition, the movie has a richness of gags and comic pantomime, including Hynkel's famous ballet with an inflated balloon that makes the globe his plaything. There is a sequence where five men bite into puddings after being told the one who finds a coin must give his life to assassinate Hynkel. None of them want to find the coin and there is cheating, but eventually—see for yourself. And there is a long, funny episode when the dictator of neighboring Bacteria, Benzini Napaloni (Jack Oakie), pays a state visit. Napaloni, obviously modeled on Mussolini, eludes an attempt to make him sit in a low chair so the short Hynkel can loom over him. And when the two of them sit in adjacent barber chairs, they take turns pumping their chairs higher than the other. There is also a lot of confusion about saluting, and Chaplin intercuts shots of the two dictators with newsreels of enormous, cheering crowds.

In 1940, this would have played as very highly charged, because Chaplin was launching his comic persona against Hitler in an attempt, largely successful, to ridicule him as a clown. Audiences reacted strongly to the film's humor; it won five Oscar nominations, for picture, actor, supporting actor (Oakie), screenplay, and music (Meredith Willson). But audiences at the time, and ever since, have felt that the film comes to a dead end when the barber, impersonating Hynkel, delivers a monologue of more than three minutes that represents Chaplin's own views.

Incredibly, no one tries to stop the fake Hynkel. Chaplin talks straight into the camera, in his own voice, with no comic touches and only three cutaways, as the barber is presumably heard on radio all over the world. What he says is true enough, but it deflates the comedy and ends the picture as a lecture, followed by a shot of Goddard outlined against the sky, joyously facing the Hynkel-free future, as the music swells. It didn't work then, and it doesn't work now. It is fatal when Chaplin drops his comic persona, abruptly changes the tone of the film, and leaves us wondering how long he is going to talk (a question that should never arise during a comedy). The movie plays like a comedy followed by an editorial.

Chaplin (1889–1977) nevertheless was determined to keep the speech; it might have been his reason for making the film. He put the Little Tramp and $1.5 million of his own money on the line to ridicule Hitler (and was instrumental in directing more millions to Jewish refugee centers). He made his statement, it found a large audience, and in the stretches leading up to the final speech, he shows his innate comic genius. It is a funny film, which we expect from Chaplin, and a brave one. He never played a little man with a mustache again.

And now a memory. In 1972, the Venice Film Festival staged a retrospective of Chaplin's complete work, with prints from his own collection. On the closing night, his masterpiece, *City Lights* (1932), was shown outdoors in Piazza San Marco. The lights were off, the orchestras were silenced for the first time in more than a century, and the film played on a giant screen to standing room only.

When it was over, and the blind flower girl could see again, and she realized the Little Tramp was her savior, there was much snuffling and blowing of noses. Then a single spotlight sprung from the darkness and illuminated a balcony overlooking the square. A little man stepped out and waved. And we cheered and cheered.

{ GROUNDHOG DAY }

Groundhog Day is a film that finds its note and purpose so precisely that its genius may not be immediately noticeable. It unfolds so inevitably, is so entertaining, so apparently effortless, that you have to stand back and slap yourself before you see how good it really is.

Certainly I underrated it in my original review; I enjoyed it so easily that I was seduced into cheerful moderation. But there are a few films, and this is one of them, that burrow into our memories and become reference points. When you find yourself needing the phrase "This is like *Groundhog Day*" to explain how you feel, a movie has accomplished something.

The movie, as everyone knows, is about a man who finds himself living the same day over and over and over again. He is the only person in his world who knows this is happening, and after going through periods of dismay and bitterness, revolt and despair, suicidal self-destruction and cynical recklessness, he begins to do something that is alien to his nature. He begins to learn.

This man is named Phil, and he is a weatherman. In a sense, he feels himself condemned to repeating the same day, anyway; the weather changes, but his on-camera shtick remains the same, and he is distant and ironic about his job. Every year on February 2 he is dispatched to Punxsutawney, Pennsylvania, to cover the festivities of Groundhog Day, on which

179

Punxsutawney Phil, the groundhog, is awakened from his slumbers and studied to discover if he will see his shadow. If he does, we will have another six weeks of winter. We usually have another six weeks of winter anyway, a fact along with many others that does not escape Phil as he signals his cynicism about this transcendentally silly event.

Phil is played by Bill Murray, and Murray is indispensable; before he makes the film wonderful, he does a more difficult thing, which is to make it bearable. I can imagine a long list of actors, whose names I will charitably suppress, who could appear in this material and render it simpering, or inane. The screenplay by Danny Rubin and Harold Ramis is inspired, but inspired crucially because they saw Bill Murray in it. They understood how he would be able to transform it into something sublime, while another actor might reduce it to a cloying parable. Ramis and Murray had worked together from the dawn of their careers, at Second City in Chicago, and knew each other in the ways only improvisational actors can know each other, finding their limits and strengths in nightly risks before a volatile and boozy audience. I doubt if Ramis would have had the slightest interest in directing this material with anyone else but Murray. It wasn't the story that appealed to him, but the thought of Murray in it.

The Murray persona has become familiar without becoming tiring: the world is too much with him, he is a little smarter than everyone else, he has a detached melancholy, he is deeply suspicious of joy, he sees sincerity as a weapon that can be used against him, and yet he conceals emotional needs. He is Hamlet in a sitcom world. *Lost in Translation*, another film that works because Bill Murray is in it, captures these qualities. So does *The Life Aquatic with Steve Zissou*, which doesn't work because Murray's character has nothing to push against in a world that is as detached as he is.

In *Groundhog Day* (1993), notice how easily he reveals that Phil (the weatherman, not the groundhog) is a perfect bastard. He doesn't raise his voice or signal through energetic acting that he's an insufferable jerk. He just is. He draws for his Punxsutawney assignment a patient angel of a producer named Rita (Andie MacDowell) and a good sport of a cameraman named Larry (Chris Elliott). Like television production people everywhere, they're accustomed to "talent" that treats them shabbily; they indulge the egos of the on-camera performers and get on with their jobs, reflecting perhaps that they can do without the big bucks if it means being a creep like Phil.

At 6 a.m. on February 2, Phil is awakened by the clock alarm in his cozy little Punxsutawney bed-and-breakfast. It is playing "I Got You Babe," by Sonny and Cher. He goes through a series of experiences: being greeted by an old classmate who wants to sell him insurance, stepping into an icy puddle, performing a stand-up on camera in front of the wretched groundhog, which he considers, not without reason, to be ratlike. Phil is rude to Rita and Larry, and insulting to his viewers (by implying they are idiots to be watching the segment). He has no liking for himself, his job, his colleagues, or the human race.

All he wants to do is get out of town. He begins to. He doesn't quite make it. What with one thing and another, he wakes up the next morning in the same bed, with the radio playing the same song, and it gradually becomes clear to him that he is reliving precisely the same day. Tomorrow and tomorrow and tomorrow, in his case, doesn't creep in at its petty pace from day to day, but gets stuck like a broken record. After the third or fourth day, the enormity of his predicament is forced upon him. He is free to change what he says and does from one February 2 to the next, but it will always be February 2 for everyone else in the world, and he will always start from the same place. They will repeat themselves unless he changes the script, but tomorrow they will have forgotten their new lines and be back to the first draft of February 2.

One night in a bowling alley, sitting at the bar, he says almost to himself: "What would you do if you were stuck in one place, and everything that you did was the same, and nothing mattered?" The sad sack next to him at the bar overhears him and answers: "That about sums it up for me."

Slowly, inexpertly, Phil begins to learn from his trial runs through February 2. Ramis and Rubin in an early draft had him living through ten thousand cycles, and Ramis calculates that in the current version he goes through about forty. During that time, Phil learns to really see himself for the first time, and to see Rita, and to learn that he loves her, and to strive to deserve her love. He astonishingly wants to become a good man.

His journey has become a parable for our materialistic age; it embodies a view of human growth that, at its heart, reflects the same spiritual view of existence Murray explored in his very personal project *The Razor's Edge*. He is bound to the wheel of time, and destined to revolve until he earns his promotion to the next level. A long article in the British newspaper the *Independent* says *Groundhog Day* is "hailed by religious leaders as the most spiritual film of all time." Perhaps not all religious leaders have seen anything by Bergman, Bresson, Ozu, and Dreyer, but never mind: they have a point, even about a film where the deepest theological observation is "Maybe God has just been around a long time and knows everything."

What amazes me about the movie is that Murray and Ramis get away with it. They never lose their nerve. Phil undergoes his transformation but never loses his edge. He becomes a better Phil, not a different Phil. The movie doesn't get all soppy at the end. There is the dark period when he tries to kill himself, the reckless period when he crashes his car because he knows it doesn't matter, the times of despair.

We see that life is like that. Tomorrow will come, and whether or not it is always February 2, all we can do about it is be the best person we know how to be. The good news is that we can learn to be better people. There is a moment when Phil tells Rita, "When you stand in the snow, you look like an angel." The point is not that he has come to love Rita. It is that he has learned to see the angel.

{ HOWARDS END }

There are two conversations in *Howards End* (1992) between Henry Wilcox, a wealthy businessman, and Margaret Schlegel, who becomes his second wife. The first is amusing, the second desperate, and they express the film's buried subject, which is the impossibility of two people with fundamentally different values ever being able to really communicate. Around these conversations revolves a story involving those dependable standbys of circa 1900 British literature: class, wealth, family, hypocrisy, and real estate.

The movie stands with *The Remains of the Day* (1993), *A Room with a View* (1985), and *A Soldier's Daughter Never Cries* (1998) among the best work by the team of director James Ivory and producer Ismail Merchant, who between 1961 and Merchant's death in May 2005 made a series of films that could be described as "Merchant-Ivory" and everyone would know what you meant.

They made high-end films with low-end budgets, which gave them freedom from studio interference, and they often began with novels by such as Henry James and E. M. Forster that had the advantage of being out of copyright. Actors would reduce their fees to work with them, knowing Oscar nominations were likely, and indeed Emma Thompson was named best actress for her performance here as Margaret, and both Thompson and

Anthony Hopkins, who plays Henry, were nominated for *The Remains of the Day*.

There was a tendency in some circles to condescend to Merchant-Ivory and their lifelong writing partner, Ruth Prawer Jhabvala. "The Laura Ashley school of filmmaking," sniffed the British director Alan Parker, to which Merchant cheerfully responded: "That is a comment that will last longer than his films."

Because they often began with literary novels, because they often made period pieces, because the art direction was rich with sumptuous costumes and seductive locations, because, as Rita Kempley wrote in the *Washington Post*, "If Merchant, Ivory and Jhabvala have anything to do with it, there'll always be an England," there was a tendency to think you knew what to expect when you went to a Merchant-Ivory.

Whether that was what you got depended on how attentive you were. *Howards End*, based on the 1910 novel by Forster, is a film seething with anger, passion, greed, and emotional violence. That the characters are generally well behaved says less about their manners than their inhibitions. That's where the two conversations between Margaret and Henry come into play. Listen to them, and you have the underlying method of the film.

In the first, the widowed Henry (Hopkins) proposes marriage to Margaret Schlegel (Thompson). They met while his wife, Ruth Wilcox (Vanessa Redgrave), was still alive, and Henry knows, but Margaret does not, that in a note scrawled on her deathbed, Ruth asked that her family home, Howards End, be left to Miss Schlegel. The note is crumpled and thrown into the fire, but Margaret becomes the mistress of the house after all, through marriage.

Henry shows Margaret through another of his houses, filled with portraits of the ancestors of the previous owners; she kindly says one "rather looks" like Henry. The tour is in the nature of a sales pitch, to underline his wealth and position. Then, awkwardly pausing on the stairs, Henry asks her: "Do you think you could be induced to share . . . I mean, is it at all possible . . ."

"Oh, yes, I see," Margaret says.

"I am asking you to be my wife."

"Yes, I know."

She kisses him. Are they in love? He is middle aged and she, while younger, is old to be single. They are middle class, he from the high middle, she from the center. Their families were neighbors in London. The marriage makes sense, is one way to put it.

The conversation displays Henry at his most awkward: he is a rigid man of conventional public principles, shy about personal matters, inclined to speak a little loudly and distinctly, as if his listeners might be deaf. Hopkins often has him bending forward from the waist and addressing people from a slightly oblique angle, as if keeping his options open. Thompson's Margaret, however, is a modern woman, raised in a German-British family where literature and music were important; she looks people in the eye, says what she thinks, is not slow to get the point.

Their strategies for addressing the world come into play during a crisis at their wedding. To set the scene, I must introduce Leonard Bast (Samuel West), who at a lecture on Beethoven has the misfortune of picking up an umbrella belonging to Margaret's high-spirited younger sister, Helen (Helena Bonham Carter).

Returning the umbrella, he is asked to tea by the Schlegels and learns secondhand that Henry thinks he should quit his job as a clerk at a firm that is "about to go smash." He quits his job, the company prospers, and he is unable to keep another job for long. Bast and his wife, Jacky (Nicola Duffett), descend into poverty and hunger, and the idealistic Helen blames it all on Henry's bad advice. "We owe Mr. Bast," she believes, although Henry is philosophical: "The poor are poor. One is sorry for them, but there it is."

The rebellious Helen brings Leonard and Jacky along when she attends Margaret's marriage to Henry, at a lavish garden party in Shropshire. The Basts are literally starving; taking Marie Antoinette's advice, they eat cake. Jacky makes good use of the punch bowl, gets drunk, and recognizes her old friend Henry. "Do you know Henry?" she's asked. "Know Henry! Who doesn't know Henry? He's had some gay old times."

Jacky is dragged away, but the furious Henry accuses Margaret of setting a trap, and "releases her" from her engagement. No need: "It's not going to trouble us," Margaret tells him. And then James Ivory embarks on a series of conversations, each one ending in a fade to black, where Henry apologizes and apologizes, and Margaret tries to calm him.

"Temptation—a fall from grace," he chokes out. "In Cyprus, I was very lonely. You can never forgive me . . ."

But she can, and does, and says they must put the past behind them, and that it has nothing to do with them, as he goes on and on, and it becomes clear that when Jacky was sixteen and parentless in Cyprus, Henry took her as a mistress and treated her badly, indeed. It is a point of the story that Leonard Bast, who has no money and no status, is a gentleman who treats Jacky with respect, and Henry, who has all the money he needs, is rotten beneath his irreproachable conventionality.

The challenge for Margaret in her marriage is to make the best of her new world, to broker communication between two sets of values. Her good heart was immediately apparent to Ruth Wilcox, who desperately urged Margaret to come down and visit the house—which she had brought with her into the marriage but did not want to leave there. When Margaret finally wanders through Howards End, old Miss Avery, the housekeeper, gets a start: "I took you for Ruth Wilcox. You have her way of walking around the house."

Forster's novel begins with the words "Only connect" on the title page, and later we read of Margaret: "Only connect! That was the whole of her sermon. Only connect the prose and the passion, and both will be exalted, and human love will be seen at its height. Live in fragments no longer."

Her task in the novel is to bridge Henry's prose and her sister Helen's passion, a passion that eventually leads to her becoming pregnant by Mr. Bast and arriving at Howards End in, to Henry, a scandalous condition. He demands to know the name of her "seducer," and later his feckless son, Charles (James Wilby), brings about the film's climax of tragedy and farce by attempting to avenge Helen, who has no wish to be avenged.

There is at this time a third conversation between Henry and Margaret during which he cannot connect. She tells him Helen wants to spend one night at Howards End before returning to Germany to have her child. He refuses. She entreats. He is rigid. "Will you forgive her as you yourself have been forgiven?" she asks him. "You've had a mistress. My sister has had a lover."

In 1910, her speech, however fair and sensible it may sound to us, was shocking. It is hard now to imagine how dangerous the novel seemed to some of its readers. The hypocrisy that Forster was illustrating had a buried meaning to him because of his own homosexuality, which he kept a secret, at least in public, until the posthumous publication of his novel *Maurice*, also filmed by Merchant-Ivory.

Howards End is of course lovely to look at. The old brick country house, not too grand, covered with vines, surrounded by lawns and flowers, is reached by big, shiny motorcars and occupied by people who dress for dinner. But this is not a story of surfaces.

What enrages Helen, and through her the audience, is that to be male and wealthy is to have privileges that the poor and the female are denied. Henry might have gotten Jacky pregnant, but if Jacky's husband dares get Henry's sister-in-law pregnant, he must be made to pay. Henry thinks he is dealing with a moral offense, but actually he is dealing with temerity: Leonard Bast must not be allowed to behave the way Henry Wilcox is entitled to, because, well, Leonard is poor, and there it is.

{ INHERIT THE WIND }

"History repeats itself, the first time as tragedy, the second time as farce."

This statement by Karl Marx admirably serves two functions: (1) it describes the difference between the two times the teaching of Darwin's theories were put on trial in this country, in Tennessee in 1925 and in Pennsylvania in 2005; (2) because it is from Karl Marx, it will automatically be rejected, along with the words to follow, by those who judge a statement not by its content but by its source. That is precisely the argument between Darwinism and creationism. Stanley Kramer's *Inherit the Wind* (1960) is a movie about a courtroom battle between those who believe the Bible is literally true and those who believe, as the Spencer Tracy character puts it, that "an idea is a greater monument than a cathedral."

The so-called Monkey Trial of 1925 put a young high school teacher named John T. Scopes on trial for violating a state law, passed the same year, prohibiting the teaching of any theory that denied the biblical account of divine creation. Darwin's theory of evolution was also therefore on trial. Two of the most famous lawyers and orators in the land contested the case. Scopes was defended by the legendary Clarence Darrow, and the prosecution was led by three-time presidential candidate William Jennings Bryan. Darrow's expenses were paid by the *Baltimore Sun* papers, home of the famed journalist H. L. Mencken, who covered the trial with many snorts and guffaws.

In Kramer's film, Darrow becomes Henry Drummond (Spencer Tracy), Bryan is Matthew Harrison Brady (Fredric March), Mencken is E. K. Hornbeck (Gene Kelly), and Scopes is Bertram T. Cates (Dick York). Another major player is the gravel-voiced Harry Morgan, as the judge. So obviously were the characters based on their historical sources that the back of the DVD simply refers to them as "Bryan" and "Darrow," as if their names had not been changed.

Seen forty-six years after its release but only a few months after Darwin was once again on trial in Dover, Pennsylvania, *Inherit the Wind* is a film that rebukes the past when it might also have feared the future. Beliefs that seemed like ancient history to Kramer have had a surprising resiliency; two recent polls show that 38 percent of American teenagers believe "God created humans pretty much in their present form within the last 10,000 years or so," and 54 percent of American adults doubt that man evolved from earlier species. There is hardly a politician in the land with courage enough to state that they are wrong.

Certainly most of the citizens in the movie's fictional town of Hillsboro, Tennessee, believe in the literal truth of Genesis. "There's only one man in this town who thinks at all," Drummond roars, "and he's in jail." The movie casts the battle as a struggle between the followers of a fundamentalist preacher (Claude Akins) and the snowy-haired agnostic Drummond, who believes Darwinism is as "incontrovertible as geometry," as indeed it seems to well over 99 percent of the world's scientists. The preacher's followers descend on the town with tents, a Ferris wheel, and a sideshow in which a monkey smokes a cigarette while a barker asks if men came from monkeys. There is a fraught romantic subplot: the defendant York is engaged to Rachel (Donna Anderson), the preacher's daughter. At one point denouncing his daughter as a creature of the devil, the preacher froths so easily that he lacks credibility.

Early scenes in the film are broadly drawn; a parade welcomes Brady to town as the band plays "That Old-Time Religion," and the Baltimore journalist speaks as if he is reading his own copy ("I'm admired for my detestability"). But once the film centers on the courtroom battle between the two old men, it finds a ferocity that is awesome; Brady and Drummond essentially engage in a debate between fundamentalism and the possibility that if God did create the world, he did so in more than six twenty-four-hour days. What is astonishing in this 1960 film is the gutsy way it engages in ideas, pulls no punches in its language, and allows the characters long and impassioned speeches. There are a lot of words here, well written and spoken, and not condescending to the audience. Both Tracy and March vent an anger and passion through their characters that ventures beyond acting into holy zeal.

I wonder if a film made today would have the nerve to question fundamentalism as bluntly as the Tracy character does. The beliefs he argues against have crept back into view as "creationist science," and it was the notion that this should be offered as an alternative to Darwinism that inspired the 2005 Pennsylvania case. In the movie and in the actual Scopes trial, Bryan was a persuasive orator who proudly defended fundamentalism; his 2005 counterparts carefully distanced themselves from religious advocacy and tried to make their case on the basis of "creationist science." Their presentation was so unpersuasive that Judge John E. Jones III (a Republican appointed by George W. Bush) not only ruled against them but added that they exhibited "striking ignorance" and "breathtaking inanity" and "lied outright under oath."

Central to the case for "alternative" theories is a misunderstanding of what a scientific theory is, and isn't. One thing it cannot do is depend on supernatural elements. That is the role of religious belief. By asking that creationism be given a place beside the theory of evolution, its supporters are asking that their beliefs be given equal standing with the scientific method. That violates the separation of church and state, as Judge Jones ruled; in claiming their science was not faith-based, he said, they lied.

What is surprising, as I watch *Inherit the Wind*, is how clearly Tracy's Drummond/Darrow character defines the same argument and persuasively wins it. After his six expert scientific witnesses are not allowed to testify, he boldly calls Brady/Bryan onto the stand as a defense witness. The bombastic Brady is unable to refuse a chance to show off, and Drummond quizzes him on biblical details, more or less destroying his credibility in the process; Brady is finally reduced to agreeing with Bishop Usher that God created the Earth at exactly 9 a.m. on October 23, 4004 BC. One might assume that calling Brady to the stand was a Hollywood gimmick, but no: Darrow really did bring Bryan to the stand and methodically ground him down.

Inherit the Wind is typical of the films produced and directed by Stanley Kramer (1913–2001), a liberal who made movies that had opinions and took stands. He was dismissed by some critics for saddling his films with pious messages, for preferring speeches to visual style and cinematic originality, but he stuck to his guns. Although his films like *On the Beach* (1959), *Judgment at Nuremberg* (1961), *Ship of Fools* (1965), *Guess Who's Coming to Dinner* (1967), and *Bless the Beasts and Children* (1971) took predictable positions on nuclear war, the Holocaust, interracial marriage, and the preservation of species, they blended ideas and entertainment in a persuasive mixture. If his messages were predictable, they were also forthright; some of today's message movies, for example the splendid *Syriana*, are so labyrinthine that viewers must sense the message almost by instinct.

Strange that forty-six years after it was made and eighty-one years after the Scopes trial, it is *Inherit the Wind* among all of Kramer's films that seems most relevant and still generates controversy. Tracy's character of Drummond in particular seems boldly drawn. There are times when he seems to be veering toward a safe harbor on the religion-versus-Darwin issue: "What goes on in this town is not necessarily the Christian religion," he says, and one of the witnesses he is not allowed to call is a Christian minister who sees no conflict between evolution and his church.

But Drummond is unswerving in his emotional courtroom scenes, arguing that "fanaticism and ignorance is forever busy, and needs feeding." When he is asked if he finds anything holy, he replies, "The individual human mind. In a child's ability to master the multiplication table, there is more holiness than all your shouted hosannas and holy of holies."

Note especially his final argument to the jury, which he performed in an unbroken shot. In the last scene of the film, Drummond stands in the empty courtroom, picks up a Bible in one hand and Darwin's *On the Origin of Species* in the other, smiles, claps them together, and packs them both under his arm. How should we take this scene? Has he reconciled the two books, or does he think he'll need them both for the appeal?

{ JOHNNY GUITAR }

Nicholas Ray's *Johnny Guitar* (1954) is surely one of the most blatant psychosexual melodramas ever to disguise itself in that most commodious of genres, the Western. Consider: no money was lavished on the production. The action centers on a two-story saloon "outside town," but we never even see "town," except for a bank facade and interior set. So sparse are the settings that although the central character (Joan Crawford) plays the tavern owner and goes through a spectacular costume charge, we never see her boudoir—she only appears on a balcony above the main floor, having presumably emerged from the sacred inner temple.

A cheap Western from Republic Pictures, yes. And also one of the boldest and most stylized films of its time, quirky, political, twisted. Crawford bought the rights to the original novel, Nicholas Ray signed on to direct, and I wonder if they even openly spoke of the movie's buried themes. One is certainly bisexualism; Crawford's tavern-owner Vienna is, it is claimed, in love with "Johnny Guitar" (Sterling Hayden), but has not seen him in five years. She effortlessly turns tough hombres into girly-men, and her bartender observes to Johnny, "I never met a woman who was more man."

Her archenemy, Emma (Mercedes McCambridge), is allegedly in love with "The Dancin' Kid" (Scott Brady) and is jealous because he is allegedly in love with Vienna ("I like you, but not that much," Vienna tells him). But there is hardly a moment when Emma can tear her eyes away from Vienna to glance at the Kid. All of the sexual energy is between the two women, no matter what they say about the men. Crawford wanted Claire Trevor for the role, but the studio, perhaps having studied the script carefully, insisted on McCambridge, who was not a lesbian but played one, as they say, in the movies.

That casting led to more Crawford bitch legends, as on the day when she threw McCambridge's costume in the middle of a highway. The chemistry of loathing is palpable, as it was between Crawford and Bette Davis in *Whatever Happened to Baby Jane*. Both women wear fetishistic black leather, silk, and denim costumes that would have been familiar enough to students of 1954 pornography: the tightly corseted waists, the high boots, the long shirts, the tight bodices, the lash of lipstick give us Meg Myles in *Satan in High Heels*.

McCambridge, said to be a "cattle baron" (not baroness), dominates her posse of cowboys and lackeys, standing before them in a wide, challenging stance. She's shorter than they are, but is always strutting in the front while they almost cower. Crawford often appears from above on her balcony, worshipped by the camera in low-angle, adored by her loyal employees, ordering Sam, her croupier, "Spin the wheel. I like the way it sounds."

Somebody has to spin it. Throughout the film, the saloon attracts no ordinary customers, only characters in the plot. Has a Western ever been more casual about its male leads? *Johnny Guitar* is about the hatred between Vienna and Emma, and Sterling Hayden seems to know it. Brought into town as firepower when Vienna fears gun trouble, he claims to have given up guns, speaks softly, talks of his onetime love of Vienna with only barely convincing regret, and is laidback, as Sterling Hayden rarely ever is. The critic Dennis Schwartz recalls: "Francois Truffaut said it reminded him of *The Beauty and the Beast*, with Sterling Hayden being the beauty."

The plot. Ridiculous. Vienna owns the saloon in a choice location outside town. We are not sure how a single woman without means paid for it, but are reminded by Marlene Dietrich in *Shanghai Express* that "it took more than one man to change my name to Shanghai Lily." Apparently Vienna is now all paid up, but the railroad is coming through, and the townsfolk fear it will run past her door and put them out of business.

The town is led by McIvers (Ward Bond) and his tool, the sheriff (Frank Ferguson), who are led by Emma as they demand what Vienna knows about a stagecoach robbery. The stolen cash was intended for her brother's bank. Since the Dancin' Kid has rejected Emma's love, it stands to reason, doesn't it, that he stuck up the bank, along with his tough sidekicks (Ernest Borgnine, Ben Cooper, and Royal Dano)?

Johnny Guitar arrives at about the same time. Coincidence? Imagine the notoriously deadly Old West and an unarmed cowboy with only a guitar. Well, he does play it once. But there is a secret: Guitar is the pseudonym for Johnny Logan, a notorious gunslinger who retired five years ago. Vienna was Guitar's lover until he "wasn't ready" for marriage (not to her, for sure). And the sheriff, McIvers, etc. are trying to frame someone—the Kid, maybe, for sticking up the stagecoach. Their suspicions are not unfounded, since there are literally no other characters in the movie, except for the faceless coots who crowd into doorways behind McIvers.

The dynamic of their investigation and their attempts to force townsfolk to testify against one another form an allegory squarely aimed at the House Un-American Activities Committee, which in 1954 was trying to force alleged communists to "name names" of other alleged communists; the screenplay was ghosted by the blacklisted Ben Maddow. A significant moment comes when Johnny Guitar acknowledges his own name.

There are extraordinary moments in the movie, not least when Crawford, who has been dressed entirely in black, suddenly appears on the balcony in a stunning white gown and cows the men with her presence and a piano recital(!).

It is also fascinating to watch her and Johnny use words as love weapons. This dialogue could have appeared in the laconic Broadway social dramas of the period:

> *Johnny:* How many men have you forgotten?
> *Vienna:* As many women as you've remembered.

Johnny: Don't go away.
Vienna: I haven't moved.
Johnny: Tell me something nice.
Vienna: Sure. What do you want to hear?
Johnny: Lie to me. Tell me all these years you've waited . . .
Vienna: All these years I've waited.
Johnny: Tell me you'd have died if I hadn't come back.
Vienna: I would have died if you hadn't come back.
Johnny: Tell me you still love me like I love you.
Vienna: I still love you like you love me.
Johnny: Thanks. Thanks a lot.

Whoa! I see Brando as Johnny, Shirley Knight as Vienna. That's not Western dialogue, it's cynicism made audible. There are other moments I will leave for you to savor, and I trust you may share my bafflement about the route from the waterfall to the hideout, but ponder this: everyone involved in this movie had made countless other films, knew all about the cliches and conventions, and must have known how many they were breaking. As the scenes come along that are clearly an indictment of HUAC, were they thinking they could get away with murder because the surrounding movie was so goofy?

It was goofy then, and very strange now. The more you think about the tavern and the "town" and the tragedy that plays out against the unpopulated landscape, the more you see them playing dice with their destinies. Spin the wheel. I like the way it sounds.

{ JULIET OF THE SPIRITS }

Fellini lore has it that the master made *Juliet of the Spirits* as a gift for his wife. Like many husbands, he gave her the gift he really wanted for himself. The movie, starring a sad-eyed Giulietta Masina who fears her husband is cheating, suggests she'd be happier if she were more like her neighbor, a buxom temptress who entertains men in a tree house.

Fellini believed the movie turned the tables on his two previous films, *La Dolce Vita* and *Fellini 8 1/2*, which were autobiographical laments about his own problems. This one, he felt, was about Giulietta. Watching it, I was reminded of Daryl F. Zanuck, who said, "But enough about me! What did you think of my movie?" *Juliet of the Spirits* is not an attempt to identify with Masina's point of view, but a bald-faced exercise in Fellini's self-justification. When Juliet has fantasies, they're Fellini's fantasies. That's why at the end it isn't Federico who is burned alive.

One clue to the movie's buried message is in the casting. Giulietta Masina plays Juliet, a chain smoker with a trim little haircut and an understated wardrobe. Sandra Milo plays her neighbor Suzy, dressed flamboyantly in tight colors, feather boas, and necklines that flaunt her charms. In *Fellini 8 1/2*, about a harassed and philandering movie director, the wife is also a chain smoker with a trim haircut—and the mistress is played by Sandra Milo, who looks exactly as she does here. In *8 1/2*, the director has a daydream in which his wife and mistress are friends who share in his care and feeding. In *Juliet of the Spirits*, Fellini seems to be suggesting that if only his wife were more like this pneumatic sex toy, she would be happier. Our conclusion: she might not be happier, but her husband certainly would be.

The movie is generally considered to mark the beginning of Fellini's decline. Some feel his great days came in the 1950s, with the neorealism of *La Strada* (1954). International success came to him with *La Dolce Vita* (1959) starring Marcello Mastroianni in his first great role as a journalist who tries to balance his job, his marriage, his mistress, his erotic daydreams, and his vague ambitions. I think it's Fellini's best movie; others would argue for *8 1/2* (1963), which is about a director trying to make a movie despite personal, professional, and health problems. By the time of *Juliet of the Spirits*, the conventional view has it, Fellini was on autopilot, using his waltzing camera and jolly Nina Rota scores to recycle his phantasmagorical visions of human grotesques on parade. The only later film widely admired is *Amarcord* (1974).

Sometimes, however, you get your best look at an artist's style when he's indulging it. *Juliet of the Spirits*, Fellini's first film in color, is the work of a director who has cut loose from the realism of his early work and is toying with the images, situations, and obsessions that delight him. It is well known that young Federico experienced some kind of psychic fixation during his first visit to the circus, and all of his films feature processions or parades. It may not be too much to suggest that the sight of bizarre characters walking in time to music has a sexual component for Fellini, who almost always composes the scenes the same way: characters in background and middle distance walk in procession in time with one another, and then a foreground face appears in frame, eager to comment.

In *Juliet*, one of the most delightful parades occurs on the seaside, where plain Juliet has gone with her sisters and their children. Across the sand, she sees Suzy in procession with her friends, admirers, servants, and followers, dressed in bright yellow, protected by gaudy parasols, setting up a tent on the sand, beckoning invitingly to her. Later, when Juliet visits her neighbor to return her strayed cat, Suzy shares her philosophy: marriage is a life sentence for a woman, Juliet should indulge herself with one of the boy-toys Suzy can make available, her husband is not worth fretting over, etc. Suzy's home includes a chute that leads straight from her bed to a swimming pool, and a treehouse with an electric hoist that hauls up her lovers in a wicker basket.

Suzy's lifestyle may or may not be the answer to Juliet's concerns, but her home certainly looks like a bordello that Fellini might like to visit. Juliet's liberating experiences also include a séance with a medium (this is an echo from *La Dolce Vita*), and fears of liturgical punishment (the fearsome nuns in one scene echo the stern priests of *8 1/2*, and both appear in flashbacks to childhood). What Fellini is doing, not subtly, is returning to his earlier films for images that he now applies to a heroine instead of a hero.

Giulietta Masina was a wonderful actress (see *La Strada* and *Nights of Cabiria*) but is it my imagination, or does she seem unhappy throughout much of *Juliet of the Spirits*? Masina and Fellini were said to be going through a difficult season of their marriage as the film was made (international fame had transformed Fellini from a hard-working Italian director to a star who welcomed his new privileges with open arms). Certainly Fellini does not present her as someone it would be fun to be married to. She's a house-proud little bourgeois Hummel figurine, meek, frumpy, sexually timid. As Juliet makes her way through scene after scene of harem fantasies and busty tarts on parade, she looks like nothing more than an unwilling housewife dragged by her husband to a strip show he is sure they will both enjoy.

This perception of Giuletta/Juliet's withdrawn unhappiness adds a melancholy undertone to the movie. She's the party pooper. What was she thinking while she made the film? That first her husband flaunts his taste in grotesque eroticism, and then expects his wife to star in a movie where she's surrounded by it? The movie's last shot shows Juliet leaving her storybook home and walking off toward the nearby woods. The director and his wife argued about the meaning of this scene. To Fellini, this meant she was free. To Giulietta Masina, we learn, it meant that she was alone, abandoned, and lonely.

This subtext makes the movie more interesting than it would have been if Fellini had been more in control of his fugitive thoughts and impulses. And it's never less than dazzling to look at. It's all pretty pictures and the music of that promenading camera. In any Fellini picture and especially those from *La Dolce Vita* onward, characters seem to glide as if moving to unheard music. In fact, they were. Fellini, like all Italian directors of his time, did not record live sound on his sets, but dubbed all the dialog and sound effects later. That meant he was essentially making silent films, and he always had an orchestra or a record player on the set to play music, instructing his actors to walk in time. The Nina Rota scores often sound like dance music, and frequently quote old standards; the result is a film that sometimes seems on the brink of bursting into a musical.

After *Juliet*, Fellini made *Fellini Satyricon* (1970). Now that both of these movies have been re-released in newly mastered and restored 35mm prints, we can see him as the master of his canvas. He was a storyteller early in his career, but became a painter of moving images, and those who fixate on plots or messages are hunting in the wrong field. *Juliet* was released in America in 1966, and some audiences no doubt attended in an expanded state of consciousness. They were in the right show: a head trip, as they said. Seen in 2001, when the party is long over, it's like a streamer from last summer's dances: still bright, still gaily waving to echoes of forgotten music.

Fellini was nominated for twelve Academy Awards, but never won one. In 1993, he was given an honorary Oscar, presented by old friends Marcello Mastroianni and Sophia Loren, and as he accepted it Giulietta wept happily in the front row. He died in October of that year. She survived him by five months.

KILLER OF SHEEP

Ordinary daily life is one of the hardest things for a movie to portray, because so many other movies have trained us to expect patterns and plots. In my own 1977 review of Charles Burnett's *Killer of Sheep*, I made that mistake of expectation, in a sentence so wrongheaded it cries out to be corrected: "But instead of making a larger statement about his characters, he chooses to show them engaged in a series of daily routines, in the striving and succeeding and failing that make up a life in which, because of poverty, there is little freedom of choice." Surely I should have seen that what Burnett chooses to show is, in fact, a larger statement. In this poetic film about a family in Watts, he observes the quiet nobility of lives lived with values but without opportunities. The lives go nowhere, the movie goes nowhere, and in staying where they are they evoke a sense of sadness and loss.

The film centers on Stan (Henry Gayle Sanders), a slaughterhouse worker who labors to exhaustion at his work and then returns to jobs at home: fixing the sink, putting down new linoleum, raising the kids. In this is he joined by his wife (Kaycee Moore), a beautiful but tired woman who freshens her makeup to welcome him home, even though he can hardly notice. Burnett regards their faces, lives, children, friends, neighbors, in a loosely strung-together series of episodes that don't add up to much, while they somehow add up to everything. His black-and-white images and deliberate editing create a sense of serene resignation; this is how it is, and ever shall be.

Killer of Sheep became a legend while hardly being seen. I cannot remember, indeed, why I was able to see it in 1977. Filmed by Burnett for $10,000 as his master's thesis at the UCLA film school, it did not find distribution because Burnett could not afford the rights to the music on his soundtrack. Now, thirty years later, the film has been beautifully restored by UCLA, and blown up from 16 to 35mm, while retaining its original music (the rights cost $150,000). The movie's Web site, killerofsheep.com, tells the story and describes the extraordinary music selection: Etta James, Dinah Washington, Gershwin, Rachmaninov, Paul Robeson, Earth, Wind & Fire.

Surely, if he wanted his film seen, Burnett could have used cheaper music? Not at all, because on a deeper level he wanted his film to be a demonstration of the breadth of music by and about African Americans. One shot at the end, with a backlit Stan and his wife (never named) dancing wearily to Dinah Washington's "This Bitter Earth," demonstrates that it had to be Dinah Washington and no one else, singing that song and no other.

You have to be prepared to see a film like this, or able to relax and allow it to unfold. It doesn't come, as most films do, with built-in instructions about how to view it. One scene follows another with no apparent pattern, reflecting how the lives of its family combine endless routine with the interruptions of random events. The day they all pile into a car to go to the races, for example, a lesser film would have had them winning or losing. In this film, they have a flat tire, and no spare. Thus does poverty become your companion on every journey.

The lives of the adults are intercut with shots of the children at play. One brilliant sequence shows a kid's head darting out from behind a plywood shield—once, twice, six times. The camera pulls back to show that two groups of kids are playing at war in a rubbish-strewn wasteland, throwing rocks at one another from behind barriers. A boy gets hit and bleeds and cries. The others forget war and gather around. He's not too badly hurt, and so they idly drift over to railroad tracks and throw rocks at a passing train. All of the scenes of children at play were unrehearsed; Burnett just filmed them.

They have few toys. One child puts on a grotesque rubber Halloween mask and wears it all day, and gets roughed up because, somehow, the mask obscures the fact that a child is inside it. At home, Stan works on projects, complains to a friend he cannot sleep, projects deep discouragement. Sitting at the kitchen table, he presses a tea cup against his face and says it reminds him of a feeling just after sex. That kind of tender thought has little place in his world. We see him at work, herding sheep to their deaths, then stringing them up on a conveyor belt, cutting their throats, watching them bleed. Later, he throws away their inner parts. It is a hard and horrible job. Is there a connection between the sheep, who are content before their ends, and the children at play, happy because they know no better, unaware of the dead end that poverty will bring to some (not all!) of them?

Other scenes. Two men want to involve Stan in a crime. He and his wife send them away. Kids playing in an alley stare as two big boys climb over a back fence with a stolen TV set. We can tell they witness such things all the time. Stan buys a used auto motor, and then the sort of thing happens that is always happening to Stan. He's running, running, just to stay in place.

For an unseen film, *Killer of Sheep* has had a lot of attention. It won the critics prize at Berlin, was one of the first fifty titles on the Library of Congress list of American films worthy of permanent preservation, and Burnett is "not only the most important African-American director but one of the most distinctive filmmakers this country has ever produced" (Andrew O'Hehir, *Salon*), and the film deserves "a secure place not only as the greatest achievement in African-American cinema but also as one of the great achievements in cinema, period" (Jeffrey M. Anderson, Cinematical). David Gordon Green names the film as an influence on his own brilliant first feature, *George Washington*; indeed, in homage, he has a kid wearing a Halloween mask.

Charles Burnett was born in 1944 in Mississippi, raised in Watts, may have learned a lot of things at UCLA but not how to film moneymakers. Among his other titles are *The Glass Shield* (1994) and *To Sleep with*

Anger (1990) and a lot of TV and documentary work; he made *The Wedding* (1998) for TV, with Oprah Winfrey producing and Halle Berry starring.

What he captures above all in *Killer of Sheep* is the deadening ennui of hot, empty summer days, the dusty passage of time when windows and screen doors stood open, and the way the breathless day crawls past. And he pays attention to the heroic efforts of this man and wife to make a good home for their children. Poverty in the ghetto is not the guns and drugs we see on TV. It is more often like life in this movie: good, honest, hard-working people trying to get by, keep up their hopes, love their children, and get a little sleep.

{ LA BELLE NOISEUSE }

Frenhofer, the great artist, has painted nothing for ten years. He threw down his brush in the middle of painting what was intended as his masterpiece, to be titled *Le Belle Noiseuse*, or "the beautiful nuisance." His model was his wife, Elizabeth, who inspired the great period of his career. "At first he painted me because I loved him," she tells a friend. "Then he painted me because he loved me." And then he stopped, perhaps because he feared that to achieve his painting would be to destroy their love. Frenhofer does not see the outsides of his models, but the insides—bones, sinew, soul.

One day three visitors call at the vast French chateau where Frenhofer still lives with Liz. They are an art dealer, a young artist, and the artist's lover, Marianne. These two have been together three years. Marianne is aloof, quiet, strong willed. There is a moment after dinner the first evening when Frenhofer regards her, and their whole relationship is contained in that look. She is walking away from him, but she is certainly aware of the look, or of the feeling behind it. He will pick up his brush again.

Jacques Rivette's *La Belle Noiseuse* (1991) is the best film I have ever seen about the physical creation of art, and about the painful bond between an artist and his muse. Winner of the Palme d'Or prize at Cannes that year, it ran to a full four hours, and so its theatrical life was limited. Rivette edited a 125-minute version titled *Divertimento*, but why bother with it? The greatness of *La Belle Noiseuse* is in the time it spends on the creation of art, and the creation and destruction of passion.

Frenhofer is played by Michel Piccoli, the saturnine French star whose eyes can bore through other actors. With his high forehead and sculpted profile, he looks intelligent, but it is a formidable, threatening intelligence. He never plays the fall-guy. He always knows the story. Marianne, the young woman who inspires him, is played by Emmanuelle Béart, who at twenty-three had electrified audiences with *Manon of the Spring* (1986). Startlingly beautiful, with sensuous lips and deep eyes under arched brows, she seems at first a prop for a familiar story: the old artist will attempt to seduce her. Ah, but he wants more than that. He wants to possess her. And he wants to draw from her irritating willfulness the inspiration for his rebirth. He must have an abrasive to create.

His wife, Elizabeth (Jane Birkin), fully understands this, and explains to the sister of Marianne's boyfriend: "It's not about the flesh. Not about nudity." She says she doesn't worry about "How do you say it? An affair." She knows him too well. She even persuades Marianne to accept her husband's invitation to model. "But do not let him paint your face," she warns. There is a whiff here of *The Portrait of Dorian Grey* in reverse: the painting will steal the vitality of the model.

What I have described so far is merely plot, and in this film plot hardly concerns us. The great central passages of the film involve creation. In his cavernous stone studio, which reminds Marianne of her boarding-school chapel, Frenhofer begins to sketch her. We observe over his shoulder. Rivette use a static camera and long takes. He rarely cuts away. We see a blank sheet of paper, and the drawing taking shape there. We see the physical process: First, Frenhofer's obsession with arranging his pens, his brushes, his inks and paints. Then the first tentative lines on the page. Impatient stabs with the sharp pen. Washes of Payne's Grey (my favorite) at various dilutions. His fingers and thumb smearing the washes into rough shapes. Later, on a larger scale, he works with charcoal. Then oil.

"In the wardrobe upstairs, there is a dressing gown," he tells her. She understands, puts it on, disrobes in front of him, and will be entirely nude for at least at hour in this film. Yes, at first we observe Emmanuelle Béart as a woman. Then we see her as a model. Slowly we come to see her as Frenhofer wants to: the woman inside, the essence, the being. There is no small talk. He positions her in poses. He yanks her arms and legs like a puppet's. "In the old days," he says almost to himself, "they tied the arms and legs of the models into place, to keep to them from moving." She complains of pain and cramps, wants to have a cigarette. He takes cigarettes out of her fingers, and pushes her into position.

Does it sound boring to watch a man simply drawing for extended periods? Yes, it does. But it is not. Suspense is building. There is a contest between them, a battle of willpower. She is a nuisance. Elizabeth says she spent some time in Quebec, where *noiseuse* means "nutty." That's what Frenhofer wants. She begins to understand. She accepts the pain to prove she is the equal of his determination. One day when he despairs, she orders him to continue. She will see this through.

The painting is completed, but how it looks need not consume us. It is enough to quote how she describes it: "A thing that was cold and dry—it was me." What he does after finishing it is astonishing. No, he doesn't destroy it. It is his masterpiece, and he knows it is. So does his wife, who quietly visits the studio and draws a cross on the back of the frame, like a grave marker. Cross-shaped shadows from a window fall on their bed that night, and across his body.

Listen to the sounds in this movie. Rivette almost never uses soundtrack music, unless there is an obvious source, like a radio. He employs room noises at a higher volume than other directors: footfalls, doors slamming, plates rattling. The scratch of the pen on the paper is loud, and grows louder with his passion. When he is painting over Liz's face on a reused canvas, the noise of his brush swells. Listen very carefully during the scene where he has Marianne kneeling on a bench in a crucifixion pose. At first she cries. Then she starts to laugh, and he does too, and under their laughter you can hear the pen scratching, even though just now he is not using it.

Truffaut said that the French New Wave came into being because of Jacques Rivette (born 1928). He has never had the fame of his generation—Truffaut, Godard, Chabrol, Varda, Resnais. His films are said to be too long and difficult. There isn't the slightest difficulty in *La Belle Noiseuse*, and I would not want it any shorter, because I have shared that combat and that bond in that studio, and its devastating outcome.

Of the performances, there is nothing to be said about Piccoli except that he communicates exactly what Frenhofer needs from his art, and doesn't need many words to do it. Emmanuelle Béart has an ethereal beauty, but it is her talent that has made her a leading actress of her generation. We quickly feel, without any dialogue or behavior to spell it out, Marianne's nuisance quality, her nuttiness if you will. Is the coldness and dryness she sees in the portrait what Frenhofer desired her for, or despaired of? Jane Birkin, born in England, at home in both countries, finds the perfect and difficult note for Elizabeth, the wife. Does she sometimes wish he had finished his great painting the first time through, even if it had destroyed their happiness? That she had been more abrasive and less loved? She believes in her husband's greatness. That explains all the unanswered questions in this film, and there are some big ones.

{ L.A. Confidential }

The opening scenes of *L.A. Confidential* are devoted to establishing the three central characters, all cops. We may be excused for expecting that they will be antagonists; indeed, they think so themselves. But the film has other plans, and much of its fascination comes from the way it puts the three cops on the same side and never really declares anyone the antagonist until near the end. Potential villains are all over the screen, but they remain potential right up to the closing scenes. What the three cops are fighting, most of the time, is a pervasive corruption that saturates the worlds in which they move.

The movie also documents a specific time when the world of police work edged into show business. These days, when we can watch video recordings of cops actually busting suspects, when celebrity trials are shown on live TV, when gossip is the prime ingredient of many news outlets, it is hard to imagine a time when crime and vice lived hidden in the shadows. But they did, and the tipping point when that era ended must have been in the early 1950s, with the rise of instant celebrities, scandalous tabloid magazines like *Confidential*, the partnership between Hollywood and law enforcement agencies, and the end of the media's reticence about seamy subject matter. *L.A. Confidential* (1997) shows the current era of sensationalism being born.

The first voice heard from the screen comes from the confiding, insinuating publisher of *Hush-Hush* magazine, Sid Hudgens (Danny De-Vito). He sets the tone: "insiders" know the score and are getting away with murder. His most valued contact is Detective Jack Vincennes (Kevin Spacey), the technical adviser on *Badge of Honor*, a *Dragnet*-style TV show. Jack also stars in some of Hudgens's scoops. They set up celebrities or politicians in compromising situations, Vincennes breaks in to bust them, and *Hush-Hush* gets the story.

Vincennes will be one of the film's protagonists. The other two cops are Officer Bud White (Russell Crowe), who believes in bending the law to enforce it, and Detective Ed Exley (Guy Pearce), a straight-arrow type whose self-righteous morality gets on the department's nerves. These three cops, so different from one another, all possess some essential quality of honor that draws them together in untangling the film's web of corruption.

For much of its running time, *L.A. Confidential* seems episodic—one sensational event after another, with no apparent connection. Mickey Cohen, the head of organized crime in L.A., has just been sent to prison, and now hit squads are rubbing out his top lieutenants. A millionaire named Pierce Patchett (David Strathairn) has sidelines in slick porn and high-priced call girls, and specializes in prostitutes who have had plastic surgery to make them resemble movie stars. A bunch of drunken cops beat up Mexican suspects and get their photos on the front page. Exley and Vincennes, for quite different reasons, testify against their fellow officers, breaking the department's code of silence. There's a massacre at the downtown Nite Owl Cafe, and a cop is one of the victims. Calling sternly for justice to be done in all of these cases is ramrod-stiff Capt. Dudley Smith (James Cromwell), who presides at morning roll call.

The plot, based on the novel by James Ellroy, can only be described as labyrinthine. For long periods, we're not even sure that it is a plot, and one of the film's pleasures is the way director Curtis Hanson and writer Brian Helgeland put all the pieces into place before we fully realize they're pieces. How could these people and events possibly be related? We don't much mind, so long as the pieces themselves are so intriguing.

Consider the business of the call girls who have been "cut" to make them look like movie stars. One of them, Lynn Bracken (Kim Basinger), looks like Veronica Lake, but the truth is, she's never had plastic surgery. White tracks her down because she's the friend of a girl who was killed at the Nite Owl. Then he pays a return visit because he is powerfully attracted to her, and they fall into bed without having had six words of personal conversation. Is that typical behavior for a hooker? Does she have another motive? As the Basinger character plays out, her motives and real feelings coil about one another, creating a deep and sympathetic character. Despite Crowe, Pearce, and Spacey, it may be Basinger who gives the film's best performance. Her speech to Exley, about how she sees Bud White, is a monologue as simple as it is touching.

White has compromised himself by sleeping with a potential witness. He is also in deep with Captain Smith, who uses him as a strong-arm man to beat up "suspects," including out-of-town mobsters (the message: go home). Vincennes compromises himself by ratting on fellow cops, something he says he would never do—until his job on the TV show is threatened. And the straight-arrow Exley believes he could never bend the official rules of conduct, until he discovers that sometimes they need bending.

It would be unfair for me to even hint at some of the directions the story takes. Let me instead describe superb moments. One of the most famous comes when Vincennes and Exley enter the Formosa Cafe, a Chinese restaurant close the Paramount lot, to question the mobster Johnny Stompanato. He's with a date, who gives them some lip. Exley tells her to shut up: "A hooker cut to look like Lana Turner is still a hooker." Notice how the camera frames Exley in foreground and holds Vincennes in background, as he confides, "She is Lana Turner." This line, one of the movie's most famous, works so well, I think, because of the particular way Spacey delivers it, and the little smile he allows himself, and because Hanson does it in the same shot; a cutaway to Vincennes would have been all wrong.

Vincennes has another emotionally wrenching experience involving a beefcake "actor" named Matt, who he first met during a bust set up by *Hush-Hush*. Now Hudgens has a scheme to lure the D.A. into a "sissy" scenario with Matt, and uses Vincennes to help convince the gullible kid this favor could open the door for him on the TV ("Like *Badge of Honor* is gonna want him after he's been cover boy for *Hush-Hush* twice in a year," Hudgens gloats). How this assignation ends, and how Spacey as Vincennes reacts, amounts to a self-contained scenario on shame.

Consider, too, the choreography after two of the characters burst into the district attorney's office. The D.A. tries to put them off with a clever line about "good cop, bad cop," until he finds out in a horrifying way what "bad cop" can really mean. I've seen endless hours of violence in movies over the years, but hardly anything to equal what happens to the D.A. in a minute or two.

L.A. Confidential is described as film noir, and so it is, but it is more: unusually for a crime film, it deals with the psychology of the characters, for example in the interplay between the two men who are both in love with Basinger's hooker. It contains all the elements of police action, but in a sharply clipped, more economical style; the action exists not for itself but to provide an arena for the personalities. The dialogue is lovely; not the semi-parody of a lot of film noir, but the words of serious people trying to reveal or conceal themselves. And when all of the threads are pulled together at the end, you really have to marvel at the way there was a plot after all, and it all makes sense, and it was all right there waiting for someone to discover it.

{ THE LAST PICTURE SHOW }

The best scene in *The Last Picture Show* takes place outside town at the "tank," an unlovely pond that briefly breaks the monotony of the flat Texas prairie. Sam the Lion has taken Sonny and the retarded boy Billy fishing there, even though, as Sonny observes, there ain't nothing in the tank but turtles. That's all right with Sam: he doesn't like fish, doesn't like to clean them, doesn't like to smell them. He goes fishing for the scenery.

"Try one?" he says, offering Sonny the makings of a hand-rolled cigarette. And then he begins a wistful monologue, about a time twenty years ago when he brought a girl out to the tank and they swam in it and rode their horses across it and were in love on its banks. The girl had life and fire, but she was already married, and Sam even then was no longer young. As he tells the story, we realize we are listening to the sustaining myth of Sam's life, the vision of beauty that keeps him going in the dying town of Anarene, Texas. The scene has a direct inspiration, I believe, for the writer-director Peter Bogdanovich. I'm sure he was thinking of the monologue in *Citizen Kane* where old Mr. Bernstein remembers a girl with a parasol who he saw once, fifty years ago, and still cherishes in his memory as a beacon of what could have been.

Sam, played by the veteran Western actor Ben Johnson, is the soul of Anarene. He owns the diner, the pool hall, and the Royal theater, and without those three places, there is no place to go in Anarene except to bed, which explains the desperate and lonely adulteries and teenage fumblings that pass for sex. Among those who treasure Sam the Lion are Sonny Crawford (Timothy Bottoms) and Duane Jackson (Jeff Bridges), co-captains of the local football team, which is so bad the local men look at them in disgust and shake their heads.

Bogdanovich's 1971 film, based on the novel by Larry McMurtry, opens on Saturday, November 12, 1951—the eve of the Korean War, and the beginning of the end for movie houses like the Royal, where Sonny grapples in the back row with his plump girlfriend, Charlene (Sharon Taggart), while enviously watching Duane kiss the town beauty, Jacy Farrow (Cybill Shepherd). On the screen are classics like *Red River* and *Wagonmaster*, which speak to the legends of this land, but already the ugly little black-and-white sets in local living rooms are hypnotizing the locals with *Strike It Rich!* and other banal trivialities that have nothing to do with their lives, or anyone's lives.

It always seems too hot or too cold in Anarene. A wind blows down the deserted main street and in through the door of the pool hall. Sam the Lion hunches his shoulders into his sheepskin jacket. Bogdanovich and his cinematographer, Robert Surtees, use a lot of horizontal pans to show the town hunkered down flat against the land; we have the feeling that emptiness surrounds these weathered buildings.

Duane and Sonny presumably have homes to go to, but their lives center around their cars—Sonny's old pickup and Duane's like-new Mercury. In high school, a valiant English teacher (John Hillerman) reads from Keats that truth is beauty and beauty is truth, but truth and beauty seem remote from their lives, and the most wonderful thing that happens to Sonny is that Ruth (Cloris Leachman), the fortyish wife of the football coach, takes him to her bed and treats him fondly. Duane, meanwhile, is toyed with by Jacy, who has her eyes on a rich kid in a nearby city and isn't above getting an invitation to his pool party by leading on the local goofball, Lester (Randy Quaid).

Jacy's parents are what pass for rich in the town, and her mother, Lois (Ellen Burstyn), is still pretty, although she spends too much time drinking on the sofa next to her TV-mesmerized husband. Lois is at least a realist, advising her daughter to sleep with Duane so she'll find out it's not as great as she thinks it is. Lois sometimes sleeps with one of her husband's oil hands, but like Ruth, she places no great faith in sex and yearns instead for tenderness and conversation and someone who has not been defeated by life.

When *The Last Picture Show* opened in 1971, it created a sensation. I saw it on its first engagement in New York, where audiences crowded in with the eagerness reserved, these days, for teenage action pictures. It felt new and old at the same time. Bogdanovich, a film critic and acolyte of Welles, shot in black and white, which gave the film a timelessness, then and now. He used a soundtrack entirely made up of pop songs, which was something new (Scorsese had tried it with his first film, in 1967). It was mostly Hank Williams who provided the soundtrack for these lives, and Bogdanovich used real sources in the scenes for the music—radios, jukeboxes—where "Cold, Cold Heart" and "Why Don't You Love Me (Like You Used to Do)" commented directly on the action.

We had not seen these faces before, except for Ben Johnson and a few other supporting players. Like *Citizen Kane* by his hero, Bogdanovich made a film introducing future stars. Cybill Shepherd was in her first film. Tim Bottoms was in his second but spent his first, *Johnny Got His Gun*, as a soldier who could not see, hear, or speak. Jeff Bridges had done nothing memorable, and Cloris Leachman and Ellen Burstyn caught fire with their roles here. For Leachman and Ben Johnson, who for years gave dependable support in the John Ford stock company, there were supporting-actor Oscars.

The film has an unadorned honesty that came as a jolt after the pyrotechnics of the late 1960s. While the *Easy Rider* generation was celebrating a heedless freedom, Bogdanovich went back to the directness and simplicity of Ford, whom he admired no less than Welles. But *The Last Picture Show* took place long after the heroics of *Red River* and the other classic Westerns. It was based on the first of many novels in which Larry McMurtry (whose hometown of Archer City, Texas, supplied the location of Anarene) charted the Texans who came after the age of heroes.

Seeing the film once again, I was struck by how many of the scenes involve sex, and how little they involve eroticism. Cybill Shepherd's celebrated striptease on a diving board got a lot of attention at the time, but her character coldly uses sex as a way to get the best deal she can out of Anarene. The only real warmth comes from the Leachman character, Ruth, combing Sonny's hair while they're both fully dressed. There is simply no way in this town to touch life and glow. The last ones who knew the secret were Sam the Lion and maybe Genevieve (Eileen Brennan), the waitress at Sam's diner. Sonny and Duane, we suspect, will grow up to drink too much, work too hard, and marry desperate women—unless Duane is killed first in Korea. There is certainly no future for gentle Billy (Sam Bottoms), who always smiles but has no reason to.

The film is above all an evocation of mood. It is about a town with no reason to exist, and people with no reason to live there. The only hope is in transgression, as Ruth knows when she seduces Sonny, the boy half her age. And then he, too, falls briefly under the spell of Jacy, leading to the powerful scene where he returns to Ruth and she hurls the coffeepot against the wall and spills out her soul. (Leachman did that scene in one take, first time, no rehearsal.)

At the end, Bogdanovich shows us brief moving shots of his stars, with titles giving their names and characters. This is a reminder of Welles's credits at the end of *Citizen Kane*. In 1971, those played simply as effective titles. Today, seeing Bridges, Bottoms, Burstyn, Leachman, Brennan, Quaid, Johnson (who died in 1996), and the others thirty-three years later, the images in the credits have a sharp poignancy. There is a line from *Citizen Kane* that comes to mind: "I was there before the beginning . . . and now, I'm here after the end."

Bogdanovich was there after the end, too. In 1990, he gathered most of the members of his original cast for *Texasville*, a sequel set in the early '80s, some thirty years after the period of the original.

{ LAST TANGO IN PARIS }

Reviewing *Last Tango in Paris* in 1972, I wrote that it was one of the great emotional experiences of our time, adding: "It's a movie that exists so resolutely on the level of emotion, indeed, that possibly only Marlon Brando, of all living actors, could have played its lead. Who else can act so brutally and imply such vulnerability and need?"

Now it is 2004 and Brando is dead. As I looked at the film yet again, Brando's most powerful scene resonated for me in an unexpected way. The scene where he confronts the body of his wife, who has committed suicide, and mourns her in an outpouring of rage and grief. "I may be able to comprehend the universe, but I'll never understand the truth about you," he says. He calls her vile names, then is torn by sobs. He tries to wipe off her cosmetic death mask ("Look at you! You're a monument to your mother! You never wore makeup, never wore false eyelashes."). He doesn't understand why she killed herself, why she abandoned him, why she never really loved him in the first place, why he was always more of a guest in her hotel than a husband in her bed.

As I watched this scene, I was struck by a strange notion. I watched it again, this time imagining that Brando was talking to his own dead body—that his anger and love, his blame and grief, were directed toward himself. I'm sure Bernardo Bertolucci, the film's director, did not have this in mind, and of course I cannot know what Brando was thinking. But here was a man who sometimes prostituted his own talent, who frustrated his admirers by seeming to scorn them, whose "eventual monstrous obesity seemed a clear sign of his hatred for Hollywood," as Stanley Kauffmann wrote in the best of the Brando obituaries. This was the greatest movie actor of his time, the author of performances that do honor to the cinema, and yet as Kauffmann notes, he was driven to disparage the profession of acting, which was the instrument of his genius.

His wife in *Last Tango in Paris* owned and ran a little hotel. "It's kind of a dump, but not completely a flophouse," he says, but the film clearly shows it as a place where prostitutes bring their clients. So he was living off a woman who lived off whores. "I moved in for one night and stayed five years," he muses. Can this refer to his love-hate for Hollywood, for acting, for his own career, for the waste he was sometimes compelled to make of his talent? Is it himself that he'll never understand the truth about?

We cannot know. These ideas exist in my mind, and it is wrong to place them in Brando's. But such a narcissistic actor never held more love and grief for anybody else than he held for himself, and I say that not as an insult but as a way of explaining his power: in his best performances, he is sorry for himself. We see the wounded little boy—quite clearly, for example, in the monologue in *Last Tango* recalling his character's childhood. Yes, at the end he was fat. A lot of people get fat. But what a thing to happen to Marlon Brando. How better to destroy an actor's vanity, how better to force us to admire him for himself and not because Stanley Kowalski looked sexy in a torn T-shirt? Did he eat as he did out of self-pity, because he felt he deserved to, because he felt deprived?

The history of *Last Tango in Paris* (1972) has and always will be dominated by Pauline Kael. "The movie breakthrough has finally come," she wrote, in what may be the most famous movie review ever published. "Bertolucci and Brando have altered the face of an art form." She said the film's premiere was an event comparable to the night in 1913 when Stravinsky's *The Rite of Spring* was first performed and ushered in modern music. As it has turned out, *Last Tango* was not a breakthrough but more of an elegy for the kind of film she championed. In the years since, mass Hollywood entertainments have all but crushed art films, which were much more successful then than now. Although pornography documents the impersonal mechanics of sex, few serious films challenge actors to explore its human dimensions; isn't it remarkable that no film since 1972 has been more sexually intimate, revealing, honest, and transgressive than *Last Tango*?

The film begins when Paul (Brando) and Jeanne (Maria Schneider) meet in a Paris apartment they are both considering renting. Paul, we will learn, is planning a move from his dead wife's hotel. Jeanne is planning marriage with Tom (Jean-Pierre Leaud), an insipid young director. Within moments after they meet, Paul forces sudden, needful sex upon her. It would be rape were it not that Jeanne does not object or resist, makes her body available almost with detachment. Indeed, it is rape in Paul's mind, Paul's sexual release seems real, here and throughout the film, but we are never sure what Jeanne feels during their sex. Although she cries during the famous "butter scene," she is not crying about the sex and indeed doesn't seem to be thinking about it.

Paul insists on "no names," no personal histories. Their meetings in the apartment are not dates but occasions for sex, which he defines and she accepts. The pairing of the twenty-year-old girl and the unkempt forty-five-year-old man seems unlikely, but Bertolucci enriches it through their extraordinary dialogue. Brando and Schneider seem natural and spontaneous. Their conversations are rare in not seeming written, not seeming to point to a purpose or conclusion; they are the sorts of things these people might really say, and it's remarkable how relaxed, even playful and sweet, Paul can be with her, when he is not dictating their brutal sexual couplings (at no point can they be said to "make love").

Schneider's performance has been discounted over the years. This is said to be Brando's film. "Both characters are enigmas," I wrote in 1995, "but Brando knows Paul, while Schneider is only walking in Jeanne's shoes." Seeing the film again, I believe I was wrong. Schneider, who plays much of the film completely nude, who is held in close-up during long scenes of extraordinary complexity, who at twenty-two had hardly acted before, shares the film with Brando and meets him in the middle. What Hollywood actress of the time could have played Brando on his own field?

In 1995 I wrote: "He is in scenes as an actor, she is in scenes as a thing." Wrong again. They are both in scenes as actors, but I was seeing her as a thing, fascinated by the disconnect between her adolescent immaturity and voluptuous body. I objectified her, but Paul does not, and neither does the movie. That he keeps his secrets, refuses intimacy, treats her roughly is explained by the scene with the body of his wife, and perhaps by his own experience of sex.

When I interviewed her in 1975, Schneider said she and Brando improvised the bathroom scene—the scene where he shaves while they talk. Brando always liked to have something to do with his hands, some kind of business, and here their dialogue is as close to overheard real conversation as it is probably possible to come. They even misspeak from time to time. There are little pauses and disconnects. The conversation seems to be finding its way.

In a film posited on two characters remaining strangers, Bertolucci and his actors achieve a kind of intimacy the movies rarely approach. Real behavior is permitted; in a scene with his wife's lover, Marcel, Paul coughs, and we sense that is Brando actually coughing, and accepting that he has coughed, and that in other movies actors never cough, except when it is in the screenplay.

The film is not perfect. The character of Tom is a caricature that only grows more distracting over the years. Leaud, the star of Truffaut's autobiographical films, behaves not as if he is a movie director, but as if he's playing one—not in this film but in another film, maybe a musical comedy. The dialogue between Tom and Jeanne seems unnatural and forced. We don't believe it, and we don't care.

What happens in the apartment between Paul and Jeanne is what the movie is about: how sex fulfills two completely different needs. Paul needs to lose himself to mourning and anger, to force his manhood on this stranger because he failed with his wife. Jeanne responds to a man who, despite his pose of detachment, is focused on her, who desperately needs her (if for reasons she does not understand). He is the opposite of Tom, who says he wants to film every moment of her life, but is thinking of his film, not of her. Jeanne senses that Paul needs her as she may never be needed again in all of her life. Her despair at the end is not because of lost romance, but because Paul no longer seems to need her.

Then there is the closing sequence, in which Paul abandons the behavior of the empty room, reveals his name, tells her about his life, seems to desire her in the banal way a middle-aged man might desire a sexy girl. That changes everything. Is it plausible, what she does to him when he follows her into her mother's apartment? I don't know, but I know the movie could not end with both of them still alive. Much has been said about Brando's death scene in *The Godfather*, but what other actor would have thought to park his chewing gum before the most important moment of his life?

THE LAST TEMPTATION
OF CHRIST

Reading my 1988 review of *The Last Temptation of Christ*, I find it is more concerned with theology than cinema. It must have driven Martin Scorsese crazy to read reviews of *The Last Temptation of Christ* in which critics appointed themselves arbiters of the manhood or godliness of Jesus Christ, and scarcely mentioned the direction, the writing, the acting, the images, or Peter Gabriel's harsh, mournful music. Or perhaps Scorsese understood. It is useful to remember the temper of the time. The film was a target of the Christian right, which accused Scorsese of blasphemy and worse. It was pulled from the MGM production schedule; after Universal reactivated the project at a smaller budget, Scorsese was targeted by death threats and the jeremiads of TV evangelists.

On vacation in London, I was invited to preview the film at a private screening for my eyes only. This was not a perk. It was a security measure. I was begged not to tell anyone the title of the movie, or even mention that a print was in England. Stopping in New York on the way home, I was directed to a pay phone on Madison Avenue, called the number I was given, and followed instructions to the town house where Scorsese was living. I was greeted at the door by a security guard.

Perhaps it was inevitable that my review defended the film against charges of heresy. Both Scorsese and I had attended Catholic schools and fell easily into the language of religion. We spoke often about Catholicism, which in pre–Vatican II days was a seductive labyrinth of logic, ritual, vision, and guilt. Pauline Kael said the most creative American directors of the 1970s (she listed Scorsese, Altman, and Coppola) benefitted from being raised within traditional Catholic imagery. Scorsese's frequent writing partner Paul Schrader grew up in a no less intense Calvinist environment. To Scorsese's image in *Mean Streets* of Charlie holding his hand over a candle flame and imagining the fires of hell, we can add Schrader's mother stabbing him with a pin and telling him hell was a million times worse and it never ended.

But all of that theological debate was twenty years ago. Watching the film again, I realized it was Scorsese's first shot largely outdoors since *Boxcar Bertha* (1972). He is a filmmaker of the city, of bars, clubs, bedrooms, kitchens, nightclubs, boxing rings, pool halls, and taxis. On location in Morocco, he found vast, hostile expanses of hard soil, distant mountains, and struggling vegetation. The sun is merciless. This is an Old Testament land, not hospitable to the message of love and forgiveness.

The character of Christ himself is radically different from most previous film portraits. He is a weary, self-doubting individual, not always willing to carry the souls of man on his shoulders. There are times when he seems not to know or believe he is the son of God, and when he does, he uses that knowledge as a reason to rebuke his mother and the memory of Joseph. He berates and hectors his followers, and confides mostly in Judas, who is radically recast in this story as a good man who is only following instructions. The film follows the bold revisionism of Nikos Kazantzakis, whose novel was placed on the church's index of forbidden books.

The film is indeed technically blasphemous. I have been persuaded of this by a thoughtful essay by Steven D. Greydanus of the National Catholic Register, a mainstream writer who simply and concisely explains why. I mention this only to argue that a film can be blasphemous, or anything else that the director desires, and we should only hope that it be as good as the filmmaker can make it, and convincing in its interior purpose. Certainly useful things can be said about Jesus Christ by presenting him in a non-orthodox way. There is a long tradition of such revisionism, including the foolishness of *The Da Vinci Code*. The story by Kazantzakis, Scorsese, and Schrader grapples with the central mystery of Jesus, that he was both God and man, and uses the freedom of fiction to explore the implications of such a paradox.

In the title role, Willem Dafoe creates a man who is the embodiment of dutiful masochism. Whether he is right or wrong about his divinity, he is prepared to pay the price, and that kind of faith is more courageous than certainty would be. Even in the last half of the film, when Jesus begins performing miracles, he seems almost an onlooker at his own accomplishments, taking little joy in them.

A key shot is when Michael Ballhaus's camera pushes past Jesus into the sepulcher of the dead Lazarus. It is black inside, contrasted with the blinding sun, and then blacker and blacker until the whole screen is filled with blackness, and held for a few seconds. I take this as an emblem of Jesus's experience of his miracles, during which he is reaching into an unknowable and frightening void.

Judas is the film's other vivid character, played by Harvey Keitel as, in a sense, Christ's manager. He does strategy, issues ultimatums, is the closest friend. One way the story commits sacrilege is by suggesting Judas was doing his duty by betraying Christ. Someone had to. Jesus doesn't have close relationships with any of the other disciples, who he seems to believe will follow along of their own accord. He is closer, I suppose, with Mary Magdalene, but their conversations seem guarded or cryptic. Scorsese's attention is more on Christ's inner struggle than his worldly role.

I am left after the film with the conviction that it is as much about Scorsese as about Christ. In his films, he performs miracles, but for years could be heard to despair that each film would be his last. The Roman Catholic Church was for him like a heavenly father to whom he had a duty, but he did not always fulfill it. These speculations may be wild and unfounded, ideas I am taking to him rather than finding in him, but particularly during Scorsese's earlier years I believe the church played a larger role in his inner life than was generally realized. Talking with me after one of his divorces, he said, "I am living in sin, and I will go to hell because of it." I asked him if he really, truly believed that. "Yes," he said, "I do."

What makes *The Last Temptation of Christ* one of his great films is not that it is true about Jesus but that it is true about Scorsese. Like countless others, he has found aspects of the Christ story that speak to him. This is the Jesus of his two most autobiographical characters, Charlie in *Mean Streets* and J. R. in *Who's That Knocking at My Door?* Both of those characters were played by Keitel. Interesting that he choose Keitel this time to play Judas. Perhaps Judas is Scorsese's autobiographical character in *The Last Temptation of Christ*. Certainly not the Messiah, but the mortal man walking beside him, worrying about him, lecturing him, wanting him to be better, threatening him, confiding in him, prepared to betray him if he must. Christ is the film, and Judas is the director.

{ LATE SPRING }

Shukichi is a professor, a widower, absorbed in his work. His unmarried daughter, Noriko, runs his household for him. Both are perfectly content with this arrangement until the old man's sister declares that her niece should get married. Noriko is, after all, in her mid-twenties; in Japan in 1949, a single woman that old is approaching the end of her shelf life. His sister warns the professor that after his death Noriko will be left alone in the world; it is his duty to push her out of the nest and find a husband who can support her. The professor reluctantly agrees. When his daughter opposes any idea of marriage, he tells her he is also going to remarry. That is a lie, but he will sacrifice his own comfort for his daughter's future. She marries.

And that, essentially, is what happens on the surface in Yasujiro Ozu's *Late Spring* (1949). What happens at deeper levels is angry, passionate, and—wrong, we feel, because the father and the daughter are forced to do something neither one of them wants to do, and the result will be resentment and unhappiness. Only the aunt will emerge satisfied, and Noriko's husband, perhaps, although we never see him. "He looks like Gary Cooper, around the mouth, but not the top part," the aunt tells her.

It is typical of Ozu that he never shows us the man Noriko will marry. In his next film, *Early Summer* (1951), the would-be bride in an arranged marriage sees the groom only in a golfing photo that obscures his face. Ozu is not telling traditional romantic stories. He is intently watching families where the status quo is threatened by an outsider; what matters to the brides is not what they are beginning but what they are ending. The women in both films are named Noriko, and they are both played by Setsuko Hara, a great star who would drop everything to work with Ozu. When the studio asked Ozu to consider a different actress for the second film, he refused to make it without Hara.

In *Early Summer*, Noriko lives with her brother, his family, and their aged parents. She has no desire to marry—at least, not the golfer. The same actor, Chishu Ryu (1904–93), plays the professor in the first film and the brother in the second; in Ozu's *Tokyo Story* (1953), he plays the grandfather and Hara is his daughter-in-law. In all three films he looks the correct age for his character; how he did that so convincingly between the ages of forty-five and forty-nine is beyond my ability to explain.

Late Spring began a cycle of Ozu films about families; the seasons in the title refer to the times in the lives of the characters, as in his final film, *An Autumn Afternoon* (1962). Did he make the same film again and again? Not at all. *Late Spring* and *Early Summer* are startlingly different. In the second, Noriko takes advantage of a conversational opening to overturn the entire plot; to avoid marrying the golfer, she accepts a man she has known for a long time—a widower with a child, whose mother's dearest wish is that her son marry Noriko. The man goes along with his mother's plan, indeed is pleased once he absorbs it; the meddling woman in this case has made two people happier.

Late Spring tells a story that becomes sadder the more you think about it. There is a tension in the film between Noriko's smile and her feelings. Her smile is often a mask. She smiles brightly during a strange early scene where she talks with a family friend, Onodera, who has remarried after the death of his wife. Such a second marriage is "filthy and foul," she says, and it disgusts her. She smiles, he laughs. Yet she is very serious.

Onodera tells the professor it's his duty to marry off Noriko, and suggests an excellent prospect: Hattori, the professor's assistant. Noriko and Hattori take a bicycle trip to the beach, and later have dinner; we think perhaps such a match will work. But when Shukichi suggests it to his daughter, she laughs and tells him Hattori is already engaged. How and when she learned that is left offscreen; what we do see is Hattori inviting her to a concert, her telling him she doesn't want to make "trouble," and Hattori at the concert with his hat on an empty seat. There is the possibility that Noriko could have married Hattori after all; she likes him, he likes her, he might leave his fiancé; the concert invitation is crucial, but she will not leave her father. This is her sacrifice, to match his later in the film.

Now Masa (Haruko Sugimura), her aunt, comes up with a new candidate, the Gary Cooper lookalike named Satake. Noriko tells her friend, "I think he looks more like the local electrician." Realizing that Noriko will not willingly leave her father, Masa proposes to the professor that he marry a younger widow, Mrs. Miwa. The professor is as happy as his daughter to remain single, but understands Masa's scheme to deceive Noriko.

Ozu brings everything to a head during an extraordinary scene at a Noh performance, where Noriko sits next to her father. The professor nods across the room to Mrs. Miwa, who smiles and nods back. Noriko observes this and loses all interest in the play; her head bows in sadness, and afterward she tells her father, "I have to go away somewhere," and all but flees from his side.

There's a later scene of uncomfortable confrontation. "Will you marry?" Noriko asks him. "Um," he says, with the slightest nod. She asks him three or four different ways. "Um." Finally, "That woman we saw today?" "Um." He defends arranged marriages: "Your mother wasn't happy at first. I found her weeping in the kitchen many times." Not the best argument for a father trying to convince his daughter to marry.

Masa the aunt, having proposed the new groom, now acts as if it is a settled thing, and begins to plan the approaching marriage. Noriko goes along, smiling as always. We see her beautiful but sad in her traditional wedding dress, but we do not see her wedding or meet her husband. Instead, we come home alone with the professor, who admits his own marriage plans were "the biggest lie I ever told." In one of the saddest scenes ever filmed by Ozu, he sits alone in his room and begins to peel an apple.

The peel grows longer and longer until his hand stops and it falls to the floor and he bows his head in grief.

The professor's decision is often described as his "sacrifice" of her. And so it is, but not one he wants to make. Nor does she want to leave. "I love helping you," she says, "Marriage wouldn't make me any happier. You can remarry, but I want to be at your side." There is an academic paper exploring the possibility of repressed incest in *Late Spring*, but I doubt that occurred to Ozu; Noriko has a hidden well of disgust about sex, I believe, which is revealed in her strong feelings about remarriage—once is bad enough. She wants to stay safe in her home with her father, forever.

Late Spring is one of the best two or three films Ozu ever made, with *Early Summer* deserving comparison. Both films use his distinctive later visual style, which includes precise compositions for a camera that almost never moves, a point of view often representing the eye level of a person sitting on a tatami mat, and punctuation through cutaways to unrelated exteriors. He almost always used only one lens, a 50mm, which he said was the closest to the human eye.

Here he wordlessly uses time and space to establish the routine and serenity of the household arrangements between father and daughter, in a sequence showing them coming and going, upstairs and down, through the rooms and central corridors of their house. They know their way around each other. Late in the film, threatened by the marriage, Noriko keeps picking things up and putting them on a table, compulsively acting out her domestic happiness.

So much happens out of sight in the film, implied but not shown. Noriko smiles but is not happy. Her father passively accepts what he hates is happening. The aunt is complacent, implacable, maddening. She gets her way. It is universally believed, just as in a Jane Austen novel, that a woman of a certain age is in want of a husband. *Late Spring* is a film about two people who desperately do not believe this, and about how they are undone by their tact, their concern for each other, and their need to make others comfortable by seeming to agree with them.

{ LEOLO }

I came in after a midnight screening this year at Cannes, and found Richard Corliss leaning over a yellow legal pad in the dining room of the Hotel Splendid. He was, he said, working on the list of the hundred greatest films of all time, which he and Richard Schickel would soon publish in *Time* magazine. "Which one are you writing about now?" I asked. "*Leolo*," he said. Yes. *Leolo*. A film that stirs in the shadows of memory for everyone who has ever seen it, a film that cannot be classified and can hardly be explained, a film left orphaned by the early death of its director, Jean-Claude Lauzon, who died with his girlfriend while piloting his Cessna in northern Canada in 1997.

He made only two features, *Night Zoo* (1987) and *Leolo* (1992). He could have made more, but spent his time shooting commercials, or fishing. He was believed to be the most gifted young filmmaker in Canada, but when the elder statesman Norman Jewison offered him a job directing Gene Hackman in a thriller, he turned it down, rudely. Ken Turan of the *Los Angeles Times* believes *Leolo* might have won the Palme d'Or at Cannes in 1992 if Lauzon hadn't made an obscene suggestion to Jamie Lee Curtis, one of the jurors. Turan tells me he heard the story from Lauzon himself: "He found himself next to Jamie Lee at the buffet at the Hotel du Cap. He introduced himself and said, as I remember it, 'What the boy in the film does to the piece of liver, I want to do to you.'" The only caveat raised by this story is that Jamie Lee Curtis is not a shrinking violet and might as plausibly have laughed as taken offense.

I met Lauzon once, at lunch after *Night Zoo* premiered at Cannes. He was long haired, outspoken, a little wild, ready to offend or take offense. His movie was about an ex-con whose father is dying; the old man's deathbed wish is to shoot an elephant, and so they break into the Montreal Zoo with his dad in a wheelchair. You get the feeling, after seeing that film and *Leolo*, that they are not a million miles removed from reality. There was mental illness all through his family, his childhood was not easy, and his hero Leolo says, "They say I am French Canadian, but because I dream, I am not. They say he is my father, but I know I am not his son because he is crazy. Because I dream, I know I am not."

Because he dreams, he thinks he is Italian, and the man posing as his father is not his real father. The boy in the movie is born Leo Lauzon, but renames himself Leo Lozone. In his dreams, his real father is a Sicilian who masturbates on a box full of tomatoes destined for Quebec. His mother falls on the tomatoes in a Montreal street market, squishing them, and nine months later Leolo is born. He spends the entire movie trying to get his family to stop calling him Leo.

If this sounds like a chapter from *Everything You Always Wanted to Know About Sex*, the film itself is not only comic but darkly angry. It centers on the adventures of Leolo (Maxime Collin) around the age of twelve, when he is not a cute teenager but a tortured and introverted boy in a family seething with insanity. His family members cycle in and out of the nearby madhouse as if it's a spa, and homelife is dominated by the belief of his father (Roland Blouin) that all human health depends upon a daily bowel movement. "Push, Leo, push!" urges his mother (Ginette Reno), a fat, good-hearted matriarch who loves the boy but is helpless to understand him. The house is tyrannized by Grandfather (Julien Guiomar), whose toenails Leolo is made to trim with his own teeth.

The boy at this age discovers masturbation, and becomes fixated by the comely neighbor, Bianca (Giuditta Del Vecchio). She is a few years too old for Leolo and many years too young for Grandfather, who nevertheless pays her to bathe and comfort him. Leolo spies on them through a window in the ceiling, and later uses this vantage point in his plan to use an elaborate system of levers and pulleys to murder the old man. Well, Grandfather has it coming; he once tried to drown Leolo in a plastic wading pool, although for Leolo the experience was not without benefits because he experienced wondrous visions.

If the movie sounds depraved and depressing to you, it is because I have failed to convey the deep amusement and even love that Lauzon conveys in his material. Leolo reminded me of the sex-crazed adolescents in Fellini's *Amarcord*, with the difference that Fellini's memories were nostalgic and his hero's family was eccentric in a lovable way. Leolo uses dreams to deny the reality of his family, and sees himself in a struggle to survive its demented grip. There seems to be no escape. His brother, Fernand (Yves Montmarquette), is humiliated by a bully, spends months turning himself into a muscle-bound bodybuilder, and then is humiliated again. "That day," says the film's narrator, speaking for Leolo, "I understood that fear lived in our deepest being."

What small portion of hope Leolo finds in his childhood comes from one book, the only book his family possesses. It comes into his life one day when an old man (Pierre Bourgault) visits their home and uses the book to prop up one leg of an off-balance kitchen table. Leolo reads it at night by the light from the refrigerator, wearing gloves and a muffler. The man, called the Word Tamer in the narration, lives in a room jammed with books and maps, and rummages in garbage cans for treasure. That is how he finds and reads Leolo's journal, which is written a page at a time and then thrown away. It is a good question whether he, Leolo, or the journal is speaking in the narration: all three, I think.

The technical brilliance of the film is astonishing. Lauzon was filled with quirks and impulses, sudden inspirations and wild inventions. Some directors with such hyperactive imagination create movies that are elaborate and yet empty; Lauzon is so motivated by his resentments and desires that everything he creates is pressed into the cause and filled with passion. There are scenes that cannot possibly exist, and yet they do. Set decoration that is a fantasy and yet insists on being a reality. A soundtrack that incorporates opera, Tom Waits, the Rolling Stones, and what sounds like Gregorian chant. Music that evokes the presence of evil so clearly that it could be a theme from *The Exorcist*. Yet everyday Montreal street life bursting with life and joy.

Reading Neil Lee's online memoir of Lauzon, I was reminded of the childhood of Francois Truffaut. Lee writes: "Lauzon's childhood was a rowboat awash in a sea of madness, driven by winds of psychosis . . . nearly all of his family—with exception of his mother—were institutionalized at one point or another. Lauzon himself escaped a life of petty street crime only through the intervention of Andre Petrowski, then the head of the NFB's French film distribution. It is to him that *Leolo* is dedicated, and rightly so, for Petrowski was the man responsible for guiding Lauzon out of the gutter of his youth and into filmmaking."

Petrowski of the National Film Board is paralleled in Truffaut's life by Andre Bazin, the film critic who guided Truffaut out of juvenile delinquency and into film. Lauzon was "a flirt, a troublemaker," Cameron Bailey remembers in a memoir. "He made demands on producers and festival directors. He didn't behave." It is perhaps not tragic that he made only two features, but remarkable that he made any at all.

When a great movie exists all by itself, it is in danger of being misplaced. We tend to want it to belong to the lifework of a director, or in the mainstream of a genre. Yet some films are singular: Laughton's *Night of the Hunter* or Jodorowsky's *El Topo*. Either you find it or you never do. You have to approach it directly, not through other films. The experience of seeing *Leolo* is, for me, like watching a high-wire act. How can Lauzon keep his balance when he careens so wildly to one extreme and then another? How can he create these characters, so grotesque, and make them human, and have sympathy for them? How can Leolo be so weird and inward, so angry and subversive, and yet somehow so noble? How can this story hurtle itself in every direction, and yet find a destination? I don't know if Jean-Claude Lauzon finished *Leolo* and decided he had nothing else he needed to say. But if he did, I can understand that.

{THE LONG GOODBYE}

Robert Altman's *The Long Goodbye* (1973) attacks film noir with three of his most cherished tools: whimsy, spontaneity, and narrative perversity. He is always the most youthful of directors, and here he gives us the youngest of Philip Marlowes, the private eye as a Hardy boy. Marlowe hides in the bushes, pokes his nose up against a window, complains like a spoiled child, and runs after a car driven by the sexy heroine, crying out "Mrs. Wade! Mrs. Wade!" As a counterweight, the movie contains two startling acts of violence; both blindside us, and neither is in the original Raymond Chandler novel.

Altman began with a screenplay by Leigh Brackett, the legendary writer of *The Big Sleep* (1946), the greatest of the many films inspired by Marlowe. On that one her co-writer was William Faulkner. There is a famous story that they asked Chandler who killed one of the characters (or was it suicide?). Chandler's reply: "I don't know." There is a nod to that in *The Long Goodbye* when a character who was murdered in the book commits suicide in the movie.

Certainly the plot of *The Long Goodbye* is a labyrinth not easily negotiated. Chandler's 1953 novel leads Marlowe into a web of deception so complex you could call it arbitrary. The book is not about a story but about the code of a private eye in a corrupt world. It is all about mood, personal style, and language. In her adaptation, Brackett dumps sequences from Chandler, adds some of her own (she sends Marlowe to Mexico twice), reassigns killings, and makes it almost impossible to track a suitcase filled with a mobster's money.

I went through the film a shot at time at the Conference on World Affairs at the University of Colorado, sitting in the dark with several hundred others as we asked ourselves, What do we know, how do we know it, and is it true? Many of our questions center on the rich, sex-drenched Eileen (Nina Van Pallandt). Does she desire the death of her husband, Roger Wade, an alcoholic writer played by the gruff old bear Sterling Hayden? Or does she only want free of him? What about that seductive dinner she serves Marlowe (Elliott Gould) on the night Wade walks into the ocean? Does she intend to sleep with Marlowe? She does in the novel, and he is later part of her alibi when she kills Wade and makes it look like suicide. But here she doesn't kill Wade. What is the link connecting Terry Lennox (the baseball star Jim Bouton), Eileen, and the gangster Marty Augustine (Mark Rydell)? Does Augustine owe Wade money, as he claims to Marlowe, or does Wade owe Augustine money, as Wade implies in a Freudian slip? What is the exact connection between any money owed to anyone and the money in the suitcase? Only a final, blunt speech by Lennox, Marlowe's unworthy friend, answers some of our questions.

Elliott Gould says on the DVD that Altman made many changes to Brackett's screenplay, but that when she saw the movie not long before she died, she said she was "more than satisfied." One change is to make Philip Marlowe, that laconic loner with a code of honor, into what Altman and Gould privately called "Rip Van Marlowe." When he awakens at the beginning of the movie, he's a 1953 character in a 1973 world. He wears a dark suit, white shirt, and narrow tie in a world of flower power and nude yoga. He chain smokes; no one else smokes. He is loyal to Terry Lennox and considers him his friend, but the movie establishes their friendship only by showing them playing liar's poker, and Lennox is no friend. Marlowe carries a $5,000 bill for most of the movie, but never charges for any of his services.

He is a knight errant, and like Don Quixote imperfectly understands the world he inhabits.

The earlier movie Marlowes (Humphrey Bogart, James Caan, James Garner, Robert Mitchum, Robert Montgomery, Dick Powell) are terse and guarded. They talk, as Chandler wrote, "with rude wit, a lively sense of the grotesque, a disgust for sham, and a contempt for pettiness." And they talk a lot, because they narrate the novels. Gould's Marlowe has these qualities, but they emerge in meandering dialogue that plays as a bemused commentary to himself. In the novel, Marlowe has no pets, but here he has a cat, and in the famous pre-credit opening sequence he attempts to convince the cat he is supplying its favorite cat food, but the cat is not fooled. In a movie that throws large chunks of plot overboard, there is no reason for this sequence, except that it establishes Marlowe as a man who is more loyal to his cat than anyone is to him.

The plot can be summarized in a few words, or endlessly. The rich playboy Lennox asks Marlowe to drive him to Tijuana. Marlowe does, and is questioned by the cops and jailed after Lennox's wife is found beaten to death. Released by the cops after Lennox's suicide in Mexico, Marlowe is visited by the gangster Marty Augustine and his goons. Augustine thinks Marlowe has money Lennox was carrying. In one of the most shocking moments in movie history, he commits an act of cruelty and says, "Now that's someone I love. Think what could happen to you."

Marlowe follows him to the Malibu beach house of the writer Roger Wade and his wife, Eileen, and is later hired by Eileen to track down Roger after he runs away to a shady drying-out sanitarium. How are Lennox, the Wades, and Augustine connected? I don't think the answer to that question concerns Altman nearly as much as the look and feel of the film. He wants to show a private eye from the noir era blundering through a plot he is perhaps too naive to understand. The movie's visual strategy underlines his confusion. Altman and his cinematographer, Vilmos Zsigmond, "flashed" the color film with carefully calculated extra light, to give it a faded, pastel quality, as if Marlowe's world refuses to reveal vivid colors and sharp definition. Most of the shots are filmed through foregrounds that obscure: panes of glass, trees and shrubbery, architectural details, all clouding Marlowe's view (and ours). The famous Altman overlapping dialogue gives the impression that Marlowe doesn't pick up on everything around him. Far from resenting the murkiness in his world, Marlowe repeats the catchphrase "It's all right with me." The line was improvised by Gould, and he and Altman decided to use it throughout the story as an ironic refrain.

There is another refrain: the title theme, which is essentially the only music heard in the film. Altman uses it again and again, with many different performers (even a Mexican marching band, with the sheet music pinned to the shirt of the man in front of them). At Boulder, the musician Dave Grusin, who worked on the film, told us Altman gathered a group of musicians on a sound stage and had them spend an evening playing around with different arrangements of the song. Why did Altman only use the one song? I've heard a lot of theories, of which the most convincing is that it amused him.

The visuals and sound undergo a shift after the suicide of Roger Wade. There is a scene on the beach where Marlowe pesters people with questions and accuses them of dishonesty; he sounds like a child, a drunk, or both. But then color begins to saturate the pale visuals, the foregrounds no longer obscure, characters start talking one at a time, and finally in the vivid sunlight of Mexico, Marlowe is able to see and hear clearly, and act decisively.

Casting is crucial in film noir, because the actors have to arrive already bearing their fates. Altman's actors are as unexpected as they are inevitable. Sterling Hayden, a ravaged giant, roars and blusters on his way to his grave. As his wife, Altman cast Nina Van Pallandt, then famous as the mistress of Clifford Irving, author of the celebrated fake autobiography of Howard Hughes. She could act, but she did more than act, she embodied a Malibu beach temptress. Mark Rydell, the director, seems to be channeling Martin Scorsese's verbal style in a performance that uses elaborate politeness as a mask for savagery. And Elliott Gould is a Marlowe thrust into a story where everybody else knows their roles. He wanders clueless and complaining, and then suddenly understands exactly what he must do.

The Long Goodbye should not be anybody's first film noir, nor their first Altman movie. Most of its effect comes from the way it pushes against the genre, and the way Altman undermines the premise of all private eye movies, which is that the hero can walk down mean streets, see clearly, and tell right from wrong. The man of honor from 1953 is lost in the hazy narcissism of 1973, and it's not all right with him.

{ MAGNOLIA }

M*agnolia* is a film of sadness and loss, of lifelong bitterness, of children harmed, and adults destroying themselves. As the narrator tells us near the end, "We may be through with the past, but the past is never through with us." In this wreckage of lifetimes, there are two figures, a policeman and a nurse, who do what they can to offer help, hope, and love.

That may not be the *Magnolia* you recall. It was not quite the film I recalled, either, and now that I have seen it again, my admiration has only deepened. On its release in 1999, our focus was perhaps distracted by the theme of coincidence, the intersecting storylines, and above all the astonishing coup with which Paul Thomas Anderson ended his film. Nor was the film a melancholy dirge; it was entertaining, even funny, always fascinating.

The central theme is cruelty to children, and its lasting effect. This is closely linked to a loathing or fear of behaving as we are told, or think, that we should. There are many major characters, but in the film's 180-minute running time, there is time to develop them all and obtain performances that seem to center on moments of deep self-revelation. Let's begin with two smart kids.

One is now an adult, still calling himself "Quiz Kid Donnie Smith" (William H. Macy). He was briefly famous as a child on a TV show and still expects people to remember him. Now he works in a furniture store, is a drunk, desperately needs money to get braces on his teeth in the forlorn hope that they will attract the bartender he has a crush on—who also wears braces. He has an outburst about his childhood, but his most touching moment is when he cries out that he knows he has love, he knows he can love, he knows he is worth loving.

The other smart kid, still about nine or ten, is Stanley Spector (Jeremy Blackman), star genius on the TV show *What Do Kids Know?* He has all the answers. But on one crucial segment, he refuses to perform because, refused a trip to the toilet, he has wet his pants and refuses to stand up. His father browbeats him.

The show's emcee is Jimmy Gator (Philip Baker Hall), who has learned he has two months to live. He hasn't seen Claudia (Melora Walters), his daughter from his second marriage, for ten years. She believes he molested her. He doesn't remember. Now she is a hopeless cocaine addict. The policeman (John C. Reilly) who appears at her door doesn't notice her nervous tics and asks her out on a date, which ends by them both confessing deep shame. And later the same cop observes Quiz Kid Donnie Smith trying to scale a pole to break into the furniture store, hears his confession, forgives him, helps him make restitution.

The show is produced by "Big Earl" Partridge (Jason Robards). His long-estranged son is the motivational huckster Frank Mackey (Tom Cruise), who fills hotel conference rooms with lectures on how to conquer women. When he was a child, his father abandoned the boy and his mother, and Frank had to nurse her through death by cancer. Now his father is dying of the same disease, attended by Phil the nurse (Philip Seymour Hoffman). His second wife (Julianne Moore), who married him for money, now finds she loves him and regrets that she cheated on him. The old man mumbles in pain to his nurse that he truly loved his first wife and hates himself for cheating on her.

But a plot description could take up all my space, and more. I have given enough to suggest the way the sins of the parents are visited on the children, how so many people lead lives of desperation, how a few try to help. The astonishing thing about this film, written and directed by Anderson when he was only twenty-eight (and had made *Boogie Nights* two years earlier and *Hard Eight* three), is that it is so wise and sympathetic. He sees that we all have our reasons.

As an act of filmmaking, it draws us in and doesn't let go. It begins deceptively, with a little documentary about amazing coincidences (including the scuba diver scooped by a firefighting plane and dumped on a forest fire). This is narrated by magician and spellbinder Ricky Jay, whose book *Learned Pigs and Fireproof Women* can be seen open before the studious little Stanley. Jay's voice appears again at the end, to remind us that coincidences and strange events do happen, and they are as real as everything else. If you could stand back far enough, in fact, everything would be revealed as a coincidence. What we call "coincidences" are limited to the ones we happen to notice.

Is the film therefore defending itself against the way its lives are intertwined? Not at all. I think it is arguing that we must mind our behavior, because it has an effect far beyond our ability to witness. A small boy, abandoned by his father, left to care for his dying mother, grows up into a complete fraud who gets rich by teaching men how to mistreat women. Why does he hate women instead of men? Tom Cruise has a scene at the deathbed of his father (deliberately framed to evoke Brando at his dead wife's body in *Last Tango in Paris*), and his hands are so tightly clenched the fingers seem bloodless. His hatred is for this man, but how has it been transferred to women?

His breakdown during a lecture is mirrored by little Stanley and Jimmy Gator, who both find themselves unable to perform on the TV show. And the second wife of Jason Robards (Julianne Moore) confesses to his nurse but cannot confess to the old man and seeks another way out. And Claudia cannot behave as she should on a date. And earlier that night, the cop has shamed himself by losing his gun and being unable to make an arrest. And Quiz Kid Donnie cannot tell another man that he loves him.

In one beautiful sequence, Anderson cuts between most of the major characters all simultaneously singing Aimee Mann's "It's Not Going to Stop." A directorial flourish? You know what? I think it's a coincidence. Unlike many other "hypertext movies" with interlinking plots, *Magnolia* seems to be using the device in a deeper, more philosophical way. Anderson sees these people joined at a level below any possible knowledge, down where fate and destiny lie. They have been joined by their actions and their choices.

And all leads to the remarkable, famous sequence near the film's end when it rains frogs. Yes. Countless frogs, still alive, all over Los Angeles, falling from the sky. That this device has sometimes been joked about puzzles me. I find it a way to elevate the whole story into a larger realm of inexplicable but real behavior. We need something beyond the human to add another dimension. Frogs have rained from the sky eight times this century, but never mind the facts. Attend instead to Exodus 8:2, which is cited on a placard in the film: "And if thou refuse to let them go, behold, I will smite your whole territory with frogs." Let who go? In this case, I believe, it refers not to people, but to fears, shames, sins.

Magnolia is one of those rare films that works in two entirely different ways. In one sense, it tells absorbing stories, filled with detail, told with precision and not a little humor. In another sense, it is a parable. The message of the parable, as with all good parables, is expressed not in words but in emotions. After we have felt the pain of these people, and felt the love of the policeman and the nurse, we have been taught something intangible, but necessary to know. That Paul Thomas Anderson thinks and creates in this way is proven again in his *There Will Be Blood* (2007). It is another film with an enigmatic ending, one that *Magnolia* teaches me I will have to think more carefully about.

{ THE MARRIAGE OF MARIA BRAUN }

—How long were you married?

—I am still married.

—I mean, it didn't last long, did it?

—Yes, it did: half a day and a whole night.

Bombs fell as Maria was married to a soldier named Hermann Braun, with the wedding party scrambling for safety. Then came more years of the war. Whatever happened to Maria Braun during those years created a woman who is strong and cruel, sad and indomitable. She is so loyal to her husband of less than a day that she kills for him, and so pitiless to her lover of many years that she drives him to death.

All the time she is keeping score: nylons and cigarettes at first, then a good job, fashionable clothes, a house in the suburbs, expensive restaurants. At the end, her desperate lover, who is also her boss and has made her rich, tries to get a word with her; as he talks, she continues to enter numbers into an adding machine.

The Marriage of Maria Braun was made by Rainer Werner Fassbinder in 1979, near the end of a career so short and dazzling that it still seems incredible he did so much and died so young. Fassbinder made at least thirty features, or many more if you count his television productions, including the fifteen-hour miniseries *Berlin Alexanderplatz*, and he did it all between 1969 and his death at age thirty-seven in 1982.

Some of his early work looks homemade ("We didn't know what we were doing, and it was like a game," remembers Hanna Schygulla, who starred in twenty of his films). Despite his production of two to three films a year, he was not a hit-and-run improviser, but a stylist who often worked with cinematographer Michael Ballhaus to create elegant, mannered visuals. His great influence, he said, was the German director Douglas Sirk, who fled Hitler and in Hollywood made a series of silky melodramas (*Imitation of Life, Written on the Wind, All That Heaven Allows*) in which, one critic observed, the characters seemed to glide within invisible glass walls that kept them from touching. Fassbinder's later films looked like elegant studio productions, although even *Maria Braun*, perhaps his most expensive, cost less than $1 million.

Fassbinder's world was one in which sex, ego, and money drove his characters to cruelty, sadism, and self-destruction. It is never difficult to discover what they want, or puzzling to see how they go about it. His occasional gentle characters, like the old woman in *Ali: Fear Eats the Soul* (1974), are eaten alive. The suggestion is that the war years and the postwar years wounded the German psyche so profoundly that the survivors wanted what they wanted, now, on their terms. Fassbinder himself was cruel and distant to those around him, particularly those who loved him, and in Maria Braun, he created an indelible monster who is perversely fascinating because she knows exactly what she is doing and explains it to her victims while it is being done.

After the brief opening wedding scene, the story rejoins Maria and her mother immediately after World War II, when they are sharing a flat carved out of a bombed building. She believes her husband, Hermann (Klaus Lowitsch), is dead, although she haunts rail stations with his photograph. The population is starving and desperate; when an American GI tosses away a cigarette butt, a dozen Germans scramble for it. Maria applies for a job in a nightclub for American soldiers; it's located in a high school gym where she once attended school, and she mounts the parallel bars, which are still in place, and more or less orders the owner to give her the job. Her mother (Gisela Uhlen) alters the hem of her skirt while fretting that Maria's father would have been heartbroken to see his daughter as a bar girl; then she says she hopes somebody gives Maria some nylons.

The B-girl joint is the first step on Maria's relentless climb to success. We follow her from about 1946 to the mid-1950s. There is a black American soldier she is fond of (they share the movie's only scene of physical affection), but when her husband unexpectedly returns and finds them in bed, she settles the matter by breaking a bottle over the GI's head. She did not plan to kill him, but he's dead. Her husband tells the court he did it and is sentenced to prison. Maria remains fiercely loyal to this absent spouse, who is essentially a stranger, for all the rest of the film; perhaps it is her form of loyalty to Germany in its defeat.

The most sympathetic character is Oswald (Ivan Desny), a manufacturer who sat out the war in comfort, perhaps in exile, and has returned to take over the reins of his business from his faithful accountant, Senkenberg (Hark Bohm). Maria crashes first class during a train ride, forces Oswald to notice her, tells him to hire her, and asks him to sleep with her: "I wanted to make the first move before you could," she tells him, and later, "You're not having an affair with me. I'm having an affair with you."

Poor Oswald would marry her, but she is married. She calls him up when she wants sex, humiliates him, says she is fond of him, and then treats him distantly. Yet all the time, she is an ideal employee, quickly rising from "personal assistant" to the company's key decision-maker. At one business meeting, translating the English of a customer, she changes it to reflect what she thinks Oswald should hear in order to do what she has decided he should do.

The cinematographer Ballhaus worked with Fassbinder on a dozen films in nine years, then "burned out," resigned, and started working for Martin Scorsese, who by comparison "was like a dream." *Maria Braun* was their final film together; observe how they like to keep the camera moving, through elegant setups in which characters and locations are arranged so that the fluid visuals flow from long shots through close-ups without cutting, often moving behind walls, peering through doors and windows, looking around posts, so that the characters seem jammed into the space around them.

Notice, too, the gradual evolution of Maria Braun from a desperate scavenger to a rich beauty; Hanna Schygulla, who met Fassbinder in school and starred in twenty of his films, had an uncanny ability to float just out of range of analysis, as if she were not acting but getting her effects through dreamy murderous impulses—that despite the fact that every shot was precisely blocked and the dialogue has the precision and brutality of a play by Neil LaBute.

Maria has a childhood friend named Betti (Elisabeth Trissenaar) who marries another friend, Willi (Gottfried John). With both of them, she sometimes returns to bombed-out buildings, where she climbs up rubble-blocked staircases in her high heels, peering down through twisted beams and remembering that this room was their classroom, and that one was—but why is she doing this? I think because she gains a savage energy from these reminders of how her world was blown to pieces. When a black marketeer (Fassbinder) offers her a rare edition of books, she says, "Books burn too fast, and they don't give any heat."

Maria is always honest, uses no deception, admits she is toying with Oswald, is coldly amused at his weakness. It is the sentimental accountant Senkenberg who loves Oswald best, but he loves the company, too, and sees that Maria is good for it. Her conversations with Oswald are like the sparkling wit of screwball comedy, rotated into psychological cruelty. She orders him to meet her at a restaurant and is already eating when he arrives. He confesses he was frightened to come; she has him so off-balance he has no idea how to please her. They quarrel. "Why don't we just leave?" he asks. "Because," she says, "you were well brought up, and I pretend that I was."

What happens to Maria and her husband in the final scene was the subject of heated discussion after the film played at Cannes in May 1979. It's a surprise, but you must admit it is as plausible an ending as any other. I remember Fassbinder late at night at a back-street bar at Cannes that year, always in his black leather jacket, surrounded by his crowd, often scowling or arguing as they tried to please him. He was Maria Braun and they were all Oswalds. But he was a genius. That much everyone admitted.

Three years later, alone in a room, naked on a mattress, surrounded by money, watching *20,000 Years in Sing Sing* on television, he gave a fatal jolt to his heart with what he phoned a friend to say would be his last line of cocaine. There should have been at least twenty-three more films.

{ MEPHISTO }

In *Mephisto*, a movie that takes place in Germany during the rise of Nazism, there are many insults, but the most wounding is simply the word "actor"! It is screamed at the film's hero by his sponsor, a Nazi general who is in charge of cultural affairs. We stare into the actor's face, but are unable to determine what he is thinking, or what he is feeling. Maybe that is what makes him a great actor and an ignoble human being.

The actor is played by Klaus Maria Brandauer, in a performance of electrifying power; he makes us intensely fascinated by his character while keeping us on the outside—until we discover there is no inside. He plays an actor named Hendrik Hoefgen, but even that's not quite right; his real name is "Heinz" until he upgrades it. ("My name is not my name," he says to himself, "because I am an actor.") Hoefgen bitterly reveals early on that what he hates most about himself is that he is a "provincial actor." Eventually he will become Germany's most famous and admired actor, and the head of its State Theater, but that progression is in fact a descent into hell.

We should begin by noting how particularly *Mephisto* (1981) makes its details vivid: the look and feel of the theater, the rise of the Nazi Party from the 1920s through the 1930s, the Berlin social life that was itself a stage. The film's Hungarian director, Istvan Szabo, demonstrates that the Nazi uniforms themselves seemed to transform some people into Nazis,

248

just as costumes and makeup can make some actors into other people. The uniforms are deliberately fetishistic; to wear them is to subjugate yourself to the system that designed them. And we sense the sadomasochistic undertones that helped seduce a ruling class into a system of evil.

The film opens in Hamburg, where Hoefgen is involved in a small-time theater scene that is later described as communist, bourgeois, decadent—everything but National Socialist. Consumed with ambition, he throws himself into his work with abandon. During a meeting to discuss the props for one production, he hears the words "lamppost" and flies into a manic fury, declaring that the lamppost, and the exploited worker woman who stands beneath it, symbolize all that is rotten with Germany. He leaps from the stage into the auditorium, screaming that the lampposts will not be confined to the stage but will extend into the orchestra!—the dress circle! the entire theater!—as their revolutionary spirit unites actors and audience. The others look at him with astonishment.

Of course this is all acting, posturing, calling attention to himself. Hoefgen as played by Brandauer has not a moment's self-doubt as an actor, although as a human being, he is nothing but doubt, fear, and abnegation. He is ruled by ambition. His first wife is the daughter of a powerful man. When the man falls from grace, the wife is divorced. His early friends are left wing; later he drops them, forgets them, or tries to shield a few from the Nazis as a gesture toward his abandoned ideals. On the day of Hitler's election, a left-wing friend asks him to join a protest movement in the theater. He can't accept, and he can't refuse: "I'd rather stay with the reserves." In fact, his early beliefs are the same as his later ones; he goes from the far left to the far right without the slightest difficulty, because he never believed anything in the first place.

Having not seen *Mephisto* since the early 1980s, I came back to it again thinking it was an anti-Nazi film. Not entirely. The Nazis are simply . . . opportunists. Hoefgen wants to be famous, rich, and admired. He purrs at praise like a cat given cream. He can discuss with himself the rights and wrongs of his situation, but it is a strategic discussion, not a moral one. All of his romances and marriages are designed to further his career, except one, which begins in Hamburg and continues unbroken into his Berlin days as the favorite actor of the Reich. This is his affair with Juliette (Karin Boyd), who had a German father and an African mother, and, as a black woman, violates all the twisted Nazi theories of racial purity.

It bothers Hoefgen not at all that he is both a Nazi puppet and a black woman's partner because his feelings for Juliette are not love—and not even lust, I think, but a certain enjoyment of the way she understands him. She has his number. They can never be seen together in public, but in her boudoir, she freely insults him. He is such a bad actor, she says, that he can't even drink a beer like a man who wants to drink a beer. And later: "Sometimes your cold, cheating eyes are those of a sad child." How does he respond to that? Almost as if it is a compliment. He looks in a mirror to see if it is true!

The key to Hoefgen's rise is the cultural czar of the Reich, referred to only as the General (Rolf Hoppe). He is oddly attracted to Hoefgen, and sees to it that the actor's leftist past is erased, he gets the best roles, he rises to lead the State Theater. The General is well into middle age, well fed, warm, with a pleasing smile and a feminine seductiveness when he pays compliments. All until his brutal speech that ends with the word "actor!" Hoppe's performance is the ideal counterpoint to Brandauer's; the actor plays every role to please, and the Nazi pleases only himself, whatever it may seem.

Hoefgen's great role is Mephistopheles, the devil. In a mask of stark white makeup, he tempts Dr. Faustus in the classic German drama by Goethe. "My Mephisto," the General calls Hoefgen fondly, over and over again. It is a rich irony, since the General is in fact playing the Mephistopheles role and throwing the world at Hoefgen's feet. Szabo illustrates this contrast in a remarkable scene. Between acts of *Faust*, Hoefgen is asked to visit the General's box in the theater. He does, in full makeup and costume. Below, the theatergoers turn and look up as the satanic figure with his red-lined cape hovers smilingly over the Nazi in full dress uniform. Szabo ends this interlude with a shot, held just long enough, showing the entire audience standing transfixed. They have witnessed the devil calling on the state.

In the energy they bring to the film, Brandauer and Szabo have made a mighty statement, but it is as much about acting, I think, as Nazism. In Hoefgen, we see an empty man, standing for nothing. This doesn't even bother him. In Paris as a spokesman for Nazi cultural affairs, he reunites with Juliette, who begs him to defect to the West. Later, on the street, he breathes the air of France with that smug contented smile and says to himself, "What could I do here? Freedom? What for?" Then he descends into the black pit of the Metro.

The lineage behind the story is interesting. Szabo adapted a satirical novel by Klaus Mann (son of Thomas), whose mother was a Jew and whose German citizenship was stripped away in 1933; he later became an American citizen. His book was said to be inspired by his brother-in-law, Gustaf Grundgens, an actor and Nazi collaborator. Szabo himself (born 1938) is a leading Hungarian director; his credits include *Confidence* (1980), *Colonel Retl* (1985), and such English-language films as *Sunshine* (1999) and *Being Julia* (2004). *Mephisto* won the Oscar for best foreign film of 1981, and richly deserved it.

As a physical production, the film is breathtaking. Szabo makes the General's office a throne surrounded by empty space. He creates elegant party scenes at which the connected people gossip about one another; they climax with a spectacular celebration at the Grunewald hunting lodge. Huge swastikas turn ordinary buildings into fearful ones. The mechanism by which some people are exiled and others "disappear" is condensed into brief, fearful automobile rides. No effort is made to depict Hitler or German militarism or large-scale persecution of the Jews; all that takes place offstage, considering that the stage is Hoefgen's life. And Szabo ends the film with a visual masterstroke in which Hoefgen is able at last to have the limelight all to himself.

{MISHIMA: A LIFE IN FOUR CHAPTERS}

Paul Schrader's *Mishima: A Life in Four Chapters* (1985) is the most unconventional biopic I've ever seen, and one of the best. In a triumph of concise writing and construction, it considers three crucial aspects of the life of the Japanese author Yukio Mishima (1925–70). In black and white, we see formative scenes from his earlier years. In brilliant colors we see events from three of his most famous novels. And in realistic color we see the last day of his life.

What he did on that day validated, in his mind, both his life and his work. A fanatic traditionalist who exalted the medieval code of the samurai, he had formed a private army to express his devotion to the emperor. With four of its members, he drove to a regimental headquarters of the Japanese army, held a general as hostage, demanded to be allowed to address the gathered troops, and then committed ritual suicide by simultaneously disemboweling himself and having an acolyte behead him.

As unorthodox as Schrader's approach to Mishima's life may be, I cannot imagine a better one. Like Hemingway and Mailer, Mishima conceived his life and his work as intimately related through his libido. In Mishima's case this process was made more complex by his bisexuality and masochism, and his "private army" combined ritual with buried sexuality;

his soldiers were young, handsome, and willing to die for him, and they wore uniforms as fetishistic as the Nazis.

Schrader has throughout his life as a screenwriter and director been fascinated by the starting point of a "man in a room," as he describes it: a man dressing and preparing himself to go out and do battle for his goals. In his screenplays for Scorsese's *Taxi Driver* and *Raging Bull*, great emphasis is placed on Travis Bickle and Jake LaMotta preparing for conflict, Bickle with his elaborate gun mounts and verbal rehearsals, LaMotta in his dressing room. In Schrader's own *American Gigolo*, his hero trains and dresses himself to seem attractive to women, and in his film *The Walker*, he shows a man carefully preparing to be a presentable companion for older women.

Mishima is his ultimate man in a room. There is the young boy, separated from his mother and held almost captive by a possessive grandmother, who won't let him go out to play but wants him always at her side. There is the writer, returning to his desk every day at midnight to write his books and plays in monkish isolation. There is the public man, uniformed, advocating the Bushido Code, acting the role of military commander of his own army. On the last day of his life, he is ceremoniously dressed by a follower and adheres to a rigid timetable that leads to his meticulously planned and rehearsed suicide, or seppuku. Considering that he is a man fully committed to plunging a sword into his own guts, he seems remarkably serene; his life, his work, his obsession have finally become synchronous.

He is insane, yes, but not confused. He thinks with the perfect clarity of the true believer, and in this case his belief is in himself and his statement. His desire is to provoke an army mutiny that will overthrow democracy and other Western infections, and restore the supreme power of the emperor. Not even the emperor agrees with him, but such is Mishima's overwhelming charisma that his army recruits want to join him in death.

Schrader contrasts this adult martinet with the shy sissy whose grandmother warned him he would get sick if he went outside. As a boy, Mishima was afflicted with a paralyzing stutter, was weakly, was the target of bullies. The film's biographical sequences show him being advised by a friend who limps to exploit his own disability as a way of making himself attractive to women. Eventually these lessons take a turn: Mishima becomes a muscular bodybuilder, a paragon of surface masculinity, to attract men—not so much as his lovers but as his followers or slaves. Their worship validates his supremacy and denies his deep-seated feelings of inferiority.

These scenes from his life find mirrors in the sequences inspired by three of his novels, *Temple of the Golden Pavilion*, *Kyoko's House*, and *Runaway Horses*. These scenes, shot on a sound stage at Tokyo's Toho Studios, are remarkably stylized, and filmed in rich basic colors. The production design is by Eiko Ishioka, who was honored at Cannes for her work on this film, won an Oscar for Coppola's *Dracula*, designed *M. Butterfly* on Broadway and the *Varakai* production for Cirque du Soleil in Las Vegas, and created the extraordinary visuals for Tarsem Singh's *The Cell* (2002).

Temple of the Golden Pavilion involves a young monk at an ancient temple who is overcome by its beauty and burns it down. The story is inspired by actual events in 1950. Ishioka's sets of dazzling red and gold include collapsing walls that open before the monk vagina-like. *Kyoko's House* is based on a 1959 novel that turned out to be prophetically autobiographical. Its hero, a bodybuilding boxer, commits suicide with his lover. *Runaway Horses* is about a young man in the early 1930s who leads a plot to assassinate government figures and restore the emperor. In one way or another, all three prefigure events in Mishima's life; the first, about the destruction of beauty, connects with his belief that a man should grow steadily more beautiful until the age of forty, when he has reached perfection and should die before decay sets in.

The title character is played as an adult by Ken Ogata (*Vengeance Is Mine*, *The Pillow Book*), who portrays the character without signaling or spin; his Mishima is self-contained, reticent, confident. Only in a voiceover does he betray his uncertainties. What we see in the "present" is essentially the persona he so elaborately created, and it is easy to think of Norman Mailer stepping into the boxing ring, running for office, head-butting Gore Vidal, stabbing a wife. The public actions somehow lend weight to the writing.

The screenplay was written by Schrader in collaboration with his brother, Leonard (1943–2006), who lived, taught, and married in Japan and also wrote *Kiss of the Spider Woman* and collaborated with Paul on

The Yakuza (1975). The Japanese dialog was co-written by Leonard's wife, Chieko. If you were to stand back and look at the mismatched facts of Mishima's childhood and adult years, and then consider the bewildering profusion of his novels, stories, plays, Noh dramas, public behavior, film acting, and self-promotion, you might despair of assembling it into a coherent screenplay. The unconventional structure of the film might seem to lead to confusion or distraction, but actually it unfolds with perfect clarity, the logic revealing itself.

Schrader, born 1946, is one of the most intelligent and fascinating figures in contemporary film. A key to his work may be his 1972 book *Transcendental Style in Film: Ozu, Bresson, Dreyer*, in which he values those directors above all others. It may seem impossible to reconcile their aesthetics with the frequent violence and sex of his work, but at a deeper level few filmmakers are more concerned with the morality of the characters. His films are often about life choices and compulsions and how they work out in real life and have unintended consequences. They spring directly out of his fundamentalist upbringing in Grand Rapids, where he had values so deeply imprinted that they have expressed themselves, however indirectly, ever since. That made him doubly sympathetic to the deep-rooted Catholicism of his lifelong collaborator Scorsese.

I remember a night after the premiere of *Mishima*, a competitor for the Palme d'Or at Cannes in 1985. The film was well received, and won an overall award for best artistic contribution (by Ishioka, cinematographer John Bailey, and Philip Glass, for one of his best scores). But Paul knew better than anyone that its chances at the American box office were slim. We met at a backstreet Japanese restaurant, where he observed that his co-producers, Francis Coppola and George Lucas, had raised $10 million "with no hope of getting it back," and indeed the film grossed only about $500,000 in the U.S.

"This may have been my last film," Schrader said, and that's also something I've heard more than once from Scorsese. It is Schrader's problem, and also his gift, to make films he believes in. Some are deeper, some entertainments, but none are merely jobs of work. He must have found Mishima's headlong dedication to his art a powerful attraction.

MON ONCLE ANTOINE

The key action in Claude Jutra's *Mon Oncle Antoine* (1971) takes place over
a period of twenty-four hours in a Quebec mining town. Although the
film begins earlier in the year, everything comes to a focus beginning on
the morning of Christmas Eve and closing on the dawn of Christmas.
During that time, a young boy has had his life forever changed. This beloved Canadian film is rich in characters, glowing with life in the midst of
death.

The town is Black Hawk, surrounded by the slag heaps of asbestos
mines. The action is "not so very long ago," the 1940s. The town is poor,
and people still live in old-fashioned ways and travel by horse, carriage, or
train. The film opens with an argument between a Quebecois mine worker
named Joe Paulin (Lionel Villenuve) and his English-speaking boss. We
soon understand that Joe hates the "English" and hates the mine, and he
quits on the spot, says farewell to his family, shoulders his ax, and heads off
to a logging camp where nobody will be on his case. We won't see much of
him again until the film's conclusion.

The central story opens with a funeral, and we are given to understand that the deceased died of lung disease, contracted in the mines. The
funeral is a sad affair; the dead man's naked body is covered with a rented

suit-front, the flowers are all fake, the undertaker takes back the rosary to be used again.

The undertaker is Antoine (Jean Duceppe) and his assistant is a robust man in his thirties named Fernand (Claude Jutra himself). They return after the ceremony to the general store that Antoine owns with his wife, Cecile (Olivette Thibault). Soon we meet Benoit (Jacques Gagnon), the orphaned fourteen-year-old who lives with them, and also the pretty young Carmen (Lyne Champagne), a clerk who boards with them.

This store will be the principal location for the movie, and it is a masterful re-creation from the period. Groceries are on the right as you enter, dry goods on the left, hardware upstairs, along with caskets for the undertaking business. The local people all know each other's business and meet here to gossip. On Christmas Eve, there is a festive air. Benoit and Carmen are up early to decorate the window. Benoit's Uncle Antoine is up later, disheveled, and repairs behind the windowpanes of the store office to pour himself a little drink.

Benoit regards him through the panes, silently. Benoit sees everything, is solemn and quiet, except with his pals or Carmen, when he is a playful boy. During this day, there will be great drama attending the unveiling of the nativity scene in the store window. Enormous excitement when Alexandrine, the accountant's wife, goes upstairs with Cecile to try on a corset. Jollity as Antoine sells an old rummy a pair of pants twice too large for him. Celebration when a young woman shyly asks to see a bridal veil. Discovery when Benoit and Carmen wrestle upstairs, he grabs her breast through her dress, she stays perfectly still, and a wordless communication passes between them.

Outside on the main street, the sour-faced, hated mine owner trots in his carriage, tossing cheap Christmas stockings at the homes of his employees. Is it an accident they mostly land in the mud? The subtext of the film is that these mine workers are all treated as serfs and are working at a deadly trade. Jutra's film was made at the height of Quebec separatism, and although it is never specific in its politics, of course they are unmistakable.

There are small human scenes. A little flirtation between Antoine and Cecile. Another little flirtation between Cecile and Fernand. Benoit's infatuation with Carmen. Carmen's sadness when her father appears to collect her wages and doesn't even wish her a merry Christmas. The ferocity with which Antoine withholds $5 for Carmen herself: "That's how it is!"

We have seen scenes at the rural home of the Paulin family and know that the eldest son is ill. The store's telephone rings, and it is Madame Paulin (Helene Loiselle), telephoning to say that her son has died. Can Antoine come to take the body? Now begins the great sequence of the film that carries all its meaning and pays off on all its implications. Benoit begs to be allowed to go along with his uncle on the carriage ride through a developing blizzard, and they head out to the Paulin home, Antoine drinking steadily. Not to fear: the horse knows the way.

This journey certainly looks like the real thing, the windblown snow cutting into their faces as they huddle in their winter fur coats. At the lonely Paulin home, Benoit as usual sees all, says nothing, as Antoine, now thoroughly drunk, uses his fingers to eat the hot meal Madame Paulin has prepared. Benoit's eyes are drawn to a corner of the room where a dark doorway stands partly open. In there, he knows, is the dead boy, scarcely older than himself.

On the journey home, the coffin is lost: it falls from the carriage bed. Antoine is too drunk to help Benoit drag it back on board and suddenly unburdens himself of a lifetime of grief: he hates the country, is afraid of corpses, his wife never gave him a child. Benoit sees how it really is, and the lessons will continue during this evening. The emergency is entirely in his hands. What he does is inevitable and responsible and leads to a heartbreaking conclusion, once again witnessed through a window with Benoit's solemn eyes.

That *Mon Oncle Antoine* is such a fine film only underlines the tragedy of the director's later life. Jutra had started full of promise. He first studied medicine, then became a student at the National Film Board of Canada (which produced this film). He worked in France as an apprentice to Truffaut. He worked with a script by Clement Perron, who was inspired by events in his own life. Jutra made other films before learning he was in the early stages of Alzheimer's. He disappeared in the winter of 1986, and his body was found in the St. Lawrence River the next spring. He was presumably a suicide. He made an earlier film in which the character leaps into the same river.

What he left behind is a film to treasure, not least because of the way it uses its locations. The slag heaps of the mines overshadow the town below, and there is a high-angle shot establishing how vast they are and how small the town is—just a few square blocks and muddy streets. It must still have been thus when he filmed. The storefronts and interiors do not look like sets—not even the store, although we know it surely is. There is not an automobile in sight, nor would one have gotten far on these roads in the winter. The faces of many of the extras betray a heavy load of work and disappointment. Social commentary is buried all through the film, as in the contrast between the working women and the haughty wife of the mine accountant.

In the loneliness and grandeur of the midnight journey of Benoit and Antoine, there is a haunting beauty. I was reminded of the moods of Willa Cather's *Shadows on the Rock*, and, indeed, in the life of the Paulin family, Cather's novels of American pioneers surviving the cold. Jutra and his screenwriter clearly know these people and this land, and tell their stories with confidence and familiarity. There is a tendency to assume a movie titled *My Uncle Antoine* will be a fond memoir of a lovable old curmudgeon. Not this time. There is that in Antoine that is lovable, and that which is happy, and that which is tragic. So it is. As Benoit learns.

{ MOOLAADE }

Moolaade is the kind of film that can only be made by a director whose heart is in harmony with his mind. It is a film of politics and anger, and also a film of beauty, humor, and a deep affection for human nature. Usually films about controversial issues are tilted too far toward rage or tear-jerking. Ousmane Sembene, who made this film when he was eighty-one, must have lived enough, suffered enough, and laughed enough to find the wisdom of age. I remember him sitting in the little lobby of the Hotel Splendid in Cannes, puffing contentedly on a Sherlock Holmes pipe that was rather a contrast with his bright, flowing Senegalese garb.

His film is about, and against, the custom of female circumcision, practiced in many Muslim lands (although Islamic law forbids it). Does that make you think you don't want to see it? Think again. Sembene embodies his subject so deeply with his characters, and especially with his heroine, Colle, that it becomes a story about will, defiance, and ancient custom.

It is never actually too specific about what would be done to the four girls who flee to Colle for moolaade, or protection. Sembene trusts us to know. He doesn't exploit blood-drenched horror scenes, and his approach is actually more effective because he limits himself to offscreen cries, or a brief glimpse of the knife used by the village's doyenne des exciseuses, the woman in charge of circumcisions. The knife is very small, wickedly hooked, hardly seen, and more frightening than a broadsword. Yet we learn that women support the removal of the clitoris because no man will marry a bride who has not been "cut." The actress Fatoumata Coulibaly, who plays Colle, has said that she herself was circumcised; the result, as with most victims, was an absence of sexual pleasure, and often pain during sex.

Why would a man insist on this mutilation? Perhaps out of deep insecurity and a distrust, even fear, of women. But *Moolaade* makes no such sweeping charges, and observes how the women themselves enforce and carry out the practice—because, of course, they want their daughters to find husbands.

Colle has refused to let her own daughter be cut, but now the girl is engaged to a man returning home from France. Will Europe have freed him of ancient barbarities, or will he demand a bride who has been cut? Since the village hopes for wealth from the returning man, there is social pressure on Colle. And just at that moment, the girls on the brink of adolescence run weeping to Colle and beg for shelter in the compound she shares with her husband and his other wives.

Colle evokes moolaade. She ties a string of yarn across the doorstep of her house, and the law says that as long as the girls stay inside, no one can enter after them. Her husband is enraged. He loses status in the village council because he cannot control his woman, but his Number One Wife supports Number Two, and he is stalemated. One of the themes coiling beneath the surface of the film is that the women in this society have great power, if they are bold enough to exercise it.

Another theme is suspicion of the West, of modernization, of the outside in general. One of the ways groups create their identities is by enforcing costume rules that conceal individuality and impose a monolithic look. Uniforms are a way of saying that those who wear them are interchangeable. One who is obviously an outsider is le mercenaire, the itinerant peddler who visits the village to sell pots and pans, postage stamps, T-shirts and toys, and to pick up and deliver mail. He has a lively eye for pretty women, suggests secret rendezvous, and in general ignores the code that a woman belongs to a man.

Among the most important items in his stock are batteries, needed for portable radios and flashlights in this district without electricity. The radio stations are in the cities, and broadcast words and music reflecting dangerous freedoms. When the frustrated all-male village council meets to ponder the challenge of Colle and moolaade, it doesn't occur to them, of course, that women might have perfectly good reasons for not wanting to be circumcised. They blame the outside. The radios. They order a sweep of the village to confiscate all the radios, which are deposited in a big pile, some of them still turned on. This pile becomes a central image of the film, and inevitably evokes bonfires of hated books, or videos, or rock 'n' roll, or people.

The construction of Sembene's film is subtle and seductive. He spends little time denouncing female circumcision, and a great deal of time studying the human nature of dissent and conformity. There is humor in the paradoxes that the men debate, and in their impotence against their women, and suspense when the prodigal son returns from Paris. On the most fundamental of levels, this is an entertaining film. Also a beautiful one, as we admire the artistry of the architecture, and appreciate how the people of the village live within the rules and respect them, even when opposing them. These people, despite some of their practices, are deeply decent and civilized, and Sembene loves them for it. The movie contains less outrage than regret.

Sembene's death at eighty-four, on June 9, 2007, brought to a close an extraordinary life, one that parallels in some ways Nelson Mandela's. Neither was born into wealth and privilege, and both achieved greatness. Although he was known for years as "the father of the African cinema," and wrote six novels before he decided films would reach a larger audience, Sembene as a young man (I learn from IMDb.com) was a mechanic, a bricklayer, a soldier for the Free French, a labor leader, an autoworker, and a stevedore. His first novel came in 1956, his first movie (*Black Girl*) in 1966.

That film told the story of the ill treatment a young Senegalese woman finds when she goes to work as an au pair in Paris. But Sembene did not devote himself to dramatizing the evils of whites against blacks on his continent. He was more interested in drama, conflicts, and comedy within the vibrant African civilization.

Consider his wonderful film *Guelwaar* (1992). In his country, Muslims live side by side with Catholics, and his story involves a mix-up that accidentally results in the burial of a Catholic body in a Muslim cemetery. When an attempt to move the body is made, the Muslims are outraged—not because the body is there, but because the removal would desecrate the cemetery. A local policeman, himself a Muslim, tries to defuse the situation and prevent a nasty fight.

This story could involve stereotypes and fan the flames of prejudice. But not with Sembene. He portrays all the characters as people who are reasonable, by their own lights, and would be content with a solution that did not violate their beliefs. And all religions contain a fuzzy area that allows common sense to sometimes win over dogma. All it takes here is a persuasive policeman, and some wise people on both sides who are weary of the hotheads. Sembene's work so often dealt with his society from the inside, with sympathy, insight, and the sly wit of a Bernard Shaw. He made political films that didn't seem political, and comedies that were very serious. His regret was that many of his films, including *Moolaade*, were not welcome in Africa. He won awards at Venice, Karlovy Vary, and many other important festivals; *Moolaade* won first place in the Un Certain Regard section at Cannes. But according to IMDb, the film has played nowhere in Africa except Morocco. The message is not heard where it is needed.

Ousmane Sembene was born into an Africa where a black man was not expected to write novels or direct films. He dedicated his life to making brave and useful films that his continent needed to see. He did that even knowing they would probably not be seen. They exist. They wait. They honor his memory.

{ My Fair Lady }

M*y Fair Lady* is the best and most unlikely of musicals, during which I cannot decide if I am happier when the characters are talking or when they are singing. The songs are literate and beloved; some romantic, some comic, some nonsense, some surprisingly philosophical, every single one wonderful. The dialogue by Alan Jay Lerner wisely retains a great deal of *Pygmalion* by George Bernard Shaw, himself inspired by Ovid's *Metamorphosis*.

This fusion functions at such an elevation of sophistication and wit that when poor smitten Freddy sings "On the Street Where You Live," a song that would distinguish any other musical, this one drops Freddy entirely rather than risk another such simplistic outburst. His sincerity seems childlike compared with the emotional fencing match between the guarded Higgins and the wary Eliza. It is characteristic that in a musical that has love as its buried theme, no one ever kisses, or seems about to.

The story involves a meeting of two egos, one belonging to the linguist Henry Higgins, the other, no less titanic, to the flower girl Eliza Doolittle. It is often mistakenly said that they collaborate because Higgins (Rex Harrison) decides to improve Eliza's Cockney accent. In fact it is Eliza (Audrey Hepburn) who takes the initiative, presenting herself at Henry's bachelor quarters to sign up for lessons: "I know what lessons cost as well as you do, and I'm ready to pay."

Even in this early scene, it is Eliza's will that drives the plot; Higgins might have tinkered forever with his phonetic alphabet and his recording devices if Eliza hadn't insisted on action. She took seriously his boast the night before, in Covent Garden: "You see this creature with her curbstone English? The English that will keep her in the gutter till the end of her days? Well, sir, in six months, I could pass her off as a duchess at an Embassy Ball. I could even get her a job as a lady's maid or a shop assistant, which requires better English." The final twist, typical Shavian paradox, is what Eliza hears, and it supplies her inspiration: "I want to be a lady in a flower shop instead of sellin' at the corner of Tottenham Court Road. But they won't take me unless I can talk more genteel."

It is her ambition, not Henry's, that sets the plot in motion, including the professor's bet with his fellow linguist Pickering, who says he'll pay for the lessons if Higgins can transform her speech. Higgins's response will thrum below the action for most of the play: "You know, it's almost irresistible. She's so deliciously low. So horribly dirty." If Henry will teach Eliza to improve her speech, she will try to teach him decency and awaken his better nature.

It is unnecessary to summarize the plot or list the songs; if you are not familiar with both, you are culturally illiterate, although in six months I could pass you off as a critic at Cannes, or even a clerk in a good video store, which requires better taste.

It is difficult to discuss George Cukor's 1964 film as it actually exists because, even now, an impenetrable thicket of legend and gossip obscures its greatness. Many viewers would rather discuss the film that wasn't made, the one that would have starred Julie Andrews, who made the role of Eliza her own on the stage. Casting Audrey Hepburn was seen as a snub of Andrews, and so it was; producer and studio head Jack L. Warner chose Hepburn for her greater box-office appeal, and was prepared to offer the role to Elizabeth Taylor if Hepburn turned it down.

One of the best-known items in the history of movie trivia is that Hepburn did not sing her own songs, but was dubbed by the gifted Marni Nixon. So notorious became this dubbing, so egregious was it made to appear, that although *My Fair Lady* was nominated for twelve Oscars and won eight (including best picture, actor, director, and cinematography), Hepburn was not even nominated for best actress; Julie Andrews was, the same year, for *Mary Poppins*, and she won.

At this remove, can we step back and take a fresh look at the controversy? True, Hepburn did not sing her own songs (although she performed some of the intros and outros), and there was endless comment on moments when the lip-syncing was not perfect. But the dubbing of singing voices was commonplace at the time, and Nixon herself also dubbed Deborah Kerr (*The King and I*) and Natalie Wood (*West Side Story*). Even actors who did their own singing were lip-syncing to their own pre-recorded dubs (and an occasional uncredited assist). I learn from Robert Harris, who restored *My Fair Lady* in 1993, that this was apparently the first musical to use any form of live recording of the music, although "only of Mr. Harrison, who refused to mouth to playbacks. His early model wireless microphone can be seen as a rather inflated tie during his musical numbers." Harrison's lips are therefore always in perfect sync, as opposed to everyone else in this film and all previous musicals.

That Hepburn did not do her own singing obscures her triumph, which is that she did her own acting. *My Fair Lady*, with its dialogue drawn from Shaw, was trickier and more challenging than most other stage musicals; the dialogue not only incorporated Shavian theory, wit, and ideology, but required Eliza to master a transition from Cockney to the Queen's English. All of this Hepburn does flawlessly and with heedless confidence, in a performance that contains great passion. Consider the scenes where she finally explodes at Higgins's misogynist disregard, returns to the streets of Covent Garden, and finds she fits in nowhere. "I sold flowers," she tells Henry late in their crisis. "I didn't sell myself. Now you've made a lady of me, I'm not fit to sell anything else."

It is typical of Shaw, admirable of Lerner and Loewe, and remarkable of Hollywood, that the film stays true to the original material, and Higgins doesn't cave in during a soppy rewritten "happy ending." Astonished that the ungrateful Eliza has stalked out of his home, Higgins asks in a song, "Why can't a woman be more like a man?" He tracks her to his mother's house, where the aristocratic Mrs. Higgins (Gladys Cooper) orders him to behave himself. "What?" he asks his mother. "Do you mean to say that I'm to put on my Sunday manners for this thing that I created out of the squashed cabbage leaves of Covent Garden?" Yes, she does. Higgins realizes he loves Eliza, but even in the play's famous last line he perseveres as a defiant bachelor: "Eliza? Where the devil are my slippers?" It remains an open question for me, at the final curtain, whether Eliza stays to listen to what he says next.

Apart from the wonders of its words and music, *My Fair Lady* is a visual triumph. Cukor made use above all of Cecil Beaton, a photographer and costume designer, who had been production designer on only one previous film (*Gigi*, 1958). He and cinematographer Harry Stradling, who both won Oscars, bring to the film a combination of sumptuousness and detail, from the stylization of the famous Ascot scene to the countless intriguing devices in Higgins's book-lined study.

The supporting performances include Wilfred Hyde-White as the decent Pickering, speaking up for Eliza; and Stanley Holloway as her father, Alfred P. Doolittle, according to Higgins "the most original moral philosopher in England." Doolittle was originally to have been played in the movie by Jimmy Cagney; he might have been good, but might have been a distraction, and Holloway with his ravaged demeanor is perfect.

What distinguishes *My Fair Lady* above all is that it actually says something. It says it in a film of pointed words, unforgettable music, and glorious images, but it says it. Bernard Shaw's *Pygmalion* was a socialist attack on the British class system, and on the truth (as true when the film was made as when Shaw wrote his play) that an Englishman's destiny was largely determined by his accent. It allowed others to place him, and to keep him in his place.

Eliza's escape from the "lower classes," engineered by Higgins, is a revolutionary act, dramatizing how "superiority" was inherited, not earned. It is a lesson that resonates for all societies, and the genius of *My Fair Lady* is that it is both a great entertainment and a great polemic. It is still not sufficiently appreciated what influence it had on the creation of feminism and class consciousness in the years bridging 1914 when *Pygmalion* premiered, 1956 when the musical premiered, and 1964 when the film premiered. It was actually about something. As Eliza assures the serenely superior Henry Higgins, who stood for a class, a time, and an attitude:

> *They can still rule with land without you.*
> *Windsor Castle will stand without you.*
> *And without much ado we can all muddle through without you.*

{ MY MAN GODFREY }

When Carole Lombard and the family maid discuss the newly hired butler, we can read her mind when she says, "I'd like to sew his buttons on
sometime, when they come off." In 1936, when elegant men's formalwear
didn't use zippers, audiences must have had an even better idea of what
she was thinking. The two women both have crushes on Godfrey (William
Powell), a homeless man whom Lombard, competing in a scavenger hunt,
discovers living at the city dump. Lombard wins the hunt by producing
Godfrey at a society ball and then, during an argument with her bitchy
sister and loony mother, hires him to be the butler for her rich family. "Do
you buttle?" she asks him, so crisply and directly that she could mean anything, or everything. Her romantic obsession is hopeless because Godfrey
has transformed himself overnight from an unshaven bum into a polished,
sophisticated man who prides himself on his proper behavior. When she
grabs him and kisses him, he regards her with utter astonishment.

My Man Godfrey, one of the treasures of 1930s screwball comedy,
doesn't merely use Lombard and Powell, it loves them. She plays Irene, a
petulant kid who wants what she wants when she wants it. His Godfrey
employs an attentive posture and a deep, precise voice that bespeaks an exact measurement of the situation he finds himself in. These two actors, who

were briefly married (1931–33) before the film was made in 1936, embody personal style in a way that is (to use a cliche that I mean sincerely) effortlessly magical. Consider Powell, best known for the *Thin Man* movies. How can such reserve suggest such depths of feeling? How can understatement and a cool, dry delivery embody such passion? You can never, ever catch him trying to capture effects. They come to him. And Lombard in this film has a dreamy, ditzy breathlessness that shows her sweetly yearning after this man who fascinated her even when she thought he really was a bum.

Like Preston Sturges's *Sullivan's Travels* (1941), Gregory La Cava's *My Man Godfrey* contrasts the poverty of "forgotten men" during the Depression with the spoiled lifestyles of the idle rich. The family Irene brings Godfrey home to buttle for is the Bullocks, all obliviously nuts. Her father, Alexander (that gravel-voiced character actor of genius, Eugene Pallette), is a rich man, secretly broke, who addresses his spendthrift family in tones of disbelief ("In prison, at least I'd find some peace"). Her mother, Angelica (Alice Brady), pampers herself with unabashed luxury and even maintains a "protégé" (Mischa Auer) whose duties involve declaiming great literature, playing the piano, leaping about the room like a gorilla, and gobbling up second helpings at every meal. Her sister, Cornelia (Gail Patrick), is bitter because she not only lost the scavenger hunt but got pushed into an ash heap after insulting Godfrey. And there is the maid, Molly (Jean Dixon), who briefs Godfrey on the insane world he is entering. She loves Godfrey, too, and perhaps down deep so does Cornelia, and so might the protégé, if he didn't like chicken legs more.

Godfrey buttles flawlessly, bringing Alexander his martinis a tray at a time, whipping up hors d'oeuvres in the kitchen, and keeping his secret. He has one. Unmasked by a Harvard classmate at a party, he turns out to be born rich but down on his fortune after an unhappy romance. The Bullocks never figure out he's too good to be a butler (or a bum) because they're all blinded by their own selfishness, except for Irene, who dreams of his buttons. Under the surface, emotion is churning. Godfrey, having come to like and admire his fellow hobos at the dump, is offended that the Bullocks flaunt their wealth so uselessly, and that leads to one of those outcomes so beloved in screwball comedy, so impossible in life.

God, but this film is beautiful. The cinematography by Ted Tetzlaff is a shimmering argument for everything I've ever tried to say in praise of black and white. Look me in the eye and tell me you would prefer to see it in color. The restored version on the Criterion DVD is particularly alluring in its surfaces. Everything that can shine, glimmers: the marble floors, the silver, the mirrors, the crystal, the satin sheen of the gowns. There is a tactile feel to the furs and feathers of the women's costumes, and the fabric patterns by designer Louise Brymer use bold splashes and zigs and zags of blacks and whites to arrest our attention. Every woman in this movie, in every scene, is wearing something that other women at a party would kill for. These tones and textures are set off with one of those 1930s apartments that is intended to look like a movie set, all poised for entrances and exits. I found myself freezing the frame and simply appreciating compositions. Notice a shot when Godfrey exits screen right and the camera pans with him and then pushes to poor, sad Irene, seen through sculptured openings in the staircase and chewing the hem of her gown. Look for another composition balanced by a light fixture high on the wall to the right. You'll know the one.

A couple of reviewers on the Web complain that the plot is implausible. What are we going to do with these people? They've obviously never buttled a day in their lives. What you have to observe and admire is how gently the film offers its moments of genius. Irene has a mournful line something like, "Some people do just as they like with other people's lives, and it doesn't seem to make any difference . . . to some people." Somehow she implies that the first "some people" refers to theoretical people, and the second refers to other people in the room. Her futile love for Godfrey shows itself in the scene where he's doing the dishes in the kitchen, and she says she wants help: "I want to wipe." I know, it sounds mundane in print, but the spin she puts on it brings buttons back to our minds.

The "implausibility" involves the complications of a theft of pearls, some swift stock-market moves, and Godfrey's plans for the city dump. OK, it's all implausible. That's what I'm here for. By pretending the implausible is possible, screwball comedy acts like a tonic. Nothing is impossible if you cut through the difficulties with an instrument like Powell's knife-edged delivery. He betrays little overt emotion, but what we glimpse is impatience with some people who will not do the obvious and, indeed, the inevitable.

The movie also benefits from the range of sharply defined characters, and the actors to play them. Even the biggest stars in those days were surrounded by other actors in substantial roles that provided them with counterpoint, with context, with emotional tennis partners. Notice here the work of Eugene Pallette, who bluntly speaks truth even though his family is deaf to him. By God, he's had enough: "What this family needs is discipline. I've been a patient man, but when people start riding horses up the front steps and parking them in the library, that's going a little too far. This family's got to settle down!" His voice is like a chainsaw, cutting through the vapors around him.

This movie, and the actors in it, and its style of production, and the system that produced it, and the audiences that loved it, have all been replaced by pop culture of brainless vulgarity. But the movie survives, and to watch it is to be rescued from some people who don't care that it makes a difference . . . to some people.

{ NANOOK OF THE NORTH }

There is an astonishing sequence in Robert J. Flaherty's *Nanook of the North* (1922) in which his hero, the Inuit hunter Nanook, hunts a seal. Flaherty shows the most exciting passage in one unbroken shot. Nanook knows that seals must breathe every twenty minutes, and keep an air hole open for themselves in the ice of the Arctic winter. He finds such a hole, barely big enough to be seen, and is poised motionless above it with his harpoon until a seal rises to breathe. Then he strikes and holds onto the line as the seal plunges to escape.

There is a desperate tug of war. Nanook hauls the line ten or twelve feet out of the hole, and then is dragged back, sliding across the ice, and pulls again, and again. We can't see, but he must have the line tied to his body—to lose would be to drown. He desperately signals for his fellow hunters to help him, and we see them running across the ice with their dogs as he struggles to hold on. They arrive at last, and three or four of them pull on the line. The seal prevails. Nanook uses his knife to enlarge the hole, and the seal at last is revealed and killed. The hunters immediately strip it of its blubber and dine on its raw flesh.

There has been some discussion among critics of a possible interruption in the filming; we never see the seal actually being pulled up to the surface. Was the quarry shot with a gun that Flaherty did not want to show, because that would affect the purity of his images of man against nature? Such questions are part of a decades-old debate about the methods of a man who has been called the father of the documentary, whose films are masterpieces, and yet whose realities were admittedly assisted.

Seeing *Nanook of the North* at the Toronto Film Festival, magnificently projected in 35mm and accompanied by a live performance of a new musical score, I did not much care about the purity of Flaherty's methods. He shot his footage in 1920, when there were no rules for documentaries and precious few documentaries, certainly none shot so far north that nothing grows except a little moss, and three hundred Inuit could inhabit a space the size of England. (At about the same time, at the other pole, a photographer named Frank Hurley was filming Shackleton's expedition, which ended with his ship, the Endurance, broken by the ice, and the crew escaping to South America on a seven-hundred-mile journey in an open boat, with not a life lost. That film is also on DVD.)

We know, because Flaherty was frank about it, that he recruited the cast for his film. Nanook was chosen because he was the most famed of the hunters in the district, but the two women playing his wives were not his wives and the children were not his children. Flaherty's first footage was of a walrus hunt, and he revealed that Nanook and his fellow hunters performed the hunt for the camera. *Nanook* is not cinema verité. And yet in a sense it is: the movie is an authentic documentary showing the creation of itself. What happens on the screen is real, no matter what happened behind it. Nanook really has a seal on the other end of that line.

The movie shows Nanook during a few weeks in the life of his family. Countless details fill in a way of life that was already dying. We see the hunters creeping inch by inch upon a herd of slumbering walruses, and then Nanook springing up and harpooning one, and then a fierce struggle in which the mate of the walrus joins the battle. Such scenes simplify Inuit life to its most basic reality: in this land the only food comes from other animals, which must be hunted and killed. Everything the family uses—its food, fuel, clothing, and tools—comes in some way from those animals, except for the knives and perhaps harpoon points, which they obtain at a trading post. They are a luxury; before there were trading posts, there were already Inuit.

One of the film's most fascinating scenes shows the construction of an igloo. Nanook and his friends carve big blocks of snow and stack them in a circle, carving new ones from the floor so that it sinks as the walls rise and curve inward to form a dome. Then he finds sheets of ice, cuts holes in the igloo walls, and inserts the ice to make windows. There is another igloo, a smaller one, for the dogs. And inside the big igloo, the tiniest igloo of all, for puppies, which the big dogs would quickly eat.

Nanook has a small son named Allee, and a baby, Rainbow, four months old; they travel inside the hoods of their mothers. There are scenes of unstudied grace and love as his wives, Nyla and Cunayou, care for the children, the children play with the puppies, and the whole family strips to crawl under their furs, which act as blankets for the night. There are also moments of hazard, as they are nearly lost in a sudden snowstorm, and times of great hunger and desperation. These are suggested in the film, but became real in the aftermath: Nanook, lost in a storm, died of starvation two years after Flaherty filmed him.

Flaherty (1884–1951), born in Michigan, traveled in northern Canada with his father as a young man, then returned as a scout looking for iron ore. He took along a camera and shot some footage of Eskimos, which was destroyed by fire. That inspired him to return and shoot a proper film, financed by a French fur-trading company. He took along a generator, developing equipment, and a projector; after filming the walrus hunt, he wrote:

> I lost no time in developing and printing the film. That walrus fight was the first film these Eskimo had ever seen and, in the language of the trade, it was a "knock-out." The audience—they thronged the post kitchen to the point of suffocation—completely forgot the picture. To them the walrus was real and living. The women and children in their high shrill voices joined with the men in shouting admonitions, warnings and advice to Nanook and his crew as the picture unfolded on the screen. The fame of that picture spread through all the country. . . . After this it did not take my

Eskimo long to see the practical side of films and . . . from that time on, they were all with me.

The film is not technically sophisticated; how could it be, with one camera, no lights, freezing cold, and everyone equally at the mercy of nature? But it has an authenticity that prevails over any complaints that some of the sequences were staged. If you stage a walrus hunt, it still involves hunting a walrus, and the walrus hasn't seen the script. What shines through is the humanity and optimism of the Inuit. One of the film's titles describes them as "happy-go-lucky," and although this seems almost cruel, given the harsh terms of their survival, they do indeed seem absorbed by their lives and content in them, which is more than many of us can say.

Flaherty went on to make more sophisticated films, notably *Tabu* (1931), an uneasy collaboration with the great German filmmaker F. W. Murnau, who was more interested in story and style than documentation; *Man of Aran* (1934), about the hard lives of the Aran Islanders off the coast of Ireland; *Elephant Boy* (1937), starring Sabu in a fiction based on a Kipling story; and *Louisiana Story* (1948), in which a young bayou boy watches as an oil rig invades his unspoiled domain. The later films are smoother and more conventionally beautiful, but *Nanook* stands alone in its stark regard for the courage and ingenuity of its heroes. Nanook is one of the most vital and unforgettable human beings ever recorded on film.

Note: the movie is available in a Criterion DVD edition, restored by David Shepard with a score by Timothy Brock. At the Toronto screening, the composer Gabriel Thibaudeau, from Quebec, led nine musicians (four flute players, a soprano, a bass, a drummer, and the Inuit throat-singers Akinisie Sivuaraapik and Caroline Novalinga) in the premiere of his score that celebrates the beauty of the land and, during scenes of crisis, expresses urgency, surprise, fear, and triumph in throat-sounds both musical and elemental. Now that do-it-yourself commentary tracks can be downloaded from the Web and played with DVDs, I wonder if this performance could be made available the same way—or offered as an alternative track on the next DVD edition.

{ ORDET }

For the ordinary filmgoer, and I include myself, *Ordet* is a difficult film to enter. But once you're inside, it is impossible to escape. Lean, quiet, deeply serious, populated with odd religious obsessives, it takes place in winter in Denmark in 1925, in a rural district that has a cold austere beauty.

The film is one of only four major features by Carl Theodor Dreyer (1889–1968), who although he made many short films, was able to make only one feature each in the 1920s (*The Passion of Joan of Arc*), the 1940s (*Vampyr*), the 1950s (*Ordet*), and the 1960s (*Gertrud*). That was enough to place him first among all directors in the minds of such as Lars von Trier and the critic Jonathan Rosenbaum, and to make him (with Ozu and Bresson) the focus of Paul Schrader's influential 1972 book *Transcendental Style in Film*. His *Joan of Arc* is often named among the ten greatest films of all time.

But there are those who prefer *Ordet*, with its two families: those of Morten Borgen, patriarch of Borgensfarm, and those of Petersen, a nearby tailor. Morten is the bearded, stern father of three sons: the sincere Mikkel, married to Inger; the mad Johannes, who believes he is Jesus Christ; and the young Anders, a quiet youth who wants to marry the tailor's daughter. The tailor, who works cross-legged sitting in his window, has a wife,

Kirstin, and a daughter, Anne. The only other characters are Mikkel and Inger's two young daughters, a pastor, a doctor, a midwife, and a servant at Borgensfarm.

I take the time to name the characters because the movie takes time to establish them, to ground them all in the very fabric of the narrative. It does not dart from one to another. It gives each full weight. When they talk, it listens, and every word is measured, none glib or careless. It's as if they're talking for the record.

The early events seem ordinary enough. Inger is pregnant again. Anders has proposed to Anne. Morten is filled with pride in his farm, and his family is known by it: "The son of Borgensfarm," etc. Anders confides to Inger that he wants to marry Anne, and Inger gently breaks this news to her father-in-law, but Morten will have none of it, because Peter the tailor is of the wrong religion. Both families are Christian, but Peter is of the fundamentalist belief, and Morten advocates a faith with more freedom and joy. In practice, both views translate to rigid dogmatism.

The unprepared audience member has long since grown a little restless, especially during the slow, mournful soliloquies of the mad Johannes, who regrets that the others do not follow him or heed his prophecies. There is a peculiar scene in which the new pastor pays a call when only Johannes is at home, and listens to one of his dire monologues. When Morten returns, the pastor immediately shakes his hand and leaves. Why did he pay the call?

Doubt is expressed by Morten about the power of prayer, because his own could not save a loved one. He blames himself: "I did not truly believe." Anders goes to Peter, asks for his daughter's hand, and is turned down: "You are not a Christian." Although Morten has refused to have his son marry the girl for exactly the same reason, the news that a son of Borgensfarm is not good enough for Peter's daughter enrages him, and he sets off with Anders to the tailor's house.

He interrupts the least cheerful prayer meeting I can imagine, with a small congregation hearing Peter's confession that he is a sinner, now born again, and then joining in a doleful hymn. The congregation files out, the two old men sit down to discuss their differences and the futures of their children, and it is *now*, although we may not have noticed, that the film has taken its grip. We will not be able to look away again until the end, and we will think of nothing else.

Morten and Peter, played by Henrik Malberg and Ejnar Federspiel, sit side by side on a bench and brutally insult each other's beliefs in deliberate, understated certainties. There is undeniable buried humor here. They have known each other for years. They know all of these disagreements already. Only at the end, when Peter goes too far, does Morten shake him by his shirt front.

These scenes are intercut with Inger going into labor back at the farm. The doctor, a tall, cool man, arrives to consult with the midwife. He intervenes to save Inger's life. His work, shielded by a sheet, is so difficult that he bares his teeth in a grimace. This is the most painful scene of medical procedure I have ever experienced in a film, even though it is only suggested, not seen.

Now I will not tell you the rest of the story, at least not in so many words. Up to this point, I have practiced more description than "criticism," because to closely observe this film is to criticize it, struggle with it, respond to it, understand it, and finally respect it. It is what it is, fearlessly, without compromise. Its characters lead their lives in their own ways, not for the convenience of the plot or the audience. They stand where they stand.

It turns out, after all, that some things are more important than others. That there are different kinds and depths of belief. That although all the adults except Johannes believe the Lord no longer works miracles, Morten may have been correct that a prayer must be believed to be successful. Dogma is meaningless without faith, but faith does not need dogma.

The lives of everyone in this film depend entirely on religion. It could be shown in any church in the world, with a few adjustments to the subtitles to supply words other than "Christian." Yet I find from Rosenbaum that Dreyer was not a particularly religious man, and this film is not intended to proselytize. It simply intends to see.

That it does astonishingly well. The rude, simple sets have the solidity of a universe. The outdoor shots, of searches for the runaway Johannes on the moors, or a buggy ride across the horizon, are almost abstractly beautiful. Much is offscreen: the Borgensfarm sow that has had piglets is much watched, never seen. Peter's house has only a sign and a doorway. The doctor's car is established only by its headlights. The grim reaper is seen only by Johannes.

The camera movements have an almost godlike quality. At several points, such as during the prayer meeting, they pan back and forth slowly, relentlessly, hypnotically. There are a few movements of astonishing complexity, beginning in the foreground, somehow arriving at the background, but they flow so naturally you may not even notice them. The lighting, in black and white, is celestial—not in a joyous but in a detached way. The climactic scene could have been handled in countless conventional ways, but the film has prepared us for it, and it has a grave, startling power.

When the film was over, I had plans. I could not carry them out. I went to bed. Not to sleep. To feel. To puzzle about what had happened to me. I had started by viewing a film that initially bored me. It had found its way into my soul. Even after the first half hour, I had little idea what power awaited me, but now I could see how those opening minutes had to be as they were.

I have books about Dreyer on the shelf. I did not take them down. I taught a class based on the Schrader book, although I did not include *Ordet*. I did not open it to see what he had to say. Rosenbaum has written often about Dreyer, but when I quote him here, it is only things he has said to me. I did not want secondary information, analysis, context. The film stands utterly and fearlessly alone. Many viewers will turn away from it. Persevere. Go to it. It will not come to you.

{ OUT OF THE PAST }

Most crime movies begin in the present and move forward, but film noir coils back into the past. The noir hero is doomed before the story begins—by fate, rotten luck, or his own flawed character. Crime movies sometimes show good men who go bad. The noir hero is never good, just kidding himself, living in ignorance of his dark side until events demonstrate it to him.

Out of the Past (1947) is one of the greatest of all film noirs, the story of a man who tries to break with his past and his weakness and start over again in a town, with a new job and a new girl. The movie stars Robert Mitchum, whose weary eyes and laconic voice, whose very presence as a violent man wrapped in indifference, made him an archetypal noir actor. The story opens before we've even seen him, as trouble comes to town looking for him. A man from his past has seen him pumping gas, and now his old life reaches out and pulls him back.

Mitchum plays Jeff Bailey, whose name was Jeff Markham when he was working as a private eye out of New York. In those days he was hired by a gangster named Whit Sterling (Kirk Douglas, electrifying in an early role) to track down a woman named Kathie Moffat (Jane Greer, irresistibly mixing sexiness and treachery). Kathie shot Sterling four times, hitting him once, and supposedly left with $40,000 of his money. Sterling wants Jeff to bring her back. It's not, he says, that he wants revenge: "I just want her back. When you see her, you'll understand better."

That whole story, and a lot more, is told in a flashback. When we meet Jeff at the beginning of the film, it's in an idyllic setting by a lake in the Sierras, where he has his arm around the woman he loves, Ann (Virginia Huston). He bends over to kiss her when they're interrupted by Jimmy (Dickie Moore), the deaf and mute kid who works for him at the station. Jimmy uses sign language to say a stranger is at the station, asking for him. This man is Sterling's hired gun, named Joe Stephanos (Paul Valentine), and he tells Jeff that Sterling wants to see him in his lodge on Lake Tahoe.

Jeff takes Ann along on the all-night drive to Tahoe, using the trip to tell her his story—his real name, his real past, how he tracked Kathie Moffat to Mexico and fell in love with her. ("And then I saw her, coming out of the sun, and I knew why Whit didn't care about that forty grand.") He tells Ann more, too: how he lied to Sterling about finding Kathie, how he and Kathie slipped away to San Francisco and thought they could live free of the past, how they were spotted by Fisher (Steve Brodie), Jeff's former partner. Fisher followed them to a remote cabin, where Kathie shot him dead, leaving Jeff behind with the body and a bank book revealing she indeed had stolen the $40,000.

The story takes Jeff all night to tell, and lasts forty minutes into the film. Then we're back in the present again, at the gates of Sterling's lodge. Ann drives away and Jeff walks up the drive to square with his past. In the lodge, not really to his surprise, he finds that Kathie is once again with Sterling. This Sterling is a piece of work. Not only has he taken Kathie back after she shot him, he wants to hire Jeff again after he betrayed him. This time he needs him to deal with Leonard Eels, an accountant in San Francisco who keeps Sterling's books, and is blackmailing him with threats involving the IRS.

The meeting between Mitchum and Douglas opens on a note of humor so quiet, it may pass unnoticed. "Cigarette?" offers Douglas. "Smoking," said Mitchum, holding up his hand with a cigarette in it. Something about that moment has always struck me as odd, as somehow outside the movie, and I asked Mitchum about it after a screening of *Out of the Past* at the Virginia Film Festival.

"Did you guys have any idea of doing a running gag involving cigarette smoking?" I asked him.

"No, no."

"Because there's more cigarette smoking in this movie than in any other movie I've ever seen."

"We never thought about it. We just smoked. And I'm not impressed by that because I don't, honest to God, know that I've ever actually seen the film."

"You've never seen it?"

"I'm sure I have, but it's been so long that I don't know."

That was Mitchum for you, a superb actor who affected a weary indifference to his work.

There is a lot of smoking in *Out of the Past*. There is a lot of smoking in all noirs, even the modern ones, because it goes with the territory. Good health, for noir characters, starts with not getting killed. But few movies use smoking as well as this one; in their scenes together, it would be fair to say that Mitchum and Douglas smoke at each other, in a sublimated form of fencing. The director is Jacques Tourneur, a master of dark drama at RKO, also famous for *Cat People* (1942) and *I Walked with a Zombie* (1943). He is working here for the third time with the cinematographer Nicholas Musuraca, a master of shadow but also of light, and Musuraca throws light into the empty space between the two actors, so that when they exhale, the smoke is visible as bright white clouds.

Mitchum and Douglas think the story involves a contest of wills between them, when in fact they're both the instruments of corrupt women. Kathie betrays both men more than once, and there is also Meta Carson (Rhonda Fleming), the sultry "secretary" of Eels the accountant. What's fascinating is the way Jeff, the Mitchum character, goes ahead, despite knowing what's being done to him. How he gets involved once again with Sterling and Kathie, despite all their history together, and how he agrees when Meta suggests a meeting with Eels, even though he knows and even says "I think I'm in a frame," and points out that he's been given a drink so that his prints will be on the glass.

The scenes in San Francisco, involving the murder of Eels, the whereabouts of the tax records, and the double dealing of Meta Carson, are so labyrinthine, it's remarkable even the characters can figure out who is being double crossed, and why. The details don't matter. What matters is the way that Jeff, a streetwise tough guy, gets involved in the face of all common sense, senses a trap, thinks he can walk through it, and is still fascinated by Kathie Moffat.

He first reveals his obsession in Mexico, when Kathie claims she didn't take the forty grand.

"But I didn't take anything. I didn't, Jeff. Don't you believe me?"

"Baby, I don't care."

And later, although he tells her, "You're like a leaf that the wind blows from one gutter to another," he is attracted to her, lured as men sometimes are to what they know is wrong and dangerous.

Film noir is known for its wise-guy dialogue, but the screenplay for *Out of the Past* reads like an anthology of one-liners. It was based on the 1946 novel *Build My Gallows High* by "Geoffrey Homes," a pseudonym for the blacklisted Daniel Mainwaring, and the screenplay credit goes to Mainwaring, reportedly with extra dialogue by James M. Cain. But the critic Jeff Schwager read all versions of the screenplay for a 1990 *Film Comment* article, and writes me: "Mainwaring's script was not very good, and in one draft featured awful voice-over narration by the deaf-mute. Cain's script was a total rewrite and even worse; it was totally discarded. The great dialogue was actually the work of Frank Fenton, a B-movie writer whose best known credit was John Ford's *Wings of Eagles*."

Listen to the contempt with which Sterling silences his hired gun, Stephanos: "Smoke a cigarette, Joe." And "Think of a number, Joe." Listen to Joe tell Jeff how he found his gas station: "It's a small world." Jeff: "Yeah. Or a big sign." Kathie saying: "I hate him. I'm sorry he didn't die." Jeff: "Give him time." Jeff's friend the cab driver, assigned to tail Meta Carson: "I lost her." Jeff: "She's worth losing." Jeff to Kathie: "Just get out, will you?

I have to sleep in this room." Kathie to Jeff: "You're no good, and neither am I. That's why we deserve each other." And in the movie's most famous exchange, Kathie telling him: "I don't want to die." Jeff: "Neither do I, baby, but if I have to, I'm going to die last."

The movie's final scene, between the hometown girl Ann and Jimmy, Jeff's hired kid at the gas station, reflects the moral murkiness of the film with its quiet ambiguity. I won't reveal the details, but as Jimmy answers Ann's question, is he telling her what he believes, what he thinks she wants to believe, or what he thinks it will be best for her to believe?

{ PAN'S LABYRINTH }

P*an's Labyrinth* is one of the greatest of all fantasy films, even though it is anchored so firmly in the reality of war. On first viewing, it is challenging to comprehend a movie that on the one hand provides fauns and fairies, and on the other hand creates an inhuman sadist in the uniform of Franco's fascists. The fauns and fantasies are seen only by the eleven-year-old heroine, but that does not mean she's "only dreaming"; they are as real as the fascist captain who murders on the flimsiest excuse. The coexistence of these two worlds is one of the scariest elements of the film; they both impose sets of rules that can get an eleven-year-old killed.

Pan's Labyrinth (2006) took shape in the imagination of Guillermo del Toro as long ago as 1993, when he began to sketch ideas and images in the notebooks he always carries. The Mexican director responded strongly to the horror lurking under the surface of classic fairy tales and had no interest in making a children's film, but instead a film that looked horror straight in the eye. He also rejected all the hackneyed ideas for the creatures of movie fantasy and created (with his Oscar-winning cinematographer, art director, and makeup people) a faun, a frog, and a horrible Pale Man whose skin hangs in folds from his unwholesome body.

The time is 1944 in Spain. Bands of anti-Franco fighters hide in the forest, encouraged by news of the Normandy landings and other setbacks for Franco's friends Hitler and Mussolini. A troop of Franco's soldiers is sent to the remote district to hunt down the rebels, and is led by Capitan Vidal (Sergi Lopez), a sadist under cover as a rigid military man.

Commandeering a gloomy old mill as his headquarters, he moves in his new wife, Carmen (Ariadna Gil), who is very pregnant, and her daughter from her first marriage, Ofelia (Ivana Baquero). The girl hates her stepfather, who indeed values Carmen only for breeding purposes. Soon after arriving, Vidal shoots dead two farmers whose rifles, they claim, are only for hunting rabbits. After they die, Vidal finds rabbits in their pouches. "Next time, search these assholes before wasting my time with them," he tells an underling. He orders Mercedes (Maribel Verdu), his chief servant, to cook the rabbits for dinner: "Maybe a stew." What a vile man.

Ofelia encounters a strange insect looking like a praying mantis. It shudders in and out of frame, and we're reminded of Del Toro's affection for odd little creatures (as in *Cronos*, with its deep-biting immortality bug). The insect, friendly and insistent, seems to her like a fairy, and when she says so, the bug becomes a vibrating little man who leads her into a labyrinth and thus to her first fearsome meeting with the faun (Doug Jones, who specializes in acting inside bizarre costumes). Some viewers have confused the faun with Pan, but there is no Pan in the picture and the international title translates as *Labyrinth of the Faun*.

The faun seems to be both good and evil; what are we to make of a huge pile of used shoes, especially worrisome in the time of the Holocaust? But what he actually offers is not good or evil, but the choice between them, and Del Toro says in a commentary that Ofelia is "a girl who needs to disobey anything except her own soul." The whole movie, he says, is about choices.

The faun fits neatly into Ofelia's worries about her pregnant mother; he gives her a mandrake root to hide under the mother's bed and feed with two drops of blood daily. The mandrake root is said to resemble a penis, but this one, in special effects that are beyond creepy, looks like a half-baby made from wood, leaves, and earth. Ofelia discovers that Carmen is aiding the rebels, but keeps her secret because she doesn't want to be responsible for hurting anyone, a trait that will benefit her.

The film is visually stunning. The creatures do not look like movie creations but like nightmares (especially the Pale Man, with eyes in the palms of his hands). The baroque organic look of the faun's lair is unlike any place I have seen in the movies. When the giant frog delivers up a crucial key in its stomach, it does so by regurgitating its entire body, leaving an empty frog skin behind. Meanwhile, Vidal plays records on his phonograph, smokes, drinks, shaves as if tempting himself to slash his throat, speaks harshly to his wife, threatens the doctor, and shoots people.

Del Toro moves between many of these scenes with a moving foreground wipe—an area of darkness, or a wall or a tree that wipes out the military and wipes in the labyrinth, or vice versa. This technique insists that his two worlds are not intercut, but live in edges of the same frame. He portrays most of the mill interiors in a cold blue-grey slate, but introduces life tones into the faces of characters we favor, and into the fantasy world. It is no coincidence that the bombs of the rebels introduce red and yellow explosions into the monotone world they attack.

Guillermo del Toro (born 1964) is the most challenging of directors in the fantasy field because he invents from scratch, or adapts into his own vision. He has made six features since his debut at twenty-nine with *Cronos* (1993), and I have admired, even loved, all of them, even those like *Hellboy*, *Mimic*, and *Blade II* that did not receive the universal acclaim of *Cronos* and *The Devil's Backbone* (a ghost story also set in Franco's Spain). He is above all a visually oriented director, and when he says "films are made of looks," I think he is referring not only to the gazes of his actors but to his own.

Born in Mexico, he has worked there and overseas, like his gifted friends and contemporaries Alfonso Cuaron (born 1961) and Alejandro Gonzalez Inarritu (born 1963). Isn't it time to start talking about a New Mexican Cinema, not always filmed in Mexico but always informed by the imagination and spirit of the nation? Think of Del Toro's remarkable films, and then consider too Cuaron's *Children of Men, Harry Potter and the Prisoner Of Azkaban* (the best-looking Potter film), *Great Expectations* (an overlooked masterpiece), and *Y Tu Mamá También*. Or Inarritu's *Amores Perros, 21 Grams*, and *Babel*.

Some of these are in one way or another genre films, but there is so much impact and intensity, and such a richness of visual imagination, that they flatter their genres instead of depending on them. The three directors trade actors and technicians, support each other, make new rules, are successful without compromise. Cuaron's 1998 *Great Expectations*, set in a Spanish-moss-dripping modern Florida and starring Ethan Hawke, Gwyneth Paltrow, and Anne Bancroft (in guess which roles), is a stunning reworking of Dickens and illustrates how all three of these directors can put hands on a project and make it their own.

What makes Del Toro's *Pan's Labyrinth* so powerful, I think, is that it brings together two kinds of material, obviously not compatible, and insists on playing true to both, right to the end. Because there is no compromise there is no escape route, and the dangers in each world are always present in the other. Del Toro talks of the "rule of three" in fables (three doors, three rules, three fairies, three thrones). I am not sure three viewings of this film would be enough, however.

{ P A T H S   O F   G L O R Y }

Stanley Kubrick's *Paths of Glory* (1957) closes with a scene that doesn't seem organic to the movie. We've seen harrowing battlefield carnage, a morally rotten court-martial, French army generals corrupt and cynical beyond all imagining, and now what do we see? Drunken soldiers, crowded into a bistro, banging their beer steins on the tables as the owner brings a frightened German girl onstage. He makes lascivious remarks about her figure and cruel ones about her lack of talent, but she has been captured and must be forced to perform. Hoots and whistles arise from the crowd. The frightened girl begins to sing. The noise from the crowd dies away. Her tremulous voice fills the room. She sings "The Faithful Hussar." A hush falls, and some of the soldiers begin to hum the notes; they know the song but not the words.

If the singing of "La Marseillaise" in a bar in *Casablanca* was a call to patriotism, this scene is an argument against it. It creates a moment of quiet and tenderness in the daily horror these soldiers occupy—a world in which generals casually estimated that 55 percent of these very men might be killed in a stupid attack and found that acceptable.

Songs at the ends of dramas usually make us feel better. They are part of closure. This song at the end of this movie makes us feel more forlorn. It is not a release, but a twist of Kubrick's emotional knife. When Truffaut famously said that it was impossible to make an antiwar movie, because action argues in favor of itself, he could not have been thinking of *Paths of Glory*, and no wonder: because of its harsh portrait of the French army, the film was banned in France until 1975.

The film, made in 1957, is typical of Kubrick's earlier work in being short (eighty-four minutes), tight, told with an economy approaching terseness. Later his films would expand in length and epic scope, sometimes to their advantage, sometimes not. It does however contain examples of one of his favorite visual strategies, the extended camera movement that unfolds to reveal details of a set or location, and continues long after we expect it to be over.

Early in the film, the camera precedes its hero, Colonel Dax (Kirk Douglas), on an inspection tour of a muddy fortified trench that goes on and on and on. Later the camera follows doomed men into No Man's Land, tracking alongside them through mud and shell blasts, trenches and craters, past bodies that drop before our eyes. Still later, there is a dolly shot through a formal ball to find a French general. And toward the end, an elaborate military parade for a firing squad, with the camera preceding three condemned men as they walk and walk and walk toward their deaths.

These shots of long duration impress the importance of their subjects upon us: the permanence of trench warfare, the devastation of attack, the hypocrisy of the ruling class, the dread of the condemned men. If some of Kubrick's later extended shots, including the endless tracking shot down long hotel corridors in *The Shining* (1979), seem like exercises in style, the shots in *Paths of Glory* are aimed straight at our emotions.

The story is simply summarized. French and German armies face each other along five hundred miles of fortified trenches. Both sides have been dug in for two years. Any attempt at an advance brings a dreadful human cost in lives. The effete little General Broulard (Adolphe Menjou) orders his subordinate, General Mireau (George Macready), to take an impregnable German position, "The Anthill," by, incredibly, the day after tomorrow. Mireau argues that it cannot be done. Broulard thinks perhaps it can be accomplished with no more than 55 percent casualties. He hints that there is a promotion and a third star for the general who does it. The two-star General Mireau goes through the motions of protest: "The lives of eight thousand men! What is my ambition against that? My reputation?" And then: "But, by god, we might just do it!"

Colonel Dax must lead the charge. He knows it is doomed, and he protests, but he follows orders. In a scene set the night before the raid, a scene that in other language might have been conceived by Shakespeare, two of his men debate the merits of dying by machinegun or bayonet. One chooses the machinegun, because it is quick; while the bayonet might not kill, it would hurt. The other says that proves he is more afraid of pain than death.

The actual assault has a realism that is convincing even now that we have seen Stone's *Platoon* and Spielberg's *Saving Private Ryan*. The black-and-white photography is the correct choice; this is a world of shapes and shadows, mud and smoke, not a world for color. The loss of life is devastating. The advance is halted. Watching from the safety of the trenches, General Mireau decides the men are cowards and orders French artillery to fire on their own men, to drive them forward. The battery commander refuses to act without a written order.

At the end of the day, to save face and protect his promotion, Mireau orders that three men, one from each company, must be executed for cowardice. One is chosen by lot. One because he is "socially undesirable." One because he was an eyewitness to the cowardice of a superior officer, who abandoned a comrade on a reconnaissance mission. Dax is outraged and asks to act as defense counsel before the military tribunal, which is, as we expect, a farce. When Dax argues for the defense that any further advance was "impossible," the prosecutor snaps, "If it was impossible, the only proof of that would be their dead bodies at the bottom of the trenches." The survivors are obviously cowards, then, because they are alive.

That night, the condemned men share the same cell. "Do you see that cockroach?" one says. "Tomorrow morning I'll be dead, and it will be alive." The film until this point has been bitter and unromantic, but we think we glimpse a turn in the plot. Dax learns of Mireau's order to fire French artillery at French troops. He finds General Broulard at a fancy ball and informs him of Mireau's artillery order. In any conventional war movie, in a film made by ninety-nine directors out of one hundred, there would be an eleventh-hour reprieve, the condemned men would be spared, and the stupid and treacherous Mireau would be publicly humiliated.

Not here. Kubrick finds a way to draw all his story threads tight without compromising his harsh and unforgiving theme. The plot is resolved, yes, but cruelty and duplicity survive, and private soldiers are still meaningless pawns. Broulard believes the executions will be "a perfect tonic" for the army: "One way to maintain discipline is to shoot a man now and then."

Paths of Glory was the film by which Stanley Kubrick entered the ranks of great directors, never to leave them. When I interviewed Kirk Douglas in 1969, he recalled it as the summit of his acting career: "There's a picture that will always be good, years from now. I don't have to wait fifty years to know that; I know it now." It has an economy of expression that is almost brutal; it is one of the few narrative films in which you sense the anger in the telling. Samuel Fuller, who fought all the way through World War II, remembered it in *The Big Red One* with nostalgia for the camaraderie of his outfit. There is no nostalgia in *Paths of Glory*. Only nightmare.

Kubrick and his cinematographer, George Krause, use sharp and deep focus for every shot. There is not a single shot composed only for beauty; the movie's visual style is to look, and look hard. Kirk Douglas, a star whose intelligence and ambition sometimes pulled him away from the comfortable path mapped by the system, contains most of the emotion of his character. When he is angry, we know it, but he stays just within the edge of going too far. He remains an officer. He does his duty. He finds a way to define his duty more deeply than his superiors would have wished, but in a way, they cannot condemn.

And then that final song. It is sung by a young actress named Christiane Harlan, who soon after married Stanley Kubrick. One day in the summer of 2000, I visited her on their farm outside London, and we walked through the garden to the boulder engraved with Kubrick's name, under which he rests. I wanted to tell her how special and powerful that scene was, how it came out of nowhere to provide a heartbreaking coda, how by cutting away from his main story Kubrick cut right into the heart of it. But it didn't seem like the moment for film criticism, and I was sure she already knew whatever I could tell her.

THE PHANTOM
OF THE OPERA

It has always been a question whether *The Phantom of the Opera* (1925) is a great film, or only a great spectacle. Carl Sandburg, one of the original reviewers, underwent a change of heart between his first *Chicago Daily News* review (he waited for the Phantom's unmasking "terribly fascinated, aching with suspense") and a reconsideration written a month later ("strictly among the novelties of the season"). It was not, he added, on the level of *The Cabinet of Dr. Caligari* or *Greed*, mentioning two of the greatest films of all time.

He was right about that, and could have added the greatest of all silent horror films, Murnau's *Nosferatu* (1922), whose vampire may have influenced Lon Chaney's performance as the Phantom. But as an exercise in lurid sensationalism, straining against technical limitations in its eagerness to overwhelm, the first of the many Phantom films has a creepy, undeniable power.

The story is simply told—too simply, perhaps, so that all of the adaptations, including the famous Andrew Lloyd Webber musical, have been much ado about relatively little. In the cellars of the Paris Opera House lives a disfigured masked man who becomes obsessed with the young singer Christine. He commands the management to give her leading roles, and when they refuse, he exacts a terrible revenge, causing a great chandelier to crash down on the audience.

Christine's lover, a pallid nonentity, is little competition for her fascination with the Phantom, until she realizes with horror that the creature wants her to dwell in his mad subterranean world. She unmasks him, is repelled by his hideous disfigurement, flees to the surface and her lover, and is followed by a Phantom seeking violent revenge. There is no room for psychological subtlety here.

It is the idea of the Phantom, really, that fascinates us: the idea of a cruelly mistreated man going mad in self-imposed exile in the very cellars, dungeons, and torture chambers where he was, apparently, disfigured in the first place. His obsession with Christine reflects his desire to win back some joy from a world that has mistreated him. Leroux and his adapters have placed this sad creature in a bizarre subterranean space that has inspired generations of set designers. There are five levels of cellars beneath the opera, one descending beneath another in an expressionist series of staircases, ramps, trapdoors, and a Styxian river that the Phantom crosses in a gondola. The Phantom has furnished his lair with grotesque fittings: he sleeps in a coffin and provides a bed for Christine in the shape of a whale boat. Remote controls give him warnings when anyone approaches and allow him to roast or drown his enemies.

To Christine, he offers wealth, luxury, and opera stardom, and she is in no peril "as long as you do not touch the mask"—oh, and she must love him, or at least allow him to possess her (although his precise sexual plans are left undefined). Perhaps warned by the fate of the hero in her current production of *Faust*, she refuses this bargain, although for an engaged woman, she allows herself to be dangerously tempted.

After taking over the leading role from an ominously ill prima donna, she follows a mysterious voice, opens a secret door behind the mirror in her dressing room, descends through forbidding cellars, is taken semiconscious by horseback and gondola deeper into the labyrinth, and sees the coffin where he sleeps. At this point, her sudden cry of "You—you are the Phantom!" inspired me to write in my notes: "Duh!"

Her lover, the Viscount Raoul de Chagny, is likewise not a swift study. After the Phantom has presumably claimed dozens of victims with the falling chandelier and threatened Christine with death if she sees him again, Raoul agrees to meet her at the masked ball. This is held in the opera house on the very next night, with the chandelier miraculously repaired and no mourning period, apparently, for the dozens of crushed and maimed. Christine tells Raoul the Phantom will murder them if they are seen together, but then, when a gaunt and spectral figure in red stalks imperiously into the grand hall, Raoul unmasks himself, which is, if you ask me, asking for trouble.

Christine determines to sing her role one more time, after which Raoul will have a carriage waiting by the stage door to spirit them safely away to England. This plan is too optimistic, as the Phantom snatches Christine from her dressing room, and the two are pursued into the bowels of Paris by Raoul and Inspector Ledoux—and, in a separate pursuit, by the vengeful stagehand Buquet (whose brother the Phantom murdered), leading a mob of torch-carrying rabble. The hapless Raoul and Ledoux are lured into a chamber where the Phantom can roast them to death, and when they escape through a trapdoor, it leads to a chamber where they can be drowned.

All of this is fairly ridiculous, and yet, and yet, the story exerts a certain macabre fascination. The characters of Christine and Raoul, played by Mary Philbin and Norman Kerry, essentially function as puppets of the plot. But the Phantom is invested by the intense and inventive Lon Chaney with a horror and poignancy that is almost entirely created with body language. More of his face is covered than in modern versions (a little gauze curtain flutters in front of his mouth), but look at the way his hand moves as he gestures toward the coffin as the titles announce "That is where I sleep." It is a languorous movement that conveys great weary sadness.

The Phantom's unmasking was one of the most famous moments in silent film. He is seated at his organ. "Now, when he is intent on the music," Sandburg wrote, "she comes closer, closer, her fingers steal towards the ribbon that fastens the mask. Her fingers give one final twitch—and there you are!" There you are, all right, as Chaney, "the Man of 1,000 Faces" and a master of makeup, unveils a defacement more grotesque than in any later version, his mouth a gaping cavern, his nose a void, his eyes widely staring: "Feast your eyes, glut your soul, on my accursed ugliness!"

The other famous scene involves the falling chandelier, which became the centerpiece of the Webber musical and functions the same way in Joel Schumacher's 2004 film version. In the original film, it is curiously underplayed; it falls in impressive majesty, to be sure, but its results are hard to measure. Surely there are mangled bodies beneath it, but the movie stays its distance and then hurries on.

Much more impressive is the masked ball sequence and its sequel on the roof of the opera house. The filmmakers (director Rupert Julien, replaced by Edward Sedgwick and assisted by Chaney) use primitive color techniques to saturate the ball with brilliant scarlets and less obtrusive greens. Many scenes throughout the film are tinted, which was common enough in silent days, but the masked ball is a primitive form of Technicolor, in which the Phantom's great red cloak sweeps through the air like a carrion bird that enfolds him. And on the roof, as Raoul and Christine plot, he hovers unseen above them on the side of a statue, the red garment billowing ominously. Chaney's movements in all of these scenes are filled with heedless bravado, and yet when he pauses, when he listens, when the reasons for his jealousy are confirmed, he conveys his suffering.

In a strange way, the very artificiality of the color adds to its effect. True, accurate, and realistic color is simply . . . color. But this form of color, which seems imposed on the material, functions as a passionate impasto, a blood-red overlay. We can sense the film straining to overwhelm us. The various scores (I listened to the music by the great composer for silent film Carl Davis) swoop and weep and shriek and fall into ominous prefigurings, and the whole enterprise embraces the spirit of grand guignol.

The Phantom of the Opera is not a great film if you are concerned with art and subtlety, depth and message; *Nosferatu* is a world beyond it. But in its fevered melodrama and images of cadaverous romance, it finds a kind of show-biz majesty. And it has two elements of genius: it creates beneath the opera one of the most grotesque places in the cinema, and Chaney's performance transforms an absurd character into a haunting one.

{ PIXOTE }

Fathered by strangers, abandoned by their mothers, thrown away by society, the children of *Pixote* live by their wits on the cruel streets of São Paolo in Brazil. They improvise their own families, forming shifting alliances based on need, fear, and even love. Their economy is based on the only two markets open to them, those for sex and drugs. Many of them are so young, they only vaguely understand sex; they are hardened to sights and experiences they don't even comprehend.

Hector Babenco's 1981 film was created in the spirit of Italian neorealism; his child actors are the real thing, discovered in the streets and essentially playing themselves. The adult characters are mostly played by professional actors, but these performances coming from completely different backgrounds seem to feed from the same desperation. There is no answer to the problem of the millions of homeless children, no remedy, no hope. It is not surprising to learn that Fernando Ramos da Silva, the illiterate eleven-year-old who plays Pixote, returned to the streets and was killed by police bullets in 1987.

The movie is told in a loosely structured, episodic style. Not every scene pays off neatly or makes a smooth connect with the next one. The jagged tone seems appropriate for these lives, which have no continuity, no balance point, no reason for something to happen today, tomorrow, or ever.

In a society of children and adolescents who have no homes and no money, crime is the natural way of survival, but they're not very good at it (the gangs in *City of God*, made twenty years later, are much more sophisticated). Their approach to crime, as to life, is thoughtless improvisation; they respond to situations, but have no control over them. We sense that Babenco isn't leading his characters but following them, and scenes don't always have a point or a purpose because neither do these lives.

We meet Pixote when he is rounded up along with other street kids after the murder of a judge. Society demands the appearance of justice and revenge, and so the murder will be pinned on one of them—never mind if it's the right one or not. Some fairly confusing dialogue indicates that one of these kids may have been involved in the crime, or witnessed it, but solving the crime is not the point of the movie, and the police despair of ever knowing who the real killer is. The code of silence, enforced by the possibility of death, is complete.

The kids are taken to a reformatory. Inside would be better for them than outside, if it weren't for the brutality of the guards, the corruption of the staff, and the crimes of one prisoner against another (on his first night, Pixote witnesses a rape).

Faces and characters form out of the crowd. The most striking is Lilica (Jorge Juliao), a transvestite whose sexual nature is accepted casually by the others. He's older—seventeen, in a nation where he can't be charged with a crime until he's eighteen. Then there are Dito (Gilberto Moura), looking cherubic under a crown of curly hair, and Chico (Edilson Lino).

Without agreeing to it, discussing it, or even really noticing it, they form a group based on their shared vulnerability and trust. When things get dangerous inside the reformatory, and it's clear some of them may die at the hands of brutal guards or cops with secrets to hide, they escape and return to the streets. It's not that hard: they go through an open window to a rooftop. (One kid, with a leg brace, decides not to escape: "It's better for me here.")

We can anticipate, more or less, what happens in the first half of the film, which is not a million miles from the poverty and crime in, say, *Oliver Twist*. The second half of the film is a descent into hell; indeed, the dominant tones become red and orange instead of the muted drabness of the earlier scenes.

Lilica is picked up by a sometime client or lover or pimp named Cristal (Tony Tornado). He can wholesale them some drugs. They snatch purses to raise the cash, prowling the city streets like a wolf pack. They ride the rails to Rio to sell the drugs, are victimized by their customers, and end up living with a deteriorating prostitute named Sueli (Marilia Pera, who won the best actress award from the National Society of Film Critics).

She is the fifth member of the family, but then it begins to shrink. Two of the boys are killed, and Lilica walks out one night—jealous because the prostitute has seduced a boy he cares for. Even earlier, Lilica was uneasy around Sueli, and indeed, he seems more feminine, more maternal, more caring than the hard woman of the streets. Lilica has a self-awareness the others lack, sighing at one point, "What can a queer expect from life?" Pixote replies, "Nothing, Lilica," but in his world no one can expect anything. Then Lilica is gone, and at the end, everyone is gone, except for Sueli and Pixote.

Pixote has obtained a gun, and he uses it. How, I will not reveal, except to say that it is shocking how impassive he seems after killing two people, one by mistake. His wide, open eyes don't seem to register the result of his actions, and his face doesn't seem to register feeling about it—until, hours later, sitting at the foot of Sueli's bed, watching TV, he throws up. And then we understand the agony inside of Pixote, the pain that is unbearable because he lacks the experience and even the words to deal with it.

The closing scenes are powerful, sad, and eventually heartless. They show without compromise the depth of Pixote's need and the totality of his loneliness. Much depends on the character of Sueli, who in the second half of the movie is really the dominant presence (Pixote throughout most of the movie is as much observer as participant).

The streets have given Sueli a hardness and coldness that close her off from real emotion, even though as an experienced prostitute she can fake it—sometimes with clients, but more often in her own life, as if she's trying to deceive herself. She has a remarkable scene, late one night when she should be in torment but gets drunk and then dances in the headlights of a stolen car, remembering that she was truly happy when she was a strip-tease performer.

Then comes her last scene with Pixote, which is so sorrowful and cruel it is barely watchable. He is still, after everything, a little boy. Sueli has recently performed an abortion on herself (she explains it in cruel detail to Pixote), but now, just for a moment, she imagines a life in which she will return to her town and family, and Pixote will be like her son. Pixote turns to her breast, not in a sexual way, but in need, and we see the child who has always hungered for a mother he never had.

It is a hushed, sacred moment, and in another film, it would be the last shot. A similar scene concludes John Steinbeck's *The Grapes of Wrath*— the novel, not the movie. But then Sueli hardens, and all the anger of her pitiful life focuses on Pixote. At this point the film fits the classical definition of tragedy, which requires the death of a hero. But Pixote is not a hero; his life has been a half-understood reaction to events. And he doesn't die, except in his heart and soul.

Babenco, born in 1946, has been one of Brazil's most successful directors. *Pixote* was his first great accomplishment, and in 1985, he made *Kiss of the Spider Woman*, with its best actor Oscar for William Hurt and a nomination for Babenco. Then came two big-budget American films with mixed receptions, *Ironweed* (1987), with Jack Nicholson and Meryl Streep, and *At Play in the Fields of the Lord* (1991). In 2003 he returned to the homeless and helpless of Brazil with *Carandiru*, set in the most notorious prison in Brazil and once again showing transvestites and thieves forming their own society in opposition to the corruption of the system.

But *Pixote* stands alone in his work, a rough, unblinking look at lives no human being should be required to lead. And the eyes of Fernando Ramos da Silva, his doomed young actor, regard us from the screen not in hurt, not in accusation, not in regret—but simply in acceptance of a desolate daily reality.

$$\left\{ \text{P L A Y T I M E} \right\}$$

Jacques Tati's *Playtime*, like *2001: A Space Odyssey* or *The Blair Witch Project* or *Russian Ark*, is one of a kind, complete in itself, a species already extinct at the moment of its birth. Even Mr. Hulot, Tati's alter ego, seems to be wandering through it by accident. Instead of plot it has a cascade of incidents, instead of central characters it has a cast of hundreds, instead of being a comedy it is a wondrous act of observation. It occupies no genre and does not create a new one. It is a filmmaker showing us how his mind processes the world around him.

At the time of its making, *Playtime* (1967) was the most expensive film in French history. Tati filmed it in "Tativille," an enormous set outside Paris that reproduced an airline terminal, city streets, high-rise buildings, offices, and a traffic circle. It was the direct inspiration for *The Terminal*, for which Stephen Spielberg built a vast set of a full-scale airline terminal. Although Spielberg said he wanted to give Tom Hanks the time and space to develop elaborate situations like Tati serendipitously blundered through, he provided Hanks with a plot, dialogue, and supporting characters. Tati made *Playtime* without a story, with dialogue (mostly in English) that is inaudible or disposable, and without a hero.

His film is about how humans wander baffled and yet hopeful through impersonal cities and sterile architecture. *Playtime* doesn't observe from anyone's particular point of view, and its center of intelligence resides not on the screen but just behind the camera lens. The most sympathetic person in the movie is a waiter who becomes a source for replacement parts. More about him later.

Tati filmed his movie in 70mm, that grand epic format that covers the largest screens available with the most detail imaginable. He shot entirely in medium-long and long shots; no close-ups, no reaction shots, no over the shoulder. He shows us the big picture all of the time, and our eyes dart around it to find action in the foreground, middle distance, background, and half-offscreen. It is difficult sometimes to even know what the subject of a shot is; we notice one bit of business but miss others, and the critic Noel Burch wonders if "the film has to be seen not only several times, but from several different points in the theater to be appreciated fully."

Playtime is Rosenbaum's favorite film, and unlike many of its critics, he doesn't believe it's about urban angst or alienation. In a lovely passage, he writes: "It directs us to look around at the world we live in (the one we keep building), then at each other, and to see how funny that relationship is and how many brilliant possibilities we still have in a shopping-mall world that perpetually suggests otherwise; to look and see that there are many possibilities and that the play between them, activated by the dance of our gaze, can become a kind of comic ballet, one that we both observe and perform."

Consider how this works in the extended opening scene. We see a vast, sterile concourse in a modern building. In the foreground, a solicitous wife is reassuring her husband that she has packed his cigarettes and pajamas, and he wearily acknowledges her concern. We understandably conclude that this is the waiting room of a hospital; a woman goes by seeming to push a wheelchair, and a man in a white coat looks doctor-like. Nuns march past in step, their wimples bobbing up and down in unison. Only slowly do these images reveal themselves as belonging to an airline terminal.

A tour group of American women arrives down an escalator. A clerk on a stool with wheels scoots back and forth to serve both ends of his counter. Impenetrable announcements boom from the sound system. Mr. Hulot's entrance is easy to miss; while babbling tourists fill the foreground, he walks into an empty space in the middle distance, drops his umbrella, picks it up, and walks off again. The bang of the umbrella directs our eye to the action. The whole sequence is alert to sounds, especially the footfalls of different kinds of shoes and the flip-flops of sandals.

Looking and listening to these strangers, we expect to see more of Mr. Hulot, and we will, but not a great deal. Tati's famous character, often wearing a raincoat and hat, usually with a long-stemmed pipe in his mouth, always with pants too short and argyle socks, became enormously popular in the director's international hits *Mr. Hulot's Holiday* (1953) and *Mon Oncle* (1958, winner of the Oscar for best foreign film). But nearly ten years passed before Tati found uncertain financing for the expensive *Playtime*, and he wanted to move on from Hulot; to make a movie in which the characters might seem more or less equal and—just as important—more or less random, the people the film happens to come across.

Mon Oncle has an ultramodern house as its setting, and in *Playtime*, we enter a world of plate glass and steel, endless corridors, work stations, elevators, air conditioning. Hulot goes to call on a man in a modern office and is put on display in a glass waiting room, where he becomes distracted by the rude whooshing sounds the chair cushions make. He takes an elevator trip by accident. A man approaches the building guard to get a light for his cigarette and doesn't realize a glass wall separates them.

Glass walls are a challenge throughout the film; at one point, Hulot breaks a glass door and the enterprising doorman simply holds the large brass handle in midair and opens and closes an invisible door, collecting his tips all the same.

Other characters are mistaken for Hulot in the film, a double is used for him in some scenes, and Hulot encounters at least three old Army buddies, one of whom insists he visit his flat. This generates a wonderful scene; the apartment building has walls of plate-glass windows, and the residents live in full view of the street. We see four apartments at once, and in a sly visual trick, it eventually appears that a neighbor is watching Hulot's army buddy undress when she is actually watching the TV.

But to explain or even recount these moments is to miss the point. They aren't laugh-out-loud gags, but smiles or little shocks of recognition.

The last long sequence in the film involves the opening night of a restaurant at which everything goes wrong, and the more it goes wrong, the more the customers are able to relax and enjoy themselves.

The sequence involves a multitude of running jokes, which simultaneously unfold at all distances from the camera; the only stable reference point is supplied by a waiter who rips his pants on the modern chairs and goes to hide behind a pillar. There he is implored by other waiters to lend them his clean towel, his untorn jacket, his shoes, and his bowtie, until finally he is a complete mess, an exhibit of haberdashery mishaps.

Some characters stand out more than others. Hulot, of course. An attractive American woman. A loud American man. A short and deliberate little man. A long-suffering restaurant owner. A very drunk man. But scenes don't center on them; everyone swims with the tide. In *Mon Oncle*, there is a magical scene where Hulot adjusts a window pane, and it seems to produce a bird song. In *Playtime*, we are surrounded by modern architecture, but glass doors reflect the Eiffel Tower, the Church of the Sacred Heart in Montmartre, and the deep blue sky. The sight of the sky inspires "oohs" and "ahs" of joy from the tourists, as if they are prisoners and a window has been opened in their cell.

Playtime is a peculiar, mysterious, magical film. Perhaps you should see it as a preparation for seeing it; the first time won't quite work. The best way to see it is on 70mm, but that takes some doing (although a print is currently in circulation in North America). The Criterion DVD is crisp and detailed, and includes an introduction by Terry Jones, who talks about how the commercial failure of the film bankrupted Tati (1909–82) and cost him the ownership of his home, his business, and all of his earlier films. Was Tati reckless to risk everything on such a delicate, whimsical work? Reckless for you, reckless for me, not reckless for a dreamer.

A Prairie Home Companion

My respect for Garrison Keillor is unbounded, so I hope he will forgive me for this admission. Preparing to watch Robert Altman's *A Prairie Home Companion* again, I unconsciously found myself picturing Altman as the host of the radio show, instead of Keillor. The film is a loving evocation of the program, and also, I believe, a farewell of sorts from Altman. Both this film and the one that preceded it, *The Company*, reflect his collaborative, elusive, almost telepathic style of directing.

There are lines in *Companion* (2006) that may indeed have been written by Keillor, but take on a special meaning now that Altman is gone. One of them is "Every show is your last show. That's my philosophy." I can hear Altman saying that. And listen to this exchange. The youngest member of the cast (Lindsay Lohan) wants Keillor to mention on the air that Chuck (L. Q. Jones), the oldest, has just been found dead in his dressing room. Keillor declines.

> *Lola:* What if you die some day?
> *Keillor:* I will die.
> *Lola:* Don't you want people to remember you?
> *Keillor:* I don't want them to be told to remember me.

Yolanda (Meryl Streep), Lola's mom, asks him: "How about just a moment of silence?" He replies: "Silence on the radio. I don't know how that works." People who have worked for years with Keillor say he often seems to exist in his own world as the show is happening. It is live, and seems to unfold spontaneously, but it is impossible to imagine anything ruffling Keillor's serenity. There may be a crisis backstage, but there can never be dead air on the radio.

Altman could and did become angry. Once on the Florida location of his *HealtH* (1980), he walked off the set and introduced me to a man leaning on a truck. "I want you to meet this man," Altman said, "because he's the highest-paid person on the movie. Even more than the actors, or me. He's the chief Teamster." But Altman never in my sight, or by report, ever grew angry with an actor. He loved them. He was capable of giving minute instructions to them, but more often he directed through the art of appreciation. Actors learned that when he praised something, that might be his way of telling them to do more of it, or less. Somehow the actors could tell.

He was a collector of people, a collaborator. He developed 16-track Lion's Gate Sound so that every cast member could be separately miked. He wanted to hear everything they said, and then in the mix he would be sure we heard what we were intended to. For a similar reason, he often wanted to see everything. On *A Prairie Home Companion* and many other pictures, he shot simultaneously with two, three cameras. We were seeing separate consecutive shots of exact moments unfolding within the same time. He also enriched his backgrounds. You have to look closely, but there is this moment in *Companion*. Having finished his performance, Chuck goes backstage. He has a quiet moment with an angel that we can see and he cannot. Foreground action develops as, now in the background, Chuck goes down to his dressing room. He carefully walks downstairs backward, the better to hold the rail. Most viewers will not see that action. But Altman did. You can bet he specified it. He wanted it back there for anyone who was looking.

A Prairie Home Companion is a lovely film about a lovely radio show. It loosely creates the format of the real program, using actors to portray performers something like Keillor uses. The onstage musicians are mostly the show's own. The film is notably missing Keillor's usual monologue about life in Lake Woebegone, perhaps because it would have taken too long and interrupted the flow. Keillor drifts onstage and off, sometimes preoccupied, always hitting his cues, talking, singing in a rich, mellow voice, exuding the comfort that the show embodies.

Altman has chosen his actors with love. Streep and Lily Tomlin play the Johnson Sisters, a singing duet who used to work with a mother they remember obsessively. John C. Reilly and Woody Harrelson are Lefty and Dusty, the cowboy singers whose songs are made of ribald jokes. Maya Rudolph is the anxiety-ridden stage manager. Kevin Kline is Guy Noir, a Keillor private eye, who narrates part of the film and plays the theater's security man. Tommy Lee Jones is Axeman, the Texas businessman whose group plans to raze the historic theater in St. Paul and has arrived to pull the plug.

And then there is the angel, played by Virginia Madsen. The credits call her the Dangerous Woman. She wears a fedora and a trench coat. We may not realize for a while that not everyone can see her. She drifts slowly, dreamily, in and out of sight. She has love and concern in her face, but telegraphs nothing. Her purpose is seemingly to ease the transition to the next life for such as old Chuck. She observes others with special interest. At the end of the film, she becomes visible to the Axeman. Yes.

Altman's multiple cameras and miking are ideal for the backstage sequences, in which characters drift in and out and talk at the same time. We get an immediate feel for the dressing room, the lulls between numbers, the history and memories that all dressing rooms contain and evoke. Streep and Tomlin have hilarious conversations with exquisite timing, and so do Reilly and Harrelson. Lohan is fresh and excited, pulled onstage for her radio debut.

The music is important, but this is not quite a musical. The songs are more performances. Toward the very end of the last show, the singers and musicians join Keillor in singing that saddest of all lovely songs, that loveliest of all sad songs, "Red River Valley." When I heard it for the first time around a campfire at a summer camp when I was about nine, I knew I would feel that way about it all of my life.

The film, as I suggested, reflects Altman's style of direction: assemble gifted actors, friends as often as possible, and make it possible for them to do what he knows that they can do. Create an atmosphere where it can happen. Support them. Fulminate against absent enemies (Teamsters, props, costumes, studio executives) but never against actors. One long afternoon I watched him transform an entire scene in a Lyric Opera production he was directing, without ever uttering a direct instruction. The actors almost feel they're doing it themselves.

Did Altman know this would be his last film? Certainly not. But he knew his time was limited. "Where the years have gone, I don't know," he told me backstage that day at the Lyric. "But they're gone. I used to look for a decade. Now I look for a couple more years." He got them. "When I'm not making a film," he told me on the set of *Gosford Park* in 2001, "I don't know how to live. I don't know what to do with the time. I don't have an assistant director taking me to this little restaurant around the corner, and a production manager telling me about my hotel, and a driver to take me where I have to go."

He said he kept track of time not by the years but by the film he was making. Given an Honorary Oscar in March 2006, he astonished his audience by revealing he had been living ten or eleven years with a heart transplant. He didn't mention that he also had leukemia, listed as his cause of death on November 20 of the same year. At the time, he had two films in pre-production.

{ REBEL WITHOUT A CAUSE }

"*You're tearing me apart! You say one thing, he says another, and everybody changes back again.*"

James Dean shouts these words in an anguished howl that seems to owe more to acting class than to his character, the rebellious and causeless Jim Stark in *Rebel Without a Cause*. Because he died in a car crash a month before the movie opened in 1955, the performance took on an eerie kind of fame: it was the posthumous complaint of an actor widely expected to have a long and famous career. Only *East of Eden* (1954) was released while Dean was alive; *Giant*, his last film, came out in 1956. And then the legend took over.

The film has not aged well, and Dean's performance seems more like marked-down Brando than the birth of an important talent. But *Rebel Without a Cause* was enormously influential at the time, a milestone in the creation of new ideas about young people. Marlon Brando as a surly motorcycle gang leader in *The Wild One* (1953), James Dean in 1955, and the emergence of Elvis Presley in 1956: these three role models decisively altered the way young men could be seen in popular culture. They could be more feminine, sexier, more confused, more ambiguous.

"What can you do when you have to be a man?" Jim Stark asks his father, the emasculated Frank Stark (Jim Backus). But his father doesn't know, and in one grotesque scene, wears a frilly apron over his business suit while cleaning up spilled food. Jim comes from a household ruled by his overbearing mother (Ann Doran) and her mother (Virginia Brissac). Early in the film, he regards his father and tells a juvenile officer: "If he had guts to knock Mom cold once, then maybe she'd be happy, and she'd stop picking on him."

As causes go, Jim's doesn't rank with civil rights and war resistance, but the movie's point is that Jim is denied even a reason for his discontent. In the early 1950s, his unfocused rage fit neatly into pop psychology. The movie is based on a 1944 book of the same name by Robert Lindner, and reflected concern about "juvenile delinquency," a term then much in use; its more immediate inspiration may have been the now-forgotten 1943 book *A Generation of Vipers*, by Philip Wylie, which coined the term "Momism" and blamed an ascendant female dominance for much of what was wrong with modern America. "She eats him alive, and he takes it," Jim Stark tells the cop about his father.

Like Hamlet's disgust at his mother's betrayal of his father, Jim's feelings mask a deeper malaise, a feeling that life is a pointless choice between being and not being. In France at the time, that was called existentialism, but in Jim's Los Angeles, rebels were not so articulate. The first time Jim talks with Judy (Natalie Wood), the girl next door, she's ready for him. "You live here, don't you?" he says. "Who lives?" she says.

And consider the scene where Jim and his new enemy, Buzz (Corey Allen), talk before the deadly game of "chicken" that will end with Buzz dead. Jim is the new kid in the high school, Buzz slashes his tire with a switchblade and challenges him to a "chickie run." The two kids will drive stolen cars toward a cliff, and the first one to bail out is the chicken.

Curiously, right before the race, Buzz tells Jim: "You know something? I like you."

"Why do we do this?" Jim asks.

"You got to do something," says Buzz.

The philosophical stage for their duel was set earlier in the afternoon, during a class trip to the Griffith Park Observatory. The subject is "The End of Man," and the lecturer happily describes the sun growing larger until it explodes and wipes out all traces of mankind. "The Earth will not be missed," the lecturer informs the students. "Through the infinite reaches of space, the problems of man seem trivial and naive indeed, and man existing alone seems himself an episode of little consequence." This is not the note of optimism they require.

The observatory speech inspires a bitter aside from the movie's other major character, the small, angry, and persecuted Plato (Sal Mineo): "What does he know about man alone?" It is clear now but may have been less visible in 1955 that Plato is gay and has a crush on Jim; at the planetarium, he touches his shoulder caressingly. After Buzz dies when his car hurtles over the cliff, the students all seem curiously—well, composed. Jim gives Plato a lift home and Plato asks him, "Hey, you want to come home with me? I mean, there's nobody home at my house, and heck, I'm not tired. Are you?" But Jim glances in the direction of Judy's house, and then so does Plato, ruefully.

There is also sexual malaise in Judy's house. In a scene at dinner, she gives her father (William Hopper) a peck on the cheek, and he reacts with embarrassment: "What's the matter with you? You're getting too old for that kind of stuff. . . . Girls your age don't do things like that." Judy responds: "Girls don't love their father? Since when? Since I got to be sixteen?" The implication is that her father is afraid of his sexual feelings for his daughter. To complete the collection of failed fathers, Plato's is dead or absent; his story changes from day to day, and he is being raised by a motherly black housekeeper.

Trying to deal with his role in Buzz's death, Jim tries to get guidance from his dad (still wearing the apron), gets in a fight with his parents, and pauses on his way out of the house long enough to kick through an oil portrait of his mother, which has helpfully been left leaning on the floor next to the door. He's on his way to the police station to talk to a sympathetic juvenile officer, but is seen by Buzz's posse. They're angry with Jim, not because the race resulted in Buzz's death, but because they think he ratted on them to the police.

Hiding from them, Jim and Judy, followed by Plato, go to a deserted mansion near the observatory. And there they engage in a curious charade in which Plato becomes a real-estate agent, and Jim and Judy play a couple being shown through the home. The subject of children comes up, and Plato advises against them, as being too noisy and bothersome. Jim agrees: "Drown 'em like puppies, eh?" He speaks in the voice of Mr. Magoo, the cartoon character voiced by Backus, who plays his father. This is beyond creepy. Later, in a tender scene, Plato goes to sleep at the feet of Jim and Judy, while she hums Brahms's "Lullaby" and Jim observes that they are like a family.

If I have quoted a lot from the movie, it's because the dialogue often seems to be making plot points that the director, Nicholas Ray, and the writer, Irving Shulman, may not have fully intended. Or perhaps they did, and guessed that some of the film's implications would not be fully recognized by 1955 audiences. Seen today, *Rebel Without a Cause* plays like a Todd Solondz movie, in which characters with bizarre problems perform a charade of normal behavior.

Because of the way weirdness seems to bubble just beneath the surface of the melodramatic plot, because of the oddness of Dean's mannered acting and Mineo's narcissistic self-pity, because of the cluelessness of the hero's father, because of all of these apparent flaws, *Rebel Without a Cause* has a greater interest than if it had been tidier and more sensible. You can sense an energy trying to break through, emotions unexamined but urgent. Like its hero, *Rebel Without a Cause* desperately wants to say something and doesn't know what it is. If it did know, it would lose its fascination. More perhaps than it realized, it is a subversive document of its time.

{ THE RED SHOES }

There is tension between two kinds of stories in *The Red Shoes*, and that tension helps make it the most popular movie ever made about the ballet and one of the most enigmatic movies about anything. One story could be a Hollywood musical: a young ballerina falls in love with the composer of the ballet that makes her an overnight star. The other story is darker and more guarded. It involves the impresario who runs the ballet company, who demands loyalty and obedience, who is enraged when the young people get married. The motives of the ballerina and her lover are transparent. But the impresario defies analysis. In his dark eyes we read a fierce resentment. No, it is not jealousy, at least not romantic jealousy. Nothing as simple as that.

The film is voluptuous in its beauty and passionate in its storytelling. You don't watch it, you bathe in it. Yes, the ending is a shocker, but you see it coming and there's no way around it; the movie tells us a fairy tale and then repeats it as real life. It's the Hans Christian Andersen fable about a young girl who puts on a pair of red slippers that will not allow her to stop dancing; she must dance and dance, in a grotesque mockery of happiness, until she is dead. This is a dire subject for a ballet, you will agree; the movie surrounds it with the hard-boiled business of running a ballet company.

The Red Shoes was made in 1948 by the team of Michael Powell and Emeric Pressburger, British filmmakers as respected as Hitchcock, Reed, or

315

Lean. Powell was the director and Pressburger, a Hungarian immigrant, was the writer, but they always took a double credit as writer-directors, and were known as The Archers; their logo was an arrow hitting its target, announcing such masterpieces as *The Life and Death of Colonel Blimp*, *Black Narcissus*, *Peeping Tom*, *The Thief of Bagdad*, and *A Matter of Life and Death*, the David Niven classic that played in America as *Stairway to Heaven*.

Pressburger had written a draft of a ballet film in the 1930s, and after the war, after their enormous success with *Black Narcissus* (1947), which made a star of Deborah Kerr and won Oscars for cinematography and art direction, they had another look at it. Powell had grown up on the French Riviera; his British father ran a hotel on Cap Ferrat, and he often saw the Russian impresario Diaghilev, whose Ballets Russes wintered nearby in Monte Carlo. The Archers used Powell's notions about Diaghilev and the earlier script to create the story of a proud, cold, distant impresario who meets his match with a fiery ballerina. Pressburger may have been inspired by a famous scandal in 1913 when Diaghilev's great but tortured star, Vaslav Nijinsky, married the Hungarian ballerina Romola de Pulszky. He fired them both.

Casting is everything when the characters must move between realism and fantasy, and *The Red Shoes* might have failed without Moira Shearer and Anton Walbrook as the stars. Shearer and Walbrook have distinctive, even idiosyncratic personalities, and they bring an emotional realism to characters who are really, after all, only stereotypes. Walbrook plays Boris Walbrook, the imperious manager of the Ballet Lermontov, a company ruled by his iron will. He is arrogant, curt, unbending, able to charm, able to chill. Shearer plays the dancer Victoria Page, whose friend Julian Craster (Marius Goring) bursts into Lermontov's office to complain that his composition has been stolen by the company's conductor. Julian is hired by Lermontov, Vicky wins an audition, and when the company's leading dancer resigns to get married, they are told "we have three weeks to create a ballet—out of nothing."

Moira Shearer, let it be said, is a great beauty: "Her cloud of red hair, as natural and beautiful as any animal's, flamed and glittered like an autumn bonfire," Powell wrote in his autobiography, the best ever written by a filmmaker. "She had a magnificent body. She wasn't slim, she just didn't have one ounce of superfluous flesh." Of Walbrook he wrote: "Anton conceals his humility and his warm heart behind perfect manners that shield him like suit of armor. He responds to clothing like the chameleon that changes shape and color out of sympathy with its surroundings."

Quite so. In *Colonel Blimp*, Walbrook makes a German aristocrat sympathetic. In Max Ophuls's great *La Ronde* (1950), he is our urbane and charming guide to a decadent society. In *The Red Shoes*, he creates a deliberate enigma, a man who does not want to be understood, who imposes his will but conceals his feelings.

Vicky Page is his opposite: joyous and open to life. Shearer, who was twenty-one when she was cast, was at the time with the Sadler's Wells Company, dancing in the shadow of the young Margot Fonteyn. She didn't take movies seriously, waited a year before agreeing to star in *The Red Shoes*, went back to the ballet, and possibly never knew how good she was in the movie, how powerfully she related to the camera. "I never knew what a natural was before," Powell told the studio owner J. Arthur Rank. "But now I do. It's Moira Shearer."

The movie tells parallel stories leading up to its seventeen-minute ballet sequence. While Vicky and Julian are falling in love, Lermontov and his company are creating the new ballet. There is a key scene where Lermontov and all his colleagues meet in his villa to hear Julian play the new ballet for the first time. "I was determined to shoot it in one big master shot," Powell wrote, and it is a masterpiece of composition, of entrances, exits, approaches to the camera, background action, and the vibrating sense of a creative team at work. "There are lots of clever scenes in *The Red Shoes*," he wrote, "but this is the heart of the picture."

The other key scenes are the ballet itself, and the sequence leading up to the ending. No film had ever interrupted its story for an extended ballet before *The Red Shoes*, although its success made that a fashion, and *An American in Paris* and *Singin' in the Rain*, among others, have extended fantasy ballet sequences. None ever looked as fantastical as the one in the *The Red Shoes*, where the little shoemaker puts the fatal slippers on the girl. The physical stage is seamlessly transformed into a surreal space, where Shearer glides and flies, enters unreal landscapes, and even does a pas de deux with a newspaper that takes the form of a dancer, turns into the dancer, and then into a newspaper again. The cinematographer Jack Cardiff wrote about how he manipulated camera speed to make the dancers seem to linger at the tops of their jumps; the art direction won an Oscar, mostly because of this scene (there was also an Oscar for the music, and nominations for best picture, editing, and screenplay).

After Vicky and Julian are married and Lermontov fires them, he persuades her to dance *The Red Shoes* one more time. Julian walks out of the premiere of his new symphony in London to fly to Monte Carlo and accuse her of abandoning him. What will she choose? The dance, or her husband? She puts on the red slippers, and in a brilliant close-up the slippers force her to turn around, and seem to lead her as she runs from the theater and throws herself in front of a train. Discussing the script, Pressburger argued that Vicky couldn't be wearing the red shoes when she runs away, because the ballet had not yet started. Powell writes: "I was a director, a storyteller, and I knew that she must. I didn't try to explain it. I just did it."

That brings us back to the tension we began with. Why does Lermontov object so violently to the marriage of these two young people? Is it sexual jealousy? Does he desire Vicky, or, for that matter, Julian? Lermontov is a bachelor with the elegant wardrobe and mannered detachment that played as gay in the 1940s, but there is not a moment when he displays any sexual feelings. He would rather die than appear vulnerable. My notion is that Lermontov is Mephistopheles. He has made a bargain with Vicky: "I will make you the greatest dancer the world has ever known." But he warns her: "A dancer who relies upon the doubtful comforts of human love will never be a great dancer—never." Like the Satan of classical legend, he is enraged when he wins her soul only to lose it again. He demands obedience above all else.

That leaves us with Vicky's choice. She can return to London with Julian, or leave him and continue her career. Why does she abandon these choices at the height of her youth and beauty, and kill herself? The answer of course is that she is powerless, once she puts on the red shoes.

A newly restored print was released in 2009 on Criterion.

{ RIPLEY'S GAME }

That's OK. I didn't expect thanks.

TOM RIPLEY, WIPING SPIT FROM HIS FACE

Tom Ripley is fascinating in the sense that a snake is fascinating. He can kill you, but he will not take it personally and neither should you. He is well educated, has good taste, is a connoisseur of art, music, food, wine, and architecture, can give a woman good reason to love him, and commits crimes and gets away with them. "I don't worry about being caught," he says, "because I don't believe anyone is watching." By "anyone," he means cops, witnesses, God, whoever.

Ripley is at the center of five novels written by Patricia Highsmith between 1955 and 1991, which have inspired as many movies: Rene Clement's *Purple Noon* (1960), Wim Wenders's *The American Friend* (1977), Anthony Minghella's *The Talented Mr. Ripley* (1999), Liliana Cavani's *Ripley's Game* (2002), and Roger Spottiswoode's *Ripley Under Ground* (2004); Ripley was played successively by Alain Delon, Dennis Hopper, Matt Damon, John Malkovich, and Barry Pepper.

The first four are splendid movies (based on only two of the novels; the Wenders and the Cavani on *Ripley's Game* and the Clement and the Minghella on *The Talented Mr. Ripley*). The fifth I haven't seen. *Ripley's*

Game is without question the best of the four, and John Malkovich is precisely the Tom Ripley I imagine when I read the novels. Malkovich is skilled at depicting the private amusement of sordid characters, but there is no amusement in his Ripley, nor should there be; Ripley has a psychopath's detachment from ordinary human values. Malkovich (and Highsmith) allow him one humanizing touch, a curiosity about why people behave as they do. At the end of the film, when a man saves his life, Ripley can think of only one thing to say to him: "Why did you do that?"

Malkovich has the face for Tom Ripley. For the movie he has lost weight and is lighted and photographed to show the skull beneath the skin. Ripley's eyes when he is angry are cold and dead, as in an early scene where he is insulted by the host at a party. When he is not angry they are simply objective, although sometimes, even during intense action, Ripley will allow his eyes to glance aside for a second. He is like an actor glancing off-stage, reminded that there is life outside his performance. When he gives pleasure, for example by taking his wife, Luisa (Chiara Caselli), to buy an antique harpsichord, he regards her in an unsettling way, not sharing the pleasure but calculating its effect. Very rarely he permits himself a childlike grin, as when remembering the triumph on the face of a dying man. When involved in violence, he has a way of baring his teeth, and you can sense the animal nature beneath the cool facade.

Tom Ripley has always been an enigma in the crime fiction genre, because a thief and murderer does not usually get away with his crimes in novel after novel, and seem on most days like a considerate lover and a good neighbor. Malkovich's philosophical Ripley is closest to Highsmith's character in the way he objectifies his actions. Why is he requested to kill a man? "Because I can." He arranges for the man who insulted him, a family man dying of leukemia, to be offered $100,000 to commit murder. The man asks him why he did that. "Partly because you could. Partly because you insulted me. But mostly because that's how the game is played."

Liliana Cavani, Italian, born in 1933, is a good choice to direct a Ripley film, because she is comfortable with depravity as a subject. Her best-known film is *The Night Porter* (1974), starring Charlotte Rampling as a survivor of the Nazi death camps, who finds one of her former guards

(Dirk Bogarde) working in a hotel, and begins a sadomasochistic relationship with him. I did not admire the film, but it shows her using some of the same objectivity about perverted values that is central to *Ripley's Game*.

It is unwise to insult Ripley. Consider. He walks into a party being given by his neighbor Trevanny (Dougray Scott). He hears himself being insulted: he is an American who has purchased a superb Palladian villa near Venice and ruined it with "too much money and no taste." Trevanny realizes he has been overheard. No matter what he says to squirm out of his rudeness, Ripley replies with one word: "Meaning?" Their verbal duel leaves Trevanny silenced and shaken. Ripley was involved three years earlier in a profitable art theft and con game in Germany. Now his hapless British partner, Reeves (Ray Winstone), has been threatened by their victims; he tracks Ripley to Italy and is trembling with fear. "Do you want to tell me what you want," Ripley asks him, "or do you want a truffling pig to find you dead in a month or two?"

Reeves wants a murder to take place. The payment is $50,000. Ripley doubles the money, and says he thinks he may have the man for the job. He has Trevanny in mind. There is a twisted logic in his reasoning: he has reason to know that Trevanny is dying, and so has less to lose, and every reason to want money to provide for his wife and child. If he is forced to commit murder for money, he will no longer be able to talk with much conviction about Ripley's wealth or bad taste.

The murders take place on a train, and play with a precision just one gruesome step this side of slapstick. "Hold my watch," Ripley tells Trevanny before the killing starts, "because if it breaks I'll kill everyone on this train." At one point there are five people, three apparently dead, in the same train toilet. We are poised between a massacre and the Marx Brothers. "It never used to be so crowded in first class," Ripley observes. Although the murders seem to be successful, Reeves and violence follow Ripley back to Italy, and in a masterful sequence using the vast lawns and interiors of the villa, Ripley prepares to greet any visitors. He is not usually capable of being surprised, but watch his eyes when Trevanny turns up to help out.

Women are an enigma in Ripley's world. He treats his wife with studious but not passionate regard, sends her out of the way when danger threatens, has apparently found a woman who never wonders how he makes his money. About Trevanny's wife, Sarah (Lena Headey), he is—well, considerate, to a degree. Sarah doesn't like or trust Ripley. When she walks in on a bloodbath, it's curiously touching the way Trevanny tells her, "It's not what you think!"

The pairing of Ripley and Trevanny joins a man capable of killing and another who doesn't think of himself in those terms. It resembles the pairing in Highsmith's first novel, *Strangers on a Train*, which inspired the 1951 Hitchcock masterpiece. In both cases, the dominant character has someone he wishes dead and wants to involve the unwilling second man in the killing. *Strangers on a Train* reflected one of Hitchcock's favorite themes, The Innocent Man Wrongly Accused. By the end of *Ripley's Game*, Trevanny is accused of nothing but has lost his innocence. Lost it, and seems almost grateful, as if proud to have passed the test Ripley set for him.

If this film had been released as intended in 2002, it would probably have made my ten-best list. Incredibly, it never opened theatrically in the United States; it finally turned up on cable in late 2003. It's said that its distributor, the Fine Line imprint of New Line, was so overwhelmed by the studio's Lord of the Rings trilogy that staff couldn't be spared to focus on it. What American audiences lost was one of Malkovich's most brilliant and insidious performances; a study in evil that teases the delicate line between heartlessness and the faintest glimmers of feeling. When Ripley smiles in the last shot, he hasn't lost his credentials as a psychopath, but he has at last found something in human nature capable of surprising and even (can it be?) delighting him.

{ THE RIVER (LE FLEUVE) }

Jean Renoir's *The River* (1951) begins with a circle being drawn in rice paste on the floor of a courtyard, and the circular patterns continue. In an opening scene, the children of a British family in India peer through porch railings at a newcomer arriving next door. At the end, the same children, less one, peer through the same railing at a departure. The porch overlooks a river, "which has its own life," and as the river flows and the seasons wheel in their appointed order, the Hindu festivals punctuate the year and all flows from life to death to rebirth, as it must.

The film is one of the simplest and most beautiful by Jean Renoir (1894–1979), among the greatest of directors. Based on the novel by Rumer Godden, who was born in India and lived there many years, it remembers her childhood seen through the eyes of a young girl named Harriet (Patricia Walters), who falls in love with the new neighbor. He is Captain John (Thomas E. Breen), an American who lost a leg in the war and now has come to live with his cousin, Mr. John (Arthur Shields).

We meet Harriet's family: her parents, her three sisters, her brother Bogey. We also meet Mr. John's daughter, Melanie (Radha), whose Hindu mother has died, and Valerie (Adrienne Corri), whose father owns the jute factory that Harriett's father manages. There are others: the family's nanny, the young Indian man who courts Melanie, the Sikh gatekeeper, the young Indian boy who is Bogey's playmate.

Although the film covers one year, the impression is of an endless summer day during which the girls play and write in their journals, observe the flow of life outside their gates, and are fascinated by Captain John. At the time of the Hindu festival of light, there is a little party at the family home with music from a wind-up phonograph, and each of the older girls asks Captain John to dance before he finally settles in a corner with Valerie. It becomes clear to young Harriet, despite her crush on the captain, that he has eyes for the red-haired Valerie. What she does not notice is that he is also attracted to his half-Indian cousin, Melanie, and she to him. One day both Melanie and Harriet follow Valerie and Captain John out into a grove, where they kiss. "It was my first kiss," Harriet remembers, "but received by another." Melanie must have felt the same.

To some degree, the girls are in love with Captain John because he is the only eligible man in their lives. No other characters appear or are discussed; that he is sad and detached they can overlook. Harriet impatiently wants to be old enough to be visible to Captain John. "I want to be outstandingly beautiful," she tells her pregnant mother. Harriet's narration is spoken by an adult voice; we understand these events take place around 1946.

Captain John has come to live in India, he tells the Anglo-Indian Melanie, because with one leg he feels like an outsider. "I'm a stranger wherever I go," he says, and she replies quietly, "Where will you find a country of one-legged men?" She is a stranger, too, because of her mixed race. "I don't know where you belong," her father tells her.

Certainly all of their lives stand apart from India; we never hear a conversation between Melanie and her Indian suitor, or between Bogey and his Indian playmate, and the nanny is limited to nannyisms; she is not even given the Indian title *ayah* by which all nannies were known. Scenes of the real India outside the compound are mostly in long shot.

The film is not constructed around high melodrama, but its deepest feelings are expressed when the two outsiders, Melanie and Captain John, speak with each other, almost in code. Melanie has an enchanted scene in which she tells a story about the meeting of Prince Krishna and his bride, named Radha. The actress Radha was a dancer, and her character's story leads into a dance scene that allows some of the color and mystery of Indian religion to enter the isolation of the British family's compound.

The River and Michael Powell's *The Red Shoes* are "the two most beautiful color films ever made," Martin Scorsese says in an interview on the new Criterion DVD of the restored print. I saw the movie for the first time when Scorsese's personal 35mm copy played at the Virginia Film Festival some years ago; when I mentioned it to him, he said, "I watch that film three times a year. Sometimes four." On the DVD, he says it reaches him more powerfully than *Rules of the Game*, considered Renoir's masterpiece. Some will agree, some will not. *The River* is like an Ozu film in the way it regards life without trying to wrest it into a plot. During the course of the year, the girls fall in love with the same unavailable man, there is a death and a birth, and the river continues to flow.

Renoir, son of the impressionist painter Pierre-Auguste Renoir, directed his first film in 1924 and was considered a grand master when he fled the Nazis and moved to Hollywood in 1941. There he worked with mixed success until, by the time he made *The River*, he was almost unemployable. The film was financed by an outsider, Kenneth McEldowney, a Hollywood florist who loved Godden's novel.

Renoir insisted on filming it on location in India, which he did with his nephew Claude Renoir as cameraman (and young Satyajit Ray as an assistant director). It was the first Technicolor film made in India. The budget was small. There were no stars, and some of the players had never acted before. Much of the atmosphere flows from Renoir's documentary footage, showing a bazaar, life along the river, annual festivals, boatmen at their work, and Hindus descending flights of stairs both grand and humble to bathe and pray in the water.

The British family lives apart from this India, and knows it. Behind the walls of their garden is a separate world, protected by the stern Sikh gatekeeper; only Bogey's young playmate climbs the walls. Together, the boys sneak out to the bazaar and watch a snake charmer, and Bogey finds another snake in the roots of the giant banyan tree right outside the garden—a tree whose roots fall down from the branches to reach for the ground, and among which gods and spirits are said to live.

There are subdued issues here involving colonialism and racism. Does Captain John shy away from romance with Melanie because she is not white? Is Harriet's father being paternalistic when he "loves" the sight of the laborers bearing their vast bundles of jute into the factory? The issues are there, but they are not called into focus, and the life Harriet shows us is the only one she knows.

The center of her world is a cubbyhole under the stairs, where she keeps her poetry and journals, and it is a betrayal when Valerie snatches away a notebook and reads Captain John some of the younger girl's love poems. India itself is on the brink of independence and partition, but Harriet is on the brink of adolescence, and that is much more important to her, as perhaps is natural.

Films have grown so aggressive and jittery that it takes patience to calm down into one like *The River*. Its most dramatic moment takes place offscreen. Renoir is not interested in emotional manipulation but in regarding lives as they are lived. Not everyone we like need be successful, and not everyone we dislike need fail. All will be sorted out in the end—or perhaps not, which is also the way time passes and lives resolve themselves.

Nothing is really finished at the end of *The River*. Despite Jane Austen's insistence that a man like Captain John "must be in want of a wife," he is still in want as the film ends. Harriet has not yet grown up. Melanie has still not found a place for herself. Renoir's way of bringing his story to a conclusion is a form of understated poetry. All three girls receive letters from Captain John. All three open them and begin to read them while sitting on the steps, and then from within the house comes a baby's cry. The nanny emerges to announce: "It's a girl!" And the three girls jump up and rush into the house, the letters fluttering forgotten to the ground behind them.

{ ROCCO AND HIS BROTHERS }

Luchino Visconti was a man of many tempers, styles, and beliefs, and you can see them all, fighting for space, on the epic canvas of his masterpiece, *Rocco and His Brothers* (1960). Visconti (1906–76) was gay, an aristocrat, a Marxist, a director of theater and opera. He was a key influence in Italian neorealism and later abandoned it to make movies of elaborate style and fantasy. He loved the subject of decadence, and yet *Rocco* is profoundly idealistic. As an aristocrat himself, he had a love of tradition that showed in his great film *The Leopard* (1962), although that film was about the slow dying of aristocracy.

The word "operatic" is often overused, but no other would apply to *Rocco and His Brothers*. It is a combination that should not work, but does, between operatic melodrama and seamy social realism, which at no point in its 177-minute running time seem to clash, although they should. We buy the whole overwrought package, the quiet truth, the flamboyant excess, even the undercurrent of homoeroticism that Visconti never quite reconciles. The excitement of the film is that so much is happening, in so many different ways, all struggling to find a fusion.

The film is an epic involving modern Italian history. In Milan one cold winter right arrives the Parondi family. Mother Rosaria (Katina

327

Paxinou) apprehensively shepherds four of her five sons from the rail station. They are Simone (Renato Salvatori), Rocco (Alain Delon), Ciro (Max Cartier), and Luca (Rocco Vidolazzi). They're on their way to the meet oldest son, Vincenzo (Spiros Focas), who has already established himself in Milan.

Their timing couldn't be worse. It is the night of Vincenzo's engagement party to the beautiful Ginetta (Claudia Cardinale), in whose home he has been made welcome. But the two mothers take an instant dislike to each other, the Parondis stalk out, and Vincenzo's engagement is temporarily broken. What follows is the most neorealist segment of the movie, as mother and sons move into a bleak basement flat and are overjoyed one morning when it is snowing, because that means work shoveling the streets.

Their living quarters improve. A friend advises them to rent an apartment, any apartment, simply to pay the rent for a few months, then stop paying, and get evicted. That way they can find public housing. It is not available, of course, to those who are homeless in the first place: "You have to be evicted." Soon they're living in spartan but spacious and clean public housing, courtesy of the socialist government, and the sons are finding their way in the world.

They meet a neighbor who is to profoundly affect the lives of the family. This is the prostitute Nadia, played by Annie Girardot, who for me creates the best performance in the film. Young, cheerful, and honest, she appeals immediately to both Simone and Rocco, although Rocco conceals his feelings and doesn't make a move until two years after Nadia and Simone have broken up.

Meanwhile, Simone is spotted as promising by a boxing promoter, a snaky and sexually ambivalent man who signs him to a contract and later invites Rocco to get into the ring as well. Simone has some success with his early fights, but is already on the road to self-destruction when he visits a laundry where Rocco has a job, and steals a shirt "just to wear for a day," he boldly tells the laundry owner when he returns it. He wanted to impress Nadia during a trip to the seaside, and she is sunny and lovely that day, and wholly sympathetic. It is Simone who turns bad, filled with low self-esteem, proud of his wins but negligent of his training—smoking and drinking too much, and finally losing both Nadia and his boxing career.

Rocco steps in behind him, starting a liaison with Nadia and also a successful boxing career (which he doesn't even want). But when Simone explodes with grief and jealousy (truly operatic, these scenes), he astonishingly breaks with Nadia, telling her she must return to his brother because "He has only you." Rocco joins the Navy, meets Nadia again by chance in a port city, resumes their romance, and then Simone, in an astonishing scene, gathers a pack of buddies, interrupts the two lovers in a secluded outdoor tryst, attacks and rapes Nadia. It is a cowardly and ruthless act, revealing how shameless he has become, and a scene in which Girardot performs heroically. But this scene, and a later murder scene, aroused the wrath of the Italian censors, who had great difficulties with the film and its seamy portrait of life.

The mother persists in dreaming that her sons will live together under her roof, but Vincenzo marries Ginetta (the result, the matriarch sniffs, of "an unfortunate accident"). Now Rocco leaves home to live with Vincenzo, and Simone moves in—with Nadia, who his mother is expected to shelter and feed, while he hangs out with louts and gets drunk.

Rocco's boxing career advances steadily, even though he despises the sport. Financially, he has little choice but to continue; the others depend on him, and the film makes a point of the serflike living and working conditions in southern Italy, and the steady migration north of those seeking jobs and wages. This theme, too, annoyed the censors, since it was more controversial at the time than it seems now.

Many, maybe most, of the best scenes in the film involve Nadia. She is cruelly abused by her love for Simone, drops from high style to degradation in her career as a prostitute, and her last meeting with Simone cries out for operatic arias to express their feelings. Another great scene comes toward the end, as Ciro, who has a job on the Alfa-Romeo assembly line, speaks with Luca, the youngest brother, of his duty to his family and his ties to the south, a "land of olives, moonshine, and rainbows," where he dreams they will someday return. In memory the south has become less harsh than the land that drove them north.

The film is shot in carefully composed black and white that fore-grounds the brothers and Nadia in many shots, showing them listening or reacting to what is happening behind them. If there is a peculiarity of the casting, it is that all five brothers are almost improbably handsome—beginning, of course, with the matinee idol Delon, then at the dawn of his career.

Rocco and His Brothers can be seen quite clearly, at this point, as an enormous influence on great American gangster films. Aspects of *The Godfather* immediately come into mind. And the critic D. K. Holm observes: "The tense, penitent relationship between Charlie (Harvey Keitel) and Johnny Boy (Robert De Niro) in (Scorsese's) *Mean Streets* is almost unimaginable without the precedence of *Rocco and His Brothers*." At a very subtle level, the love between the brothers seems almost sexual, as in a late scene where Simone confesses to Rocco and Rocco fights with Ciro and vows to defend him. These feelings are well concealed by the film, but they are there.

There's a great passage near the end, when Rocco has a great tri-umph on the same night when Simone ruins himself. Two fights, in a sense, are intercut. The neighbors pour out onto the balconies to cheer Rocco as a new champion, and then Simone comes home in wretched defeat to the always forgiving arms of his mother. The way the two story strands come together is manipulative, yes, but deeply effective.

The experience of watching *Rocco and His Brothers* is rather over-whelming. So much happens, at such intensity and complexity, with such an outpouring of emotion, that we do feel we're witnessing an opera. Like many operas, it has too much melodrama in too little time. That can be exhausting but it can be exhilarating as well.

{ SAFETY LAST }

It is by general agreement the most famous shot in silent comedy: a man in a straw hat and round horn-rimmed glasses, hanging from the minute hand of a clock twelve stories above the city street. Strange, that this shot occurs in a film few people have ever seen. Harold Lloyd's *Safety Last* (1923), like all of his films, was preserved by the comedian but rarely shown; having been through most of Charlie Chaplin and virtually everything by Buster Keaton, I viewed it for the first time last week, and it was my first Harold Lloyd. Others got their chance, as a retrospective of Lloyd's work, meticulously restored, tours the country in advance of a DVD package.

Lloyd was "the third genius," the silent-film historian Kevin Brownlow declared in a documentary of the same name. Lloyd's films outgrossed those of Chaplin and Keaton in the '20s, if only because he made many more than Chaplin, and his everyman appealed to a wider audience than Keaton. But he is not a genius in their sense, creating comedy out of inspiration and instinct and an angle on the world.

"He had to think it all out," Walter Kerr says of Lloyd in his invaluable 1975 book *The Silent Clowns*. "Lloyd was an ordinary man, like the rest of us: ungrotesque, uninspired. If he wanted to be a successful film comedian, he would have to learn how to be one, and learn the hard way."

Lloyd played an early would-be Chaplin character named Lonesome Luke, then saw a silent film where the character calmly replaced his glasses after an action scene, and adopted the glasses as his own. To the degree Lloyd's famous character has a name at all, it is "Glasses," and in *Safety Last*, he is billed merely as The Boy. The glasses make distinct a face that is otherwise pleasant, even handsome, but not remarkable in the way that Keaton's deadpan gaze and Chaplin's toothbrush moustache are distinctive.

Nor was Lloyd's character remarkable—not in the sense of Chaplin's Little Tramp, whose every movement expressed an attitude toward life, or Keaton's characters, always on the run, always deadly earnest about goals of overwhelming importance. The Glasses character in *Safety Last* would have blended with the background of the department store where he worked if it had not been for action imposed upon him. But what action!

The plot: The Boy promises The Girl (Mildred Davis, Lloyd's real-life wife) that he will go to the city, make good, and send for her. He gets a lowly job as a dry-goods clerk, but impresses her with such inventive letters that she hurries to the city to join him. The Boy poses as the manager of the store, is exposed, and decides to risk everything for a $1,000 prize offered to anyone who can lure more traffic to the store. His idea: have his roommate (Bill Strother), a human fly, climb the building.

This is a splendid idea, as far as it goes. It doesn't take into account that the roommate has earlier angered a cop (the silent veteran Noah Young) and escaped from him by climbing up the side of the building. Now, as the roommate prepares to repeat the stunt, the cop appears and gives chase, and The Boy is forced to substitute as the climber. The theory is that the roommate will replace him on the second floor, or the third, or sooner or later, but Glasses ends up scaling the entire building, despite hazards on every floor. A child showers him with peanuts, which attract hungry pigeons. A mouse climbs up his pants leg. A window swings out and almost brushes him to his death. A weathervane changes direction and nearly dooms him. And finally there he is, hanging from the clock. A little later, he does some remarkably casual walking or even dancing on the building's roof ledge.

It looks real. That is the whole point. It seems to really be Harold Lloyd, really climbing the building, over a real drop that would be fatal.

Kerr emphasizes in his book: "virtually every shot in it keeps the street below in view."

Well, was it Lloyd? It certainly wasn't special effects, which were not capable in 1923 of creating such illusions. In many shots, it is clearly Lloyd because we can see his face. In longer shots, as Kerr points out, the climber is certainly not the shorter and stockier Strother, who was a human fly in real life.

Analysis of the camera angles suggests that the height was exaggerated by using a building on a hill and by selecting dramatic camera angles. Lloyd himself said he had a platform with mattresses on it placed one, two, or three stories below him. After his death in 1971, according to the critic Dennis Schwartz, "it was finally revealed that the famous climb up the 12-story building was done with the aid of a stuntman." With the aid. What exactly does that mean? Having seen a high-resolution 35mm print in which I am clearly looking at Harold Lloyd much of the time, I am prepared to believe that certain shots may have been doubled, but that in others the star himself was in mortal danger.

That was not unique for the period. Buster Keaton did virtually all of his own stunts, allowing a building to fall around him in a hurricane, running on the top of a train, dangling over a waterfall. I accept without question that there were times in *Safety Last* when Harold Lloyd could have fallen to his death. The question becomes: is that funny?

I didn't find myself laughing, but I watched in fascination. I don't love the Glasses character with the intensity I reserve for Buster and the Little Tramp. But I was there with him every inch of the way up that building, and I shared the physical joy of his triumph at the top. I could understand why Lloyd outgrossed Chaplin and Keaton in the 1920s: not because he was funnier or more poignant, but because he was merely mortal and their characters were from another plane of existence. Lloyd is a real man climbing a building. Keaton, as he stands just exactly where a building will not crush him, is an instrument of cosmic fate. And Chaplin is a visitor to our universe from the one that exists in his mind.

While Chaplin and Keaton seemed to float on waves of inspiration and invention, "Lloyd knew that he didn't know what he was doing," Kerr wrote, "and detested himself for it. . . . In due time, Lloyd acquired skills that were superb of their kind. But they were acquired skills. He got no gift from the gods." Perhaps that is what makes him special: he is determined to be a great silent comedian, and succeeds by experimentation, courage, and will. His films are about his triumph over their making.

Now I can test that theory. I have all the rest of Harold Lloyd still ahead of me. I would rather have all of Keaton or all of Chaplin, and yet I am pleased to have Lloyd still to explore. In a way that later films could never duplicate, silent films, especially comedies, have a documentary level beneath their fictions: they're often shot on real locations and use the locations, and the backgrounds are often unrehearsed and real. Into this actual universe steps a character who for reasons of his own will do extraordinary things.

Born in 1893, Lloyd began as an extra by mingling with a crowd of other extras returning from their lunch break. He met another extra named Hal Roach, later to become a giant among early producers, and was assigned by Roach to be a comedian. He made dozens of shorts before finding his rhythm and footing. He worked steadily to establish his character, had no time for Chaplin's perfectionism, had a better head for business than the dreamy Keaton.

He saved his money, preserved his films, kept them out of release for decades, was unconcerned when his legacy seemed to be falling behind those of the other two geniuses. His granddaughter Suzanne is now supervising the re-release of films that were never lost, never threatened with decay or destruction, and essentially look as fresh as the day they were premiered. It is like going to new movies that happen to have been made eighty years ago.

{ SAMURAI REBELLION }

The tension in *Samurai Rebellion* is generated by deep passions imprisoned within a rigid social order. The words and movements of the characters are dictated to the smallest detail by the codes of the time, but their emotions defy the codes. They move formally; their costumes denote their rank and function; they bow to authority, accept their places without question, and maintain ceremonial distances from one another. The story involves a marriage of true love, but the husband and wife are never seen to touch each other.

The visual strategy of the film reflects the rules of its world. The opening shots show architectural details, all parallel lines or sharp angles, no curves. It is the year 1725, in the Tokugawa Dynasty, which from 1603 to 1868 enforced a period of peace that depended on absolute obedience to authority. The story takes place in a remote district where Lord Matsudaira enforces his whims on all those beneath him.

We meet the Sasahara household. We see its master, Isaburo (Toshiro Mifune), in an opening scene with his best friend, Tatewaki (Tatsuya Nakadai). More precisely, we see his sword, its point and then its blade, and then the focus shifts to show his fierce eyes behind it, and then shifts to the blade again. They stand in a field before a straw man, which Isaburo cuts in two with one blow. They are testing swords. Walking back home, they talk of their boredom, and Isaburo notes he has been "henpecked for twenty years."

Yes, this samurai warrior, said to be the deadliest swordsman of his clan, lives unhappily under the thumb of his wife. The film is so concerned with family life that in Japan it was released in 1967 as *Rebellion: Receive the Wife*. This title was intended, says the critic Donald Richie, to attract women moviegoers who traditionally avoided samurai films. In America, the film was retitled *Samurai Rebellion*, to attract martial arts fans. In the mind of its director, Masaki Kobayashi, its only title was *Rebellion*.

It is a film of grace, beauty, and fierce ethical debate, the story of a decision in favor of romance and against the samurai code. The plot involves the sexual convenience of the lord, who first forces the Sasahara family to accept his discarded mistress and then wants her back again. Lady Ichi (Yoko Tsukasa) was forced to become the lord's lover, bore him a son, and then in anger struck the old man, pulled his hair, and disgraced herself. The lord decrees she must be banished, and orders her to marry Yogoro (Go Kato), one of the two sons of the Sasaharas.

This does not please the family, but they obey the lord. After the marriage, Isaburo sees a way out of his unhappy subservience to his wife. He retires and names Yogoro head of the family. Yogoro explains to Ichi that his father dislikes his mother, "but has borne everything." Now Ichi will be the woman who manages the household: "You needn't hold back because of the old woman." To everyone's surprise, Ichi and Yogoro learn to love each other, and their marriage is blessed with a daughter named Tomi. When Yogoro asks his wife why she attacked the lord, she replies simply: "I felt as if a hairy worm was crawling over me."

Edicts from the lord are delivered by the steward (Shigeru Koyama). One day he arrives with news: the lord's heir has died, and the son he had by Ichi is the new heir to the throne. The steward says Ichi must leave the Sasaharas and return to the castle, for it would be improper for the heir's mother to be married to a vassal. As Ichi learns the news, we see her seated in the angle of two rice-paper walls, ominous shadows crawling behind her like insects. She refuses to return. She is supported by her husband and, unexpectedly, by her father-in-law: Isaburo calls it a "cruel injustice," and tells them he has been moved by "your tender love for each other," so unlike his own marriage. So begins the rebellion of the title: father, son, and wife refuse to obey the lord, although Isaburo's wife, Suga (Michiko Otsuka), and their other son are in favor of sending her back to the castle.

I was reading Anthony Trollope's *Doctor Thorne* when I saw the film, and was struck by how the two plots are similar in the way romance is opposed by a ruthless pragmatism, with social class being used to enforce what the characters should feel. The world of the samurai is far away from us, even further than Trollope's Barsetshire, but the feelings of the characters are universal and fundamental.

When we think of samurai movies, we think of swordplay, but *Samurai Rebellion* consists almost entirely of domestic life and diplomatic maneuvering until the film's final bloodbath. Isaburo believes he can protest the autocracy of the lord at the court of the emperor, in Edo, and the lord's steward is not eager to see this happen. A period of extraordinary negotiation opens, with bluff and counterbluff, and we see family councils as the Sasahara relatives gather to try to talk the three rebels into accepting the lord's will. Lies are told, intrigues are carried out, Lady Ichi is kidnapped, and yet true love will not be denied.

There is also a curious change in the appearance of Mifune, the most famous of all Japanese stars. In early scenes, he looks so meek, so defeated by his marriage, that we hardly recognize him. As his resolve grows, as he supports Yogoro and Ichi, his famous face seems to take form, and he looks stern and angry, like the Mifune we know.

There is a key turning point. He is walking along the brick pathways in his enclosed stone garden. As he tells Ichi he will support her, he leaves the path, and his sandals make footprints in the carefully raked sand. He has broken the rules, refused to stay between the lines, and placed his own will above that of the lord.

The director Masaki Kobayashi (1916–96) was himself a rebel. I learn from Ephraim Katz's *Film Encyclopedia* that Kobayashi was a pacifist during World War II. After being drafted into the army and sent to Manchuria, "in a courageous act of personal defiance, he refused promotion and remained a private for the duration."

Defiance would be a subject of his films. His *The Human Condition* (1959) is a three-part, nine-hour film about a conscientious objector who serves in Manchuria just as Kobayashi did and acts not in obedience to the emperor but out of loyalty to his men.

He is best known for the elegant ghost stories in *Kwaidan* (1964) and the samurai drama *Harakiri* (1962), which many feel is better than *Samurai Rebellion*. Richie disagrees, praising Kobayashi's use here of 2:35-to-1 widescreen compositions to "even more effectively hem in his rebellious characters." The film's black-and-white cinematography is somber and beautiful, arranging the characters within visual boxes of space and architecture that reflect their relationships. Notice how when they are seated at meetings, their positions and body language precisely reflect their status, and how the departure of one character upsets the balance. Notice, too, the symbolism involved when Isaburo and his son prepare to do battle with the lord's men, and begin by disrupting the stark verticals and horizontals of the architecture with crisscrossed bamboo poles that make jagged barriers across the windows.

Samurai Rebellion can be seen as a statement against the conformity that remained central in Japanese life long after this period. It is the story of three people who learn to become individuals. Consider the dramatic moment when the lord's steward returns to the Sasahara household, bringing with him the kidnapped Ichi, who has been ordered to plead for a divorce. She has been told the only alternative is that her husband and father-in-law will be ordered to commit seppuku, or suicide. Centuries of tradition require her to follow the script, but "They lie!" she cries out. "I am still the wife of Yogoro!"

The ending is tragic, resulting in death that is not glorious but obscure and hidden, leaving no record. Isaburo's dying words are gasps of advice to Tomi, his granddaughter. He tells her how brave her mother and father were, but Tomi is too young to understand. In another sense, the ending is triumphant: the three heroes of the story have expressed their will and their sense of right and wrong. We remember Isaburo shouting, "For the first time in my life I feel alive!"

{ SANSHO THE BAILIFF }

Kenji Mizoguchi's *Sansho the Bailiff*, one of the best of all Japanese films, is curiously named after its villain, and not after any of the characters we identify with. The bristle-bearded slavemaster Sansho is at the center of two journeys, one toward him, one away, although the early travelers have no suspicion of their destination. He is as heartless a creature as I have seen on the screen.

The film opens on a forest hillside, where Tamaki, the wife of a kind district administrator, is discovered with her young son, Zushio, her younger daughter, Anju, and their servant, making their way down a difficult path. The dense underbrush here is reflected throughout the film, which is set in eleventh-century feudal times, and reflects the director's feeling that humans and nature are the sides of a coin. The little group has had to flee for their lives after her husband drew the wrath of the cruel Sansho and was exiled. They hope to rejoin him.

In this shot, and throughout the film, Mizoguchi closely observes the compositional rules of classic cinema. Movement to the left suggests backward in time, to the right, forward. Diagonals move in the direction of their sharpest angle. Upward movement is hopeful, downward ominous. By moving from upper left to lower right, they are descending into an unpromising future.

They stop for the night, build a rough shelter from tree limbs, and start a small fire. In the darkness, wolves howl. Their little domestic circle in the firelight is a moment of happiness, however uncertain, that they will not feel again. Then an old priestess finds them, and offers them shelter in her nearby home. In the morning, discovering their destination, she suggests that a boat journey will greatly diminish the distance. She knows some friendly boatman. As they leave her house, a furtive dark figure, almost unseen, darts behind them in the shrubbery.

The delivery to the boatmen is a betrayal. The woman and servant are captured by body merchants, the women to be sold into prostitution, the children into slavery under Sansho. He runs a barbaric prison camp of forced labor, and it here that the children will spend the next ten years. Sansho is an unlovely man, a bully and sadist, who is surrounded by servile lackeys, all except for his son.

Flashbacks have shown us something of the captured children's early life under their father, a good man who gave his son an amulet representing the Goddess of Mercy, and taught him that all men are created equal. That same familiar concept is enshrined in the Japanese Constitution, imposed by the American occupation in 1947 and still in force, not a word changed, sixty years later. When Mizoguchi made his film in 1954 the words must have been alive in his mind, reflecting his obsession with the rights of women throughout his career, and serving to condemn Sansho's slave camp (which mirrors those the Japanese ran in the Second World War). The story, we're told in a prefatory note, took place in "an era when mankind had not yet awakened as human beings." By that Mizoguchi may be referring both to the story and to aspects of traditional Japanese totalitarian society, in which everyone's role was rigidly defined, and authority flowed from the top down.

As the plot unfurls, we see Zushio and Anju trying to escape, lured by an evocative song that is sung to them by a recent prisoner from their village, and echoed too in a bird cry: "Zushio, Anju, come back, I need you." It is their mother's ghostly voice. The film incorporates this mystical summons into images of startling cruelty under Sansho, who causes prisoners to be branded on their foreheads if they try to escape. One who does not agree with this practice is Sansho's son, Taro, and it is an irony of the film that while Taro embraces resistance, Zushio begins to identify with Sansho and becomes the tyrant's surrogate son. Then he has a conversion, in a scene of surpassing beauty and emotion, as the film moves toward its final journey.

Kenji Mizoguchi (1898–1956) is considered, with Ozu and Kurosawa, one of Japan's greatest directors; for this film, and also *Song of Oharu* (1952) and *Ugetsu Monogatari* (1953), he won the Silver Lion, the grand prize, three years in a row at Venice, which was and remains unheard of. He is known for the elegance of his compositions and the tact of his camera movement, and his theory "one scene, one shot," as in a famous scene in *Sansho* where the suicide by drowning of one of the characters is not shown, but merely indicated by ripples on the surface of a lake. Remarkably, since his characters always seem carefully composed within the frame, we learn that he never instructed the actors about where to move or stand, but simply indicated the desired result and let them move and place themselves. No doubt this leads to a subtly sensed feeling of unstudied natural movement.

Ozu of course also adheres to "one scene, one shot," but his camera never moves, and framing and composition are everything. Mizoguchi's elegant camera movement almost creates the illusion that we are not only looking along with him, but sometimes looking away, choosing not to see. The camera does not move away from certain actions so much as decline to notice them, often because they are too painful or personal.

Mizoguchi made about seventy-five films, but of them all, *Sansho* may contain the most autobiographical impulse. Living in poverty, Wikipedia reports, his family placed his older sister for adoption, and the adoptive family sold her as a geisha. His father treated the family brutally. Here are perhaps the reasons why the story of *Sansho*, based on a five-hundred-year-old folk tale, resonated so strongly in the director's mind.

Sometimes it is difficult to say exactly why a story strikes us with such power. In the case of *Sansho the Bailiff*, it may be the unrelieved tragedy that strikes this good family for no good reason. They are not destroyed instantly, in a natural cataclysm, but separated for long years to know and experience their fates. That gives us time enough to know and believe the depth of Sansho's cruelty. Some humans are born without kindness or mercy, and do with pleasure what others could not do at all.

At dinner last night a man of around sixty recalled an event when he was six. His beloved cat gave birth to a litter on his stomach during the night. On awakening, he saw the miracle of the tiny mewing specks of life, and wondered that his cat would so trust him as to give birth there, and not in a hidden corner, as is the nature of cats. The man's voice trembled as he told what happened then. His beast of a stepfather took the kittens and, in the boy's full view, smashed them with a hammer. I tell the story only to capture the sadism of Sansho, who takes pleasure in his work, and mirrors some of the stories Mizoguchi must have heard about wartime atrocities.

Does the story have a happy ending? No. But it has resolution, reconciliation, forgiveness (although not of Sansho). It has the conversion of Zushio, and the spectacular turn his fortune takes. After all of that more still happens, but for that you must see the film. At some point during the watching, *Sansho the Bailiff* stops being a fable or a narrative and starts being a lament, and by that time it is happening to us as few films do.

Anthony Lane, the film critic for the *New Yorker*, did a profile of Mizoguchi a few years ago in which he wrote these extraordinary words: "I have seen *Sansho* only once, a decade ago, emerging from the cinema a broken man but calm in my conviction that I had never seen anything better; I have not dared watch it again, reluctant to ruin the spell, but also because the human heart was not designed to weather such an ordeal."

{ SANTA SANGRE }

To call *Santa Sangre* (1989) a horror film would be unjust to a film that exists outside all categories. But in addition to its deeper qualities, it is a horror film, one of the greatest, and after waiting patiently through countless Dead Teenager Movies, I am reminded by Alejandro Jodorowsky that true psychic horror is possible on the screen—horror, poetry, surrealism, psychological pain, and wicked humor, all at once.

The movie involves the perverse emotional and physical enslavement of a son by his mother—a control all the more macabre when we learn, late in the film, the secret of its actual nature. It is also about an instinctive hatred between characters representing lust and chastity, which are both seen as perversions in a world without a sane middle way. This bold subject matter is orchestrated by Jodorowsky in a film that inspires critics to make lists, calling it Jungian, surrealistic, Felliniesque, Buñuelian, sadomasochistic, expressionist, and strongly flavored by such horror classics as *The Beast With Five Fingers*, *The Hands of Orlac*, and the film that guides the hero's fantasies, *The Invisible Man*.

The story involves Fenix, the boy magician at the Circus Gringo, a shabby touring show in Mexico. Played by two of Jodorowsky's sons (Adan at about eight, Axel at about twenty), Fenix is the child of the beautiful trapeze artist Concha (Blanca Guerra) and the bloated circus owner and

343

knife thrower Orgo (Guy Stockwell). Always at Fenix's side is the dwarf Aladin (Jesus Juarez), who acts as his assistant and moral support. The little magician's best friend is Alma (Faviola Elenka Tapia and, when older, Sabrina Dennison). She is a deaf-mute mime, the daughter of the carnal tattooed lady (Thelma Tixou), who works as the target for Orgo's knives.

One night when Concha is suspended above the circus ring by her hair, she sees Orgo caressing the tattooed lady and screams to be brought back to earth. In a rage, she surprises them in bed and throws acid on Orgo's genitals. Bellowing with pain, he severs her arms with mighty thrusts of two knives. Then he kills himself, the acid having rendered him uninteresting to women tattooed and otherwise.

Concha's mutilation is a cruel irony: she is the leader of a cult of women who worship a saint whose arms were cut off by rapists. Their church contains a pool of blood, no doubt suggesting menstrual fluid (Concha's name is Mexican slang for the vagina); its members wear tunics with crossed, severed arms. When authorities arrive to bulldoze the church, there is a clash between the women and the police, and then a shouting match between Concha and the local monsignor, she screaming that the pool contains holy blood, he replying that it is red paint.

The bulldozing reveals the shabby construction of the church, mostly made of corrugated iron and possibly reflecting the film's limited budget. If Jodorowsky's funds were limited, however, his imagery and imagination are boundless, and this movie thrums with erotic and diabolical energy. Consider the scene where the circus elephant dies after hemorrhaging from its trunk. In a funeral both sad and funny, the beast's great coffin is hauled by truck to a ravine and tipped over the edge—to the delight of wretched shanty-dwellers, who rip open the casket and throw bloody elephant meat to the crowd. An image like this is one of the reasons we go to the movies: it is logical, illogical, absurd, pathetic, and sublimely original. For Alejandro Jodorowsky, all in a day's work.

Now seventy-four and at work on his first film in fourteen years, Jodorowsky is a legendary man of many trades. Born in Chile, living mostly in Mexico and Paris, he works here in English, which has been imperfectly dubbed; oddly enough, the oddness of the dubbing adds to the film's eerie quality.

Jodorowsky has occupied the edges of the arts. He was a clown and puppeteer, studied under the mime Marcel Marceau, filmed a mime version of Thomas Mann's play *The Transposed Heads*, was a friend of the surrealist Arrabal, and is, in his own words, a "very famous comic-strip artist," the author of graphic novels that have become legendary.

He is also the author of the legendary cult film *El Topo* (1970), which was both saved and doomed by John Lennon. Saved, because Lennon admired it so much, he asked his manager, Allen Klein, to buy and distribute it. Doomed, because after the film became a worldwide sensation (Jodorowsky told me in 1989), "Klein made it disappear. He says, 'I am waiting until you die, and then I am going to have a fortune.' He thinks he's immortal. If he dies first, I get the film back." So far, both men are still alive and only recently has *El Topo* been made available on video.

Jodorowsky's visionary world owes much to the surrealists, but even more to the quirky films that Luis Buñuel made during his Mexican exile, films showing men quietly obsessed with the details of their fetishes. Fenix, his hero, is literally a man whose world is defined by his obsessions. The witness to his mother's mutilation and his father's suicide, he is in an insane asylum when the film opens, perched atop a tree trunk. When he returns to the world, it is to play the role of his mother's arms and hands. He walks behind her, slips his arms through the sleeves of her garments and feeds her, plays the piano, gestures, and even caresses her body as if it is his own. Axel Jodorowsky and Blanca Guerra do this with such perfect timing that the hands seem to sense the next thought of the mother. But Fenix has no identity except as her instrument, which is why *The Invisible Man* appeals so strongly.

The first half of the film is filled with Felliniesque exuberance, celebrating the circus with its tawdry charms and sad clowns. The second half is somber and creepy, as in a scene where Fenix and four young men with Down syndrome are taken on a movie outing that ends (not unhappily) with cocaine and a visit to the red-light district.

Fenix eventually moves with his mother into a house where timbers lean everywhere at crazy angles for no apparent reason, except to evoke expressionism. And here he begins his revolt. As his mother jealously uses his hands to kill one woman after another, he recruits a muscular giantess who will be able, he thinks, to fight off any attack.

This giantess is pretty clearly a man in drag, but the movie makes no notice of that fact, and indeed many oddities pass unremarked, including the omnipresent doves and the ability of the tattooed lady, the dwarf, and the deaf-mute girl to materialize in Fenix's life when and how he needs them. All is finally made clear at the end, revealing how fearlessly Jodorowsky has married magic realism to Freud, in a film that is like a shriek against Momism.

Of course the movie is rated NC-17. I believe more horror films should be made for adults, so that they are free to deal with true malevolence in the world, instead of retailing the pornography of violence without consequences. A generation is growing up that equates violence with action, instead of with harm. Not long ago *The Exorcist* was re-released and some young moviegoers laughed all the way through it. A society that laughs at evil eventually laughs at good, and then it loses its way.

The quality that Jodorowsky has above all is passionate sincerity. Apart from his wildly creative style, apart from his images, apart from his story inventions, he has strong moral feelings. He has an instinctive sympathy for Fenix, who was born into a world of fanaticism and cruelty, and has tried, with the help of a deaf girl and a dwarf, to get back the soul that was warped by his father and trapped by his mother. Maybe one difference between great horror films and all the others is that the great ones do not celebrate evil, but challenge it.

{ THE SCARLET EMPRESS }

"It is a relentless excursion into style," Josef von Sternberg said of his *The Scarlet Empress* (1934). That's putting it mildly. Here is a film so crammed with style, so surrounded by it and weighted down with it, that the actors peer out from the display like children in a toy store. The film tells the story of Catherine the Great as a bizarre visual extravaganza, combining twisted sexuality and bold bawdy humor as if Mel Brooks had collaborated with the Marquis de Sade.

The film is the sixth of seven collaborations between von Sternberg and Marlene Dietrich, and the strangest. It juxtaposes a Russia of gigantic grotesque gargoyles and overdressed towering Hussars with the giggling imbecility of the Grand Duke Peter and lingering fetishistic close-ups of Dietrich's cold, erotic face. It provides Peter's domineering mother, the Empress Elizabeth, with the manners of a fishwife, and paints Catherine as a sexual adventuress who is assigned to provide Peter with a male heir and produces a child who is a male heir, right enough, but not Peter's.

The movie was released in 1934, just as the Hays Office began to police Hollywood films for morals violations. Von Sternberg must have had a friend on the force; he gets away with murder. Although the movie wisely sidesteps the famous legend of the empress's sub-equestrian death, a title does inform us, in sublime understatement, "Catherine coolly added the army to her list of conquests."

We see her inspecting the troops with particular attention to their nether regions, and when she meets the handsome Captain Orloff she says she's "heard" of him and asks what his job is. "I'm in charge of the night watch, your majesty." Dietrich's reply is a sensuous purr: "It must be . . . cold . . . at night . . ." To be sure we get the point, we see Peter playing with toy soldiers, and then it's observed of Catherine, "she's always picking up the archduke's soldiers."

Von Sternberg (1894–1969) was one of the true Hollywood characters, sometimes a great director, always a great show. He dressed in costumes appropriate to the films he was directing, made his assistants remove their wristwatches because he could hear the ticking, and calmly claimed he did it all himself: direction, photography, lighting, sets, costumes, props, the works. "It takes me a lot of time," he sighed. Of course he had the usual craft professionals assigned to all of those jobs, but he certainly controlled the look of his films, and in *The Scarlet Empress* he compensates for the lack of a vast canvas by filling a small one to bursting.

His interiors suggest the Russian imperial household without showing us much more than a throne, some corridors, a dining room, a grand staircase, and some bedrooms. We're reminded of how Orson Welles created Kane's Xanadu out of shadows, props, tricks, and mirrors. The fixtures in Sternberg's rooms are boldly overscale; rough stone sculptures of monstrous gargoyles tower over the characters, surround them, leer at them. The doors are so heavy it takes two men or six women to swing them open. And the fur costumes of the wicked Count Alexei (John Lodge) look so heavy, it's a good thing he's over six feet tall and strong enough to wear them.

Alexei is the one who journeys to the hinterlands to fetch the beautiful "young princess," then called Sofia Frederica, who has been commanded to become Peter's bride. Sofia has already had quite a childhood; her doctor was also the hangman, and her bedtime stories involved tortures of the rack and the stake. In a montage imagining these grisly agonies, a prisoner is hung upside down and used as the clapper for a bell, and that image dissolves into Sofia swinging back and forth at play. No sooner do Alexei and

Sofia meet than she looks at him with long fascination, in a close-up where she takes forever to close a door. The next day, Alexei boldly kisses her. "Why did you do that?" she asks. "Because I've fallen in love with you, and now you must punish me," he says, promptly handing her a whip as if the kiss was the price he had to pay for his reward. Later, on their long journey to the palace, her mother sees them together at a roadside inn, Sofia again holding his whip. "What are you two doing down there?" she asks, adding quickly: "Never mind; I don't want to know."

Arriving at the court, Sofia and her mother are greeted by Empress Elizabeth (Louise Dressler, with a no-nonsense Midwestern American accent). A court doctor immediately plunges under her hoop skirt to make sure all is in order for a royal pregnancy. Elizabeth renames her Catherine, "a good Russian name," and awards her the Order of St. Catherine: "May you wear it in good health. And be careful it doesn't scratch you."

Soon her betrothed Peter the Great (Sam Jaffe) enters, a grinning, simpering simpleton dismissed by his mother as a "half-wit." His principal royal duty is to produce an heir, something he is apparently unequipped to do, as von Sternberg hints in a scene where Peter is so desperate for a glimpse of his wife that he drills a spy hole through the eye of a mosaic in his mother's bedroom, which I think is a Freudian trifecta.

Dietrich exists surrounded but untouched by this madness, as a locus of carnal insinuations. She rarely engages the other actors physically; von Sternberg likes to isolate her in fetishistic compositions of lace, feathers, fur, and fire (notice the shot in which she gazes steadily at Alexei from behind her veil; the candle flame a few inches from her mouth trembles as she begins to breathe more heavily). One dress seems made of black-tipped white fur spikes, which undulate when she moves, like a dreamy underwater porcupine. There is something both contented and demented in her narcissism; perfectly made up and exquisitely lighted, she poses for us in von Sternberg's close-ups, regarding us with contemptuous passivity while we commit sins of thought by contemplating sins of deed.

Some of her erotic moments are more than passing strange. She and Alexei find themselves in a stable, where she plunges into the hay, then rights herself, and puts a straw in her mouth sideways. He takes it away.

She puts another straw in her mouth sideways. He also takes that away. She goes through five sideways straws and five Alexei removals. I have no idea what obscure communication is taking place here, but there's a payoff later in the film when, to taunt him, she boldly inserts a straw in her mouth not sideways but stem first, and twirls it with her tongue. Yowza!

As drama, *The Scarlet Empress* makes no sense, nor does it attempt to. This is not a resource for history class. Its primary subject is von Sternberg's erotic obsession with Dietrich, whom he objectified in a series of movies (*The Blue Angel, Morocco, Dishonored, Shanghai Express, Blonde Venus, The Scarlet Empress*, and *The Devil Is a Woman*) that made her face one of the immortal icons of the cinema. Whether she could act was beside the point for him; it would have been a distraction.

Von Sternberg has a slapdash way with some scenes, as if impatient when his attention is called away from Dietrich. Notice his several crowd scenes, in which peasants materialize on demand, mill about in frenzied turmoil, and are then forgotten. There is almost no sense of a real society outside the palace walls, and little enough within, where some of the arrangements would be at home in a Marx Brothers movie. For the long winter journey to the palace, for example, Count Alexei supplies piles of furs for Catherine, and then dismisses her mother with a hot-water bottle.

When Dietrich is onscreen, however, nothing is too good for her; not only do von Sternberg's lighting and cinematography make her the center and subject of every scene, but he devises extraordinary moments for her, as when, clad in a fur uniform and cape, with an improbable sable military hat, she mounts a horse and leads a cavalry charge up the grand staircase. "It took more than one man to change my name to Shanghai Lily," she says in *Shanghai Express*, but it only took von Sternberg to make her Marlene Dietrich.

{ SECRETS & LIES }

Too much attention is paid to Mike Leigh's famous method for "devising" his screenplays. It is well known that he imagines characters and a situation, casts actors to play the characters, joins with them in workshops where the dialogue and the plot take shape, and only then writes the screenplay. Quite true, but that doesn't mean he's winging it; his *Secrets & Lies* (1996) reveals a filmmaker who works with the most delicate precision to achieve exactly what he desires. The payoff for his method comes in scenes like the film's two very long and unbroken takes, when he calls on his actors to use the disciplines of the stage as well as the screen.

Leigh, born 1943, made his first feature, *Bleak Moments*, in 1971. He made his second, *High Hopes*, in 1988. In between, he worked constantly for television and the theater but couldn't get a film financed because the backers wanted to see a script, and of course he didn't have one. When I saw *Bleak Moments*, I knew I was watching a masterpiece by a great director and wrote a long review for the *Sun-Times*. This turned out to be the film's first review; Leigh had been ignored at home in England. In the seventeen years between features, he perfected what he instinctively began with: tragicomic portraits of discontented people in trying circumstances, and an embarrassment in social situations that borders on pathology.

Although he makes some characters into caricatures, there is a compassion in his work that acts like a safety net. Characters who seem over the top in one scene have a way of rounding out later in a film. That's true of Brenda Blethyn's performance in *Secrets & Lies* as Cynthia Purley, a factory worker who rattles discontentedly around the little rowhouse she was born in and regards Roxanne, her twenty-year-old daughter, with despair. Cynthia seems an anthology of raw sadness and worry, but she will be transformed when her worst nightmare comes true.

This happens when she receives a phone call from Hortense Cumberbatch, who Cynthia bore out of wedlock at sixteen and gave up for adoption without ever seeing her. Hortense (Marianne Jean-Baptiste) is a black woman, now in her late twenties, an optometrist. After the death of her mother, she decides to seek her birth mother, and the long-held secret of Cynthia's first child is threatened. This secret has been guarded not only by Cynthia but by her younger brother, Maurice (Timothy Spall), and his wife, Monica (Phyllis Logan).

Cynthia breaks into tears and hangs up on Hortense. Her daughter calls back. Cynthia fearfully agrees to meet with her. At first she cannot believe her daughter is black: "There's been some mistake, sweetheart. Why, look at me." When she first saw her adoption papers, Hortense also thought there was a mistake: "It says here my mother is white." Hortense and Cynthia go into a cafe for a cup of tea, and here begins the film's first long unbroken shot, the camera never moving from a medium two-shot, no one else ever in the frame, Cynthia saying she had never slept with a black man ("I'd remember something like that, wouldn't I?"). Then her face changes. A buried memory has surfaced. She begins to sob.

The way the two women play this scene is fascinating. They're acting in real time, creating a new relationship on the spot, Cynthia feeling the first inner stirrings of this daughter who is an optometrist, when her layabout Roxanne is a street sweeper.

Scenes of the two women, together and apart, are intercut with scenes of Maurice and Monica, childless, with a coldness between them. An unusual amount of screen time is devoted to the photographs Maurice takes in his portrait studio. They're interesting in themselves; a woman whose face was scarred in a traffic crash says she wants to look "as bad as possible" for insurance purposes. Then there is an odd visit from a down-and-out drunk who sold Maurice the business. Why do these scenes exist? They lay the foundations for Maurice's outburst near the end, beginning with "I've spent my life trying to make people happy."

Maurice and Monica, who live in a spacious new house, hardly ever see his sister and her daughter. They decide to invite them over for Roxanne's twenty-first birthday. Cynthia urges her daughter to bring her boyfriend: "I wouldn't know him if he stood up in my soup." Then she rings up Maurice and asks if she can bring "a mate from work." This will be Hortense, who is reluctant to attend a family function where there might be difficulties.

Soon comes the second very long, unbroken take, focused on a crowded picnic table in Maurice's backyard, as the guests uneasily settle down. The tension is palpable, and not only because of the unexplained Hortense. Cynthia, who brought up Maurice as her "little brother," hates Monica, and the feeling is returned. Roxanne doesn't like Maurice. Paul (Lee Ross), the boyfriend, had only a little mumbled dialogue, but watch him closely: he is terrified, his hands clenching, his chin twitching, as he bolts his food. And then later, inside around the birthday cake, Cynthia drops her bombshell: Hortense is her daughter.

How this plays out and what it leads to is encompassed in the film's title. What is interesting is that there is no sign of racial prejudice; the fact that Roxanne is learning that she has a half-sister is quite enough. The shock of the announcement spreads through the room, jarring loose other family secrets and lies.

Observe this scene as an illustration of what I mean by Mike Leigh's delicate precision. Every camera setup, every close-up, the size and timing of every close-up, the editing of the whole, works to unfold the scene powerfully. Material enough for a season of soap opera is handled in several minutes and never seems forced or arbitrary.

The tricky thing with many Leigh films is to process the comedy. In his more upbeat films like *Life Is Sweet* (1991) and *Topsy-Turvy* (1999), the comedy is evident. In his darker films, like this one, *Bleak Moments*, *High Hopes* (1988), and, of course, *Vera Drake* (2004), the humor is there, but often repressed and insidious, the kind of humor that in a social situation tempts you to laugh when it's inappropriate. One of Leigh's favorite devices is to contrive some sort of party, dinner, or gathering in which all the story strands emerge, sometimes with great inconvenience.

Bleak Moments is now finally available on DVD, as is Leigh's celebrated BBC film *Abigail's Party* (1977). Social embarrassment in both is palpable; are we supposed to laugh or wince? That sort of choice can make a film hypnotic. Consider an extended scene in *Bleak Moments* when the heroine, a beautiful, severe, reserved woman (Ann Raitt), goes on a first date with a painfully shy teacher (Eric Allen). In their paralysis in a Chinese restaurant, and in their confrontation with a waiter, you can sense all of Leigh's career lying in wait.

In my review of *Bleak Moments*, I wrote that the film "is not entertaining in any conventional way. This is not to say for a moment that it is boring or difficult to watch; on the contrary, it is impossible not to watch." That describes so much of his work. A fellow critic at that long-ago festival screening told me, "I was riveted to the screen. I could not stop watching the movie. But I could never sit through it again."

I could, I wrote then, and I have. The kind of fascination Mike Leigh generates is unlike almost anything else in the cinema, because it takes such chances, goes so deeply, explores the human comedy for its tears.

{ THE SHINING }

Stanley Kubrick's cold and frightening *The Shining* (1980) challenges us to decide: who is the reliable observer? Whose idea of events can we trust? In the opening scene at a job interview, the characters seem reliable enough, although the dialogue has a formality that echoes the small talk on the space station in *2001*. We meet Jack Torrance (Jack Nicholson), a man who plans to live for the winter in solitude and isolation with his wife and son. He will be the caretaker of the snowbound Overlook Hotel. His employer warns that a former caretaker murdered his wife and two daughters, and committed suicide, but Jack reassures him: "You can rest assured, Mr. Ullman, that's not gonna happen with me. And as far as my wife is concerned, I'm sure she'll be absolutely fascinated when I tell her about it. She's a confirmed ghost-story and horror-film addict."

Do people talk this way about real tragedies? Will his wife be absolutely fascinated? Does he ever tell her about it? Jack, wife Wendy (Shelley Duvall), and son Danny (Danny Lloyd) move into the vast hotel just as workers are shutting it down for the winter; the chef, Dick Hallorann (Scatman Crothers), gives them a tour, with emphasis on the food-storage locker ("You folks can eat up here a whole year and never have the same menu twice"). Then they're alone, and a routine begins: Jack sits at a typewriter in the great hall, pounding relentlessly at his typewriter, while Wendy and Danny put together a version of everyday life that includes breakfast cereal, toys, and a lot of TV. There is no sense that the three function together as a loving family.

Danny: is he reliable? He has an imaginary friend named Tony, who speaks in a lower register of Danny's voice. In a brief conversation before the family is left alone, Hallorann warns Danny to stay clear of Room 237, where the violence took place, and he tells Danny they share the "shining," the psychic gift of reading minds and seeing the past and future. Danny tells Dick that Tony doesn't want him to discuss such things. Who is Tony? "A little boy who lives in my mouth."

Tony seems to be Danny's device for channeling psychic input, including a shocking vision of blood spilling from around the closed doors of the hotel elevators. Danny also sees two little girls dressed in matching outfits; although we know there was a two-year age difference in the murdered children, both girls look curiously old. If Danny is a reliable witness, he is witness to specialized visions of his own that may not correspond to what is actually happening in the hotel.

That leaves Wendy, who for most of the movie has that matter-of-fact banality that Shelley Duvall also conveyed in Altman's *3 Women*. She is a companion and playmate for Danny, and tries to cheer Jack until he tells her, suddenly and obscenely, to stop interrupting his work. Much later, she discovers the reality of that work, in one of the movie's shocking revelations. She is reliable at that moment, I believe, and again toward the end when she bolts Jack into the food locker after he turns violent.

But there is a deleted scene from *The Shining* that casts Wendy's reliability in a curious light. Near the end of the film, on a frigid night, Jack chases Danny into the labyrinth on the hotel grounds. His son escapes, and Jack, already wounded by a baseball bat, staggers, falls, and is seen the next day, dead, his face frozen into a ghastly grin. He is looking up at us from under lowered brows, in an angle Kubrick uses again and again in his work. Here is the deletion, reported by the critic Tim Dirks: "A two-minute explanatory epilogue was cut shortly after the film's premiere. It was a hospital scene with Wendy talking to the hotel manager; she is told that searchers were unable to locate her husband's body."

If Jack did indeed freeze to death in the labyrinth, of course his body was found—and sooner rather than later, since Dick Hallorann alerted the forest rangers to serious trouble at the hotel. If Jack's body was not found, what happened to it? Was it never there? Was it absorbed into the past, and does that explain Jack's presence in that final photograph of a group of hotel partygoers in 1921? Did Jack's violent pursuit of his wife and child exist entirely in Wendy's imagination, or Danny's, or theirs?

The one observer who seems trustworthy at all times is Dick Hallorann, but his usefulness ends soon after his midwinter return to the hotel. That leaves us with a closed-room mystery: in a snowbound hotel, three people descend into versions of madness or psychic terror, and we cannot depend on any of them for an objective view of what happens. It is this elusive open-endedness that makes Kubrick's film so strangely disturbing.

Yes, it is possible to understand some of the scenes of hallucination. When Jack thinks he is seeing other people, there is always a mirror present; he may be talking with himself. When Danny sees the little girls and the rivers of blood, he may be channeling the past tragedy. When Wendy thinks her husband has gone mad, she may be correct, even though her perception of what happens may be skewed by psychic input from her son, who was deeply scarred by his father's brutality a few years earlier. But what if there is no body at the end?

Kubrick was wise to remove that epilogue. It pulled one rug too many out from under the story. At some level, it is necessary for us to believe the three members of the Torrance family are actually residents in the hotel during that winter, whatever happens or whatever they think happens.

Those who have read Stephen King's original novel report that Kubrick dumped many plot elements and adapted the rest to his uses. Kubrick is telling a story with ghosts (the two girls, the former caretaker, and a bartender), but it isn't a "ghost story," because the ghosts may not be present in any sense at all except as visions experienced by Jack or Danny.

The movie is not about ghosts but about madness and the energies it sets loose in an isolated situation primed to magnify them. Jack is an alcoholic and child abuser who has reportedly not had a drink for five months but is anything but a "recovering alcoholic." When he imagines he drinks with the imaginary bartender, he is as drunk as if he were really drinking, and the imaginary booze triggers all his alcoholic demons, including an erotic vision that turns into a nightmare. We believe Hallorann when he senses Danny has psychic powers, but it's clear Danny is not their master; as he picks up his father's madness and the story of the murdered girls, he conflates it into his fears of another attack by Jack. Wendy, who is terrified by her enraged husband, perhaps also receives versions of this psychic output. They all lose reality together. Yes, there are events we believe: Jack's manuscript, Jack locked in the food-storage room, Jack escaping, and the famous "Here's Johnny!" as he hatchets his way through the door. But there is no way, within the film, to be sure with any confidence exactly what happens, or precisely how, or really why.

Kubrick delivers this uncertainty in a film where the actors themselves vibrate with unease. There is one take involving Scatman Crothers that Kubrick famously repeated 160 times. Was that "perfectionism," or was it a mind game designed to convince the actors they were trapped in the hotel with another madman, their director? Did Kubrick sense that their dismay would be absorbed into their performances?

"How was it, working with Kubrick?" I asked Duvall ten years after the experience.

"Almost unbearable," she said. "Going through day after day of excruciating work, Jack Nicholson's character had to be crazy and angry all the time. And my character had to cry twelve hours a day, all day long, the last nine months straight, five or six days a week. I was there a year and a month. After all that work, hardly anyone even criticized my performance in it, even to mention it, it seemed like. The reviews were all about Kubrick, like I wasn't there."

Like she wasn't there.

{ THE TERRORIST }

Malli is only nineteen, a young woman who has spent all of her life within the closed world of a movement. She accepts its values without question. Her brother died for the cause. She has killed for it, comfortable with weapons, moving through the jungle where her guerrilla unit operates. When she is not fighting, she is simply a young girl, giggling with her friends. There is nothing hardened about her. We look in her enormous eyes and see they are open to life and love.

One day, her group is summoned to a meeting. A volunteer is needed to become a suicide bomber, who will place a garland of flowers around the neck of a political leader and detonate explosives that will kill them both. Malli volunteers. Her girlfriends cluster around in excitement, as if she has won a beauty contest. There is no greater honor than to die for the cause.

Santosh Sivan's *The Terrorist* (1999) was filmed in India in the Tamil language. He says it was inspired by the assassination of the Indian prime minister Rajiv Gandhi in 1991. But in the movie, no country is identified, no name is attached to her target, and no ideology or religion is attached to her movement.

This is not a film about the rightness or wrongness of her cause or the political situation that inspired it. It simply and heartbreakingly observes for a few days as a young woman prepares to become a suicide bomber. Her story is told with a minimum of onscreen violence and little in the way of action scenes; if Truffaut was correct, and war movies argue for war by making it look exciting, *The Terrorist* looks the other way.

I watch the film in horrified fascination. To die of disease, age, accident, or even in combat is a condition of the human destiny. But to choose the moment of your own death and take other lives because you believe an idea is bigger than yourself: what idea could justify that? At least in battle you hope to survive. To me, consciousness is the all-encompassing idea; without it, there are no ideas, and to destroy it is to destroy all ideas.

A movement that encourages suicide so that it can benefit from that annihilation is monstrously selfish: let people like The Leader, who thanks Malli for her death by treating her to lunch, blow himself up, if he is so sure someone must.

But my discussion is outside the terms of the movie. *The Terrorist* is anchored in the everyday reality of Malli, played by Ayesha Dharker so expressively that we identify with her feelings even as we deplore her mission. Her "unforgettable face, with her wide, full mouth and enormous dark eyes, appears in nearly every frame," writes A. O. Scott, "often filling most of the screen, as if we might be able to find our way into Malli's mind through her pores."

After she volunteers for death, she is passed by a network of movement members to a farm where she will spend the last four days of her life. On this journey she is helped by a young boy named Lotus (Vishwas), who knows the territory; they wade in a river to avoid land mines, and he knows where all the booby traps are. He tells her that everyone he has guided has eventually been killed. He weeps: "There will be blood everywhere."

On this journey, she meets a young fighter who has been mortally wounded. She does what she can, cradling him in her arms. He tells her he has never been so close to a woman before. This is a love scene, really; they love each other because they share the same cause, and his death in a way is a consummation.

She arrives at the farm, which is run by the jolly Vasu (Parmeshwaran). His wife has been in a coma for seven years, but he always sets a place for her at dinner. He has a crony, and when the two men talk, we are reminded of the dialogue of the great Indian novelist R. K. Narayan, which feasts on amusing contradictions. All the time, the wife on her bed watches with open eyes. What does she see, what does she hear?

Malli's trainers fit her for clothing that will conceal the explosives and show her how to detonate them. As she goes through this training, she is an obedient student, awed by the seriousness of her study, pleased to be treated as such an important person. When the trainers leave, she enters into the life of the farm. Vasu, like many Indians, is a natural philosopher. "A flower is the earth smiling," he tells her. Does he know she has been assigned to blow herself up? The movie never answers this question. I think it's quite possible he doesn't know the nature of her mission; he gabs too much to be entrusted with secrets.

Now two events happen that are treated with such subtlety and delicacy that we understand, if we didn't before, how gently Santosh Sivan tells his story. (You may want to see the movie before reading further.) Malli discovers that she is pregnant. And, in an almost inexplicable way, she receives a communication from Vasu's wife. The everyday human life of the farm absorbs her. Then the day of her destiny arrives, and she sets off on her mission.

Does she detonate the bomb? Does she succeed in killing the politician? In real life, Rajiv Gandhi and his assassin were killed. But *The Terrorist* is not the story of that event and must find its own conclusion. It finds, I think, the only conclusion that it can, but do not conclude that you therefore know what that must be.

Santosh Sivan, the director, is one of India's most successful cinematographers, a master of the color, dance, and music of Bollywood; he shot Gurinder Chadha's *Bride and Prejudice*. He is also a thoughtful and quixotic person whose Web site, santoshsivan.com, involves technique, wit, and philosophy. He made *The Terrorist* in seventeen days on a budget of $25,000, using mostly non-actors, although the beautiful Ayesha Dharker later won a role in *Star Wars: Episode II—Attack of the Clones* and starred in *Bombay Dreams* in London and New York.

Despite its limited budget, *The Terrorist* is visually breathtaking: "The most beautiful film from India in years (maybe ever)," wrote David

Overby, who selected it for the Toronto festival. Sivan shot some scenes in the jungle and others "in his own backyard," Dharker told me, when I showed the film at my 2000 Overlooked Film Festival. She did her own stunts and broke her leg during one of them. There is a lot of water in the film, a lot of rain, rivers, some tears; "the movie was shot in an actual drizzle," Sivan says on his Web site. "No sprinklers."

In an interview with David Walsh, Sivan notes: "Most of the films that deal with violence end up showing a great deal of it and then say, at the end, 'No, it's not right.'" Sivan deliberately avoided violence to focus on the story of Malli, who he says comes from "a group of young people, mostly teenagers. They are deprived of any kind of education, sex life, smoking; everything is considered harmful. All of them are made to believe that being a martyr is the biggest thing to happen, and they're given fantastic funerals. It is like the ultimate high for a person in that kind of environment."

I admire *The Terrorist* because it sidesteps the ideology, the question of which side is right and which side is wrong, the political motives, the tactical reasons and simply says: here is a young woman who has decided to kill and be killed for a cause. Look in her eyes, listen to her voice, watch her as she lives for a few days, and ask yourself what motivates her, and why. Every time I see the film, I feel a great sadness, that a human imagination could be so limited that it sees its own extinction as a victory.

{ THE THIEF OF BAGDAD }

To begin with a story: our grandson Taylor was deeply immersed in a video game on his laptop. I began to watch *The Thief of Bagdad* on DVD. At first he ignored it. Then I saw him glancing at the screen. Then he closed the laptop and watched full time. During the spider sequence, only his eyes were visible above the neck of his T-shirt. "That was a good movie!" he told me. "What did Taylor say when he found out it was almost seventy years old?" his mother, Sonia, asked me. "I didn't tell him," I said.

This 1940 movie is one of the great entertainments. It lifts up the heart. An early Technicolor movie, it employs colors gladly and with boldness, using costumes to introduce a rainbow. It has adventure, romance, song, a Miklos Rozsa score that one critic said is "a symphony accompanied by a movie." It had several directors; as producer, Alexander Korda leaped from one horse to another in midstream. But it maintains a consistent spirit, and that spirit is one of headlong joy in storytelling.

The story is loosely borrowed from Douglas Fairbanks Sr.'s *The Thief of Bagdad* (1924), itself a great film. Fairbanks Jr. told me it was his father's favorite. One major change is crucial: in the silent film, the thief and the romantic lead were one and the same, played by Fairbanks. In the 1940 film, they are made into two characters. The thief, Abu, is played by the Indian

363

child star Sabu, then about fifteen. The king, Ahmad, is played by John Justin with a Fairbanksian mustache. This is an invaluable change, for both dramatic purposes and practical ones: the silent character needs no one to talk to. The 1940 characters become allies drawn from the top and bottom of society, making Sabu essentially the star of the film, although he doesn't receive top billing. The most compelling character, as he should be, is the villain Jaffar, played by the German emigré Conrad Veidt with hypnotic eyes and a cruel laugh. The beautiful, passive heroine, a princess desired by both men, is played by June Duprez.

The story in my mind moves from one spectacular special-effects sequence to another: the Sultan's mechanical toy collection. The flying horse. The storm at sea. The goddess with six arms. The towering genie released from a bottle. Abu's assault on the temple that contains the All-Seeing Eye. His climb up a mountainous statue. The battle with the gigantic spider. The flying carpet.

Half of the the shots in *Citizen Kane* used special effects, according to Robert Carringer, who wrote a book on the film. There is rarely a shot in *The Thief of Bagdad* without them. The film was a breakthrough in technique and vision, influential in shaping the entire genre. There are few effects in *Star Wars* (1977) that cannot be found in *Thief*. Some of them, such as blue screen, were still being perfected. Other effects, such as matte paintings, had been in use for years.

The Criterion DVD offers interviews with three effects experts, including Ray Harryhausen, who discuss the film's techniques. It is especially eye opening to see stills revealing the "hanging matte" technique, which creates a background or completes a composition by suspending a matte painting in front of the camera. The camera's 2-D eye is fooled by the painting into making us see foreground as background. Other techniques are simplicity itself: the genie is made to tower over Abu by using an optical printer to combine a shot of the genie (Rex Ingram) close to the camera, and Abu hundreds of feet away. Both are filmed from a static camera on the same beach.

The use of blue screen may seem primitive compared to today's computer-generated animation, but it has the advantage of using real-world subjects. The flying horse, for example, is a real horse, with a real actor mounted on it. The flying carpet is a real carpet, with Abu standing on it. Both the genie and the thief seem real in all of their shots, because they are.

The point here is that all of the effects, supervised by the wizard Lawrence W. Butler, are used to further and deepen the story. Consider the remarkable beauty of several scenes showing magnificent cities climbing hills in the background. The cities may be tinted peach or blue, which makes them all the more fantastical. They are all mattes.

Once on a visit to the Disney Studios, I met the famous matte artist Peter Ellenshaw, who was a young assistant artist on *Thief*. He told me how his paintings used not only a forced perspective, but such devices as deliberate blurring to create the illusion of depth. When two lovers are standing in a balcony in front of a matte cityscape, it would be a mistake to make the painting in a photorealistic style. Its indistinct qualities make it seem farther away.

Korda, a Hungarian emigré who had earlier run Britain's Denham Studios, was now an independent, powerful in the Mayer, Selznick, or Goldwyn mode. He used his brother Vincent as his art director, his brother Zoltan as a director. The already legendary art director William Cameron Menzies also worked on the film, and is said to have directed some scenes. Together they made a film of breathtaking beauty. It is done so well that it does not date. Never mind that today similar vistas could be painted with CGI. These are so gorgeous that we cannot imagine them being improved.

Korda often employed others from overseas. Veidt (1893–1943) was a famous German silent actor who fled Hitler in 1933, became a British citizen, worked in Hollywood, was a major star. Sabu (1924–63) was born in Mysore, India, and as a boy was a servant for a maharajah. In 1937, he was cast by Robert Flaherty in the title role of the quasi-documentary *Elephant Boy*, an international hit. He was signed by Korda, for whom he made *The Drum* (1938), *Thief*, and the great success *Jungle Book* (1942). Rex Ingram (1895–1969), the genie, was a well-known African American stage and screen actor who graduated from Northwestern University. He achieved fame in films like *Green Pastures* and *Cabin in the Sky*.

The energy centers on the film are clearly supplied by Sabu and Veidt, as a boy bubbling with enthusiasm and innocent guile and a man steeped in bitterness and cruelty. Both performances are perfectly pitched to the needs of the screenplay. The romance between Duprez and Justin, as the princess and Ahmad, is rather bloodless, centering on abstract vows; their greatest passion is shown in the scene where they're bound to opposite walls, and under sentence of death. The same low-flame romance was mirrored in Disney's *Aladdin* (1992), greatly influenced by both versions of the *Thief*, combining Abu and Ahmad as Aladdin.

Although the film had so many directors (including Michael Powell, two Kordas, and Menzies), it seems the work of one vision and that must have been Korda's. It remains one of the greatest of fantasy films, on a level with *The Wizard of Oz*. To see either film is to see the cinema incorporating every technical art learned in the 1930s and employing them to create enchanting visions. Today, when dizzying CGI effects, the Queasy-Cam, and a frantic editing pace seem to move films closer to video games, witness the beauty of *Thief of Bagdad* and mourn.

{ Top Hat }

There are two numbers in *Top Hat* where the dancing on the screen reaches such perfection as is attainable. They are by Fred Astaire and Ginger Rogers for "Isn't This a Lovely Day?" and "Cheek to Cheek." Because Astaire believed that movie dance numbers should be shot in unbroken takes that ran as long as possible, what they perform is an achievement in endurance as well as artistry. At a point when many dancers would be gasping for breath, Astaire and Rogers are smiling easily, heedlessly. To watch them is to see hard work elevated to effortless joy: the work of two dancers who know they can do no better than this, and that no one else can do as well.

The movie has three other dance numbers, two solos by Astaire that are wonderful but not transcendent, and a final duet with Rogers ("The Piccolino"), where one of Irving Berlin's lesser songs is redeemed by the sight of Astaire and Rogers dancing all over a huge set that is intended to represent a canal-side hotel in Venice and looks every bit as realistic as the Grand Canal Shoppes at the Venetian in Las Vegas.

The movie's plot depends on a misunderstanding that is all but impossible: Ginger falls in love with Fred, then mistakenly decides he is the cheating husband of her best friend, Madge. "How is it that Ginger has never met her best friend's husband?" Alan Vanneman reasonably asks in the *Bright Lights Film Journal*. "Well, Europe is a big place."

Yes, and Madge and her husband, Horace, spend long periods living separate lives of luxury. That Horace is a womanizer seems, strangely, to cheer Madge, perhaps because none of the sex in this movie seems to require body parts. That's why she gives her blessing to what Ginger thinks is adultery. She even pushes the couple onto the dance floor for the "Cheek to Cheek" number.

This is an Idiot Plot, yes, which could be cleared up at any moment by one line of sensible dialogue, but there are times when nothing but an Idiot Plot will do, and we are happy to play along. The movie, made during the Depression in 1935, features characters so rich that even their butlers are gentlemen of leisure. Astaire plays Jerry Travers, who is opening in a London musical being produced by his best friend, Horace Hardwick (Edward Everett Horton), which means he doesn't know his best friend's wife, either.

For reasons utterly contrived, Jerry is staying in Horace's hotel suite, which is why Dale Tremont (Rogers) finds Astaire when she rings Horace's doorbell. As the film opens, Horace advises Jerry on the pleasures of marriage, and Astaire insists on the joys of bachelorhood with "No Strings," a Berlin song with lyrics that could have been written by the naughty Cole Porter:

> *Bring on the big attraction*
> *My decks are cleared for action*
> *I'm fancy free and free for anything fancy.*

His tap dancing during this number disturbs Dale, who is sleeping directly below them in a bedroom that looks like where Botticelli's Venus spends her nights when the clamshell gets damp. She comes upstairs to complain, he falls in love, and the next day buys out the hotel flower shop to fill her room. "I wonder what Mr. Beddini is going to say about this," the shop owner muses to an unbilled Lucille Ball. "The desk clerk has intimated that Mr. Beddini provides Miss Tremont with all the niceties, including her clothes. And her niceties are very nice."

Alberto Beddini, who often speaks of himself in the third person, is played by Erik Rhodes as a dress designer who pays Dale's expenses in return for her showing off his gowns at fancy watering holes. That he is gay goes without saying, and in 1935, it did. At one point, fed up with Dale, he declares, "Never again will I allow women to wear my dresses."

Jerry and Dale meet in the hotel lobby, where she's on her way to riding lessons. He pursues her to the park, where her ride is interrupted by a sudden shower. She takes refuge in a pavilion where he finds her, and as the rain pours all around them, he sings "Isn't This a Lovely Day?" She tries to remain aloof, but when he begins to dance she begins, reluctantly at first, to join him.

When discussions come up about which of the two was the better dancer, people often quote a line that became famous after a 1982 *Frank and Ernest* comic strip: "Ginger Rogers did everything Fred did, and she did it backwards and in high heels." Although she is wearing riding boots and not heels in this scene, what is remarkable is how supremely the two dancers work together. The dance begins as a solo by Astaire and then becomes a conversation in dance, each one performing a dazzling step that the other reproduces, until they are in perfect synchronicity. After watching this scene, there is only one thing to be done, and that is to watch it again.

Dale is now in love with this man, whoever he is. Then a hotel clerk points out "Mr. Hardwick" on the mezzanine, she thinks he's pointing to Jerry, and is furious to have been romanced by a married man. She confesses all to Madge (played by Helen Broderick, who was the mother of Broderick Crawford, and we can believe it). But Madge is elated by the news, the latest in a series of dalliances by Horace that result in payoffs of diamonds and furs for her. Horace, who doesn't know about the mistaken identity, thinks Jerry and Dale are simply having an affair, and assigns his butler, Bates (Eric Blore, an ingratiating busybody), to shadow them and keep Jerry out of trouble before his show's big opening night. Astaire arrives late at the theater, just in time for his "Top Hat, White Tie and Tails" dance number, which provided his signature song.

And why am I bothering to describe this plot, which exists as such silly froth it makes P. G. Wodehouse look ponderous by comparison? Perhaps because the actors give it such goofy playfulness. Events conspire to transport all of the principals to Venice, created on a gigantic Venetian set where gondolas travel for yards at a time and seaplanes land at restaurants.

It was here that Madge intended to introduce them; she still doesn't know they've met under Dale's impression that Jerry is Horace. I love writing sentences like that. "You two run along and dance," Madge tells them, "and don't give me another thought." That's when Dale decides, "If Madge doesn't care, I certainly don't." Jerry replies, "Neither do I. All I know is . . ."

Heaven, I'm in Heaven . . .
And my heart beats so that I can hardly speak . . .

And then comes their third great dance number, covering most of the visible real estate in Venice and conveniently clearing a dance floor for their pas de deux. This is the number featuring Rogers's famous gown made mostly of ostrich feathers, which Astaire hated because they distracted from the clean lines of the dance (in "Swing Time," one of her beaded costumes actually swipes him in the face). The feathers are a challenge for Rogers, too, who has to work with and not against them. Her choreography causes them to undulate as if she herself is almost in flight; at the moments when, in Astaire's arms, she bends over backward almost to the floor, they underline the appearance of surrender.

Because we are human, because we are bound by gravity and the limitations of our bodies, because we live in a world where the news is often bad and the prospects disturbing, there is a need for another world somewhere, a world where Fred Astaire and Ginger Rogers live. Where everyone is a millionaire and hotel suites are the size of ballrooms and everything is creased, combed, brushed, shined, polished, powdered, and expensive. Where you seem to find the happiness you seek, when you're out together dancing cheek to cheek. It doesn't even matter if you really find it, as long as you seem to find it, because appearances are everything in this world, and . . .

Let the rain pitter patter
But it really doesn't matter
If the skies are gray.
Long as I can be with you,
It's a lovely day.

{ TRIUMPH OF THE WILL }

"By general consent [one] of the best documentaries ever made."

So I wrote in 1994, in a review of what in fact is a better documentary, Ray Muller's *The Wonderful Horrible Life of Leni Riefenstahl*. I was referring to Riefenstahl's *Triumph of the Will* (1935), about the 1934 Nazi Party congress and rally in Nuremberg. Others would have agreed with me. We would all have been reflecting the received opinion that the film is great but evil, and that reviewing it raises the question of whether great art can be in service of evil. I referred to *Triumph* again in the struggle I had in reviewing the racist *Birth of a Nation*.

But how fresh was my memory of *Triumph of the Will*? I believe I saw it as an undergraduate in college, and my memory would have been old and fuzzy even in 1994, overlaid by many assertions of the film's "greatness." Now I have just seen it again and am stunned that I praised it. It is one of the most historically important documentaries ever made, yes, but one of the best? It is a terrible film, paralyzingly dull, simpleminded, overlong, and not even "manipulative," because it is too clumsy to manipulate anyone but a true believer. It is not a "great movie" in the sense that the other films in this group are great, but it is "great" in the reputation it has and the shadow it casts.

Have you seen it recently, or at all? It records the gathering together, in September 1934 in Nuremberg, of hundreds of thousands of Nazi Party members, troops, and supporters, to be "reviewed" by Adolf Hitler. "Reviewed" is the operative word. Great long stretches of the film consist merely of massed formations of infantry, cavalry, artillery groups, and even working men with their shovels held like rifles. They march in perfect, rigid formation past Hitler, giving him their upraised right arms in salute and having it returned. Opening sections of the film show Hitler addressing an outdoor formation, and the conclusion involves his speech in a vast hall at the closing of the congress.

Try to imagine another film where hundreds of thousands gathered. Where all focus was on one or a few figures on a distant stage. Where those figures were the objects of adulation. The film, of course, is the rock documentary *Woodstock* (1970). But consider how Michael Wadleigh, that film's director, approached the formal challenge of his work. He begins with the preparations for this massive concert. He shows arrivals coming by car, bus, bicycle, foot. He shows the arrangements to feed them. He makes the Portosan Man, serving the portable toilets, into a folk hero. He shows the crowd sleeping in tents or in the rough, bathing in streams, even making love. He shows them drenched with shadows and wading through mud. He shows medical problems. He shows the crowds gradually disappearing.

By contrast, Riefenstahl's camera is oblivious to one of the most fascinating aspects of the Nuremberg rally, which is how it was organized. Yes, there are overhead shots of vast fields of tents, laid out with mathematical precision. But how did the thousands eat, relieve themselves, prepare their uniforms and weapons, and mass up to begin their march through town? We see overhead shots of tens of thousands of Nazis in rigid formation, not a single figure missing, not a single person walking to the sidelines. How long did they have to stand before their moment in the sun? Where did they go and what did they do after marching past Hitler? In a sense, Riefenstahl has told the least interesting part of the story.

There is a lesson, to be sure, in the zombielike obedience of the marching troops, so rigidly in formation they deny their own physical feelings. One searches the ranks for a smile, a yawn. But all are stern and serious, and so is Hitler, except once when he smiles as the horses are marching past. But what else does the film contain, apart from the march-pasts? There is a long series of close-ups near the beginning, of Nazi party officials mouthing official platitudes. There are two speeches by Hitler, both surprisingly short, both lacking all niceties, both stark in their language: the party must be "uncompromisingly the one and only power in Germany."

One searches for human touches. Riefenstahl had no eye for human interest. Individuality is crushed by the massed conformity. There are occasional cutaways to people smiling or nodding, but rarely ever speaking to one another. There is no attempt to "humanize" Hitler. In his closing speech, sweat trickles down his face, and we realize that there was no perspiration in earlier shots. Is it possible that he posed for some of the perfectly framed shots of him reviewing troops? A 35mm camera and crew would have been a distracting presence in the street next to his car; one filming him from a high pedestal would have had to be crane-mounted, and shot out of synchronicity with the event.

"If you see this film again today, you ascertain that it doesn't contain a single reconstructed scene." So says Riefenstahl in her film's defense in the Muller documentary. What does she mean by "reconstructed"? Certainly we would not think the massed march-bys would be reconstructed. But what of such scenes as the Workers' Brigade, where the men chant in unison, presumably to Hitler, that they labor in the swamps, in the fields, etc., and then, in response to the barked question "Where are you from?" individuals answer with the names of their towns or districts. They could not have all heard the question; each answer would have been a separate set-up.

There are also questions of spontaneity. During one Hitler speech, he is interrupted by *sieg heil!* exactly six times, as if there were an applause sign to prompt them when to begin and end, and we note that throughout the film, there are no scatterings of individual voices at the start or finish of *sieg heil!* Only a single massed voice, in unison. I found myself peering intently to observe other moments of the film revealing its mechanism. Although Riefenstahl used thirty cameras and a crew of 150, only one camera appears to be visible on screen; during the outdoor rally before three gigantic hanging swastika flags, you can see the camera on an elevator between the first and second, its shadow cast on the second. And in a shot of a man who has climbed up a pole to get a better view of a parade, she cuts back to him giving the right-arm salute; I reflected that he could not hold on without both hands, and realized that his left foot is out of frame in both shots—standing on a support, undoubtedly. Among minor details: everyone on screen seems to have a fresh haircut.

That *Triumph of the Will* is a great propaganda film there is no doubt, and various surveys have named it so. But I doubt that anyone not already a Nazi could be swayed by it. Being a Nazi, to this film, means being a mindless pawn in thrall to the godlike Hitler. Yet it must have had a persuasive effect in Germany at the time; although Hitler clearly spells out that the Nazis will be Germany's only party, and its leader Germany's only leader for a thousand years to come. At the end, there is a singing of the party anthem, the Horst Wessel Song; under Nazi law, the right-arm salute had to be given during the first and fourth verses. We see a lot of right-arm saluting in *Triumph of the Will*, noticing how Hitler curls his fingers back to his palm before withdrawing the salute each time, with a certain satisfaction. What a horrible man. What insanity that so many Germans embraced him. A sobering thought: most of the people on the screen were dead within a few years.

{ VENGEANCE IS MINE }

The title *Vengeance Is Mine* poses an implied question that is never answered: vengeance for what? This portrait of a cold-blooded serial killer suggests a cruel force without motivation, inspiration, grievance. Unlike most sociologically oriented films in the true crime genre, it lacks the Freudian explanation for everything and shows us pure evil, remote and inhuman. A few scenes from the killer's boyhood feel almost like satirical demonstrations of how any "explanation" would be impossible.

The 1979 film details the violent career of Akira Nishiguchi, who committed a series of murders in Japan in late 1963 and early 1964. Named Iwao Enokizu in the film, he is played by the powerful actor Ken Ogata, who uses two dominant emotional states, passivity and rage. Sometimes he can be persuasive and even charming, but only to gain his goals of theft or murder. His face is a mask concealing—what? Perhaps concealing nothing.

The film is by Shohei Imamura (1926–2006), considered with such as Ozu, Kurosawa, and Mizoguchi among the greatest Japanese directors. He was once named an entomologist by a French critic, and not just because of his famous film *The Insect Woman* (1963), which regarded a prostitute as prey in an unthinking, deadly world. His killer Enokizu is also like an insect, doing what he does because it is what he does. We realize how

375

much we desire such stories to explain their evil, and what resolve it takes a storyteller to deny us.

In a pre-title sequence, we see Enokizu in the back seat of a police car, after his capture. He had been the subject of a national manhunt for seventy-eight days, his photograph everywhere, and yet he looked so anonymous with his regular features, his glasses, his hat, and overcoat that even when people thought they recognized him, they doubted themselves. Enokizu sings in the police car, speculates on the date of his hanging, refuses to go along with the questions of the police. His theory: he committed the crimes, he deserves to die, everything is as it should be.

After the titles, Imamura shows us the first murders. Enokizu hitches a ride with two truck drivers, makes up a story about gambling, leads one to a wooded hillside near railroad tracks, and stabs him to death. The murder is committed with great difficulty, the victim struggling desperately, the killer almost overcome, blood everywhere. He leads the second man to the same area, and kills him, too. He washes up and changes, cool and impassive.

The film will indicate all of his murders, but only once again in such detail; like Hitchcock in *Frenzy*, Imamura knows that once you bring violence onto the screen, it can later be more effective simply to evoke its memory. There is an interlude in which Enokizu poses as a bail bondsman, befriends the family of a man in court, separates the mother from her daughter, and obtains all of the cash she brought for bail; he does it smoothly, as throughout the film, he is able to improvise, disguise himself, successfully pose as a lawyer or professor. With another victim, an old lawyer, he befriends him, then murders him, seals him into a cabinet, makes himself at home in the man's apartment, and then flies into a frenzy when he cannot find the can opener. He was not angry with his victim, but the can opener makes him furious because it cannot be killed.

There are subplots involving two families, one Enokizu's own, another a mother and daughter in whose inn he hides. Both of these stories involve the amorality of the parents and the corruption of the children. Enokizu's marriage is lifeless, his mother is in the hospital, and there has long been a powerful attraction between his wife, Kazuko, and his father,

Kayo. Although the two come close to sex during an interlude in a hot bath, they resist because of their Catholic values. Such values, however, do not prevent the father from suggesting to a friend that Kazuko would be willing to have sex with the other man. Kazuko resists, until the man tells her he has the approval of Kayo. Then she submits, as if submitting to the father himself.

The inn where Enokizu takes refuge is run essentially as a brothel. The mother is an ex-convict, released after a sentence for murder. The daughter, Haru, arranges prostitutes for the clients of the inn, and is herself the mistress of a businessman, who pays their lease. The two women are absolutely matter-of-fact about this arrangement, and it leads to some extraordinary dialogue. The girl falls for Enokizu, even after she knows he is a wanted killer. Observing, "I know absolutely nothing about you," which is true, she nevertheless says, "Shall we die together, professor? I'm serious."

The mother goes for a walk down a bleak canal path with Enokizu. "When I killed the old battle axe, I really felt great," she tells him. "Is that how you feel now?" "No," he says. "So you haven't yet killed who you really want to kill?" "Maybe not." "Then you're a wimp."

The film gathers fearful force. Ordinary human values have been set aside for all the major characters, and that is tested above all when the rich businessman rapes Haru, with Enokizu and the mother in the next room. Haru cries for help. Enokizu seems emotionless, fixates on a dripping faucet, tightens it, and then finally reaches for a knife—but the mother stops him. She does not want to lose the man's financial support.

When the film was released in 1979, it was sometimes called the Japanese *In Cold Blood*. Not at all. Richard Brooks's 1967 film offers motivations for the characters—greed in one, childhood wounds in another. It contains a famous line: "I thought Mr. Cutter was a very nice gentleman. I thought I so liked the old man. I thought so right up to the time I cut his throat." What is most disturbing about Enokizu is that he has no feelings at all about his victims. It is simply in his nature to kill.

Seeing *Vengeance Is Mine* soon after seeing Paul Schrader's *Mishima* again, I was reminded of the Japanese fascination with death. I stare into Enokizu's eyes, which are a blank slate, and imagine his thoughts. Does he have such contempt for life that he is killing innocent strangers simply to be hanged by the state? Maybe his victims also create ideas about him in their own minds. Certainly the girl Haru has been given no reason to believe he loves, likes, or even much notices her. He never says a single kind thing to her; indeed, he says as little as possible, speaking mostly in epigrams. Insectlike, she is drawn to the candle flame.

Imamura made another great film about death named *Ballad of Narayama*, which won the Cannes Film Festival in 1983 (another of his films, *The Eel*, won in 1997). In *Nayarama*, a village traditionally determines that the time has come for an old person to die, and ceremoniously abandons him or her in the wilderness, even in winter. It is, curiously, a life-affirming film, lacking the rage of *Vengeance Is Mine*, but sharing its absorption in death. *The Eel* is about a barber who finds his wife with her lover and stabs them both to death. Released on parole, he begins a new life shadowed always by the awareness that he may kill again.

As a stylist, Imamura is a master of unobtrusive camera strategies. His POV is sometimes a little above eye level, which has the effect of diminishing his characters, presenting them perhaps as entomological specimens. In other shots, he will use low angles to include backgrounds in deep focus, as in the scene where Enokizu smolders in the kitchen while Haru is raped; the dripping faucet is placed and lighted to draw his, and our, attention. During the murders, his camera holds a middle distance, not moving, once looking straight down. He does not indulge in shock cuts or quick moves; he regards objectively. You can no more attribute motives to him in this film than to his subject.

On the DVD, there is an interview with Imamura, some years later. It is utterly unhelpful and unrevealing, and for that reason fascinating. What does he think of Enokizu? He will not say.

{ WAKING LIFE }

It is hard to say how much of Richard Linklater's *Waking Life* (2001) is a dream. I think all of it is. His hero keeps dreaming that he has awakened. He climbs out of bed, splashes water on his face, walks outside, and finds himself dreaming again. But the film isn't one of those surrealist fantasies with pinwheels coming out of the hero's eyes or people being sucked down into the vortex. It's mostly conversational, and the conversation is all intriguing; the dreamer must be intelligent.

Or perhaps not. Perhaps he's channeling it from outside. A woman in a coffee shop tells him her idea for a soap-opera plot, and he asks her how it feels to be a character in his dream. She doesn't answer, because how can she, since she's only a character in his dream? On the other hand, where did she come up with that plot? He tells her he could never have invented it himself. It's like it came to him in a . . . no, that doesn't work. It's like it came in from outside the dream.

And what is dreaming, anyway? A woman in the film speculates that when we dream, we are experiencing ourselves apart from our physical bodies. After we die, she says, doesn't it make sense that we would keep on dreaming, but that we'd never stop dreaming because now we were apart from our bodies? No, it doesn't make sense, I think, because our dreams take place within our physical brains. Maybe not. Maybe we only think they do.

Waking Life is philosophical and playful at the same time. It's an extravagantly inventive film that begins with actual footage of real actors and then translates them into animated images; it's called motion-capture, and you can see it in *Beowulf* and *300*, but it was startling when Linklater made his film in 2001, and showed it didn't need to cost millions. A founding member of the Austin, Texas, filmmaking crowd, he collaborated with a software genius named Bob Sabiston, who did it all on Macs. It's visually bright and alive—a joy to regard.

Linklater likes to listen to people talk. His standard for what they say is very high. His early film *Slacker* (1991) followed one character around Austin until that character encountered another, and then followed the new character, and so on, while they were all the time acting out their everyday lives. It was fascinating; I'd only seen that done before by Buñuel, in *The Phantom of Liberty* (1974). In Linklater's famous *Before Sunrise* (1995) and *Before Sunset* (2004), he followed Julie Delpy and Ethan Hawke around first Vienna and then Paris as they talked all night and then all day. They turn up in *Waking Life* in an impossible scene, because it shows them together between the two movies; perhaps that's a clue this is Linklater's own dream.

His characters seem engaged in all the conversations we ever had in school, or should have had. In *Waking Life*, the hero (never named, played by Wiley Wiggins) does more listening than talking: in college lectures, bars, coffeehouses, on the sidewalk, to musicians, to philosophers, even— in a quick jump in space—to a guide on the Brooklyn Bridge. That one's easy to explain; he must have seen *Cruise*, the documentary about the self-appointed king of tourist guides, Speed Levitch, who of course appears as himself. That's how dreams work.

There are also scenes with abrupt disconnects. An angry man with a red face prowls a jail cell issuing imprecations at the world. An activist drives the streets shouting at people through the loudspeakers on top of his car, but there are no people on the streets and eventually he just stops. A man who despairs of life sets himself on fire, and the hero stares at him, and then his dream continues elsewhere. Dreams often cut out in midstream.

There's a crucial scene where the hero is told a story involving synchronicity. A novelist meets a woman at a party who has the same name as a character in his novel, and her husband has the same name, and the man she's having an affair with has the same name, and so on and on. That can happen in dreams. Strangely, I've been involved for a few weeks with ongoing discussions on my blog about free will, the afterlife, politics, existentialism, the theory of evolution, and what it is to be alive. I sat watching the movie and realized the characters were discussing the same topics, sometimes in the same language. Cue *Twilight Zone* music. We've been discussing man's place in the tree of life; a biologist argues that there is more of an intelligence gap between Plato and an ordinary human than between that human and an intelligent chimpanzee. I'm a subscriber to Darwin, but I wouldn't go that far. Still, it makes you think.

Linklater has fun with the inevitable paradoxes of dreaming. The hero complains to a friend that he feels trapped in his dream, and keeps waking up into another dream. How can he break free? The friend warns him it is easy to be deceived by dreams. You can direct them and change them, but whatever you do with them, they seem to be happening now, and your changes seem to flow naturally, even when you detour to Brooklyn or start floating above Austin. The one thing you can't change, his friend says, is the lighting. If you try to turn a light switch on and off, and it doesn't work, you're dreaming. It's a test that never fails.

The hero thanks him for this advice and gets up to leave the room. He tries to switch off the light, but he can't. Of course he can't. But is there anything to the original advice, or is this dream logic at work? Maybe he was able to turn off the lights in earlier dreams, but now that he knows the rule, he'll never be able to do it again.

The film opened in October 2001, with 9/11 still a wound in our minds. It was a soothing flow of intelligence, of questioning, of curiosity and imagination. There was a paralysis and hopelessness that seemed to descend upon us. The images of the towers collapsing belonged in a nightmare, but no, they were real. *Waking Life* was a jolt, or nudge, a reminder that we could usefully ask big questions and propose possible answers. It affirmed our need to think for ourselves and not give in to dead-end despair.

Richard Linklater is one of the best directors we have. He makes commercial films (*The Bad News Bears*, with Billy Bob Thornton). He makes wry films that are applied sociology (his *SubUrbia*, with a screenplay by Eric Bogosian, was about a crowd of teenagers who hang out pointlessly at a strip mall). He makes quirky comedies (*The School of Rock*). He makes bold experimental films (*Tape*, which starred Ethan Hawke, Uma Thurman, and Robert Sean Leonard as three friends in one motel room for continuous talk and dispute, shot with a hi-def video camera). He makes period films (his *Me and Orson Welles*, one of the best films at Toronto 2008, re-creates the early days of Welles's Mercury Theatre and his brilliant but sometimes not pleasant behavior).

Above all, Linklater is a man who doesn't like to be bored and doesn't want to bore us. You can tell that from his films. He's intensely interested in his subjects. You may think you'd know all about *The Bad News Bears* just by reading the title, but you wouldn't. In my review, I said Billy Bob's character "is like a merger of his ugly drunk in *Bad Santa* and his football coach in *Friday Night Lights*, yet he doesn't recycle from either movie; he modulates the manic anger of the Santa and the intensity of the coach and produces a morose loser who we like better than he likes himself." That's not boring. Linklater has never made a formula story, and I don't believe he ever will.

Now here's an intriguing thing. The final shot in *Waking Life* isn't a POV shot. I wonder what that means.

Linklater himself appears near the end, as the pinball player.

{ WERCKMEISTER HARMONIES }

Bela Tarr's *Werckmeister Harmonies* (2000) is maddening if you are not in sympathy with it, mesmerizing if you are. If you have not walked out after twenty or thirty minutes, you will thereafter not be able to move from your seat. "Dreamlike," Jim Jarmusch calls it. Nightmarish as well; doom-laden, filled with silence and sadness, with the crawly feeling that evil is penetrating its somber little town. It is filmed elegantly in black and white, the camera movements so stately they almost float through only thirty-nine shots in a film of 145 minutes.

To know where we stand as the film begins, we should start with these words by the director, Tarr: "I despise stories, as they mislead people into believing that something has happened. In fact, nothing really happens as we flee from one condition to another. . . . All that remains is time. This is probably the only thing that's still genuine—time itself; the years, days, hours, minutes and seconds."

And what is time anyway but our agreement to divide one rotation of the Earth around the Sun into units? Could there be hours, minutes, seconds, on a planet without our year? Why would one Earth second need to exist except as part of one Earth year? Perhaps such questions lead us into the extraordinary, funny, ingenious eleven-minute shot at the start of the picture.

It is the dead of winter, almost closing time in a shabby pub. An eclipse of the Sun is due, and Janos (Lars Rudolph), the local paper carrier, takes it upon himself to explain what will happen in the heavens. He pushes the furniture to the walls, and enlists a drunk to stand in the center of the floor and flutter his hands, like the Sun's rays. Then he gets another pal to be the Earth, and walk in circles around the Sun. And then a third is the Moon, walking in his own circles around the Earth. All of these circles stagger around, the drunks rotating, and then the Moon comes between the Sun and the Earth, and there is an eclipse: "The sky darkens, then goes all dark," Janos says. "The dogs howl, rabbits hunch down, the deer run in panic, run, stampede in fright. And in this awful, incomprehensible dusk, even the birds . . . the birds too are confused and go to roost. And then . . . complete silence. Everything that lives is still. Are the hills going to march off? Will heaven fall upon us?"

Janos continues, and the others listen in befuddlement, because in their village at this hour there is nowhere else to go, nothing else to do. And now I've got you through the first eleven minutes of your twenty- or thirty-minute test, and you certainly haven't left yet. The pub owner announces closing time and throws them all out, and Janos goes to the newspaper office to pick up his papers. There, and at a hotel that is his first stop, he begins to hear alarming rumors, almost Shakespearean portents, that all is not right on heaven and earth, that a circus is coming to town with a huge stuffed whale and "the Prince," who has darkling powers. Whole families have started to disappear . . .

The shot of the arriving circus truck is haunting. It appears for a long time as a huge, square shadow on the house fronts. I was reminded of the monster shadow in *The Third Man* that turns out to be only a balloon vendor. Then headlights. Then the truck itself, outsize, gargantuan, large enough to hold, well, a whale. Its full length passes Janos as he stands and regards.

Janos is well liked in the town. "How's our Janos?" he's asked. He receives a visit from his Auntie Tunde (Hanna Schygulla), who insists he visit her estranged husband, Uncle Gyorgy (Peter Fitz), and enlist him in leading the townspeople against unnamed but imminent threats. She gives him a suitcase to take along, a case that is never opened or explained. Uncle Gyorgy is a musicologist who believes the world went wrong when Andreas Werckmeister (1645–1706) popularized a system of harmonics that clashed with the music of the celestial spheres. Janos and Gyorgy walk to the town square, both held in frame in a very long shot, until they arrive at clumps of people hunched in the cold around the truck containing the whale. Later, when Janos buys his ticket and goes inside, he regards the whale's enormous, lifeless, staring eye.

Bela Tarr (born 1955) is a Hungarian director more talked about than viewed, in part because few audiences have an appetite for, and few theaters the time to play, his films like *Sátántangó* (1994), which is 415 minutes long. For all of my time on the festival circuit, I had never seen one of his films until this one, which I obtained on DVD through Facets Multimedia of Chicago. When you're at a festival and seeing one film means missing four others, you tend to take the path of least resistance. But Tarr's name kept swimming reproachfully into my view, even in that book *1001 Movies You Must See Before You Die*, where I proudly checked off movie after movie until I came to . . . Bela Tarr.

And now I find that Tarr does, in fact, make films both unique and original, and in a style I find beautiful. I prefer the purity of black and white to color, I like very long takes if they serve a purpose and are not simply stunts, I am drawn into an air of mystery, I find it compelling when a film establishes an immediate, tangible time and place. For all of its phantasmal themes, *Werckmeister Harmonies* is resolutely realistic. Every person, every room, every street, every action, every line of dialogue feels as much like cinema verité as the works of Frederick Wiseman.

There is a state of film reverie that longer films can create (and at 145 minutes, *Werckmeister* is, after all, shorter than, say, *Zodiac*). You are lured away from the clock ticking in your mind and drift in a nontemporal state. Tarr's camera drifts as well; it is rock steady (even though handheld at times), and glides smoothly through unbroken takes that become long shots, tracking shots, close-ups, framing shots, all without haste or indecision, all without a cut. (Average shot length, if you're one of David Bordwell's ASL collectors: 3.7 minutes, as compared to, say, *The Bourne Supremacy* at 1.9 seconds.)

So do you just sit there, friends ask, and look at the shots? Well, yes, that's what everybody does when they watch a film. But they don't always see the shots as shots. Bela Tarr's style seems to be an attempt to regard his characters with great intensity and respect, to observe them without jostling them, to follow unobtrusively as they move through their worlds, which look so ordinary and are so awesome, like ours.

{ # WHAT EVER HAPPENED TO BABY JANE? }

The staircase should be billed along with the stars in Robert Aldrich's *What Ever Happened to Baby Jane?* (1962). On a claustrophobic set, it dominates many shots, separating the upstairs captivity of the paraplegic Blanche from the downstairs lair of her deranged sister, Jane. Although the two sisters live in a "mansion" that allegedly once belonged to Valentino, it is jammed between nosy neighbors and seems to consist only of a living room, a kitchen, a hallway, and a bedroom for each sister. In this hothouse a lifelong rivalry turns vicious, in one of Hollywood's best gothic grotesqueries.

The story involves sisters who were once movie stars, played by Bette Davis and Joan Crawford. The casting is one of the crucial successes of the film, although it is hard to imagine how Aldrich convinced the two divas to appear together. Rivals since the 1930s, competitive, vain, and touchy, they by all accounts hated each other in real life. Indeed, a book was written about their mutual disdain, *Bette and Joan: The Divine Feud* (1989). It is claimed on IMDb.com that in the scene where Jane kicks the helpless Blanche, Davis kicked Crawford so hard a cut required stitches. This is surely an urban legend, since the actual contact takes place below frame and Crawford would not have been present for the shot.

What wasn't an urban legend was that the two were fiercely competitive; it's possible that each agreed to do the picture only because she was jealous of the other's starring role. In the event, it was Davis who emerged on top, winning an Oscar nomination as the former child star who was now a shrill gargoyle with makeup pancaked all over her face. Davis was nothing if not courageous, as she abandoned all shreds of vanity and overacted her heart out. Crawford plays the quieter, kinder, more reasonable sister—and, it must be said, the less interesting.

The movie begins in the days of vaudeville, when Baby Jane Hudson was a child star famous for her saccharine performance of "I've Written a Letter to Daddy"—a letter she seals with a kiss and mails to heaven. Off-stage, she was a spoiled monster, screaming for ice cream, ridiculing her plain sister, Blanche. But in their twenties it is Blanche who becomes the Hollywood queen, and Jane whose appeal fades and whose movies flop. Their lives change forever when, in a mysterious incident, their car crushes Blanche against a gate, paralyzing her from the waist down.

Why she is put in charge of the "care" of her sister is hard to under-stand, despite some mumbling about a studio "cover-up." What results is the situation for the rest of the film, with Blanche trapped in a wheelchair in an upstairs bedroom, and Jane calling the shots. Blanche has two contacts with the world: her telephone and their kind maid, Elvira (Maidie Norman). But as Jane's hatred grows more venomous, she rips out the phone, sends Elvira away, and beats the maid when she bravely tries to return.

At some point during this descent into madness, *What Ever Hap-pened to Baby Jane?* stops becoming a "camp classic," which is how it's often described, and starts becoming the real thing, a psychological horror story. Davis tilts her performance toward Jane's pathological ego, which is dis-played in a macabre adult performance of "I've Written a Letter to Daddy." It also emerges in her behavior toward a peculiar gentleman caller, Edwin Flagg (Victor Buono), whom she proposes to hire as a pianist to accom-pany her during a comeback. She flatters herself that Edwin is attracted to her, failing to see that he is not the marrying kind. (The real Buono famously said, "I've heard about actors being asked 'Why have you never married?' They answer with the immortal excuse 'I just haven't found the right girl.' No one's asked me yet. If they do, that's the answer I'll give. After all, it was good enough for Monty Clift or Sal Mineo.") Edwin towers over his elderly mother, the tiny Marjorie Bennett, in a relationship as closed-off as the sisters'.

Upstairs, Blanche grows more desperate. She tries to toss a note to their next-door neighbor, but Jane finds it in the driveway. She hopes for help from Elvira, but Jane drives her away. She wheels her chair to the top of the staircase, which looms vertiginously below her. Her horrors are only beginning. I will not reveal what her sister serves her at one meal, but the next day, when she complains of hunger, Jane tells her, "You're not gettin' your breakfast because you didn't eat your din-din." When the next meal finally arrives, we stare with as much horror as Blanche does at the silver dome concealing whatever is on her plate.

The impact of *What Ever Happened to Baby Jane?* was considerable in 1962. Today's audiences, perhaps not familiar with the stars, don't fully realize how thoroughly Crawford, and especially Davis, trashed their screen images with the coaching of Aldrich. Imagine two contemporary great beauties—Julia Roberts and Cate Blanchett, say—as aged crones. The personal dislike between Crawford and Davis no doubt deepened the power of their onscreen relationship; the critic Richard Scheib observes: "The irony that only came out in later years is that the roles were uncommonly close to the truth upon the parts of both actresses—Crawford and Davis were both utterly vain, particularly when it came to their own celebrity, both abused their own family members and both had daughters who wrote books about the cruelty of their parents."

The film functions among other things as a demonstration of the need both women had to appear before the camera. In a career that began in 1925, Crawford (1905–77) was capable of making *Trog* (1970), where she was given top billing as an anthropologist on the trail of a surviving troglodyte. I cannot forget Crawford on hands and knees in a tailored pantsuit, crawling into a cave crying out, "Trog! Here, Trog!"

Davis (1908–89) had a more suitable image in her next-to-last film, the touching *The Whales of August* (1987), where she and Griffith's silent star Lillian Gish (1893–1993) played sisters. It, too, gave rise to an anecdote. Its director, Lindsay Anderson, told me that one day he said, "Miss Gish, you have just given me a perfect close-up." Davis observed, "She should. The bitch invented 'em."

Robert Aldrich (1918–83) was a master of Hollywood genres; his credits include *Vera Cruz* (1954), with Gary Cooper and Burt Lancaster; *Kiss Me Deadly* (1956), a Mickey Spillane classic; *Hush . . . Hush, Sweet Charlotte* (1964), which was intended to reunite Davis and Crawford before Crawford fell ill (one story) or was fired because she fought with Davis (possibly apocryphal); *The Dirty Dozen* (1967); *The Longest Yard* (1974); and the underrated *Hustle* (1975). None of them were art pictures, but most of them were popular, profitable, well crafted, and splendid examples of their genres. He was one of the first mainstream directors to insist on autonomy in selecting stories, actors, and editors.

Making *What Ever Happened to Baby Jane?* he possibly thought of Billy Wilder's *Sunset Boulevard* (1950), which starred Gloria Swanson as an aging movie queen, living on in her mansion. He began with a novel by Henry Farrell, which moved its aging queens further down on the artistic and financial scale, and emphasized the violence over the pathos. He knew he was asking for trouble by pairing Davis and Crawford, but he guessed, correctly, that trouble would translate into a better film. And at the end of the day it was Davis who won the ancient battle, by upstaging Crawford, winning the nomination, and making the pseudo-sequel *Charlotte*. She may not have been a pretty sight mincing her way through an old-age version of "I've Written a Letter to Daddy," but she was a trouper, and no one who has seen the film will ever forget her.

An elaborate two-disc special edition DVD was released in 2006, including a documentary on Davis written by David Anson and narrated by Jodie Foster; a thirty-minute British talk show with Crawford; a documentary about their feud; footage of Aldrich directing and Davis performing a Chubby Checker twist version of the title song on a 1962 *Andy Williams Show*. There is a commentary track by Davis impersonator Charles Busch and John Epperson (*Lypsinka*).

{ WITHNAIL & I }

In my drinking days, some of us would gather around noon on Saturdays at Oxford's Pub for what we called Drunch. We would commence with shots of creme de menthe and pint glasses of real Coke, in the hope that a combination of alcohol, sugar, and caffeine would restore us. Then we would laugh until the tears ran down our faces about the hilarity of the dreadful things that had happened the night before. In doing this, I would often quote "We laugh, that we may not cry," although just now I have discovered that no one originally said that. I always thought it was Shakespeare. It was me.

I relate this story to explain why I identify with *Withnail & I* (1987), which conveys the experience of being drunk so well that the only way I could improve upon it would be to stand behind you and hammer your head with two-pound bags of frozen peas. It is said that Bruce Robinson, the film's writer and director, based it largely on his friendship in the 1960s with Vivian MacKerrell, a usually unemployed actor and full-time alcoholic. They shared lodgings and misery in London, where Robinson recalls being down to one light bulb and taking it with him from room to room. The critic Mark Morris, in an article titled "The Real Withnail," writes: "Robinson knew it had to end when MacKerrell returned from a trip home to Scotland armed with bottles of a drink—200 percent proof, Robinson claims—that distillery workers made by sticking used whiskey filters into spin driers. Deranged by the drink, Robinson and MacKerrell, armed with a hammer and an artificial leg, smashed down one of the walls of their house. It still took another six months for Robinson and MacKerrell to work up the will go their separate ways."

In the film as in life, Withnail and "I" live in poverty and disarray and do not waste valuable drinking time by doing anything else. Since drink costs money, and Withnail (Richard E. Grant) can be quick to order "four quadruple whiskeys and a couple of pints," there is the presumption that he receives funds from his well-off homosexual uncle Montague Withnail (Richard Griffiths). It is to Uncle Monty that they appeal for the loan of his country cottage, when they are seized by the need for a change of scene. Perhaps they are seeking a geographical cure.

Robinson based the character of "I" on himself. Students of the film have learned from one glimpse of a telegram that the character's name is Marwood; it never appears in the dialogue. Marwood has within himself the seeds of sanity and prudence. He drinks heavily, but Withnail is consumed by an unslakable thirst. Withnail is also possessed by fury. He is angry at everyone and everything almost all the time, except when a brief window sometimes opens between his last hangover and his next binge. He drops the f-bomb as punctuation, and his face reveals bitter resentment. What does he resent? That the world and everyone in it, except possibly Marwood, have conspired to make his life miserable.

The performance by Richard E. Grant is a tour de force. *Withnail & I* was his second film. IMDb lists more than eighty other credits, but it is his destiny to be forever linked with this early role that has become iconic. To this day there must be those who imagine Grant himself to be hostile and furious, yet in person, he is just another talented acting bloke. Withnail could possibly have become a comic drunk in the wrong hands. Richard E. Grant never, ever, not for a second, breaks character; he is relentlessly wounded and aggressive. He never goes too far, he never relaxes, he aims at the end of the movie and charges.

Paul McGann, as Marwood, reflects a tenuous grip on reality. And he makes the right choices in the role; he doesn't play a straight man or a sparring partner, but a fellow trekker on a daily journey to oblivion. He retains shreds of common sense. When Withnail snatches a can of lighter fluid and squirts it down his throat, Marwood is horrified. When Withnail starts looking for antifreeze, Marwood cries out: "Don't mix your drinks!" Incredibly, not even this scene is invented; Vivian MacKerrell did drink lighter fluid and went blind for several days; Robinson thinks that may have contributed to his death from throat cancer at fifty-one. That, and his smoking. Withnail smokes as if his cigarette is the source of life.

Their sojourn in the country cottage is the centerpiece. They are hopelessly inadequate for such tasks as building a fire and cooking, and our last sight of a rooster being placed in the oven is not one we shall soon forget. They have difficulties with the locals, including the poacher who is accused by Withnail in a pub: "You've got an eel down your leg!"

Uncle Monty comes to visit and grows amorous toward Marwood: "I mean to have you even if it must be burglary!" Robinson says this advance was inspired by the romantic overtures of Franco Zeffirelli when he was playing Benvolio in his *Romeo and Juliet*. Richard Griffith is wonderful in the role, plummy and insinuating, self-effacing in an affected way. (Withnail says, "Monty used to act," and he replies: "I'd hardly say that. It's true I crept the boards in my youth, but I never had it in my blood.")

The dialogue is famous and quoted; in the UK, certain lines are widely recognized. "I can't get my boots on when they're hot," "Those are the kind of windows faces look in at," "I have been known to weep in butchers' shops," "Warm up? We may as well sit round this cigarette," "My thumbs have gone weird!" and Danny the drug dealer's "Hairs are your aerials. They pick up signals from the cosmos and transmit them directly into the brain. This is the reason bald-headed men are uptight."

Danny (Ralph Brown) has dialogue that speaks to the bottom line of the movie: "We are ninety-one days away from the end of the 1960s, the greatest decade in human history." The film is a time capsule, not least because booze is more central than drugs, although Danny's theory of the politics of uppers and downers is prophetic. Withnail and Marwood share the delusion that release and elation can be found in a bottle. If you asked them if it made them happy to drink, they would probably claim that it did, and that's why they do it.

Well, maybe not Withnail. For reasons remaining obscure and certainly never mentioned by him, he seems to be courting suicide. He pours bottles down his throat, sucks on cigarettes, alienates the world, always looks enraged. At the end of the film, he has a famous scene when he stands in the rain beside a fence and performs the Hamlet soliloquy including, "What a piece of work is a man!" He is one of the rare characters in modern films who can quote it with accuracy about himself.

That scene reflects on a quality in the film: Withnail, Marwood, and Monty, for that matter, are well educated, steeped in literature and drama, and so their speech is not sodden but shows intelligence and wit even in the worst of times. (Marwood, after being threatened by a man in a pub: "I don't consciously offend big men like this. And this one has a decided imbalance of hormone in him. Get any more masculine than that and you'd have to live up a tree.")

Why does the film, which I have made sound so depressing, remain so popular after more than twenty years? It achieves a kind of transcendence in its gloom. It is uncompromisingly, sincerely itself. It is not a lesson or a lecture, it is funny but in a consistent way that it earns, and it is unforgettably acted. Bruce Robinson saw such times, survived them, and remembers them not with bitterness but fidelity. In Withnail, he creates one of the iconic figures in modern films. Most of us may have known someone like Withnail. It is likely that Withnail never knew someone like us. His mind was elsewhere.

{ A WOMAN'S TALE }

The old woman has just come from attending a funeral and knows her own is not far in the future. She is speaking with the young nurse who visits her daily. The actress, Sheila Florance, could be describing herself. She is bone thin, her arms like sticks, her face deeply lined. She was once a great beauty, but now what she has left is character.

Paul Cox's *A Woman's Tale* (1991) tells the honest, brave, and profoundly touching story of the last days of a seventy-eight-year-old woman named Martha (Florance), who lives with her memories and treasured possessions in a few rooms in a Melbourne rental complex and defiantly guards her independence. She knows she is dying and has shrugged off the last course of cancer treatment. She is in pain, but doesn't complain, and spends her days taking care of others: Billy, her senile neighbor, surrounded by his memories of the war; Miss Inchley, a sweet old lady as innocent as Martha is knowing; and even, in a way, her nurse, Anna (Gosia Dobrowolska).

The movie looks calmly and with love at the fact that life ends. It provides not one of those sentimental Hollywood deaths, poetic and composed, but a portrait of a woman who faces her decline with fierce pride. Florance herself was dying when the movie was made, knew it, and died a few days after winning an Australian Academy Award as best actress in 1991.

She was a grande dame of the Australian theater, a friend of Paul Cox's since the 1970s, and the film plays like her final testament—not least since some of Martha's memories are actually her own. She describes an aerial dogfight during the Battle of Britain, and it becomes immediate for us: the lumbering German bombers, the little Spitfires appearing out of nowhere, the noise! the noise! of the roaring engines and the guns and the explosions, and the shreds of airplane and body parts raining down on those below.

Martha is very ill, but gets around. She helps poor Billy (Norman Kaye), who is forever locking himself out of his room or wetting his pajamas. She is a good companion for Miss Inchley, who is ninety, taking her for walks in the park, where they chat with Martha's friend, the local prostitute. ("Do you know what a whore is, Miss Inchley?" "Isn't that a rude word?" "Yes, it is.") Martha's nights are sleepless, and she passes them with her cigarettes and her cat, Sam, listening to talk radio. When a suicidal sixteen-year-old girl phones in, Martha calls to speak with her, to tell her how much there is to live for.

Martha's son, Jonathan (Chris Haywood), cares for her, but is very busy and has a wife who has long since fallen out with Martha. Jonathan thinks his mother would be better off in a nursing home. "Do you know how hard we work to keep these people out of homes?" asks the nurse Anna. She fights for Martha's independence because she respects it; she loves the old woman and has become like her daughter. Martha, in turn, lets Anna use her bedroom for an affair the nurse is having with a married man. "I'm going to die in this bed," she says, "and I want you to love in it."

Billy has a daughter, who never visits him. "We saw him at Christmas," the daughter tells Martha. "That was the one day we didn't see him," Martha replies tartly. She is a woman of power and confidence, a woman who insists on her dignity when the world wants her to give up and admit she is sick and go off somewhere convenient to die.

What a feisty defense she makes of her cigarettes in a no-smoking restaurant! She hides the worst of her pain from everyone, but we see her wracked with agonizing spells of coughing. In a scene of extraordinary courage, Cox and Florance show us Martha naked in her bath, her body pitifully gaunt, her mouth that must once have been so sensuous, now without lipstick, an anguished slash in a wrinkled face.

Her memories are of the war, when she was in Britain. "In Bristol," she tells Anna, "my ten-month-old baby was killed. A German dropped a bomb, and her lungs exploded." There is a nightmare in which she wanders in a wood, and restless dreams of falling water. She visits a waterfall with Miss Inchley and observes how the water seems to pause for a moment at the precipice, before disintegrating into exploding, falling drops, only to reassemble at the bottom as if nothing had happened. Is that what happens when we die? *A Woman's Tale* is too realistic and tactful to make such a greeting-card statement; it allows us to conclude what we will about Martha and her story.

The performance by Dobrowolska is essential to the film's impact. We see that she is efficient, a good visiting nurse, but that isn't the point. The point is that she loves and admires Martha and will fight for her, and Dobrowolska brings a natural, unforced sweetness and tenderness to the role. "How I envy your youth!" Martha says, and Anna smiles and says, "I'm not that young." Ah, but she is, and Martha tells her, "Life is so beautiful. Keep love alive."

Anna visits old Billy every day, and one day Billy's hand touches her cheek and then falls slowly toward her breast. Anna removes it, and tells Martha, "Billy tried to touch my breast." "Oh, dear, why didn't you let him?" Martha says. "What difference does it make?" This conversation results in a later scene that is sweet, sad, and quietly moving.

When I say that Florance's performance is courageous, I do not mean simply that she made the movie even though she was dying. That took strength and resolve, but what takes courage is to reveal her character as she does, to let us see Martha stripped of vanity. All women, actresses especially, want to look their best; Florance shares her frail body with us like a sacrament.

The character's vanity, we realize, is expressed not through her appearance, but through her independence, through her determination to fight through every day without giving up and going off to an institution to die. That she cares for Billy and Anna and Miss Inchley and the girl on the talk radio is her reason for holding on: she can still be of use, and that's worth living for.

Paul Cox is one of the heroes of modern cinema, a Dutch-born Australian who makes his way independently of the mainstream production and distribution channels. In a world of fiercely marketed product and manufactured cinematic artifacts, his films embrace all the wonder and complexity of everyday human life. Consider his *Man of Flowers* (1983), also starring Norman Kaye (who is in most of his films), as a particular and eccentric man who lives alone and pays for sex in a way that, once we understand it, becomes touching (to know all helps us to forgive). Or his *Vincent* (1987), one of the best documentaries ever made about an artist, and his *Diaries of Vaslav Nijinsky* (2001), an almost surreal effort to penetrate the mind of the great dancer. Or his wonderful *Innocence* (2000), with its evocation of a romance that begins between two teenagers and continues when they meet again in old age.

His film *The Human Touch* played at Cannes 2004. It deals with a love affair, but a very particular one, between an uneasily married woman and a brilliant older man who is impotent, but whose caresses excite her as never before. All well and good, but who but Cox would think to transport his characters from Australia to France, and send them into a cave that is 110 million years old, where they are awed by the distance between their brief lives and lusts and the overwhelming span of time that humbles them? Directors like Cox validate the cinema in an age of commercialism; his struggle to carry on making his films his way shows the same kind of courage that Martha has in *A Woman's Tale*. He knows he can be of use.

{ WOODSTOCK }

Abbie Hoffman: I live in Woodstock Nation.
Defense attorney: Will you tell the court and the jury where it is?
Hoffman: Yes, it is a nation of alienated young people. We carry it around with us as a state of mind, in the same way the Sioux Indians carry the Sioux Nation with them.

That's how I began my review of *Woodstock* when it opened in 1970. Twenty-five years later, when it was revived in a director's cut, here is how I closed: "And look what happened to the Sioux."

After another ten years, I wonder how many people even remember who Abbie Hoffman was? Those who were twenty at Woodstock are sixty-one, and many of those who performed are dead, not least Jimi Hendrix, whose electric guitar solo of "The Star-Spangled Banner" folded protest and patriotism within its anguish.

It is perhaps necessary to note that for three days in the summer of 1969, a rock concert was given on an upstate New York farm, and four hundred thousand people attended—far more than were anticipated, far more than paid, far more than could be fed or sheltered or cared for after injuries or drug overdoses. It rained, there was mud, all traffic in and out was gridlocked, and the music continued, night and day. It was filmed by

399

a director named Michael Wadleigh and a team that included a young Martin Scorsese and the editor Thelma Schoonmaker, who would later edit all of Scorsese's movies. They exposed 120 miles of film, shot with sixteen cameras.

Had it not been for this movie, Woodstock would be vaguely remembered as a rock concert that produced some recordings. Wadleigh's *Woodstock* created the idea of "Woodstock Nation," which existed for three days and was absorbed into American myth. Few documentaries have captured a time and place more completely, poignantly, and, for that matter, entertainingly. It has a lot of music in it, photographed with a startling intimacy with the performers, but it's not simply a music movie. It's a documentary about the society that formed itself briefly at Woodstock before moving on, showing how the musicians sang to it, the Hog Farm commune fed it and the Portosan man provided it with toilet facilities.

The remarkable thing about Wadleigh's film is that it succeeds so completely in making us feel how it must have been to be there. It gives us maybe 60 percent music and 40 percent about the people who were there, and that is a good ratio, I think. Wadleigh and his editors allowed each performer's set to grow and build and double back on itself without interference; this isn't a "greatest hits" doc, and the director's cut is even more expansive; for the first time, we learn that the notes of "Taps" were associated with the Hendrix solo.

The Hendrix guitar solo is the most famous single element in the film, which uses it as a form of closure. As Hendrix begins, we see the concert grounds after most of the four hundred thousand have left, leaving behind acres of debris, muddy blankets, lost shoes. Then the chronology reverses itself to show the field filling, until finally we see the whole expanse of the mighty crowd, as Hendrix's guitar evokes rockets bursting in air.

The concert was democratic in its choice of performers. Country Joe, pokerfaced, leads the crowd through the anti-Vietnam "I Feel Like I'm Fixin' to Die Rag." Sha-Na-Na does a tightly choreographed 1950s version of "At the Hop." And Joe Cocker and everybody else on the stage and in the crowd sings "With a Little Help from My Friends." The director's cut adds an additional forty-five minutes, including sets by Janis Joplin and

Jefferson Airplane, which were not in the original: Janis, so young, so filled with fierce energy, so doomed.

The editors led by Schoonmaker weren't stuck with the concert shot that had become standard—a fixed camera in front of the stage, pointing up at a singer. They could cut to reaction shots, multiple images, simultaneous close-ups when two members of a band did a mutual improvisation. Split screen was an innovation then, and they used it, taking full advantage of their wide screen. It hadn't really worked in the fiction films that tried it in the late 1960s, maybe because when we're being told a story, we don't want to be told another one at the same time.

But in *Woodstock*, it's used in other ways: as counterpoint, as ironic commentary, as a way to see the same performers from several different points of view. Wadleigh also uses it to compress his narrative, showing the sky clouding up on one screen, while people hold down a windblown canvas on another.

Of course, there was also the option of remaining simple, even shy, when the material called for it. One of the most moving moments in the film is Joan Baez singing the old Wobblies' song "Joe Hill," and then putting down her guitar and singing "Swing Low, Sweet Chariot," with that voice that was surely the purest and sweetest of its time. *Woodstock* just lets her sing it. No tricks. No fancy camera angles. Just Joan Baez all alone on an enormous, pitch-black screen.

At other times, the movie follows the music wherever it goes. When Santana gets into an intricate rhythm, Wadleigh uses triple screen, and frames the drummer with two bongo players. All in synchronized sound (which is not anywhere near as easy as it sounds under outdoor-concert conditions). The editing rhythm follows the tense, driving Santana lead. The filmmakers were right there, right on top of what the performers were doing.

Watch, for example, the way Richie Havens is handled. We see him backstage, tired, a little down. Then he starts singing "Freedom," and we don't see his face again, but his thumb on the guitar strings, punishing them. And then an unbroken shot pans down to his foot in a sandal, pounding with the beat, and then up to the fingers, and only then the face, and now this is a totally transformed Richie Havens, possessed by energy.

Intercut with the music, paralleling it sometimes on a split screen, are more traditional documentary aspects of *Woodstock*. There are the townspeople, like the man who says, "Kids are hungry, you gotta feed 'em. Right?" And the farmer who make his land available. And kids skinny dipping, and getting high, and eating and sleeping and (in a famous long shot) making love. With all that film to choose from in the editing room, Wadleigh was able to give us dozens of tiny unrehearsed moments that sum up the Woodstock feeling. There's Hugh Romney (aka Wavy Gravy) from the Hog Farm ("Folks, we're planning breakfast in bed for four hundred thousand people"). The famous warning about "bad acid." The Portosan man, who, after swabbing out a few units, confides to the camera that he has a son out there in the crowd somewhere—"and another one in the DMZ, flying helicopters." There were the townspeople who took carloads of food to the park. The children. The dogs, running loose. Swami GI, and three nuns giving the peace sign. Cops eating popsicles. The Army dropping blankets, food, and, yes, flowers from helicopters.

The structure of the documentary is roughly chronological. We see the fields being prepared, the stage being built, the traffic jams forming. We see crowds trampling over the fences, and there is the moment when the event, conceived as a profit-making enterprise, is officially declared a "free concert" because obviously there was no other option. (There is a moment when Bill Graham, a San Francisco concert promoter who always kept his eye on the gate, advises the organizers, facetiously I think, to fill ditches with flaming oil to keep the gate-crashers out.)

Woodstock is a beautiful, moving, ultimately great film. It seemed to signal the beginning of something. Maybe it signaled the end. Somebody told me the other day that the 1960s has "failed." Failed at what? They certainly didn't fail at being the 1960s. Now that the period is described as a far-ago time like "the 1920s" or "the 1930s," how touching it is in this film to see the full flower of its moment, of its youth and hope. The decade began with the election of John F. Kennedy and ended as the last bedraggled citizens of Woodstock Nation slogged off the muddy field and thumbed a ride into a future that would seem, to many of them, mostly downhill.

WR—MYSTERIES OF THE ORGANISM

"When I started making films, sex and humor were considered as very serious matters—even high treason." Dusan Makavejev is remembering the uproar over his *WR—Mysteries of the Organism* (1971), a film of sex and comedy that had a mixed reaction: best director at the 1971 Chicago festival, around-the-clock screenings at Cannes, an uproar in New York by followers of Wilhelm Reich, banned in Yugoslavia and at the Venice Film Festival, denounced as pornographic, irresponsible, anti-Soviet, anti-American, anti-cinema.

"Maybe it is like a mirror," Makavejev told me late one night in Chicago. "People hold it up to themselves and see reflected only what they are most offended by." That has a way of happening with his work. *Sweet Movie* (1974) was described by *Time* as "not a movie—a social sickness." At that crucial period in history spanning the late 1960s to the late 1970s, Makavejev (born 1932) was the most eclectic, eccentric, impenetrable, jolly anarchist to come out of Eastern Europe.

He was from Yugoslavia, that late country, and ethnically Serbian, but international to the core. The director of the first Serbian talkie has a line in Makavejev's *Innocence Unprotected* (1967) that could apply to Makavejev himself: "Gentlemen, I assure you the entire Yugoslavian cinema came out of my navel. In fact, I have made certain inquiries, and I am in a position to state positively that the entire Bulgarian cinema came out of my navel as well." The movie, a comic treasure, contains most of the footage of the 1944 talkie, about an acrobat whose daring stunts were recycled as patriotic resistance to the Nazis. Makavejev revisits the director, the acrobat, and others who were involved.

That night in Chicago we were walking up Lincoln Avenue to see the Biograph Theater, where Dillinger was shot by the FBI. Makavejev was in the city for a retrospective of his work at Facets Multimedia, and eventually he and several Facets workers ended up in my kitchen, eating vegetable soup and solving the problems of the cinema.

In a real way, Makavejev is his films. Like Andrei Tarkovsky, Guy Maddin, Russ Meyer, or Alejandro Jodorowsky, he cannot help but make the films he makes, and no others. In his early career in Yugoslavia, in movies like *Love Affair; or, the Case of the Missing Switchboard Operator* (1967), he delighted in sneaking political parallels past the censors; he was not anticommunist but anti-authority. The man in charge of film funding in Yugoslavia was an old classmate of Makavejev's. Faced with one of his scripts, the man sighed: "Dusan, Dusan, Dusan! I know what you are really saying in this screenplay, and you know what you are really saying. Now go home and revise it so only the audience knows."

Bald, burly, and bearded, Makavejev has fashioned a career out of poverty, windfalls, luck, and genius. The year *Sweet Movie* played at Cannes, he had a suite at the Carlton Hotel. The next year, I asked him if he was staying at the Carlton again. "Wife and I have tent on beach," he said. "Some years Carlton, some years beach."

The plots of his earlier movies are almost impossible to describe, although such later titles as *Montenegro* (1981) and *The Coca-Cola Kid* (1985) are more linear. *Montenegro*, a brilliant seriocomedy, is about a bored American wife in Stockholm (Susan Anspach) who escapes her marriage and spends two wild, liberating nights in a nightclub frequented by Serbo-Croatian immigrants. *The Coca-Cola Kid* stars Eric Roberts as a man from headquarters in Atlanta who is dispatched to Australia to find out why one district drinks absolutely no Coke. The critic Jonathan Rosenbaum speaks of Makavejev's method as materials in collision; he combines documentary, fiction, found footage, direct narration, and patriotic music in ways startling and puzzling. The movie is about whatever impression you leave it with.

WR, for example, begins as a documentary about the Austrian analyst Wilhelm Reich, once Freud's first assistant, later a communist, later an anti-communist, eventually an American, who believed the orgasm was the key to freedom and happiness, and possibly a cure for disease. His Orgone Accumulator was a box the size of a phone booth, wood on the outside, lined with metal, which he believed concentrated orgasmic energy within anyone sitting inside of it. Reich's science was condemned by the FDA, his books were burned by the U.S. government, and he died in prison. You see how dangerous sex is.

Makavejev's film strays from Reich to investigate the wilder shores of modern sex. There is a sequence involving the once-infamous practice of "plaster casting." Reflections by the transvestite Jackie Curtis. Poetry (bad) by Tuli Kupferberg as he stalks Manhattan streets with a toy machinegun. And a fictional subplot about a love affair between a Yugoslavian named Milena (Milena Dravic) and the Russian figure skater Vladimir (Ivica Vidovic). After she supplies him with an orgasm, he chops off her head with one of his ice skates. ("Nickel-plated Champions," a cop says. "The finest made.") Not to worry: her severed head continues to speak.

To list *WR* as a great movie will stir outrage from some. "I never, in all my years of moviegoing, booed a film, no matter how bad, boring or insipid the film might have been," wrote David Bienstock in the *New York Times*. "Sometimes the crime being committed in the name of cinema seemed outrageous enough to justify such a response, but I restrained myself." *WR* offended him principally because of its distortions of the teachings of Reich, which he felt amounted to character assassination. That Bienstock took the film as being serious about Reich, or anything else, is surprising.

"Collage," Rosenbaum calls Makavejev's style. Yes. Materials from anywhere come together to create whatever it is you get from it. The movie embodies the very essence of the hippie and flower-power period, which is maybe why it was a box-office hit (the nudity and X rating didn't hurt, although there is no specifically erotic material). It is as evocative of its time as *Woodstock*. I think Makavejev's purpose is to ridicule authorities in the areas of sex and politics (Stalin comes in for some rough sledding), and to suggest we'd get along just fine without anyone issuing us instructions in either area.

Movies like this are impossible now, unless they are made marginally, on small indie budgets. Makavejev's own later films had stars like Roberts and Greta Scacchi, and I liked them, and they made money, but they lacked the anarchy. He hasn't made a feature in ten years, but is still a frequent visitor and juror at film festivals, where somehow he seems to be the host. In recent years he has taught at Harvard.

The editions of Makavejev's films in the Criterion Collection include fascinating supplementary material, not least a little documentary on the "improved" version of *WR*. The movie was purchased by the BBC's Channel Four, which asked Makavejev to reedit some of the more graphic scenes. He was happy to oblige. Key elements of the "plaster casting" scene are obscured by starbursts of psychedelic colors. And an opening nude sequence from an old silent sex film is tidied up with goldfish swimming past the crucial areas.

There is also Makavejev's own short doc about the experience of leaving the dissolving Yugoslavia and finding himself in Hollywood. Monique Luddy, wife of the co-founder of the Telluride Film Festival, takes him to buy some trendy clothes. He looks dubiously at a colorful shirt. She encourages him: "If the producer doesn't like you, maybe he'll like the shirt."

A YEAR OF THE QUIET SUN

When the actor Scott Wilson went to Poland to make *A Year of the Quiet Sun* (1984), he found the country still slowly rebuilding from World War II. "The war was a fresh memory for them," he says, and poverty and rationing were still facts of life. Perhaps that is why Krzysztof Zanussi's film has such an immediate, palpable presence: set in 1946, it shows its characters at the beginning of that long postwar period, living in shabby rooms of half-destroyed buildings, struggling for the few loaves at the local bakery, spying on one another in a world of bribery and betrayal. What we remember about the film's love scene is that the American soldier spreads his Army overcoat over himself and the woman he loves, because it is so cold.

Wilson plays a man named Norman, a private, assigned as a driver to a commission seeking the mass grave of American airmen executed by the Nazis. The Army seems to have forgotten him half the time, and he drives around the half-deserted village in a Jeep. He meets Emilia by accident. Played by the great actress Maja Komorowska, she is a war widow, living with her mother (Ewa Dalkowska) in a single room; her neighbor Stella (Vadim Glowna) is a prostitute, and Emilia has a job baking cakes. Norman brings her gifts: tubes of paint, for she is an artist, and sugar, for her cakes. They do not speak each other's languages, but they fall in love wordlessly, and quickly.

Zanussi surrounds this love story with details of life under the emerging communist government. The most vile character in his story is a well-dressed man of about forty, his salt-and-pepper hair neatly cut, his overcoat warm, his tie nicely knotted, who (although the movie never says so) seems to be the local party representative. He commands two goons who steal the small amount Emilia and her mother have saved for their dream of escaping to the West. He keeps an eye on the prostitute, who sleeps with a German who fixes such escapes, and who is a Jewess who survived the concentration camps by working in a Nazi officer's brothel. "Don't judge people," Emilia tells the party man. "Let the past be past."

The courtship between Norman and Emilia involves kindness, sexual urgency, soulful looks, a few words of English and Polish. "I thought Norman should not be an articulate man," Wilson says in an interview on the DVD of the film. "He does not depend on dialogue. Even if they spoke each other's languages, he might not have much to say."

What he does say sounds honest and sincere right down to the bottom of his soul; he has no one back in America, he tells her, and nothing to go home to ("until you came along, I was an empty man"), but he knows how to farm, and "I promise I will work hard for you." He imagines them on their own little farm.

This love story, sweet as it is, seems clouded by the penetrating gloom of the times. The mother is dying of an infected leg. The prostitute is victimized by her clients. Emilia is reluctant to leave Poland, having finally returned home after years as a displaced person. In a field outside the town, the grave of the dead airmen is excavated, and in a startling scene, the corpses are examined and then, in a twilight montage, seem to bear witness to their murder.

The cinematography, by Slavomir Idziak, is masterful in its use of light and color to evoke the cold, sad mood of the film. Browns, blacks, deep olives, and blues are a backdrop to pale, undernourished faces. There is often a bright light source, like a bare bulb, to cast hard light on the characters while enveloping them with shadows. The camera was almost always handheld, we learn from the Wilson interview; even tracking shots are done with Idziak sitting on the dolly and holding the camera. Yet we are almost never aware it is handheld; instead of moving his camera incessantly as unwise young American independent directors do, under the impression that they have found a useful style, Idziak holds it steady. That it inevitably moves slightly, unnoticeably, creates a subtle form of urgency, of personal involvement, and we are reminded of Scorsese's belief that a locked-down camera is objective, but a camera moving however slightly is subjective.

Idziak's camera loves the actors' faces, which instruct us how to feel: Komorowska, with sad eyes, displays a great weariness, but her sensuous lips cannot conceal delight and surprise when she discovers the G.I. has come to visit her, and not Stella. And Wilson, who often seems filled with a great melancholy, and who plays his simple soldier as a man determined to be good. Perhaps one of the reasons he wants to rescue this woman is explained by a nightmare he has, in which as a prisoner of the Germans, he soils his pants with fear. This is a great performance from Wilson, so underused by Hollywood, whose debut was *In Cold Blood* (1967) and whose work includes *The Right Stuff* (1983) and *Shiloh* (1996).

A Year of the Quiet Sun, which won the Golden Lion as the best film at the 1984 Venice Film Festival, was not entered for the Academy Awards, because the Polish government was boycotting the Oscars after a film by Andrzej Wajda, critical of the government, was entered. Zanussi, born 1939, no less critical of the communist regime and (with Komorowska) a strong supporter of the Solidarity movement, succeeded in making films because, as he explains with a quiet smile, "I was diplomatic."

Indeed he ran a Warsaw film studio that used government money to make anti-government films, with disguised messages Poles had no trouble in translating. A close friend of Pope John Paul II, Zanussi filmed the pope's play *Our God's Brother* in 1997, once again choosing Scott Wilson as the star.

As a producer and mentor, Zanussi helped inspire a new generation of Polish filmmakers, including Krzysztof Kieslowski (Zanussi acted in his *Camera Buff*) and Agnieszka Holland (she began as his assistant). Together with Wajda, Andrzej Munk, and others, they formed the Cinema of Moral Anxiety, creating a group of films about the dilemma of being a good person in a bad time. Kieslowski's *Decalogue*, ten hour-long films about ethical dilemmas, is paralleled by Zanussi's *Weekend Stories*, eight films also about impossible moral situations.

One of the remarkable qualities of *A Year of the Quiet Sun* is the way it tells its love story without resorting to the devices of cheap romance. These are two middle-aged people of dignity, who have been through unspeakably painful experiences; at one point, Emilia asks her priest, "Does a person have a right to happiness?"

One answer, which the priest does not think to provide, is that a person must be willing to be happy. This is something Emilia's mother knows, and Ewa Dalkowska is luminous as a dying woman of little sentiment, great humor, and hard realism, who encourages the romance and despairs that her daughter will not act decisively to accept a better future.

I will try to discuss the ending of the film without revealing how the story concludes. It is a fantasy scene that takes place in Monument Valley, where John Ford shot his great Westerns, and indeed the one film that Emilia and her mother mention in the movie is *Stagecoach*. We learn from Wilson that Zanussi and the Russian director Andrei Tarkovsky visited Monument Valley on their way to the Telluride Film Festival in 1983, and indeed I remember them there, Tarkovsky dressed in jeans and cowboy boots, Zanussi as always in dark blue suit and tie.

Both directors vowed to film there someday. Tarkovsky died before he could. Zanussi traveled to the valley with only his cameraman, his two stars, and Wilson's wife, Heavenly, as crew, and they filmed the ending, which is poetic in the way it visualizes the hope of the two lovers while reflecting the poignancy of their fates.

{Yojimbo}

Almost the first thing the samurai sees when he arrives is a dog trotting down the main street with a human hand in its mouth. The town seems deserted until a nervous little busybody darts out and offers to act as an employment service: he'll get the samurai a job as a yojimbo—a bodyguard. The samurai, a large, dusty man with indifference bordering on insolence, listens and does not commit. He wants sake and something to eat.

So opens *Yojimbo* (1961), Akira Kurosawa's most popular film in Japan. He was deliberately combining the samurai story with the Western, so that the windswept main street could be in any frontier town, the samurai (Toshiro Mifune) could be a gunslinger, and the local characters could have been lifted from John Ford's gallery of supporting actors.

Ironic, that having borrowed from the Western, Kurosawa inspired one: Sergio Leone's *A Fistful of Dollars* (1964), with Clint Eastwood, is so similar to *Yojimbo* that homage shades into plagiarism. Even Eastwood's Man With No Name is inspired, perhaps, by the samurai in *Yojimbo*. Asked his name, the samurai looks out the window, sees a mulberry field, and replies, "Kuwabatake Sanjuro," which means "thirty-year-old mulberry field." He is thirty, and that is a way of saying he has no name.

He also has no job. The opening titles inform us that in 1860, after the collapse of the Tokugawa Dynasty, samurai were left unemployed and wandered the countryside in search of work. We see Sanjuro at a crossroads, throwing a stick into the air and walking in the direction it points. That brings him to the town, to possible employment, and to a situation that differs from Hollywood convention in that the bad guys are not attacking the good guys because there are no good guys: "There is," the critic Donald Richie observes, "almost no one in the whole town who for any conceivable reason is worth saving." It's said Kurosawa's inspiration was Dashiell Hammett's novel *Red Harvest*, in which a private eye sets one gang against another.

Sanjuro's strategy is to create great interest about himself while keeping his motives obscure. He needs money and so presumably must hire himself out as a bodyguard to one of the two warring factions. There is the silk dealer and the sake merchant, both with private armies, who occupy headquarters at either end of the town. In between, the townspeople cower behind closed shutters and locked doors, and the film's visuals alternate between the emptiness of the windswept street, shots looking out through the slats of shutters and the chinks in walls, and shots from outdoors showing people peering through their shutters.

Richie, whose writings on Kurosawa are invaluable, notes that Kurosawa's shots are always at right angles to what they show; they either look straight up and down the street, or straight into or out of the buildings, and "there are very few diagonal shots." The purpose may be to emphasize the simplicity of the local situation: two armies face each other, the locals observe the main street as if it's a stage, and the samurai himself embodies the diagonal—the visitor who stands at an angle to everyone and upsets the balance of power. Indeed, in a crucial early scene, as the two sides face each other nervously from either end of the street and dart forward fearfully in gestures of attack, Sanjuro sits high above the action in the central bell tower, looks down, and is vastly amused.

His strategy is to hire himself out as a yojimbo to first one side and then the other, and do no actual bodyguarding at all. His amorality is so complete that we are a little startled when he performs a good deed. A farmer and his wife, possibly the only two good people in the town, are kidnapped. Sanjuro, employed by the side that kidnapped them, kills their six guards, frees them, tears up a house to make it look like there was a fierce struggle, and blames it on the other side. Disloyal to his employer? Yes, but early in the film, he is offered fifty ryo by one of the leaders, only to overhear the man's wife telling him, "We'd save the whole fifty ryo if we killed him after he wins."

Sanjuro's strategy is an elaborate chess game in which he is playing for neither side but plans instead to upset the board. "In this town, I'll get paid for killing," he muses, "and this town would be better off if they were dead." His planning is upset by the unexpected appearance of Unosuke (Tatsuya Nakadai), the younger brother of one of the sake dealer's bodyguards. The samurai often walk about with their empty sleeves flapping at the sides, their arms folded inside their kimonos. (Eastwood, in the Leone movies, always keeps one hand under his poncho.) When Unosuke finally reveals one of his hands, it holds a pistol—the first one seen in the village. This upsets the balance of power and tilts against Sanjuro's plans, which depend on his skill as a swordsman who can kill any number of the others without being wounded himself.

The gun provides Unosuke with a sneaky kind of self-confidence, and he produces the weapon gloatingly from time to time. Occasionally, he kills people in cold blood, just to prove that he can, in events leading up to a final bloodbath. One of the first people Sanjuro meets in the town is the coffin maker, and there is a nice moment when he first goes out to do battle and advises him, "Two coffins. Noon, maybe three." By the end there is no business for the coffin maker, because there is no one to pay for coffins.

That kind of dark humor is balanced in the film by other moments approaching slapstick, as when the injured Sanjuro is smuggled away in a large barrel; when his bearers pause in the middle of the street, the samurai tilts up the lid of the barrel to provide a droll commentary on the progress of the manhunt for him.

Richie believes *Yojimbo* is the best-photographed of Kurosawa's films (by Kazuo Miyagawa, who also shot *Rashomon* and such other Japanese classics as Ozu's *Floating Weeds* and Mizoguchi's *Ugetsu*). The wide screen is fully employed for dramatic compositions, as when the armies face each other across an empty space. And there is a dramatic sense of depth in scenes where Sanjuro holds the foreground while forces gather in the background. Shutters, sliding doors, and foreground objects bring events into view and then obscure them, and we get a sense of the town as a collection of fearful eyes granted an uncertain view of certain danger.

Yojimbo was followed quickly by Kurosawa's *Sanjuro* (1962), which also stars Mifune, the greatest modern Japanese actor, playing the same character or one so similar as to make no difference. He acts as the adviser for nine uncannily similar brothers who are remarkably inept samurai. The choreography in *Sanjuro* is one of its best jokes; the brothers do everything together: nod, recoil, agree, laugh, gasp, and they follow Sanjuro in a kind of conga line, until he snaps, "We can't move around like a centipede."

The difference between the two films is that *Sanjuro* is a comedy in which ancient samurai traditions are exposed as ludicrous by the pragmatic hero, while *Yojimbo* is more subversive: the samurai were famed for their unyielding loyalty to their employers, but Sanjuro, finding himself unemployed because of the collapse of the feudal system, becomes a modern man and is able to manipulate both sides because they persist in thinking he will be faithful to those who pay him.

There is a moment at the end when old and new hang in the balance. The wounded Sanjuro no longer has his sword, but we have seen him practicing with a knife—skewering a bit of paper as it flutters around a room. He faces Unosuke, the gunman. Without revealing precisely what happens between them, let me ask you to consider the moment when Unosuke aims his pistol at Sanjuro. It may be loaded, it may not be. Sanjuro cannot be absolutely sure. He is free to move away or to disarm Unosuke, but instead he sits perfectly motionless, prepared to accept whatever comes. This, it strikes me, is the act of a samurai aware that his time has passed and accepting with perfect equanimity whatever the new age has to offer.

ESSAYS APPEARING IN
THE GREAT MOVIES (2002)

415

Greed

A Hard Day's Night

Hoop Dreams

Ikiru

It's a Wonderful Life

JFK

La Dolce Vita

The Lady Eve

Last Year at Marienbad

L'Atalante

L'Avventura

Lawrence of Arabia

Le Samourai

M

The Maltese Falcon

Manhattan

McCabe & Mrs. Miller

Metropolis

Mr. Hulot's Holiday

My Darling Clementine

My Life to Live

Nashville

Network

The Night of the Hunter

Nosferatu

Notorious

On the Waterfront

Pandora's Box

The Passion of Joan of Arc

Peeping Tom

Persona

Pickpocket

Pinocchio

Psycho

Pulp Fiction

Raging Bull

Red River

Schindler's List

The Seven Samurai

The Seventh Seal

The Shawshank Redemption

The Silence of the Lambs

Singin' in the Rain

Some Like It Hot

Star Wars

Sunset Blvd.

Sweet Smell of Success

Swing Time

Taxi Driver

The Third Man

Trouble in Paradise

Un Chien Andalou

The "Up" Documentaries

Vertigo

The Wild Bunch

Wings of Desire

The Wizard of Oz

Woman in the Dunes

A Woman Under the Influence

Written on the Wind

Essays Appearing in *The Great Movies II* (2005)

12 Angry Men

The Adventures of Robin Hood

Alien

Amadeus

Amarcord

Annie Hall

Au Hasard, Balthazar

The Bank Dick

Beat the Devil

Being There

The Big Heat

The Birth of a Nation

The Blue Kite

Bob le Flambeur

Breathless

The Bridge on the River Kwai

Bring Me the Head of Alfredo Garcia

Buster Keaton

Children of Paradise

A Christmas Story

The Color Purple

The Conversation

Cries and Whispers

The Discreet Charm of the Bourgeoisie

Don't Look Now

The Earrings of Madame de …

The Fall of the House of Usher

The Fireman's Ball

Five Easy Pieces

Goldfinger

The Good, the Bad and the Ugly

GoodFellas

The Gospel According to Matthew

The Grapes of Wrath

Grave of the Fireflies

Great Expectations

House of Games

The Hustler

In Cold Blood

Jaws